Proceedings of the
Danish Institute at Athens

Proceedings of the Danish Institute at Athens

VOLUME IX

Edited by

Kristina Winther-Jacobsen & Nicolai von Eggers Mariegaard

Athens 2019

Proceedings of the Danish Institute at Athens Volume IX

General editor: Kristina Winther-Jacobsen
Graphic design: Jørgen Sparre
Typeset: Ryevad Grafisk
Cover illustration: View from the north over Monastiraki Square, Plaka and the Acropolis.
Printed at Narayana Press, Denmark

ISSN 1108 149X
ISBN 978 87 7184 818 2

AARHUS UNIVERSITY PRESS
Langelandsgade 177
DK-8200 Aarhus N
www.unipress.dk

Oxbow Books Ltd.
The Old Music Hall 106–108
Cowley Road Oxford, OX4 1JE
United Kingdom
www.oxbowbooks.com

ISD
70 Enterprise Drive
Bristol, CT 06010
USA
www.isdistribution.com

This volume was financed by a private Danish foundation wishing to remain anonymous.

Table of Contents

Reports on Danish Fieldwork in Greece

Preface

In 1992, the combined efforts of representatives of several institutions and the Minister of Education Bertel Haarder succeeded in establishing The Danish Institute at Athens. DIA, as we call ourselves, has its judicial seat at the Ministry of Higher Education and Research and its board consists of nine representatives from the Ministry of Higher Education and Research, the Ministry of Education, the Ministry of Culture, the National Museum, The Universities of Aarhus, Copenhagen and Southern Denmark and the Academy Council of the Royal Academy of Fine Arts. The board represents the Danish interests also reflected in the aims of The Danish Institute at Athens, which is both an academic institution and a cultural institute. According to its statute, DIA aims to promote research, education and culture in Greek and Mediterranean archaeology, history, language, literature, visual arts, architecture and cultural traditions. The Danish Institute at Athens exists because many Danes believe the Classical world still has much to teach us. Yet ideas and ideals change; as of 2019, Modern Greek language and culture is no longer offered at university level in Denmark.

It has long been the ambition of the Board of the Institute to broaden the scope of the Institute, and the 25th anniversary in 2017 provided a suitable occasion to turn our attention more formally towards the recent periods of Greek history and culture. In 2016, DIA appointed Birgit Olsen as its vice-director, whose research is dedicated to Modern Greek traditions of storytelling, folktales and literature. In 2018 the vice-director co-organised a conference dedicated to the analysis of aspects of orally produced and diffused stories from the Greek tradition, from Antiquity up to the storytelling communities in the 20th century, in collaboration with the Kapodistrian University of Athens.

Also in 2016, the Carlsberg Foundation generously offered a three-year post-doctoral grant at the Institute, starting January 2017. This grant was awarded to Nicolai von Eggers Mariegaard, who holds a PhD in the history of ideas, to work on a project dedicated to analysing Classical Greek conceptions of politics, sovereignty, civil war and revolution, and to show us what this might mean to our contemporary understandings of politics. He has organised two workshops dedicated to politics and how to approach Antiquity, and a large international conference in 2019 dedicated to the topic of contemporary democracy and social movements on a global scale.

Finally, 2017 also provided another opportunity to focus on more recent interactions between Denmark and Greece. In November, the Institute hosted a seminar on the Danish pressure on the Greek Military Junta (1967-74) in the European Council and NATO in relation to the Junta's violations of human rights, co-ordinated with Norway, Sweden and The Netherlands in 1967-69, when Greece left the European Union. This topic is also the focus of a large international conference in December 2019 entitled *The 'Greek Case' in the Council of Europe: A Game Changer for International Law and Human Rights?*, which is being co-organised with the Netherlands Institute, The Swedish Institute, The Norwegian Institute, and the Marangopoulos Foundation for Human Rights.

Over the years many Danish scholars specialising in more recent aspects of Greek history and culture have moved through the Institute, and with the current volume of Proceedings we wish to acknowledge our commitment. Apart from the reports on Danish archaeological projects in Kalydon (Olympia Vikatou, Søren Handberg, Neopto-lemos Michaelides & Signe Barfoed) and Rhodes (Ana-stasia Dreliossi-Herakleidou & Lisa Betina), this volume is dedicated to "Modern" Greece.

Two articles focus on personalities involved in the world of archaeology: John Lund's article on the Danish Consul General Christian Tuxen Falbe, who was also an eager antiquarian, and Alexandra Kankeleit's article on numismatist Willy Schwabacher and his correspondence during his exile in Copenhagen in 1939 with archaeologist Berta Segall, whom he had met and befriended in Greece.

Four articles focus on different types of reception of ancient Greek culture. The role and function of Classical Antiquity is analysed in the music of Carl Nielsen (Paolo Muntoni), in contemporary sculpture (Bente Kiilerich), in the American television series Star Trek (Evanthis Hatzivassiliou) and in contemporary Hellenic polytheism in Modern Greece (Tao Thykier Makeeff). Each in their own way, these articles remind the reader how diffused and yet how profound the link between ancient Greek culture and contemporary society is, on a global scale, and that in order to understand contemporary society it is sometimes necessary to understand its relation to its Classical past.

The remaining articles discuss different aspects of Modern Greece that are not related to Antiquity. In her article, Birgit Olsen analyses a fairytale from Kos and discusses the Greek tradition of storytelling and folk-tales. John Lund, in his second contribution to this volume, introduces the reader to Danish Philhellene and participant in the Greek Revolution Adam Friedel, who made portraits of the 24 Protagonists of the Greek Rev-olution in the years 1821-32. Finally, Mogens Pelt gives a detailed overview of Greece's international relations with Denmark, and Danish interest and involvement in Greek affairs from the foundation of the modern nation state in the 1820s up to the recent financial crisis.

Proceedings volume 9 is published by Arhus University Press; its production was made possible by the generous support of a foundation that wishes to remain anony-mous, and to which we are very grateful.

Kristina Winther-Jacobsen, Director of the Danish In-stitute, and Nicolai von Eggers Mariegaard, Post.Doc., January 2019

Art Historical Studies and Modern Greece

Christian Tuxen Falbe:

Danish Consul-General and Antiquarian in Greece, 1833-5*

JOHN LUND

Abstract

The topic of the paper is Christian Tuxen Falbe's tenure as Danish Consul-General in Greece from 1833 until 1835. It draws on sources in Danish archives as well as on previous publications by other scholars. Falbe fulfilled his duties in Greece diligently, but his efforts were not always appreciated by the authorities in Copenhagen, and they decided to terminate the position and recall him in the summer of 1835, because Danish shipping and trade in the Aegean had turned out to be negligible. Falbe's letters give a valuable and vivid firsthand account of life in the formative period of Modern Greece, and they reflect the roles played by Danes in this process. Special attention is given to Falbe's not entirely successful efforts to acquire antiquities for Denmark; those he managed to collect are kept in the Danish National Museum.

Introduction

Christian Tuxen Falbe (Fig. 1) was Danish Consul-General in Greece from 1833 until 1835, during which time he made efforts to acquire antiquities and coins for Danish collections. His role in this respect was similar to that of the British consuls in the Aegean, who were equally active in excavating and collecting antiquities for the British Museum at about the same time.[1] Indeed, from the point of view of the creation of the Collection of Classical and Near Eastern Antiquities of the National Museum of Den-

mark, the first half of the 19th century has been referred to as the age of the Consular–Collectors.[2]

The primary documentary sources on Falbe's stay in Greece are his letters to various individuals in Denmark as well as his reports to the Royal Commerce Department [Kommercekollegiet & Departementet for de udenlandske Sager], which was responsible for the consular service in the then Ministry of Foreign Affairs.[3] Most of these letters are unpublished, except for excerpts quoted (mainly in Danish) by the scholars who have previously

---

* I wish to thank Pia Johansen for comments on an early draft of this paper. I am grateful also to Dyfri Williams for sending me the manuscript of his forthcoming article on the fragment of part of a horse's lower leg and hoof in the National Museum (see *infra* note 126) and to the anonymous reviewer for helpful suggestions.

1   Gunning 2009.

2   Bundgaard Rasmussen & Lund 2002 [2004], 172-3 and Lund 2015 [2016]; other Danish consuls, e.g. Alfred Friedrich von Dumreicher and Abraham Jacob Polack in Alexandria, and Peter Julius Löytved in Beirut, likewise collected antiquities for Danish museums. The French vice-consul in Athens, Louis François Sebastien Fauvel, and other diplomats from the then major European powers did the same.

3   Kjølsen 1970, 302-6.

dealt with this subject.[4] In a publication that came out in 1951, Niels Breitenstein focused on the antiquities in the Danish National Museum that were acquired by Falbe in Greece.[5] Viveca Liventhal included a brief account of Falbe's Greek years in her biographical sketch from 1986,[6] and Ida Haugsted gathered a good deal of the relevant evidence in her comprehensive publication on Danish antiquaries, architects and artists in Greece in the 19th century, which was published in 1996.[7] This contribution seeks to place Falbe's Greek interlude in its historical setting, against the background of the relations between Denmark and the Greek state that emerged after the War of Independence (1821-32).[8]

Few Danes had visited the Aegean in the preceding centuries, when Greece was part of the Ottoman Empire.[9] But some 20 Danish officers – of whom Moritz Hartmann is the most renowned – participated in the Venetian expedition to the Morea from 1685 to 1687.[10] In 1737 only eight out of 4000 objects in the Royal Danish Kunstkammer originated from regions that formed part of the Ottoman Empire, and of these only two came from Greece: two marble heads from the Parthenon, which Moritz Hartmann acquired in Athens.[11] Carsten Niebuhr crossed the Aegean with his travel companions on his way to Arabia Felix in 1761.[12] However, the most consequential Danish traveller to Greece before the War of Independence was the archaeologist and philologist Peter Oluf Brøndsted, who arrived in July 1810 accompanied by his prospective brother-in-law, Georg Koës. The latter died at Zakynthos in September 1811, but Brøndsted stayed on until the Spring of 1813, and after his return to Copenhagen promulgated

Fig. 1. *Portrait of Christian Tuxen Falbe painted by Adam Müller in 1830, reproduced with the kind permission of the owner.*

his firsthand experience of ancient and contemporary Greece to a captivated Danish audience.[13] The architect Jørgen Hansen Koch, who travelled in Greece from 1818 to 1819,[14] was followed by a dozen or so Danish Philhellenes who participated in the Greek War of Independence,[15] and after the liberation by the theologian Johannes Ferdinand Fenger, who published one of the first books in Denmark on Modern Greece in 1832.[16]

---

4   The archival resources are listed in the bibliography. For a list of the letters see Haugsted 1996, 355-6 nos. 44-76.

5   Breitenstein 1951, 106-9; for an updated discussion see Lund 2000a, 124-7.

6   Liventhal 1986, 343-4. See also Christiansen 2000, 47-48.

7   Haugsted 1996, 89-137.

8   Gallant 2001, 16-26 dates the end of the War of Independence to 1828. Brewer 2001 opts for 1833. In my view, 1832 – the year of the Treaties of London and Constantinople – constitutes a more logical end date.

9   Brewer 2010; Greene 2015; Gallant 2015.

10   Bobé 1933, 61-7; many of these originated in parts of the then Danish realm, which are no longer included in the Danish state. In the present essay all such persons are regarded as Danish.

11   Gundestrup 1990, 48 and 53.

12   Niebuhr 1774, 34-42; Haslund Hansen & Rasmussen (eds) 2005, 225-33.

13   Brøndsted 1844; see further Haugsted 1996, 11-46, 347 and 349-50; Bundgaard Rasmussen 2000; Haugsted 2000; Bundgaard Rasmussen et al. (eds) 2007 and Lund forthcoming with references to previous publications.

14   Haugsted 1996, 47-62.

15   Krarup 1985; Pelt 2000; Ghazaleh 2005; Papanikoláou-Kristensen 2010, 2540; Koukíou-Mitropoúlou 2014; my article in this publication on Friedel. St Clair 2008 scarcely refers to the Danish Philhellenes. For Frederik von Scholten's journeys in the Aegean, 1824-1829, see Lund 2014.

16   Fenger 1832; Haugsted 1996, 77-8, 348.

Greece in the decade after the War of Independence

Greece underwent a turbulent period in the wake of the War of Independence, but in 1832 Britain, Russia and France agreed to a Convention in London guaranteeing the existence of Greece as a monarchical and independent state,[17] and a Treaty signed in Constantinople in July 1832 laid down the borders of the new nation.[18]

The three signatory powers offered hereditary sovereignty of Greece to Otto, the 16year-old second son of King Ludwig I of Bavaria.[19] But since he was a minor, King Ludwig appointed a Regency of three members, who were to rule until Otto came of age on 1 June 1835: Count Joseph-Ludwig von Armansperg, who emerged as the Regency's undisputed leader, the law professor Georg-Ludwig Ritter von Maurer and the general Carl-Wilhelm von Heideck, with Karl-August Ritter von Abel and Johann-Baptist von Greiner as supplementary members.[20] Maurer and Abel were later recalled following internal quarrels and intrigues, to be replaced by Egid von Kobell and Johann Baptist von Greiner.[21]

3500 Bavarian soldiers accompanied Otto to Greece to guarantee his safety, and Bavarian officers were given the task of training the Greek army.[22] In the words of the historian Thomas W. Gallant: "the war for 'liberation' from a foreign yoke had resulted merely in a change of masters".[23] The government was autocratic and most of the administrative branches were dominated by Germans, Greek politicians being largely relegated to roles in the three political factions which emerged: the French, the English and the Russian party. The Regency officially pursued a policy of impartiality towards all the powers, but in reality often seems to have favoured the French party.[24]

The establishment of a Danish Consulate General in Greece

On 28 October 1829, the Commerce Department asked the Ministry of Foreign Affairs if the time had come to establish a Danish General Consul in Greece. The Ministry of Foreign Affairs initially rejected the proposal, but the Commerce Department submitted a new enquiry on 26 March 1831 with reference to the importance for Danish shipping of having a General Consul in Greece to "watch over the rights and security of the Danish citizens there". This time the response was positive. On 29 April 1831 the Ministry of Foreign Affairs concluded that the Greek state was by now sufficiently stable to make the creation of such a position desirable,

in particular if the man who might be chosen for this post, was to possess mercantile and diplomatic as well as other personal qualities enabling him to handle the interest of Denmark in general and also with wisdom and force to further the requirements of those countrymen who might need his protection.

Falbe must have been aware of the possible outcome of the deliberations, because he applied to King Frederik VI for the post in April 1830,[25] and was appointed Danish Consul General in Greece on 17 September 1831, with an annual salary of 5000 silver rix-dollars.

Falbe's background

Born in Elsinore in 1791, Falbe had been educated at the Naval Academy in a wide range of skills, including mathematics, languages and the drawing of maps.[26] He resigned from the Navy in 1821 with the rank of Commander in order to become Danish Consul General in Tunis,[27]

---

17   Clogg 2013, 39-41; Brewer 2000, 350-1; Angeláki 2010, 137-45.

18   Gallant 2001, 28.

19   Bower & Bolitho 1939, 29; Friedrich 2015.

20   Bower & Bolitho 1939, 30; Petropulos 1968, 155-8; Dickopf 1995; Kotsowillis 2007, 18-26; Friederich 2015, 102-23.

21   Bower & Bolitho 1939, 65-8; Petropulos 1968, 157-8; Dickopf 1995, 86; Friedrich 2015, 125-38.

22   Hildebrandt 1995. An interesting pictorial record of the presence of the Bavarian soldiers in these years are the albums with watercolours by Ludwig Köllnberger, cf. Heydenreuter 1995; Baumstark 1999, 388-92 no. 228 and Παπασπύρου-Καραδημητρίου 2000.

23   Gallant 2001, 32-3; Petropulos 1968, 162-5; Bastéa 2000, 18-23; Clogg 2013, 43, 273-4; for a more positive assessment, see Kotsowillis 2007, 57-63.

24   Petropulos 1968, 192-201 and 215-7.

25   Letter from Falbe written in Copenhagen on 2 April 1830 kept in The Danish State Archives, "Det kongelige General-toldkammer og Commerce-Collegium, Grækenland Danske konsuler 1829-1845", like the other documents referred to below.

26   Steensen 1951, 170-86.

27   Lund 1992.

Fig. 2. *Nauplion seen from the sea in March 1825; watercolour by Frederik Scholten in the Maritime Museum of Denmark. Photo: John Lee.*

where he developed an interest in Antiquity thanks to the influence of Frederik Münter, a professor of theology and Bishop of Zealand.[28] Falbe initiated excavations and undertook the difficult task of surveying the site of ancient Carthage. The resulting map was highly accurate and secured him enduring international recognition after it was published in 1833.[29]

While in Tunisia, Falbe received a letter from the Danish Prince Christian Frederik, the future King Christian VIII, who during a tour of Italy in 18201 had developed a keen interest in coins and antiquities, in particular Greek and South Italian vases. Christian Frederik encouraged

Falbe to continue his antiquarian studies in Tunisia, urging him to collect antiquities and to ship them to Denmark. The latter was more than happy to comply and from then on regularly corresponded with the Prince.[30]

When on leave in Copenhagen, Falbe began working in the Vase Cabinet of the prince, and he continued this work after his term as Danish Consul General in Tunisia ended in 1832.[31] The Prince presented Falbe with a diamond brooch valued at 100 rix-dollars on 26 May 1833 (shortly before his departure for Greece), in recognition of the presumably unpaid work that he had carried out in his beloved Vase Cabinet.[32]

28   Lund 1992, 91-2.
29   Falbe 1833. Cf. Freed 2011, 39-41.
30   Lund 2000a, 121-4.
31   Falbe writes in a letter to Christian VIII dated 7 February 1847 that he has had the honour of working for the Vase Cabinet for nineteen years; cited by Breitenstein 1951, 154.
32   Breitenstein, 1951, 106.

In Nauplion, 1833-4

Nauplion was one of the few towns in Greece that had emerged relatively unscathed from the War of Independence,[33] and Ioannis Kapodistrias, the first president, chose this town (alternately with Aegina) for the seat of his government.[34] On his arrival in February 1833,[35] Otto made Nauplion the first provisional capital of Greece.[36]

Falbe arrived at Nauplion (Fig. 2) at the end of November 1833, accompanied by his wife, their five children and two Danish servants.[37] Christoph Heinrich Detlef Fabricius – a Danish Philhellene who was now employed by Otto – helped Falbe rent a house;[38] the price was reasonable, but Falbe compared the lodgings to a poorly constructed house of cards, "full of windows and doors, none of which can be closed, and rain comes through the roof", and he was obliged to spend 8000 rix-dollars on settling down, without any refund from the Treasury.[39] He and his wife were both afflicted by daily headaches and their children caught measles.[40] Moreover, Falbe was unhappy about his position – he felt that it would have added to his prestige if he could have travelled to Greece on board the Danish Corvette Galathea –[41] and as a mere General Consul, he was not part of the diplomatic corps, and this was a draw-back in his dealings with the Greek officials.[42] Due to this lack of diplomatic status, Falbe was not invited to Otto's New Year audience on 13 January 1834. However, the British Resident, E. J. Dawkins, intervened on his behalf and he was summoned to a separate audience at very short notice immediately afterwards.[43] Falbe characterised the young king as "neither *short–sighted nor bandy–legged*, even if he is hard of hearing on his left ear and lisps slightly".[44] He found him a pleasant enough person with nice manners, who spoke with thoughtfulness and sense.[45] Other observers were far more critical.[46] Falbe also came in contact with the Regency, in particular Count von Armansperg, reporting home that its members had been stupid enough to let the public become aware of their difficulties in working together, something that he considered detrimental not only to its own reputation but also to that of the king.[47] Maurer and Abel turned against von Armansperg, and the two were recalled to Bavaria in late July 1834.[48] Falbe was satisfied with this turn of events, noting that he and his wife, together with the English emissary, had been the only ones among the foreign ministers and agents "who had not acted as a turncoat towards the Count and his family".[49] Ludwig Ross noted that Falbe's wife had been so eager to wait on Armansberg's wife that she

---

33 Woodhouse 1973, 347.

34 Woodhouse 1973, 415, 488-507.

35 Bower & Bolitho 1939, 37-41; Haugsted 1996, 82-4; Baumstark (ed.) 1999, 355-61 nos. 188-93; Brewer 2001, 350; Kouria 2007, 191-3 figs 153-5, 194-6 figs 156-8.

36 Bower & Bolitho 1939, 42: "The population of Nauplia did not exceed six thousand before Otho landed there. But when the news of his arrival spread through the country-side, strangers of all nationalities swarmed to the town." See also Ross 1863, 68; Kouria 2007, 190, 198 and 199 with figs 160 and 161.

37 Haugsted 1996, 90.

38 Militært repertorium 2.r.II, 1845 216-20; Krarup 1985, 51 and *passim*; Haugsted 1996, 89 note 1, 291-2 and *passim*; Pakkanen 2006, 101, 142-3; Παπανικολάου–Κρίστενσεν 2010, 40.

39 Letter to Prince Christian Frederik written in Nauplion on 10 March 1834.

40 Letter to Prince Christian Frederik, Copenhagen, 24 December 1833, Haugsted 1996, 91. See also a letter from Falbe in The Danish State Archives, the archive of R.A. Adler.

41 Letter to Prince Christian Frederik written in Nauplion on 28 January 1834.

42 Letter to Hans Krabbe-Carisius from Nafplia dated 22 January 1834; letter to Prince Christian Frederik written in Nauplion on 28 January 1834. The Ministry of Foreign Affairs were probably reluctant to change Falbe's status because of the additional expenses this would have involved.

43 Letter to Hans Krabbe-Carisius from Nauplion dated 22 January 1834. Ross 1863, 70-71 reports the same incident, but with the added information that Falbe actually turned up at the same time as the diplomats, demanding to be presented with them and making a fool of himself when he was refused.

44 Letter to Prince Christian Frederik written in Nauplion on 24 December 1833. Haugsted 1996, 91.

45 Haugsted 1996, 91.

46 Bower & Bolitho 1939, 72-3 and 77-8; Petropoulos 1968, 230-3; Christiane Lüth described him as a loveable man but slow and pedantic, see Clausen & Rist (eds) 1926, 98-9; Detlevsen 1978, 66; Lüth 1988, 56.

47 Letters to J.G. Adler dated 31 March and 14 July 1834 in The Danish State Archives, the archive of R.A. Adler.

48 Bower & Bolitho 1939, 65-7.

49 Letter to Prince Christian Frederik, written in Nauplion on 4 August 1834.

was referred to in Nauplion as "*die erste Hofdame der Gräfin–Mutter*".[50]

At the same time, Falbe also had dealings with Greeks. In January 1834, he informed the Danish Ministry of Foreign Affairs of his meetings with the Minister of the Interior, Ioannis Kolettis,[51] who had reassured him that "the influence of the administration will succeed against the rebellious party, dreaming of the independence of the country, who assault it and have revolted against the Regency".[52] Kolettis was referring to a suspected insurrection by the Russian Party led by Theodoros Kolokotronis, who had been arrested with other suspects in the late summer of 1833.[53] Falbe also reported on the arrival of a deputation from Samos, which was excluded from the territory of independent Greece, asking for asylum for the Greek families on the island that would prefer to emigrate rather than submit to Turkish rule. They were invited to settle in a ruined town and on nearby land in Euboea in compensation for what they had lost.[54]

An excursion to Mantineia, Tegea and Sparta

One of the persons Falbe met in Nauplion was the philologist and archaeologist Peter Wilhelm Forchhammer (1801-94), a Dane from Husum in Schleswig, who had come to Greece with financial support from the "Fonden ad usos publicos".[55] More consequential, however, was his encounter with "Mr. Ross, Doct: Filos".[56] The person in question was Ludwig Ross from Holstein, at the time a Duchy in personal union with Denmark. Falbe regarded

him as Danish,[57] but Ross did not consider himself so, and today he is claimed for German scholarship.[58] He had come to Greece in 1832 with a grant from the "Fonden ad usos publicos", and he served as the Ephor of Antiquities of the Peloponnese from November 1833 to May 1834, with responsibilities for Arcadia, Laconia, parts of Argolis and Elis. In 1834 he was appointed Keeper of all the antiquities in Greece.[59]

On 28 January 1834, Falbe wrote to Prince Christian Frederik:

Tomorrow I shall depart on a small tour to Mantineia, Tegea and Sparta with Doctor Ross. I cannot expect to obtain any antiquities on this journey because he [Ross] wishes to keep everything for the state. This zeal cannot be tempered by my persuasive arguments … I hope … that my present modesty and deference to the needs of the state may stand me in good stead when I, in time, might wish to acquire something really valuable that they hold in duplicate in the state collections."[60]

In this respect the journey was a disappointment to him. Upon his return, Falbe wrote:

"My trip to Tripolitza and Mistra gave so little result that it is hardly worth reporting upon. Anything in the way of an antiquity was requisitioned by Dr Ross on behalf of the government. The government traces all antiquities and makes such great demands that all private individuals must hand over objects to the State Museum that is to be set up, and the officials have orders to reserve everything that is found so that there is very little prospect of obtaining any marbles, inscriptions, vases or bronzes.[61]

---

50 Ross 1863, 71.

51 Baumstark (ed.) 1999, 385 no. 223; Clogg 2013, 269-70.

52 Haugsted 1996, 91.

53 Kolokotronis was condemned to death but pardoned in 1835; see Petropulos 1968, 201-12; Clegg 1992, 245.

54 Letter to J.G. Adler written in Nauplion on 31 March 1834. His source may well have been reports in *Le sauveur*, a newspaper published in Nauplion; the story appears in a cutting he sent home to Denmark.

55 Haugsted 1996, 91-2, 348.

56 Letter to Prince Christian Frederik written in Nauplion on 24 December 1833. Haugsted 105 note 20.

57 Christian Hansen also regarded Ross as a Dane, cf. Papanicolaou-Christensen 1994, 60.

58 Goette & Palagía(eds) 2005. Dyson 2008, 73-4 refers to him as "German".

59 Letter to Johan Gunder Adler, 4 November 1834. Haugsted 1996, 138 note 1: "I am, however, in a position to notify our most gracious Prince of something good. – The Danish Doctor Phil. Ross has been named Keeper of all Antiquities of Greece, a post which is honourable and gives him a secure salary of 500 rix-dollar species." See further Pántov & Kreeb 2005.

60 Breitenstein 1951, 106; Lund 2000a, 124-7. For the journey to Sparta, see also Ross 1869, 72-4 and Lund 2000a, 124-7.

61 Letter to Prince Christian Frederik, 10 March 1834. Breitenstein 1951, 106-8; Haugsted 1996, 92, 356 no. 47; Lund 2000a, 124-7. For the Greek government's restrictions on the export of antiquities in the 19th century, cf. Kvist 1997.

relief[63] and an inscription[64] from Tegea, a fragment of a sculpture[65] and a piece of an inscription from Tripoli,[66] as well as two fragments of inscriptions from Sparta.[67] Moreover, an entry for 1842 in the inventory of the Collection of Classical and Near Eastern Antiquities informs us that nine pieces of gold jewellery were handed in by Com. Capt. Falbe, "who had acquired them in Nauplia in 1834. They had been found in tombs in Aegina."[68] In the same year, he also got hold of objects from the Cycladic island of Serifos:[69] pottery[70] and oil lamps from different periods,[71] a terracotta figure[72] and some bronzes (Fig. 3).[73] These antiquities were the contents of the two boxes, "one with stones and the other with pots and potsherds", which he sent to Prince Christian Frederik via the Danish Vice-Consul in Marseille.[74] Unfortunately, one item of the "medals, terracottas and tombstones" was missing when the objects were loaded on the Danish ship "Ludwig" in November.[75]

But Falbe's visit to Sparta paid off in another respect. The Regency embarked on an ambitious programme involving the foundation of numerous new towns initiated by Kapodistrias,[76] and the re-foundation of Sparta was decided by a decree of 20 February 1834.[77] During the trip with Ross, Falbe had surveyed the terrain of the new town, and his plan "found the approval of Count von Armansperg; he used it to point out the terrain where he intends to re-build Sparta".[78] Falbe's plan from 1834 seems to be preserved in a copy from 1882 published by Alexander Papageorgiou-Venetas, who was unaware of its origin.[79]

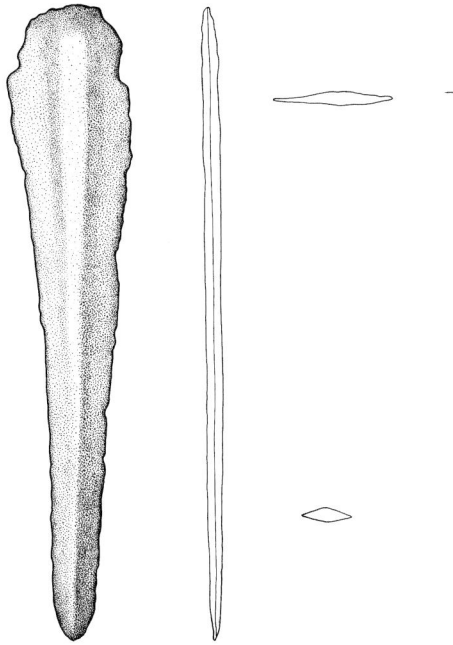

Fig. 3. *Bronze dagger allegedly from Seriphos, The National Museum of Denmark, Collection of Classical and Near Eastern Antiquities, I.n. Aba 341, drawn by Poul Wöliche.*

Despite the restrictions,[62] Falbe was able to acquire some antiquities from the Peloponnese during this trip, which he later presented to Christian Frederik. They are now part of the Danish National Museum: fragments of a grave

---

62   It is highly unlikely that Falbe could have acquired the rather bulky antiquities in question without the knowledge and permission of Ross, who himself presented two Cycladic figurines and other antiquities to Prince Christian Frederik (later King Christian VIII), cf. Riis *et al.* 1989, 26-9 nos. 12-3.

63   Collection of Classical and Near Eastern Antiquities, Inventory number (I.n.) ABb 119.

64   I.n. ABb 121.

65   I.n. ABb 135.

66   I.n. ABb 120.

67   I.n. ABb 117, 122.

68   I.n. ABa 208-15.

69   There is no indication in Falbe's correspondence that he himself visited Seriphos, as tentatively suggested in Lund 2000a, 125.

70   I.n. Chr. VIII 387, 418, 438 and 631; Chr. VIII 383 originates from Aegina or Seriphos.

71   I.n. Chr. VIII 577, 581, 588-589.

72   I.n. Chr. VIII 716.

73   I.n. ABa 267-72, 283-7, 341-3. For the illustrated dagger, I.n. 341, see Dietz *et al.* 2015, 22 no. 12.

74   Letter to Johan Gunder Adler written in Nauplion on 7 July 1834. Haugsted 1996, 92.

75   Letter to Johan Gunder Adler written in Nauplion on 4 November 1834.

76   Bastéa 2000, 43-68.

77   Papanicolaou-Christensen 1994, 60 note 29.

78   For the new town plan of Sparta, see Haugsted 1996, 95; Papageorgiou-Venetas 2009, 206-10.

79   Papageorgiou-Venetas 2008, 208 fig. 86: "Urheber nicht gesichert". The draughtsmanship is highly similar to the plans made by Falbe in Tunisia, cf. Lund 2000b.

Fig. 4. *Perspective view of Athens, sketch and watercolour by Christian Hansen, 1836, The Danish National Art Library, Architectural Drawings S 18545.*

A Danish Institute at Athens?

In his first letter from Nauplion written on Christmas Eve 1833, Falbe informed Prince Christian Frederik of the Regency's plan to transfer the capital to Athens.[80] He looked forward to this, because the climate in Nauplion did not agree with him. Greek families who also wanted to move there were putting pressure on the Government to set things in motion and so were 150 families from Chios, who wished to settle in the Piraeus.[81]

Falbe later reported home that the members of the Regency used all occasions to "urge the foreign envoys and everybody else to build in Athens", arguing that this would be cheaper than renting. He claimed that a building lot might be bought at a reasonable price and that most of the wood and iron needed for construction work could come from Denmark. Moreover,

"the Royal Danish Academy of Fine Arts, the Royal Academy of Sciences and Letters and the Royal Museum in Copenhagen might wish to have a place in Athens, where scientists and

artists could deposit their things and where one could receive and lodge *high*–ranking persons who wished to visit the town".

Falbe urged immediate action,[82] noting the expenditure involved in building a consulate would repay itself after eight years in comparison with the money to be paid for renting.[83]

Regrettably, nothing came of Falbe's proposal, which in a way anticipated the founding of the Danish Institute in Athens in 1992.[84] It is not without interest that the first foreign Archaeological School in Greece, the École française d'Athènes, was not established until 1846, followed by the Deutsches Archäologisches Institut in 1874, the American School of Classical Studies in 1881 and the British School in 1886.[85]

Athens 1834-5

Around 1800, Athens had about 9000 inhabitants and 1200 to 1300 houses,[86] but the town was subsequently

---

80 Athens was first spoken of as the future capital of Greece in a German newspaper in October 1832, according to Mackenzie 1992, 128. The idea was enthusiastically endorsed by Ludwig I of Bavaria, the father of King Otto, cf. Bower & Bolitho 1939, 73; Papageorgiou-Venetas 1999, 69; Bastéa 2000, 6-9; Kotsowillis 2007, 40-1; Papageorgiou-Venetas 2008, 31-41.

81 Letter to Prince Christian Frederik, Copenhagen, 24 December 1833, Haugsted 1996, 91.

82 Letter to Prince Christian Frederik, Copenhagen, dated 28 January 1834. Liventhal 1986, 344; Haugsted 1996, 98, 109 note 50.

83 Letter to Prince Christian Frederik, 10 March 1834,

84 Lehmann 1994, 3: "It is said, albeit with a certain reservation, that the Danish General Consul in Athens, Christian Tuxen Falbe, was the first to suggest the establishment of a Danish Institute in Athens already in the 1830'ies."

85 Korka (ed.) 2005.

86 Lund 2009, 75.

Fig. 5. *Hadrian's Library and the Tzistarakis mosque, watercolour by General Carl Wilhelm von Heideck, dated 15 April 1835 and presented to Christine Stampe. Copenhagen, the Royal Museum of Fine Art, Nysø Album Td 145.*

destroyed during the War of Independence, and it was said to have no more than 6000 inhabitants in 1832 (Figs 4-5).[87] Two years later, Athens hardly comprised 150 small houses and the same number of miserable huts, which made it difficult and expensive to find lodgings there.[88] Falbe described the incredibly chaotic conditions of the transfer from Nauplion in mid-winter during rain and sleet in December 1834, comparing the scene to Napoleon's retreat from Moscow in 1812.[89] The furniture and luggage of 3000 people, which had been sent to the Pireaus, had been left on the beach because of the absence of "storage magazines, wagons to transport the goods and a road to transport them on" (Fig. 6). A new road from Piraeus to Athens had been decreed, but not completed, whereas the old road had been made impassable. The ship carrying Falbe's family from Salamis to Athens was very nearly wrecked, and they only reached Piraeus after five hours of rowing, wet through due to bad weather; they then had to endure one and a half hours in an open carriage to Athens, where they had to spend the night in the allotted house without bedclothes or spare clothes.

---

87 Kairophílas 2011, 41; Bower & Bolitho 1939, 73-4; Mackenzie 1992, 105-26; Papageorgiou-Venetas 1999, 69; Angelomátis 2007. Bastéa (2000, 10-14) paints a somewhat more positive picture.

88 Letter from Falbe in The State Archives, The Archive of Christian VIII; Mackenzie 1992, 125: "only about a hundred and fifty [houses] were still in a reasonable condition"; Papageorgiou-Venetas 1999, 71: "Nach Ende des Unabhängigkeitskrieges waren nur and die 25 der etwa 1200 Hauser in der Altstadt intakt geblieben". According to Bastéa (2000, 6), Athens had a population of about 12,000 in 1834.

89 The State Archives, The Archive of Christian VIII.

Fig. 6. *The harbour of Piraeus, sketched by Christian Hansen in 1834, The Danish National Art Library, Architectural Drawings S 18543.*

Two of the children are ill, and I am surprised that we are not all. For the time being everything is in a state of great confusion, and a couple of months must pass before a little quiet and order can come to pass; but we would then have only three months until the day when the king reaches the age of majority.

When Otto arrived in Athens on 1 December,[90] he passed through the gate of the Emperor Hadrian, of which one side is inscribed: "This is the Athens of Theseus", and the other: "This is not the city of Theseus but the one built by Hadrian". Otto was celebrated by a temporary addition of a board over the ancient marble gate with a painted inscription proclaiming: "This is now neither the city of Theseus nor that of Hadrian, but the Athens of Otto" (Fig. 7).[91] The newspapers were nevertheless full of complaints about disturbances caused by the billeting of the soldiers.[92] A few months later Falbe reported to Prince Christian Frederik that the State had no money; the foreign subsidies having been spent and that

there is often unrest in the provinces. Here in Athens, a Vespro Siciliano against all Germans had been scheduled for the 6th of April; however, it was too publicly known to be realised. Still, there had been fights and maltreatments three nights in a row before the appointed day, during which some Germans lost their lives, and the Greeks were up to no good.[93]

These were early expressions of a growing anti-German sentiment among the Greeks, which erupted more forcefully in the late 1830s and 1840s.[94]

---

90 Bastéa 2000, 6-7; Kairophílas 2011, 82-5.

91 Letter to Prince Christian Frederik written in Athens in December 1834. Haugsted 1996, 128 note 44. According to Bastéa (2000, 10), the gate had been adorned with a similar inscription at a previous visit Otto made to Athens.

92 The State Archives, The Archive of Christian VIII. See also Mackenzie 1992, 129.

93 Letter to Prince Christian Frederik written in Athens on 16 April 1835.

94 Clogg 2013, 50-1. For an example of this sentiment on the Peloponnese in 1834, see Ross 1863, 73-4. In 1840 Christiane Lüth wrote that "Immediately after the New Year a conspiracy was uncovered, which had as its purpose to drive all Germans out of Greece, because the Greeks thought that they could themselves take care of the positions, which had been given to the Bavarians. And in many ways they were right", cf. Clausen & Rist (eds) 1926, 80; Lüth 1988, 40.

Fig. 7. *Temporary wooden arch erected in commemoration of King Otto's arrival. In the background the Arch of Hadrian. Drawn by Christian Hansen on 1 December 1834, The Danish National Art Library, Architectural Drawings S 18540.*

According to Falbe, as late as July 1835 there were only four good houses in Athens built by foreigners, no public buildings, and no thoughts had been given to water conduits or drains (Figs 8-9). "The Palace is not yet begun, nor the pipe lines or drains. All the filth remains in the houses or piles up in the streets among building material which is never taken away." He added that the Greeks were only building half–timbered houses with shops on the ground floor and some rooms on the upper floor, and that most houses were painted ochre yellow.[95] One of the most successful Danish residents at the time was the architect Christian Hansen,[96] who lived in Greece from August 1833 to August 1850, drawing ancient and modern monuments (Fig. 10). He was the Government's architect from 1834 to 1843 and designed numerous private hous-

es, churches and public buildings in Athens, notably the University.[97]

Consular business

The first and, in the eyes of the Commerce Department in Copenhagen, only duty of Danish consuls was to protect and assist Danish traders and sea-merchants, but Falbe's letters from Greece contain few references to such matters, presumably because hardly any such trade existed. In fact, he reported to the Commerce Department that Greece would not yield any advantage as far as Danish trade was concerned for many years to come, suggesting – without success – that Denmark might follow the example of the Dutch in establishing a joint-stock company to

95 Letter to Prince Christian Frederik, written in Athens on 7 July 1835. Haugsted 1996, 129 note 51.

96 In the summer of 1834, Hansen had come to Nauplion where Falbe instructed him in how best to take imprints of inscriptions. Letter to Jacob Christian Lindberg written in Nauplion on 28 September 1834. Haugsted 195 note 21.

97 Papanicolaou-Christensen 1994; Haugsted 1996, 348-9.

98 Letter to Prince Christian Frederik written in Athens on 16 April 1835.

99 According to Allgemeine Wochenblatt of Aabenraa no. 1211 on 30 July 1835; cf. Haugsted 1996, 125 note 57: "it was stated that the officers Motz and Gainer worked in a surveyor's office in Athens, Joh. Müller worked as a bricklayer and Christoph Richter as a carpenter, and the Officer Wachenhausen was looking for employment. Major Fabricius, who was now doing service in Athens, was visited by his two brothers; one was a theologian and tutor in Syros, the other, Lieutenant Theodor Fabricius, was doing service in Piraeus. The naval officer C. Köster served at Poros, and the soldiers Renouard, Bonnet and Lange were employed in Nauplia and Megara."

21

Fig. 8. *View of the city of Athens with Lykabettos in the background, drawn by Christian Hansen in 1834. The Danish National Art Library, Architectural Drawings S 18543.*

trade with the Levant.[98] Nevertheless, Falbe did his best to help his compatriots who came to Greece at the time – in July 1835 there were reportedly 29 Danes living in Greece (including individuals from Schleswig-Holstein).[99] He lent money to Hansen to see him through until his stipend from the Academy arrived from Copenhagen,[100] and he also helped others in the same way, but he regretted the arrival of former Danish officers, because the employment of strangers had stopped "and the Greeks are clearly hostile towards foreign soldiers". More and more were coming, but no jobs were to be found for them, and the Commerce Department refused to compensate him for what he had given to those in need, because he was only supposed to help shipwrecked sailors in this way.[101] Falbe

still managed to find employment as a surveyor for the Danish lieutenant Sames,[102] and he reported home that a law had been passed stipulating that anyone who had fought in the Greek War of Independence was entitled to receive national property to the price of 2000 drachmae. He wanted to find out if the Danish Philhellenes or their heirs could lay claim to this sum.[103] Another Dane – like Ross a native of Holsten – who came to Athens at the time was the librarian and law student Adolph Ludvig Køppen, who was trying to perfect his knowledge of Modern Greek.[104] Falbe helped Køppen find employment as a teacher at the Military Academy on Aegina by introducing him to the Minister of War, and Køppen was duly appointed professor there on 28 November 1835.[105]

---

100 Papanicolaou-Christensen 1994, 59 note 24; Haugsted 1996, 92 note 20 and 94. Ludwig Ross had invited Christian Hansen to accompany him and Falbe on their excursion to Sparta in 1834, but Hansen had to decline due to lack of money; cf. Papanicolaou-Christensen 1994, 60.

101 Letter to Christian Frederik written in Athens on 16 April. The Danish consulates abroad did not as a rule receive compensation for money given to anyone other than seamen in need, cf. Kjølsen 1970, 310-1.

102 Letter to Jacob Christian Lindberg written in Nauplion on 28 September 1834. Haugsted 1996, 125 note 52.

103 Letter to Prince Christian Frederik dated 7 July 1835. The law also applied to all native-born Greek heads of families, see Gallant 2001, 35-7.

104 Haugsted 1996, 350.

105 Letter to Christian Frederik written in Athens on 16 April 1835. Cf. Haugsted 1996, 123-4 and Papanikoláov-Kristensen 2015, 18-27.

Fig. 10. *View of the Lion Gate Entrance to the Acropolis of Athens, drawn by Christian Hansen in 1833-1834. The Danish National Art Library, Architectural Drawings S 18543.*

Fig. 9. *A street in Athens, drawn by Christian Hansen in 1833-1834. The Danish National Art Library, Architectural Drawings S 18540.*

A good deal of Falbe's time was consumed by attending tedious (one would think) duties of a ceremonial nature, such as his presence on 4 May 1835 at the inauguration of a monument in the Piraeus honouring Georgios Karaïskakis, a hero of the War of Independence, who had been killed in action on 23 April 1827.[106] Falbe reported that:

The remains of Karaïskakis, which were on the island of Salamis, were together with others brought here and placed in a common grave under the monument. The King made a short speech, and at the end he took the Cross of Our Saviour, which he himself carried, and put it in the open coffin of Karaïskakis. This sign of respect for one of the best soldiers of Greece pleased everybody.[107]

---

106 Brewer 2001, 312-3.
107 Haugsted 1996, 136.

Fig. 11. *The Temple of Hephaistos from the southeast, sketched by Christian Hansen in 1836. The Danish National Art Library, Architectural Drawings S 18541.*

In the Early Christian period, the temple of Hephaistos had been converted to a church dedicated to Aghios Georghios, which later served as a burial ground for some of the foreigners who died in Athens (Fig. 11). But it was decided in November 1834 that the church should be made into an archaeological museum, which it was from 1835 to 1874,[108] and plans were being laid to establish a special Protestant cemetery elsewhere.[109] Falbe tried in vain to persuade his superiors in Copenhagen to contribute 200 rix-dollars to this initiative, which involved England, Prussia, Bavaria, Sweden and the Netherlands. He had seen remains of the deceased being disturbed by pigs and jackals and argued that such a cemetery would be appropriate where so many Danes were living, and where

Danish artists and scholars would be frequent guests in the future.[110] We do not know why Falbe was unsuccessful in drumming up Danish support for the initiative. A Protestant cemetery was eventually established, after his departure from Greece and without Danish support; it was situated close to the Ilissos River, opposite the Panathenaic Stadium.[111] As foreseen by Falbe, a number of Danes came to be buried there, e.g. Christian Friederich Thomas Fabricius (Fig. 12), presumably a relative, perhaps the brother, of Christoph Detlef.[112] Another brother of his, Theodor Fabricius, was doing service in Piraeus,[113] and yet another, Carl Fabricius, was employed as a tutor in Syros at first, and later in Nauplion and Athens.[114] Two children of Christiane Lüth were also buried in this cem-

---

108 Papanicoulaou-Christensen 1994, 63 note 46; Haugsted 1996, 132-4; Kókkou 2009, 170-4.

109 Lund 2006.

110 Letter to Prince Christian Frederik written in Athens on 7 July 1835.

111 The area can clearly be made out on old photographs of the area; see Papanicolaou-Christensen 2004, 94 fig. 73.

112 The inscription on the preserved tomb stone reads "GEBOREN IN FRIEDRICHSTADT IN DAENNEMARK DEN 14 MAI 1806 GESTORBEN IN ATHEN DEN 11 NOVBR 1836". I have not been able to find any other information about him.

113 Haugsted 1996, 125.

114 Lüth 1988, 132 note 152a. See also Haugsted 1996, 136 and 350.

Fig. 13. *Bronze bracelet, The National Museum of Denmark, Collection of Classical and Near Eastern Antiquities, I.n. Aba 319, drawn by Poul Wöliche.*

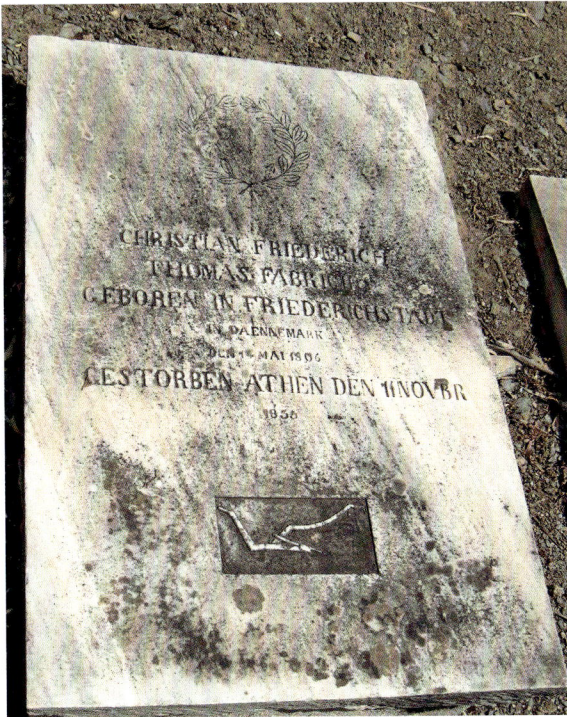

Fig. 12. *Tombstone of Christian Friederich Thomas Fabricius, who died in Athens on 11 November 1836. Photo: John Lund.*

etery, and their tombstones are preserved to this day.[115] She was the Danish wife of A.H.F. Lüth, the priest of King Otto's Queen Amalia.[116] In the early 19th century, the protestant cemetery was moved to within the confines of the First Cemetery of Athens.

The most auspicious official event in Athens in 1835 was the coming of age of Otto on 1 June.[117] The Regency was abolished at the same time, but Otto retained Count Armansperg as "Arch–Chancellor" and the German influence on Greek affairs did not diminish. Athens was decorated with myrtle and olive to celebrate the occasion, arches were erected in the streets, and the King received the Diplomatic Corps in the palace.[118] Falbe's lack of dip-

lomatic status possibly barred him from taking part in this event, because it is not mentioned in his letters, though it is possible that he described the coming of age celebrations in the lost first eight pages of the letter he wrote to Prince Christian Frederik on 7 July 1835.

Collecting antiquities and coins

In Athens, Ludwig Ross accorded Falbe plaster casts of two slabs of the Parthenon frieze, which were sent to The Royal Academy of Arts in Copenhagen.[119] They reached Denmark in the spring of 1836.[120]

One of Falbe's most persistent desires was to acquire genuine antiquities and coins for collectors and collections in Denmark, but – as he had already learnt in Nauplion – this was a difficult pursuit because of the Government's restrictions. Still, he did manage to acquire some antiquities from Athens, which subsequently entered the Danish

---

115 Lund 2006.
116 Falbe had long left Greece when Otto married Amalie Marie von Oldenburg (1818-1875) in 1836; cf. Kairophílas 2011, 102-110 and Baumstark 1999, 406-49.
117 Petropulos 1968, 218-33.
118 Bower & Bolitho 1939, 79-80; Kairophílas 2011, 92-3.
119 Papanicolaou-Christensen 1994, 66.
120 Haugsted 1996, 137.

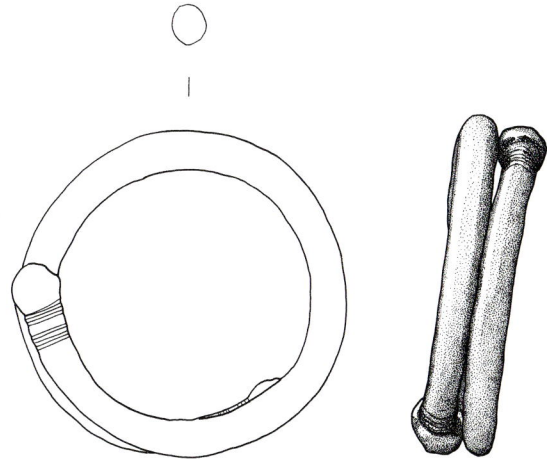

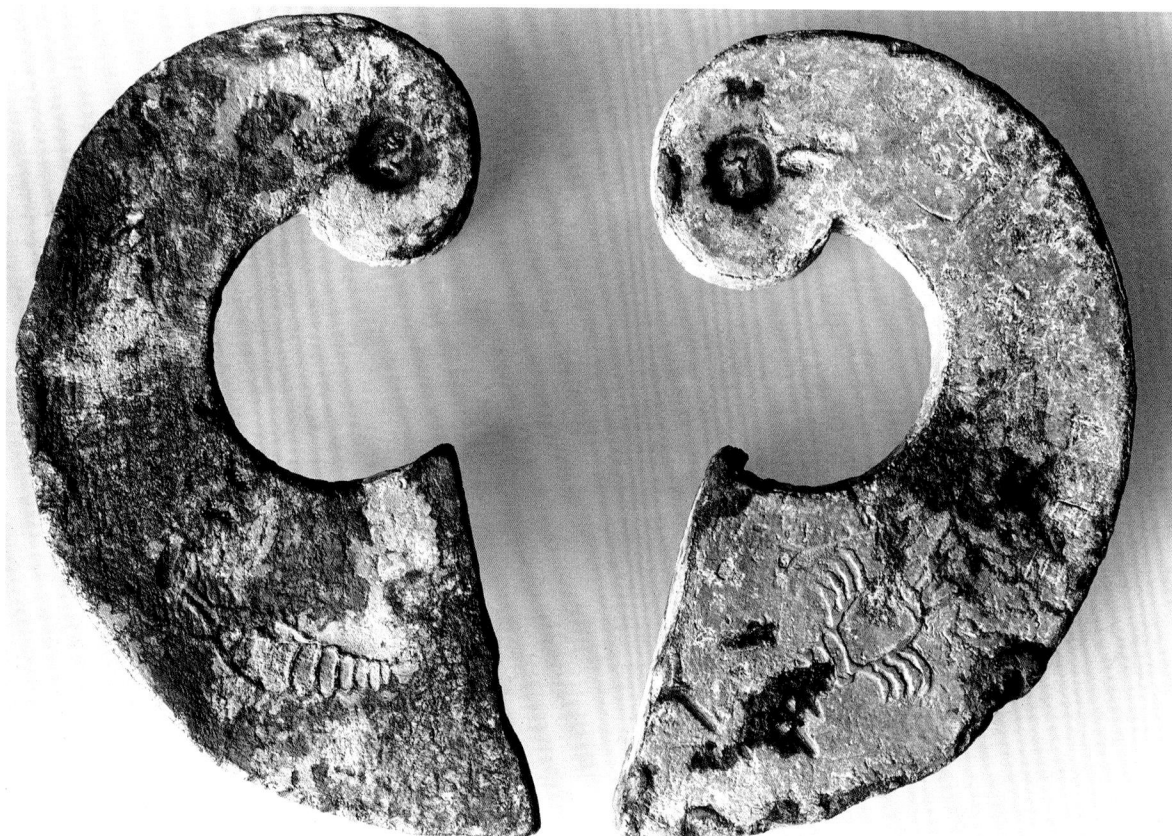

Fig. 14. Halteres *of lead with scorpions, I.n. Aba 364. Photo: Sophus Bengtsson.*

National Museum: pottery,[121] an oil lamp,[122] a terracotta figure,[123] a pre-Mycenaean bracelet (Fig. 13)[124] and two jumping-weights of lead (Fig. 14).[125] Perhaps the most interesting find is described as follows in the inventory: "Foot of a horse with hoof of excellent workmanship. Now made up of three pieces, the old bronze nails fixed with lead solder, for fastening this foot to the figure, can still be seen". The fragment was supposedly found near the Parthenon temple on the Acropolis, near the Parthenon (Fig. 15).[126] Epidaurus is given as the provenance for two pottery finds and a glass bottle,[127] and Aegina for some ceramics,[128] an oil lamp,[129] a grave relief and a fragment of sculpture.[130] A fragment of a Doric column drum with parts of three flutes comes from the temple of Aphaea.[131]

---

121 Collection of Classical and Near Eastern Antiquities, Inventory numbers Chr. VIII 300, 315, 318, 389, 412, 427, 430, 450, 492, 510. Chr. VIII 388 has Attica as provenance.

122 I.n. Chr. VIII 591.

123 I.n. Chr. VIII 709.

124 I.n. ABa 319. Dietz *et al.* 2015, 35 no. 80.

125 I.n. ABa 364. Lund & Rasmussen 1995, 56.

126 See Williams forthcoming; the information about the provenance of i.n. ABb 130 no doubt goes back to that supplied by Falbe himself. Also from Athens are i.n. ABb 133 and i.n. ABb 144.

127 I.n. Chr. VIII 542.

128 I.n. Chr. VIII 317, 380, 382, 424, 660, 666, 677, 686.

129 I.n. Chr. VIII 580.

130 I.n. ABb 132.

131 Without i.n., Riis 1936, 231 no. 3.

Fig. 15. *The Parthenon with the mosque inside, drawn by Martinus Rør-bye in 1835. The National Museum of Denmark, Collection of Classical and Near Eastern Antiquities, a gift from the Ny Carlsberg Foundation.*

Throughout his stay, Falbe eagerly collected coins and medals for Prince Christian Frederik, despite being cheated by forgers on Syros "with an Attic Gold-medal, a couple of inedited silver coins and ancient Lead-medallions".[132] Perhaps he was more successful as a collector of coins than antiquities,[133] but this aspect of his activities has not yet formed the subject of a special investigation.[134] However, in the spring of 1935, Falbe informed the Danish Prince of an unexpected encounter in Athens with a fellow officer (and numismatist):

Lieutenant Giede is among those who think they can find a career in Greece. He arrived here at the beginning of March. His broad knowledge and ability make him really fit for instruction, which he also applies for. Although I can take no responsibility for him (and the reason for this Your Majesty knows), I cannot deny him a certain assent, which his learning deserves.[135]

Giede had been educated at the Naval Academy, but was found temperamentally unfit for service in the Danish Navy in spite of his undoubted abilities. Falbe's reservations were probably caused by an immature streak in Giede's character. The captain and officers of the naval cadet ship "Najaden" concluded that his temperament and attitude made him incapable of accepting the strict military discipline, and he later fell into bad company after having come into an inheritance.[136] Still, Giede had been interested in numismatics since his youth, and he had assisted Falbe when he was in charge of the private collection of Prince Christian Frederik in the Amalienborg Castle from 1831 to 1833.[137] Giede went on to become director of the first Greek Coin Cabinet, which was established in the new Mint built by Hansen, but he died in Athens on 18 November 1836.[138] His tomb has not been preserved.

Falbe's circle of acquaintances

Falbe seems to have associated mainly with other European envoys in Nauplion and Athens. He met members of the Regency and other Government officials from time to

---

132 Letter to Prince Christian Frederik written in Athens on 16 April 1835.

133 Cf. Haugsted 1996, 92: "Mostly, when Falbe was in the country, he procured only coins."

134 Neither Mørkholm 1981 nor Steen Jensen 2000 refer to Falbe's activities as a numismatist in Athens. He is known to have presented gifts to the new Numismatic Museum in Athens, see Kókkou 2009, 259 note 1.

135 Letter to Prince Christian Frederik from Athens, dated 16 April 1835; Haugsted 1989-90 [1994], 13; Haugsted 1996, 125.

136 Haugsted 1989-90 [1994], 6-8; Haugsted 1996, 348 and *passim*.

137 Haugsted 1989-90 [1994], 8-11.

138 Haugsted 1989-90 [1994], 16-7; Kókkou 2009, 259-60.

27

time, and the letters of support to him written by Count von Armansperg on the eve of his recall (see below) suggest that the court held him in a high regard.

Falbe had attended meetings with Ioannis Kolettis in Nauplion, and met him again in August 1835, on the ship which took the Falbe family from Athens to Italy. Kolettis, who was on his way to Paris as a Greek envoy, had formerly been a doctor; when Falbe's eldest son broke his leg on the ship, Kolettis helped him and comforted his wife.[139] Incidentally, this son was reportedly the only member of the family who spoke passable Greek.[140] Falbe was fluent in French, and probably learnt some Arabic during his stay in Tunisia, but there is no evidence that he himself learned Greek. Newspapers published in Greece were apparently a prime source of information for him, and he enclosed a cutting from *Le sauveur* in Nauplion in one of his letters, but the text is bilingual (in Greek and French).

Falbe's social life was probably otherwise restricted to his family and the Danes who resided in or visited Greece during his stay. He seems to have been on good terms with all of these, except perhaps Forchhammer, and in his memoirs, Ludwig Ross characterised him as *"nicht ohne Talent, auch ein tüchtiger Numismatiker, aber wie fast alle Dänen von einer unglaublichen Eitelkeit und Selbstliebe, und voller Ansprüche"*.[141]

Falbe is recalled

Complaints about the exorbitant living expenses in Greece are a recurring theme in Falbe's letters home. He quoted statements to the effect that Nauplion was even more expensive than London, and stated that he and his family had to go without the simplest of things. "If things are to continue thus it will lead to my destruction."[142] The Commerce Department had not given him the financial support usually granted for the establishment of consulates, and Falbe threatened in 1834 to "send my wife and children home and let them live at the expense of their relatives" while he himself remained in Greece – unless he was granted more money.[143] Things were just as bad in Athens.[144] In October 1835, Christian Hansen noted that living expenses there were about twice as high as in Copenhagen, and the excessive cost of living in the new capital is well documented by other sources.[145]

The Commerce Department was not moved by Falbe's constant complaints, though it took steps to find out whether the General Consul in Greece of Sweden and Norway had received a raise in payment. In the end the Department concluded that the annual expenditure in maintaining a presence in Greece might well exceed 7000 rix-dollars, a sum that was deemed too high to justify keeping a Danish Consul General in Athens. This seems to have contributed to the decision to abolish the post in 1835. In fact, The Commerce Department sent a note as early as 22 November 1834 to the Ministry of Foreign Affairs acknowledging that the hopes nurtured in 1829 with regard to the potential importance of the "New Greek" state to Danish trade and shipping had not been realised. A reference was made to Falbe's reports, which concluded that Greece would not yield any advantage as far as trade was concerned for many years to come. The Commerce Department accordingly concluded that the costs involved in maintaining a Danish General Consul in Greece were unjustified and wished to see the post abolished.

King Frederik VI formally decided to recall Falbe on 3 March 1835, but news about the decision reached Athens well before that date.[146] Falbe informed Adler about it in a letter dated 19 February 1835, and he notified Prince Christian Frederik on 16 April that "rumours about my recall have reached Athens from Copenhagen", explaining that that Theodor Kjerstrup von Ruhmor, a journalist at the *Statstidende* had been very well informed about the

---

139 Haugsted 1996, 136.

140 Letter to Prince Christian Frederik written in Athens on 16 April 1835.

141 Ross 1863, 70; cf. Haugsted 1996, 90.

142 Letter to Prince Christian Frederik, Copenhagen, of 24 December 1833, Haugsted 1996, 91.

143 Letter to Prince Christian Frederik, Copenhagen, dated 28 January 1834.

144 It is possible that the Greeks may have been better able to cope with the fluctuating prices, see Papageorgiou & Minóglou 1988.

145 Papanicolaou-Christensen 1994, 64 note 56; Kairophílas 2011, 73-81.

146 According to a document dated 28 July 1840 in the State Archives, Departementet for udenlandske anliggender. Grækenland. Danske konsuler 1829 – Danske konsuler 1845.

matter.[147] Von Ruhmor was the brother-in-law of Liutenant Sames in Athens, who was presumably Falbe's source.

The Greek authorities tried to have the decision changed. Before the end of March, Count von Armansperg asked the Greek representative in Paris to inform the Danish ambassador that the Greek court was delighted to have a Danish presence in Athens – in particular in the person of Falbe, and that the Greek king wished for him to stay on as a *chargé d'affaires* after Otto's coming of age. And on 18 May, von Armansperg instructed the Greek consul in Copenhagen to notify the Danish king of this wish. But he was informed by the Commerce Department on 9 June that Frederik VI regretted that it was too late for the decision to be changed.[148] Falbe, who was well aware of these interventions on the part of the Greeks, had delayed his departure from Athens until the matter was settled, and the outcome had still not been communicated to him by the beginning of July.[149] But he must have been notified shortly afterwards, because he and his family left Greece for good in August 1835.

Mission impossible

During his less than two years in Greece, Falbe managed – despite his lack of diplomatic status – to establish good relations with the leading member of the Regency, von Armansperg, and he was apparently also appreciated by King Otto. Falbe was also well connected with the other European envoys in Greece, and he assisted resident Danes and those who came to Greece in those years to seek their fortune to the best of his ability. Some of them he helped to find employment, he lent money to others and attempted to find out if any Danish Philhellenes or their families were entitled to receive the national property at the price of 2000 drachmae to which they were entitled by Greek law. As far as is known he was unsuccessful in this endeavour.

Falbe foresaw that Athens would attract Danish scholars and artists in the future, and he proposed building a

Consulate in the city, where their luggage could be stored and visiting dignitaries could be housed. He had Christian Hansen in mind as the architect of this building, which – had it been realised – would have anticipated the establishment of the Danish Institute in Athens in 1992 by more than 150 years. Moreover, Falbe foresaw that some of the Danish visitors would die during their stay in Athens and argued that Denmark should contribute financially to the establishment of a new protestant cemetery. Nothing came of this suggestion either.

All of this mattered little to the Commerce Department in Copenhagen, which recalled Falbe in the summer of 1835. In the eyes of the Department, his sole responsibility as Consul General was to look after the interests of Danish shipping and trade,[150] but such commerce had turned out to be nearly non-existent, and Falbe himself acknowledged that Greece would not yield any advantage as far as trade was concerned for many years to come. Moreover, it had emerged that the costs of maintaining a Danish presence in Greece were far higher than anticipated. The Ministry of Foreign Affairs in Copenhagen could have chosen to let Falbe stay on as a *chargé d'affaires*, as the Greek court wished, but it was unwilling to take this step, perhaps because the Director of the Department felt that Falbe was not the right person for the job, or perhaps because of the financial situation.

Conclusion

Falbe certainly made the best out of his time in Greece, and if the results were in many respects less than hoped for, the blame rests not with him but with the bureaucrats in the Ministry of Foreign Affairs in Copenhagen and their lack of understanding of the role an emerging state such as Greece could have played for Danish shipping and trade. Indeed, it is difficult to comprehend – even without the benefit of hindsight – how and why the Commerce Department could have formed its initial optimistic view of these prospects, that is to appoint a Danish Consul

---

147 Letter to Prince Christian Frederik from Athens written 16 April 1835.

148 The relevant documents are kept in the file entitled "Departementet for udenlandske anliggender. Græenland. Danske konsuler 1829 – Danske konsuler 1845".

149 Letter from Falbe to Bülow on 18 March 1835; and to Adler on 5 March and again on 6 April 1835. Letter to Prince Christian Frederik written on 7 July in Athens.

150 According to the consular instruction, his duty was to "seek to the utmost of his abilities to further the benefit of our realm and countries in general and more specifically the commerce and sea-trade of our subjects", cf. Kjølsen 1970, 300-1.

General in Greece in the first place. Falbe's relatively short stay in Greece left a permanent mark on Denmark in the form of the coins and antiquities he collected. These are kept in the Danish National Museum, and the objects on display in the Collection of Classical and Near Eastern Antiquities help to inform Danish audiences about the civilisation of ancient Greece. Moreover, his letters from Greece give valuable and in some cases vivid firsthand accounts of life in Greece from 1833 to 1835, a crucial period in the formation of Modern Greece. They also reflect the roles played by Danes in this process. This contribution has deliberately focused on these aspects of Falbe's undertakings, instead of exploring the poten-

tial of integrating a Danish perspective into the recent postcolonial research about Greece in the 19th century. Such an attempt would surely be worthwhile, but it calls for separate treatment.

JOHN LUND
Collection of Classical and Near Eastern Antiquities
Ancient Cultures of Denmark and the Mediterranean
The National Museum of Denmark
Frederiksholms Kanal 12
DK–1220 Copenhagen K
John.Lund@natmus.dk

Bibliography

Archival sources

THE NATIONAL MUSEUM OF DENMARK

BESKRIVELSE over DE ÆGYP-TISKE, GRÆSKE OG ROMERSKE OLDSAGER i det KONGELIGE KUNSTMUSEUM April 1826 Indbe-fattende Antiksamlingens Forögelse til Aaret 1856

THE STATE ARCHIVES

Letters written by C.T. Falbe to Prince Christian Frederik, Haugsted 1996, 355-6 nos. 44, 46, 47, 50, 51, 54, 61, 71, 74, 75.

Letters written by C.T. Falbe to Johan Gunder Adler, Haugsted 1996, 356 nos. 48, 52, 56, 58, 59, 62, 65, 66, 68, 70, 72.

Letters written by C.T. Falbe to Hans Krabbe–Carisius, Haugsted 1996, 355 nos. 45, 49, 69.

Letter written by C.T. Falbe to F.C. von Bülow, Haugsted 1996, 356 no. 67.

Departementet for udenlandske anlig-gender. Grækenland. Danske konsuler 1829 – Danske konsuler 1845.

THE ROYAL LIBRARY

Letter written by C.T. Falbe to Peter Oluf Brøndsted, Haugsted 1996, 356 no. 60.

Letters written by C.T. Falbe to Jacob Christian Lindberg, Haugsted 1996, 356 nos. 53, 55, 57, 63, 64, 73.

Printed sources

Angeláki, R. 2010
'Άπο τον Καποδίστρία στον Όθωνα', in *1821: Η γεννοή ενος έθνους–κράτος Δ' τόμος*, Σ. Βασιλείου, Κ. Παπανικουλάου & Ρ. Αγγελάκη (eds), Αθήνα, 113-59.

Angelomátis, Ch. 2007
Η Απελευθέρωση των Αθηνών: Ο Μεντρεσές και οι αναμνήσεις του, Αθήνα.

Bastéa, E. 2000
The Creation of Modern Athens: Planning the Myth, Cambridge, New York & Melbourne.

Baumstark, R. (ed.) 1999
Das neue Hellas: Griechen und Bayern zur Zeit Ludwigs I, München.

Berner, M.L. 1997
'Lysavlede fuldtegninger. Fotografi, kunst og naturvidenskab i Danmark 1839-40', *Fund og Forskning i Det kongelige Biblioteks samlinger 36*, 133-92.

Bobé, L. 1933
Moritz Hartmann MDCLVI–MDCXXV. Dansk og venetiansk Orlogs-kaptajn, Ridder af San Marco og Gouverneur i Trankebar: Danmarks forbindelser med Republiken Venedig, København.

Bower, L. & G. Bolitho 1939
Otho I: King of Greece. A Biography, London.

Breitenstein, N. 1951
'Christian VIII's Vasecabinet', in *Antik-Cabinettet 1851 udgivet i hundredaaret af Nationalmuseet*, København, 57-176.

Brewer, D. 2001
The Flame of Freedom: The Greek War of Independence 1821-1833, London.

Brewer, D. 2010
Greece, the Hidden Centuries: Turkish Rule from the Fall of Constantinople to Greek Independence, London.

Brøndsted, P. O. 1844
P.O. Brøndsted's Reise i Grækenland i Aarene 1810-1813, N.V. Dorph (ed.), København.

Bundgaard Rasmussen, B. 2000
'P.O. Brøndsted – 'den lille professor Worm' – arkæolog og antikvar', in *København–Athen tur/retur: Danmark og Grækenland i 1800-tallet* (MedKøb Ny Serie 2), København, 87-97.

Bundgaard Rasmussen, B. & J. Lund 2002 [2004]
'On the creation of the Collection of Classical Antiquities in the Danish National Museum', *Pharos, Journal of the Netherlands Institute in Athens 10*, 169-78.

Bundgaard Rasmussen, B., J. Steen Jensen & J. Lund (eds) 2000
Christian VIII & The National Museum: Antiquities. Coins. Medals, Copenhagen.

Christiansen, J. 2000
The Rediscovery of Greece: Denmark and Greece in the 19th century, Copenhagen.

Clausen, J. & P. F. Rist (eds) 1926
Fra Fredensborg til Athen. Fragment af en Kvindes Liv, (Memoirer og Breve XLVIII), Kjøbenhavn.

31

Clogg, R. 2013
A Concise History of Greece (3rd ed.), Cambridge.

Detlevsen, K. H. 1978
Rejsen til Athen. Danske i Grækenland i 1800-tallet, København.

Dickopf, K. 1995
'Die bayerische Regentschaft in Griechenland (1833-1835)', in *Die erträumte Nation. Griechenlands Wiedergeburt im 19. Jahrhundert*, R. Heydenreuter, J. Murken & R Wünsche (eds), München, 83-95.

Dietz, S., T. J. Papadopoulos & L. Kontorli–Papadopoulou 2015
Prehistoric Aegean and Near Eastern Metal Types. The National Museum of Denmark Collection of Classical and Near Eastern Antiquities, Aarhus.

Dyson, S.L. 2008
In Pursuit of Ancient Pasts: A History of Classical Archaeology in the Nineteenth and Twentieth Centuries, New Haven & London.

Falbe, C. T. 1833
Explorations sur la site de Carthage, Paris.

Fenger, J. F. 1832
Om det nygræske Folk og Sprog: Erindringer fra en Reise i Grækenland i Aaret 1831, Kjøbenhavn.

Freed, J. 2011
Bringing Carthage Home: The Excavations of Nathan Davies, 1856-1859, Oxford.

Friedrich, R. 2015
König Otto von Griechenland: Die bayer-ische Regentschaft in Nauplia 1833/1834, München.

Gallant, T. W. 2001
Modern Greece: From the War of Independence to the Present, London.

Gallant, T. W. 2015
The Edinburgh History of the Greeks, 1768 to 1913, Edinburgh.

Ghazaleh, M. F. 2005
Danmark og den Græske Frihedskrig: Den dansk philhellenistiske bevægelse i 1820erne, Thesis, University of Copenhagen.

Goette, H. R. & O. Palagía (eds) 2005
Ludwig Ross und Griechenland. Akten des Internationalen Kolloquiums Athen, 2.–3. Oktober 2002, Rahden/Westf.

Greene, M. 2015
The Edinburgh History of the Greeks, 1453 to 1768: The Long Nineteenth Century, Edinburgh.

Gundestrup, B. 1990
'Egyptian, Greek and Roman Antiquities in the Oldest Royal Kunstkammer Collection in Denmark', *Acta Hyperborea* 2, 43-56.

Gunning, L. P. 2009
The British Consular Service in the Aegean and the Collection of Antiquities for the British Museum, Farnham & Surrey, VY.

Haslund Hansen, A. & S. Rasmussen (eds) 2005
Min Sundheds Forliis: Frederik Christian von Havens Rejsejournal fra Den Arabiske Rejse 1760-1763, København.

Haugsted, I. 1989
'Lysets spor', *Objektiv* 45, page numbers.

Haugsted, I. 1996
Dream and Reality: Danish antiquaries, architects and artists in Greece, London.

Haugsted, I. 1989-90 [1994]
'Second Lieutenant Christian Giede – a Danish numismatist in Athens', *Nordisk Numismatisk Årsskrift* 94, 5-26.

Haugsted, I. 2000
'"Landet er alt for guddommeligt skjønt" – Brøndsted og Köes i Grækenland', in *København–Athen tur/retur: Danmark og Grækenland i 1800-tallet* (MedKøb Ny Serie 2), København, 69-86.

Heydenreuter, R. 1995
'Soldat und Maler: Ludwig Kollnberger (1811-1892) und seine griechischen Aquarelle', in Heydenreuter *et al.* (eds), 113-65.

Heydenreuter, R., J. Murken & R. Wünsche (eds) 1993
Die erträumte Nation – Griechenlands Wiedergeburt im 19. Jahrhundert, München.

Hildebrandt, M. 1995
'"Jetzt fahren wir ins Griechenland". Bayerische Soldaten in Griechenland in Tagebiichern und Volksliedern', in Heydenreuter *et al.* (eds), 103-11.

Kairophílas, G. 2011
Η Αθήνα στου Όθωνα τα χρόνια, Αθήνα.

Kjølsen, K. 1970
'Tidsrummet 1770-1905', *Den danske Udenrigstjeneste 1770-1970* (Bind 1), K. Kjølsen & V. Sjøqvist (eds), København, 1-312.

Korka, E. (ed.) 2005
Ξένες αρχαιολογικές σχολές στην Ελλάδα. 160 χρόνια. Foreign archaeological schools in Greece. 160 years, Αθήνα.

Kόκκου, A. 2009
Η μέριμνα για τις αρχαίοτητες στην Ελλάδα και τα πρώτα μουσεία (Β' έκδοση), Αθήνα.

Kotsowillis, K. S. 2007
Die Griechenbegesiterung der Bayern unter König Otto I, München.

Koukíou-Mitropoúlou, D. 2014
Οι Έλληνες του Adam Friedel: προσωπογραφίες αγωνιστών της Ελληνικής Επανάστασης (Ιστορική και εθνολογική εταιρία της Ελλάδος) (Β' έκδοση επαυξημένη), Αθήνα.

Kouria, A. 2007
The Nauplion of the foreign travellers, Athens.

Krarup, E. V. 1985
Dansk Filhellenisme. Dansk engagement i den græske frihedskamp 1821-1830, Thesis, University of Copenhagen.

Kvist, K. 1997
Arkæologi og politik. En analyse af tysk og græsk arbejde med Grækenlands antikviteter i perioden 1828-1881, København.

Lehmann, H. 1994
'Forord', *Beretning 1992-1993. Det danske Institut i Athen*, København, 3-4.

Liventhal, V. 1986
'C.T. Falbe – søofficer og arkæolog: En dansk mandsskæbne fra det forrige århundrede', *Klassisk arkæologiske studier* 56, 337-61.

Lund, J. 1986
'The Archaeological Activities of Christian Tuxen Falbe in Carthage in 1838', *CahÉtAnc* 18, 8-24.

Lund, J. 1992
'C.T. Falbe: Dansk agent og antikvar i Tunesien 1821-1832', in *Rejsen*, K. Grinder–Hansen (ed.), København, 89-101.

Lund, J. 2000a
'Royal connoisseur and consular collector: the part played by C.T. Falbe in collecting antiquities from Tunisia, Greece and Paris for Christian VIII', in Bundgaard Rasmussen *et al.* (eds), 119-49.

Lund, J. 2000b
'Archaeology and Imperialism in the 19th Century: the Case of C.T. Falbe, A Danish Agent and Antiquarian in French Service', in *Aspects de l'archéologie française Au XIXème siècle, Actes du colloque international tenu à La Diana à Montbrison les 14 et 15 octobre 1995*, P. Jacquet & R. Périchon (eds), Montbrison, 331-50.

Lund, J. 2006
'At rejse er at dø – den protestantiske kirkegård i Athen', *Sfinx* 29, 148-53.

Lund, J. 2009
'Et besøg i det tyrkiske Athen', *Sfinx* 32, 72-7.

Lund, J. 2014
'Frederik von Scholtens akvareller og tegninger fra Grækenland, 1824-1829', *Nationalmuseets Arbejdsmark*, 112-27.

Lund, J. 2015 [2016]
'Tunisia under Danish eyes: The role of Christian Tuxen Falbe and other Danes in the incipient archaeological exploration of Tunisia', in *Under Western Eyes. Approches occidentales de l'archéologie nord–africaine (XIXᵉ– XXᵉ siècles)* (Philainos 1), H. Dridi & A.M. Andreose (eds), Bologne, 33-59.

Lund, J. forthcoming
'P.O. Brøndsted – og de første danske udgravninger i Grækenland', *Store danske arkæologer – på jagt efter fortidens byer*, E. Mortensen & R. Raja (eds).

Lund, J. & B. Bundgaard Rasmussen 1995
Greeks, Etruscans, Romans: Near Eastern and Classical Antiquities, Copenhagen.

Lüth, C. 1988
Μιά Δανέζα στην Αυλή του Οθωνα: Μαρτυρία της εποχής, σημειωματάριο, ημερολόγιο, γράμματα, Αθήνα.

Mackenzie, M. 1992
Turkish Athens: The Forgotten Centuries 1456-1832, Reading.

Mørkholm, O. 1981
'The Danish Contribution to the Study of Ancient Numismatics 1780-1880', *Den kongelige Mønt– og Medaillesamling 1781-1981*, O. Mørkholm (ed.), København, 9-122.

Niebuhr, C. 1774
Carsten Niebuhrs Reisebeschreibung nach Arabien und andern umliegenden Ländern Erster Band, Kopenhagen.

33

Pántou, M. & M. Kreeb 2005
'Ο Λουδοβίκος Ρόσς ως Γενικός Έφορος Αρχαιοτήτων: τα πρώτα χρόνια', in Goette & Παλαγγιά (eds), 73-83.

Papageorgíou, S. P. & I. P. Minóglou 1988
Τιμές και αγαθά στην Αθήνα (1834) κοινωνική συμπεριφορά και οικονομικός ορθολογισρός της οικογένειας Μαυροβουννιώτη, Αθήνα.

Papageorgiou-Venetas, A. 1999
'"Ottonopolis" oder das Neue Athen. Zur Planungsgeschichte der Neugründug der Stadt im 19. Jahrhundert', in Baumstark (ed.), 69-90.

Papageorgiou-Venetas, A. 2008
Friedrich Stauffert: Städte und Landschaften in Griechenland zur Zeit König Ottos (Peleus 21), Ruhpolding.

Papanicolaou-Christensen, A. 1994
Christian Hansen. Breve og tegninger fra Grækenland, København.

Papanicolaou-Christensen, A. 2004
The Panathenaic Stadium – Its History over the Centuries, Athens.

Papanikoláou-Kristensen, A. 2013
Ένας Δανός κοσμοπολίτης διδίδσι τα ελληνικά χραμμάτα. Αθήνα

Παπασπύρου-Καραδημητρίου, Ε. 2000
Εικόνες από την Ελλάδα 1833-1838. Υδατογραφίες του από Hans Hanke το έργο του Ludwig Köllnberger, Αθήνα.

Pelt, M. 2000
'Vi er alle sammen grækere: Den europæiske filhellenisme fra passion og politik til pædagogisk projekt', in *København–Athen tur/retur: Danmark og Grækenland i 1800-tallet* (MedKøb Ny Serie 2), København, 30-42.

Pakkanen, P. 2006
August Myhrberg and North–European Philhellenism. Building the Myth of a Hero (Vol. 10), Helsinki.

Petropulos, J.A. 1968
Politics and Statecraft in the Kingdom of Greece 1833-1843, Princeton, New Jersey.

Riis, P. J. 1936
'Greek and Roman Architectural Fragments in the Danish National Museum', *ActaArch* 7, 229-43.

Riis, P. J., M. Moltesen & P. Guldager 1989
The National Museum of Denmark Department of Near Eastern and Classical Antiquities: Catalogue of Ancient Sculptures I. Aegean, Cypriote and Graeco–Phoenician, Copenhagen.

Ross, L. 1863
Erinnerungen und Mittheilungen aus Griechenland mit einem Vorwort von Otto Jahn, Berlin.

St Clair, W. 2008
That Greece Might Still Be Free. The Philhellenes in the War of Independence (New Edition), Cambridge.

Steen Jensen, J. 2000
'Christian VIII as numismatist: his collections of coins and medals', in Bundgaard Rasmussen *et al.* (eds), 45-77.

Steensen, R. S. 1951
Søofficersskolen gennem 250 aar 1701-1951, København.

Williams, D. forthcoming
Falbe's Parthenon Fragment.

Woodhouse, C. M. 1973
Capodistria: The Founder of Greek Independence, London, New York & Toronto.

"Copenhagen amuses itself, seemingly as always, on the edge of the abyss":

Two German Archaeologists in Exile in May 1939

ALEXANDRA KANKELEIT

Abstract

This article offers a snapshot from 1939, shortly before the outbreak of World War Two, when two Jewish archaeologists from Germany swapped stories about their experiences in exile. Berta Segall and Willy Schwabacher became acquainted and clearly grew fond of one another while they were living and working in Greece several years earlier. After years of great uncertainty, Willy Schwabacher landed in Denmark in spring 1939 and clearly felt at home there. His reports from Copenhagen illustrate how both archaeologists, despite precarious living conditions and frequent changes of location, remained open, creative and productive in their academic work. It becomes apparent that research and intellectual exchange functioned as anchors, providing these exiles with a firm basis for existence in turbulent times.

Introduction

Rummaging through archives can sometimes lead to surprising, unforeseen and, in part at least, happy discoveries.[1] One such treasure, which, with the agreement of the Antikensammlung Basel, I would like to present here, is a letter from Willy Schwabacher to Berta Segall from 1939.[2] Both archaeologists were German Jews.

Willy Schwabacher was born in Frankfurt am Main in 1897. His father was a businessman and numismatist, his mother the daughter of the numismatist Adolph E. Cahn. His uncles (Julius and Ludwig Cahn) and cousins (Herbert and Erich Cahn) were also both esteemed numismatists. From 1916-18 Schwabacher served in World War One and was distinguished for his service several times.[3] Berta Segall was born in East Prussia (Kirchenjahn bei Allenstein) in 1902. Her father was a manufacturer who supported his daughter generously in her studies and travels.[4]

---

1   In the context of the project "Reappraising the history of the DAI Athens during the National Socialist Era", material from the time is currently being systematically gathered, studied and scientifically analysed. The findings are due to be published later in a critical monograph. I am deeply grateful to the Deutsches Archäologisches Institut and in particular the director of the DAI Athens, Katja Sporn, for supporting this project. I would also like to thank Kristina Winther-Jacobsen for accepting this article for the journal *Proceedings of the Danish Institute at Athens* (*PoDIA*).

2   I particularly wish to express my sincere gratitude to Esau Dozio for his assistance and generous cooperation.

3   For more on Willy Schwabacher: Boehringer 1973; Boehringer 2014; a detailed curriculum vitae can be found in the "Antrag auf Wiedergutmachung [Request for compensation]", Entschädigungsbehörde Berlin, Akte [file] 78 053, Juni 1952.

4   For more on Berta Segall: Documents in the Entschädigungsbehörde des Landes Berlin, Akte [file] 353 814; Schmidt 1977; Wendland 1999, 639-41; Hochwarter 2008; Rochau-Shalem 2013, 76-7. Renate Rosenthal-Heginbottom is currently working on a short biography of Berta Segall as part of the "Jüdischen Miniaturen [Jewish Miniatures]" series of the Berlin publisher Hentrich Verlag.

During the era of the Weimar Republic, both of them studied at various highly esteemed universities in the German-speaking world and successfully completed their doctorates. Schwabacher attended universities in Darmstadt, Munich and Berlin. In 1924 he completed his doctorate under Paul Wolters on the topic of "The Tetradrachmenprägung von Selinunt [The tetradrachm coinage of Selinunte]". Berta Segall studied in Berlin, Freiburg, Leipzig, Hamburg and Vienna and completed her dissertation "Zur Handzeichnung des Mittelalters [On hand-drawings in the Middle Ages]" in 1927 under the art historian Julius von Schlosser. Schwabacher was an expert on ancient coins. Segall specialised in jewellery and gold work. Everything – their career paths, positive references and the special knowledge that they attained during their studies and in their first years of professional life – pointed to an academic career in Germany.

During the 1920s Schwabacher was able to gain valuable experience in museums, collections and the coin trade. In 1932 he received a travel grant from the Deutsches Archäologisches Institut [German Archaeological Institute] and spent time working on the German excavations in Athens (Kerameikos) and on the island of Samos (Heraion). From 1928 Segall worked for the Staatliche Museen [State Museums] in Berlin: first as a trainee in the Kupferstichkabinett [Museum of Prints and Drawings], then as an employee in the Antiquarium of the Altes Museum [Old Museum]. As a result of the "Gesetz zur Wiederherstellung des Berufsbeamtentums [Law for the Restoration of the Professional Civil Service]"[5] both were suddenly deprived of any professional future in Germany.[6] Emigration seemed to offer the only possible escape from this hopeless situation.

Both landed in Greece, where they were able to stay until spring 1938. After the National Socialists seized power in 1933 many German-speaking exiles sought temporary refuge in Greece, including the archaeologists Berta Segall (1902-1976), Willy Schwabacher (1897-1972), Peter Kahane (1904-1974) and Anton Raubitschek (1912-1999). They cultivated contact with other exiles (e.g. artists and writers), employees of German-language institutes (DAI and ÖAI) and, in particular, with English-language institutes in Greece (BSA and ASCA). Thanks to support from Otto Walter, some exiles found a home at the Österreichisches Archäologisches Institut [Austrian Archaeological Institute]. Most of them left Greece in 1938. Whether the annexation of Austria in March 1938 was the cause of this requires further investigation.[7] The theory that "increasing anti-semitism in Greece" was another contributing factor has not been proven by academic research.[8] Several reports seem to contradict this theory, including the writings of Henry Miller, who spent several months in Greece in 1939.[9]

In 1938 their paths diverged: Segall emigrated to the USA, while Schwabacher obtained a temporary position at the British Museum in London. After just one year, in April 1939, he answered a call to go to Denmark. This is the background against which the following letter arose.

A letter from Copenhagen shortly before the outbreak of World War Two

Willy Schwabacher's letter is a declaration of love towards Denmark, its rich culture, traditional hospitality and social achievements. After years of uncertainty in Greece and England, Schwabacher finally seemed to have found hope, security and recognition, as well as an interesting field to work in. In addition, his closest relatives (mother and sister) had recently managed to flee Germany –

5 English translation of the "Gesetz zur Wiederherstellung des Berufsbeamtentums": http://www.yadvashem.org/odot_pdf/Microsoft%20Word%20-%202146.pdf (Accessed September 2018). The law's aim was to exclude all Jewish civil servants from working for the state. As Margarete Bieber wrote to Wilhelm Dörpfeld on 18 December 1933: "as you may have already heard, [I am] no longer professor in Giessen [...], as the Hessian authorities, in a letter received by me on 30th June, informed me that my employment was terminated as of 1st July this year." See Stadtarchiv Wuppertal, NDS 23, Kasten 1.
6 For more on Schwabacher's "voluntary" resignation in 1933: DAI Berlin, Archiv der Zentrale, Nachlass Carl Weickert, letter from Willy Schwabacher to Carl Weickert, 14 November 1949; Entschädigungsbehörde Berlin, Akte 78 053, June 1952.
7 See Boehringer 2014, 308.
8 See Wendland 1999, 640; Freyberger & Rochau–Shalem 2013, 77.
9 See Miller 1941. Torsten Israel, to whom I owe gratitude for tips on this matter, is currently researching the subject of "German exiles in Greece during the National Socialist era".

though it entailed giving up everything they possessed, as Schwabacher tersely notes in the letter.

Despite difficult personal circumstances and the looming threat of war, Schwabacher's writing style is humorous and cheerful, with a mildly ironic undertone. It is necessary to read the German original to fully appreciate his wit.[10] He coins his own phrases (e.g. "Armutswohnstrassen", "Atomzertrümmerer", "Aufsatzspäne", "Entrierung" and "von autorativsten englischen Stellen rekommandiert"), rather unorthodox diminutive forms ("Sterbchen", "Ländchen" and "Sterbenswörtchen") and many Anglicisms, which he presumably picked up during his stay in London (e.g. "city", "job" and "copies").[11]

The high esteem in which he holds Berta Segall is evident from the letter. He regards her as talented, adaptable and tactful: ever capable of creating her "own social and intellectual centre".

Other German archaeologists with whom Schwabacher evidently worked closely in Greece are also positively judged. For example, Schwabacher suggests that in Olympia in 1939 Emil Kunze struck his Danish colleague Vagn Poulsen as both friendly and reflective. The reader gets the impression that Kunze felt burdened by the political situation. Praise is also given to Ernst Homann-Wedeking, who despite the atmosphere of terror and anti-Jewish laws in Germany remained loyal to his Jewish friends.[12]

Schwabacher's letter is a private one, but although he and Segall are clearly on good terms, no truly personal details are revealed. That they are interested not only in archaeological matters, but also political and economic questions, is clear from the extensive description of the living standards in Copenhagen and the wry remark that

"man is a product of his living conditions".[13] The two exiled friends clearly aim to help others who suffer from a similar plight. Indeed, it is evident from the letter that this aspect of mutual support, the cultivation of networks and regular contact with colleagues and relatives, is a prerequisite for coping with life in exile.[14]

In May 1939 World War Two is looming into view. However, at this moment no one could have predicted that Schwabacher's stay in Copenhagen would be a relatively brief one. Now we will let the archaeologist himself offer us insight into the situation at that time:

Copenhagen, 1st May 1939
Aaboulevard 3, Pension Solborge

Dear Miss Segall,
Unfortunately, it took a long time before your letter from 12th March was forwarded on to me, and I didn't receive it until 20th April. And then its contents led to some inquiries in London, the answers to which I only received today.

I was delighted to get all your news, and regard the handful of less happy descriptions as part and parcel of the inevitable side effects that occur everywhere in life under these bearable, if not exactly satisfying circumstances! Above all, I was very happy to hear about your triumph in Baltimore and your private reception there.[15] I can well imagine how skilfully you arranged the whole thing. Do you happen to have a leaflet left over? If so, it would of course be of g r e a t interest to me. I hope soon to be able to return the favour with a reprint of a larger article which recently appeared as the lead article in the 100year anniversary edition of the "Numismatic Chronicle", and which was also my first major

---

10   I would like to thank Neil Bristow for his thorough and sensitive translation.

11   The text stands in favourable contrast to other German-language documents of the time and seems remarkably modern and cosmopolitan.

12   Contact between Berta Segall and Ernst Homann-Wedeking continued after the war; for more information, see various documents (letters, maps and formal writing specimens) in the Antikensammlung Basel and the Staatsarchiv des Kantons Basel-Stadt. Almost all former DAI Athens colleagues were positively appraised by Willy Schwabacher in the 1950s. He wrote the following to the DAI president in 1949: "among friends and colleagues, who were sincere and full of character, I detected hardly any interruption of normal and scientifically fruitful personal relationships"; see DAI Berlin, Archiv der Zentrale, Nachlass Carl Weickert, letter from Willy Schwabacher to Carl Weickert, 14 November 1949. At the Entschädigungsbehörde in Berlin he listed his former, and still living, employers Georg Karo and Walther Wrede as referees. He also stressed the "good will" of his supervising authority (the DAI) at that time; see Entschädigungsbehörde Berlin, Akte 78 053, June and 21 September 1952; see also DAI Berlin, Archiv der Zentrale, Biographica-Mappe Willy Schwabacher, letter from Willy Schwabacher to Erich Boehringer, 12 May 1954.

13   This is presumably a reference to Karl Marx's preface to "A Contribution to the Critique of Political Economy"; see Marx 1979: "The mode of production of material life determines the social, political and intellectual life process in general. It is not the consciousness of men that determines their being, but, on the contrary, their social being that determines their consciousness."

14   For more information, see Obermayer 2014, 11. 18. 21-3.

15   For more on Segall's stay in Baltimore see Note 50.

article in English. The publication has been out for one month and I've already received a series of letters with questions and compliments – but I still haven't received any copies, so you will have to be a bit patient. Two more articles will soon appear in the same publication.

Yes, I've been happily settled here now for 5 weeks. I feel really very happy here and prefer the rather continental style of life, as you know, to the "Chinese" ceremonies of Old England!

However, I certainly don't wish to be ungrateful: the 10 months in England and in particular the friendly English people gave me so much. All in all, it was an extremely important time for me over there with endless experiences, insights and impressions, which have greatly enriched my life. For this – but make no mistake, for this only! – I'd even like to thank "our" Führer, as long as he hurries up and croaks before plunging the world into total destruction….

Copenhagen is a lovely town. People are rather quiet and less excited in this country, knowing that their fate entirely depends on decisions taken elsewhere! What's more, the Danes have a naturally cheerful temperament and Copenhagen amuses itself, seemingly as always, on the edge of the abyss. What other option does it have? I live very comfortably in a guesthouse, with windows that shut properly, a 20th-century invention called central heating, a modern and always functioning bathroom etc. etc. and all at a relatively affordable price – all things that while by no means to be regarded as culture, are nevertheless pleasant accompaniments in life and which in dignified and time-honoured but old-fashioned London are almost nowhere to be found, unless you have access to an income of, say, 800 pounds or more!! Here every worker (and even the few unemployed) can enjoy these benefits.

[page 2]
There is a truly amazing level of social equality here, which I have never experienced to such a degree and which, particularly after seeing the situation in England, seems both uplifting and forward-thinking: when you see that a small agricultural country with little industry can achieve such a thing, even in

the midst of such an unhealthy global situation, you have to ask – what else would be possible if the world came to its senses? … True, there isn't as much wealth as in ~~Denmark~~ England, but far less blatant poverty and the large majority of the population live <u>contentedly</u> amidst an amazingly high general standard of living! What wonderfully modern residential areas surround the splendidly built city! There are really few very impoverished, olden style residential streets in the city. Everyone can afford, up to a certain point, modern technological hygiene facilities and a healthy life in well-built mass housing with green areas. (Copenhagen has almost 1 million inhabitants). What is truly incredible is the amount of so-called cultural offerings that this small country also provides to its public: two universities, galleries and museums as numerous as the grains of sand on a beach, and scientific institutions that are a great testament to the community spirit of the major industries here! Danish beer makes a particularly notable contribution. For example, today all revenue from the large Carlsberg brewery is invested in science,[16] while the Rask-Ørsted Fondet,[17] which is the source of my income, and which, for example, has provided the world-famous atom splitter Prof. Niels Bohr[18] with a highly modern experimental physics institute, is also worthy of mention. I could continue with this hymn of praise. But I can already hear you – perhaps justly – saying "man is a product of his living conditions: when he's doing well, everything looks a bit too rosy, and when he's doing poorly everything quickly appears dour…."

My work has begun quite satisfactorily. The National Museum is a highly modern and well-led organisation and the coin collection in particular has a wonderful department head and large, splendid rooms, complete with a specialist library, all journals etc. Right beside it (in the same building!) is Professor Johansen's[19] archaeological university institute with an equally impressive library, and 5 minutes away is the NY Carlsberg Glyptotek with its wonderful treasures in the areas of ancient sculpture and modern painting (along with another specialist, archaeological library!). And anything you don't find there you will almost certainly find in the excellent Royal

---

16   For more on the history of the Carlsbergfondets [Carlsberg Foundation]: http://www.carlsbergfondet.dk (Accessed September 2018).

17   The state-funded Rask-Ørsted Fondet [Rask-Örsted Foundation] was founded in 1919 to support research that involved multiple countries. It was named after the Indo-Germanic specialist Rasmus Christian Rask and the scientist and natural philosopher Hans Christian Ørsted, and it remained in existence until 1972.

18   Niels Bohr (1885-1962) was a Danish physicist. In 1922 he received the Nobel Prize for "his services in the investigation of the structure of atoms and of the radiation emanating from them". During the German occupation of Denmark (April 1940 until May 1945) he was involved in the Danish resistance.

19   Knud Friis Johansen (1887-1971) was a Danish classical archaeologist. From 1926 he was a professor at the University of Copenhagen.

Library! – I have no fewer than about 25,000 Greek coins to analyse, which since the Renaissance have been lying here effectively waiting to be roused from their slumber, though thankfully well looked after, and were last (in 1816) discussed by Ramus,[20] a pupil of Eckhel,[21] in a Latin catalogue! I'm sharing this work – in accordance with the Rask-Ørsted Fondet regulations – with a Danish colleague,[22] who, however, as curator of the museum's antiquities department, is also blessed with lots of other work… Naturally, as with every kind of cataloguing (the results are supposed to appear in the "Sylloge" series, edited by E.S.G. Robinson[23] and published by the British Academy), numerous little problems and scraps of material for articles arise. Shortly – it is the work kind of work I like to do!

But to return quickly to your letter! Hinks,[24] of course, only gave up his position at the BM [British Museum] for good when he had already secured a new position, one both appealing and worthy of him, at the Warburg Library in London! So that *idea is a non-starter. However,*

[page 3]

I'd like to offer you the "particulars" of an extraordinarily likeable and talented German compatriot in suffering, who, as you will see, meets the approval of the highest echelons of English society and with whom I often spent time in London. Furthermore, I know the family from Munich and Augsburg and thus know from what stock the man comes. In a word, he seems ideally suited to fulfil the conditions you allude to. He also writes to me that only recently his name was men-

tioned at the Bliss's[25] and so will surely be fresh in the memory: his friend Albi Rosenthal[26] (son of Erwin R.)[27] had paid a visit there and in answer to similar questions about a Coptic specialist mentioned his name and sang his praises….. Kitzinger[28] has excellent, by now thoroughly English manners, speaks the language fluently and without any accent – all he would have to do now is pick up an American one!

As you will see, there is no great urgency to the matter, as K. currently has a highly respectable and even rather lucrative job at the BM. [British Museum] – but that's highly unlikely to be a long-term position, and like everyone else he longs to get away and regards the BM., quite correctly, as the best springboard. It is truly amazing how he "got in" there and is regarded by the upper brass as t h e charming young blond German whose human qualities and specialist abilities – as far as they can be observed and made use of there! – should be supported. – And so you can see what's possible; with your special skill in such things, your tactfulness and discretion, you really have the chance to achieve something! Naturally, K. requests in particular that the last of those qualities be observed, not least because of his current position at the BM., which shouldn't be undermined in any way by this matter getting around …

By now, hopefully, you will have settled into life in W.[29] I imagine you as being capable of living according to your "style" anywhere in the world within a short space of time and then having the satisfaction of creating your own social and intellectual centre and one that clearly bears your imprint! Have you heard anything from our joint friends scattered across the world? My most intensive contact is with Ms. Philippson.[30]

20   Christian Ramus (1765-1832) was a Danish numismatist. Schwabacher refers here to the standard work "*Catalogus Numorum Veterum Græcorum et Latinorum Musei Regis Daniæ*, Copenhagen 1816, vols I-II".

21   The Austrian Joseph Hilarius Eckhel (1737-1798) is considered a pioneer in establishing numismatics as a modern science.

22   The Danish colleague was Niels Breitenstein.

23   Edward Stanley Gotch Robinson (1887-1976) was a British numismatist.

24   Roger Hinks (1903-1963) was a British art historian. Due to damage caused by improper cleaning of the "Elgin Marbles" he had to resign from his post at the British Museum in 1939.

25   The family in question is presumably that of the American archaeologist Frederick Jones Bliss (1859-1937), see https://www.pef.org.uk/profiles/frederick-j-bliss-1859-1937 (Accessed October 2018).

26   Albi Rosenthal (1914-2004) was a music scholar and bookseller who emigrated from Germany to England in 1936. In 1945 he was granted British citizenship.

27   Erwin Rosenthal (1889-1981) was an art historian and bookseller who emigrated to the USA.

28   The art historian Ernst Kitzinger (1912-2003) left Germany in 1934. From 1935 to 1940 he resided in England and worked for the British Museum. In 1941 he finally found a position in the USA; see https://www.kunstgeschichte.uni-muenchen.de/forschung/ausstellungsprojekte/archiv/einblicke_ausblicke/biografien/kitzinger/index.html (Accessed September 2018).

29   The reference may be to the Walters Art Gallery in Baltimore, Maryland.

30   Paula Philippson (1874-1940), paediatrician and religious scholar, made several trips to Greece between 1933 and 1938, where she presumably made friends with Segall and Schwabacher. In November 1938 she fled to Switzerland and settled in Basel in 1939; see Möbius 1949 for more on the death of Paula Philippson.

Did she send you her lovely new work "Greek Divinities in their Landscapes" [original title: "Griechische Gottheiten in ihren Landschaften"], Symbolae Osloenses Fasc.Supplet. IX?[31] Otherwise I have more contact with my English friends. Vagn Poulsen[32] was recently in Athens and sent greetings from many who are there – however, on Young's[33] advice, he had to abruptly cut short his trip due to the looming threat of war and hurry home with his young wife. He had good things to report about the Americans (Homer Th.[34] and Lucie T.[35]), even though the situation has them all full of trepidation… In Olympia he found Kunze[36] particularly charming – and silent regarding the less uplifting matters! He didn't see Welter[37] on this occasion. – I haven't heard a peep from Petros[38]… And from Guiol[39] etc. I don't expect anything! Wedeking[40] dutifully keeps up his correspondence from Rome – inwardly they are all in a rather worse state there than we are….

I really hope to hear from you again soon. Forgive me for the over-long letter – as the classic saying goes, "I didn't have time to write a shorter one"!

Your Willy Schwabacher

[handwritten in left margin:] How are your siblings doing in G. [Germany]?? My mother and sister can now – finally! – move to London this month once they have handed over everything they possess…

Fig. 1. *Willy Schwabacher, 1897-1972 (Source: Boehringer 2014).*

The fate of two "stateless" persons[41]

Willy Schwabacher (1897-1972)

Willy Schwabacher was not granted a quiet life: after six years in Greece, one in England and an additional five in Denmark, the threat posed by German occupation grew ever more ominous. The plan was made to begin mass deportations of Danish and foreign Jews in autumn 1943. At almost the last possible moment, on 5 October 1943, the Danish resistance assisted Schwabacher in escaping to neutral Sweden.

---

31 Philippson 1939.

32 Vagn Poulsen (1909-1970) was a Danish classical archaeologist and director of the Ny Carlsberg Glyptotek.

33 Rodney Young (1907-1974) was an American archaeologist and Middle East specialist.

34 Homer Armstrong Thompson (1906-2000) was an American archaeologist and for many years the director of the American School of Classical Studies at Athens; see http://www.ascsa.edu.gr/index.php/archives/thompson-finding-aid/ (Accessed September 2018).

35 The reference may be to the American archaeologist Lucy Talcott (1899-1970), who was involved in the Athenian Agora excavations for over twenty years.

36 Emil Kunze (1901-1994) was a German classical archaeologist. From 1929 to 1933 he worked for the DAI Athens. From 1937, together with Hans Schleif (1902-1945), he led the so-called Führergrabung [Führer Excavation] in Olympia. In 1951 he was appointed First Secretary of the DAI Athens.

37 Gabriel Welter (1890-1954) was a German classical archaeologist who was in Greece from 1920.

38 It has thus far not been possible to establish the identify of Petros (a Greek native?).

39 The reference may be to the botanist F.G. Guiol, who conducted research into herbaria in Greece in the 1930s; see https://www.bgbm.org/sites/default/files/documents/3994636.pdf, page 841 (Accessed September 2018). Segall herself mentions him (1938, 5).

40 Ernst Homann-Wedeking (1908-2002) was a German classical archaeologist. From 1936-1938 he worked for the DAI Athens. He then switched to the DAI's Rome branch.

Despite extremely difficult conditions in the early stages, he settled in Stockholm and remained there for the rest of his life. In 1952 he married Annemarie Rosenbaum née Schoenlank, who had survived the Holocaust. In 1954 the couple were granted Swedish citizenship.[42] From the 1950s onwards Schwabacher received a regular income and worked at the Royal Coin Cabinet and Stockholm University.

His attempts to re-establish a professional footing in Germany after the war were unsuccessful. Like many other Jewish emigrants, he discovered that he was not welcomed there. When it came to the allocation of jobs in the area of classical archaeology, quality was not always the main criteria. In 1949 Schwabacher looked set to be offered the position "Konservator für Antike Münzen" [Curator of Ancient Coins] at the Staatliche Münzsammlung [State Coin Collection] in Munich. However, the position went to Gerhard Kleiner, who up to that point had published hardly anything about coins and in Schwabacher's view was a "non-specialist" who possessed little "practical experience in the analysis of original ancient coin material". Schwabacher expressed his displeasure in letters to the president of the DAI, along with his supposition that Kleiner had attained the position as a result of the intervention of Ernst Buschor, who had supervised his doctoral work, and that Kleiner only wanted to use the position as a springboard. In this case he seems to have been right, as Kleiner left Munich after two years to pursue other work.[43] In those days Schwabacher was pushed into the role of a needy foreigner, whose personal fate was a matter of utter indifference to the authorities at the time.[44] Nevertheless, he did not become bitter, and continued to publish large numbers

Fig. 2. *Berta Segall, 1902-1976 (Source: Archiv Antiken-sammlung Basel und Sammlung Ludwig).*

of specialist articles on Greek coins, articles that even today specialists in the field continue to cite and use as a basis for their research.[45]

Berta Segall (1902-1976)

Thanks to the National Socialists' anti-Jewish laws and World War Two, Berta Segall was also forced into a nomadic life in exile, one in which she never truly settled. Exile led her first (with the support of the DAI) to Eng-

---

41   I received support from many sides concerning my research into Berta Segall and Willy Schwabacher. In addition to those already mentioned above, I would like to sincerely thank the following people and institutions: Christoph Manasse (Staatsarchiv des Kantons Basel-Stadt), Stephan Zakow (Entschädigungsbehörde des Landes Berlin), Martin Maischberger (Antikensammlung der Staatlichen Museen zu Berlin), Michaela Hussein-Wiedemann (Zentralarchiv Staatliche Museen zu Berlin), Frank Hildebrandt (Museum für Kunst und Gewerbe Hamburg), Christof Boehringer (Georg-August-Universität Göttingen), Johanna Mueller von der Haegen (DAI Berlin), Katharina Brandt, Joachim Heiden and Jutta Stroszeck (DAI Athens).

42   Boehringer 2014, 316.

43   See DAI Berlin, Archiv der Zentrale, Nachlass Carl Weickert, letters from Willy Schwabacher to Carl Weickert, 31 October 1949, 14 November 1949 and 25 November 1949; Boehringer 2014, 312-3; the detailed description of the situation in Schwabacher's Antrag auf Wiedergutmachung [Request for compensation], Entschädigungsbehörde Berlin, Akte 78 053, June 1952.

44   This attitude is clearly reflected in the letters of the then DAI president Carl Weickert; see DAI Berlin, Archiv der Zentrale, Nachlass Carl Weickert, letter from Carl Weickert to Willy Schwabacher, 4 November 1949.

45   For more on his extensive scientific oeuvre: Boehringer 1973; Boehringer 2014; https://www.coingallery.de/Schriftenverzeichnisse/Schwabacher.htm (Accessed September 2018).

land,[46] and afterwards to Greece. In Athens she created the catalogue on goldwork in the Benaki Museum.[47] In the introduction she expresses sincere gratitude to her former employer at the Altes Museum in Berlin (Robert Zahn) and the former director of the DAI Athens (Georg Karo). Presumably both archaeologists had some involvement in her getting the support of Antonis Benakis and attaining work at the Benaki Museum in Athens.[48] During her time in Greece, in 1936, Segall returned to Germany once to study material in Berlin relevant to her research in Greece.[49]

In 1938 she left Europe and emigrated to the USA, where she resided at various times in Baltimore, Washington, Boston, Princeton New Jersey and New York.[50]

In 1956 Segall returned to Germany and became curator at the Museum für Kunst und Gewerbe [Museum of Art and Design] in Hamburg.[51] As early as 1950 she

had returned to Greece and other European countries, as evidenced by various stamps in her American passport.[52] Presumably she was motivated by the desire to see Europe again, as well as the possibility of studying the objects of her research in the places where they were located. It is also not clear what other professional opportunities were open to her in the America of the 1950s. However, she only stayed in Hamburg for three years and appears to have left her position there of her own accord.[53] In 1959, at the age of 57, she moved to Basel[54] and continued her work there on an independent basis, without firm ties to any institutions. Her archive in Basel shows that she maintained a lively correspondence with various major intellectuals of her time: archaeologists,[55] orientalists,[56] arabists,[57] philosophers,[58] writers[59] and publishers.[60] She had a particularly close relationship with her brother Max Segall, who lived in Australia.[61] She also had contact with archaeologists in Basel,[62] though

---

46 The DAI financed her trip to England: "The president has attained special funds [...] Dr. Segall 3000 marks for trip to England"; DAI Berlin, Archiv der Zentrale, Altregistratur 11-03, Sitzungen Protokolle ZD, 1926-1941, handwritten protocol from 14 July 1933.

47 See Segall 1938.

48 Antonis Benakis (1873-1954), founder of the Benaki Museum in Athens: https://www.benaki.gr/index.php?option=com_landings&view=founder&Itemid=820&lang=en (Accessed September 2018)

49 My gratitude to Torsten Israel, who found a letter relating to the matter in the Benaki Museum archive, for drawing my attention to this. Concerning a passport from the German embassy in Athens from 15 December 1936, see a letter from the General Consulate of the Federal Republic of Germany in Basel from 14 April 1964: Staatsarchiv Basel-Stadt PD-Reg 3a 161467.

50 Schmidt 1977; more details on her career are available at the Entschädigungsbehörde des Landes Berlin, Akte 353 814; see also her letter to Georg Steindorff from 8th January 1947 in the Universität Leipzig Archiv, Ägyptologisches Institut, https://zenon.dainst.org/Record/001476678 (Accessed September 2018).

51 Detailed information on this position can be found in Segall's file at the Entschädigungsbehörde des Landes Berlin and in her archive at the Antikensammlung Basel.

52 Berta Segall's invalidated passport can be found in the Entschädigungsbehörde des Landes Berlin, Akte 353 814.

53 The decision of the Entschädigungsbehörde in Berlin played a seemingly decisive role in her departure from Hamburg. Her lawyer informed her on 12 February 1959 that her employment was "beneath her station" and "non-tenured", whereas she had a right to a position as a "department head in a state museum on a permanent basis". She would receive "full benefits" if she gave up her current, inferior position. Her archive, which is kept in the Antikensammlung Basel, includes a full box of business cards from the Hamburger Museum. On the cards, which were presumably never used, Segall bears the title of "Leiter der Antiken-Abteilung am Museum für Kunst und Gewerbe" [Head of the Antiquities Department at the Museum of Art and Design].

54 Ernst Homann-Wedeking, Karl Schefold, Herbert Cahn-Vögeli and Hans Jucker all wrote in support of her stay in Switzerland in 1959; see references in the file on Berta Segall in the Staatsarchiv Basel-Stadt PD-Reg 3a 161467.

55 Among the archaeologists were, for example, Pierre Amandry, Hans Diepolder, Ernst Langlotz, Reinhard Lullies, Bernhard Schweizer, Henri Seyrig, Homer Thompson, Arthur D. Trendall and Violette Verhoogen. German, French and English were the languages of communication.

56 Albrecht Goetze.

57 Adolf Grohmann.

58 Hannah Arendt; see Arendt 2017.

59 Hermann Broch; see Broch 2010, 82.

60 Daniel Brody and Günther Wasmuth.

61 In Segall's archive in Basel there are dozens of letters from her brother, sent from all over the world and always beginning with the affectionate "Mein liebes Bertachen" [My dear little Berta]. Her replies, if they are still in existence, are presumably in the family's possession.

62 The diary and letters offer evidence of the following meetings and events: a birthday at Otto Rubensohn's; a meeting at the Schefolds'; talks and events at the Archaeological Institute at the University of Basel. In the last years of her life she was particularly close to Margot Schmidt; see Schmidt 1977.

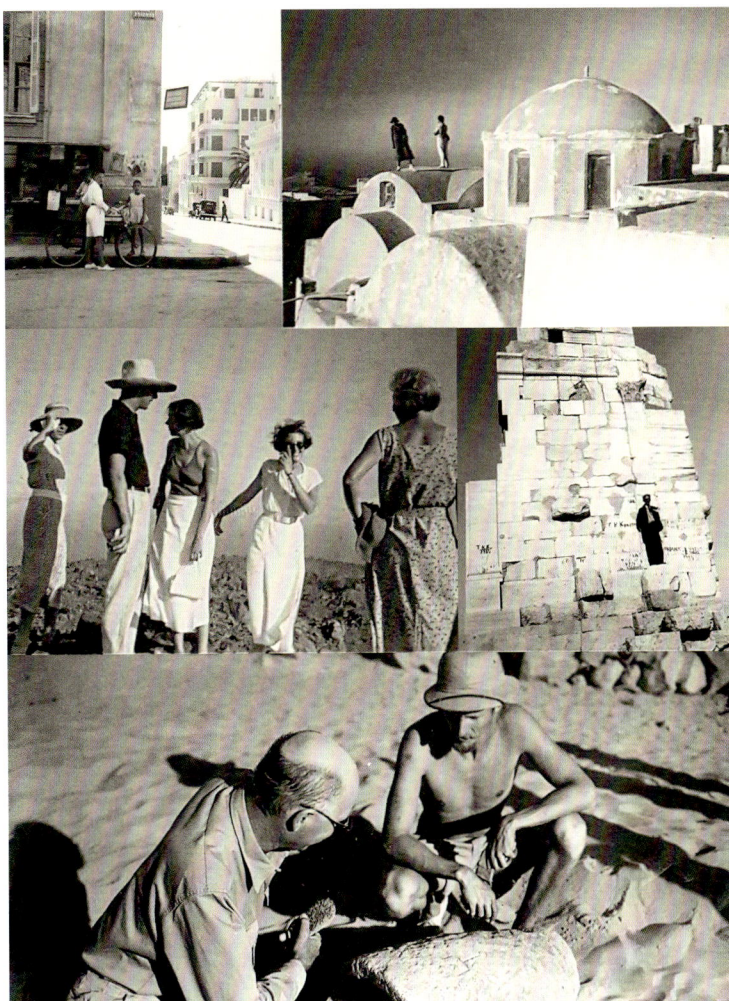

Fig. 3. *Snapshots from seemingly happier times: Greece in the inter-war period*[64] *(Source: Berta Segall archive at the Antikensammlung Basel und Sammlung Ludwig).*

one entry in her diary from 1966 is worth noting: in the field "To be notified in case of an accident" she has put the name of her sister Lotte Jacoby, with an address in Jerusalem, Israel. It is difficult to say whether Berta Segall felt lonely in Basel. It seems she lived in her own orbit and created, as Schwabacher puts it in his letter from Copenhagen, her own "intellectual centre".

It is to be hoped that more thorough research will offer additional insight into the life and intellectual world of Berta Segall. While examining documents relating to the DAI Athens during the National Socialist era, I stumbled upon a letter from Ernst Homann-Wedeking from 1937. The former employee at the DAI Athens asked the central office in Berlin whether articles from "non-Aryan Germans" were allowed to be published in the *Athenische Mitteilungen*. The specific case related to a contribution from Berta Segall, who at that time was working for the Benaki Museum in Athens and was on good terms with Homann-Wedeking.[63] As was to be expected, Segall's text did not appear in the DAI's *Athenische Mitteilungen*, but was instead published in the USA.

---

63   See DAI Berlin, Archiv der Zentrale, Altregistratur Ordner 10-40, letter from Ernst Homann-Wedeking to Martin Schede, 29 October 1937.

64   Street scene in the Odos Solonos in Athens (above left), excursion to Santorini (above right and centre left), with an acquaintance at the Philopappos Monument in Athens (centre right), cleaning of an archaeological relic on a sandy beach (below). The sporty-looking topless man may be the Austrian Alfons Hochhauser (1906-1981), who lived in Greece from 1924 (my thanks to Torsten Israel for his assistance in this matter); see http://www.alfons–hochhauser.de (Accessed September 2018).

This episode prompted me to investigate further. I was interested in the following questions: Who was Berta Segall? How and via what paths had she come to Greece? What was her experience of the inter-war period there? What kind of relationship did she have with the DAI Athens? I had many questions, some of which remain unanswered – it has to be said that in comparison to Willy Schwabacher, relatively little is known about her person and life.

It is thus a happy coincidence that Berta Segall's archive is located in the Antikensammlung Basel. Largely untouched and unsorted, these papers contain treasures that are in need of thorough scientific analysis. It is also reasonable to suppose that letters written by Segall lie undiscovered in archives throughout the world. Further research and publications on this matter are planned for the future.

In any case, the images, letters and notes from Segall's archive in Basel give the impression that her time in Greece (1934-1938) contained enjoyable moments, despite the ever-present dangers.

Conclusion

The letter from Willy Schwabacher to Berta Segall from 1939 that is presented here offers insight into the lives of two German archaeologists in exile. It shows the issues that occupied them and their attempts to deal with the permanent threat posed to their existence. Despite regular changes of residence and professional and financial uncertainty, they manage to retain their interest in the world and their professional field as well as their ability to take pleasure in life, not least thanks to communication and solidarity with those enduring a similar fate.

This is a correspondence between two intellectuals who in various ways are processing the loss of their former lives and their homeland. Schwabacher expresses enthusiasm about Copenhagen, which against the backdrop of a shattered system and desperate times seems to shimmer on the horizon as a symbol of a possible brighter future.

It is to be hoped that similar reports will soon come to light about Athens and the rest of Greece, where a number of German-Jewish exiles resided in the interwar period.

The original letter of Willy Schwabacher

Copenhagen, 1. Mai 1939
Aaboulevard 3, Pension Solborge

Liebes Fräulein Segall,

es hat leider sehr lange gedauert, bis man mir Ihren Brief vom 12. März hierher nachsandte, sodass ich ihn erst gegen den 20. April erhielt. Und dann verursachte sein Inhalt erst einige Nachfragen in London, die nun heute eintrafen.

Ich freute mich sehr mit allen Ihren Nachrichten und halte die paar weniger erfreulichen Schilderungen für die überall im Leben mitauftretenden Complementärerscheinungen zu im Ganzen doch sicher erträglichen, wenn nicht zufriedenstellenden Umständen! Vor allem Ihr Triumph in Baltimore und Ihre private reception dort haben mich gefreut. Ich kann mir gut vorstellen, mit welchem Geschick sie das alles arranged hatten. Haben Sie noch eines der leaflets übrig? Dann würde es mich natürlich s e h r interessieren. Ich hoffe mich baldigst mit dem reprint eines grösseren Aufsatzes revanchieren zu können, der kürzlich an der Spitze des 100sten Jahrganges des "Numismatic Chronicle" erschien, zugleich der erste grössere in Englisch. Das Heft ist schon 1 Monat heraus und ich hatte schon eine Reihe von Briefen mit interessierten Anfragen und Complimenten – aber ich erhielt noch immer keine copies, sodass Sie noch etwas warten müssen. Zwei andere kommen demnächst ebendort heraus.

Ja, seit 5 Wochen bin ich nun hier sehr glücklich installiert. I feel really very happy here and prefer the rather continental style of life, as you know, to the "Chinese" ceremonies of Old-England!

Aber ich will gewiss nicht undankbar sein: die englischen 10 Monate und besonders die befreundeten englischen Menschen haben mir unendlich viel gegeben. Es war im Ganzen eine äusserst wichtige Zeit für mich dort drüben und ich bin um unendlich viele Lebenserfahrungen – Einsichten und Eindrücke reicher. Dafür – aber gewiss nur dafür! – will ich sogar "unserm" Führer danken, vorausgesetzt dass er nun doch bald sein Sterbchen macht, ohne vorher die Welt ins Verderben gestürzt zu haben …

Copenhagen is a lovely town. People are rather quiete and less excited in this country, knowing that their fate entirely depends on decisions taken elsewhere! Zudem haben die Dänen durchschnittlich ein von Natur heiteres Temperament und Copenhagen amüsiert sich, wie wohl stets, am Rand des Abgrunds. Was will es auch machen? Ich wohne sehr hübsch in einer Pension, in der es gut schliessende Fenster, eine Erfindung des 20. Jahrhunderts genannt Centralheizung, moderne und stets funktionierende Badeeinrichtung etc. etc. alles für verhältnismässig erschwingliches Geld gibt – ~~alles~~ Dinge, die zwar noch lange keine Kultur, aber doch erfreuliche Begleiterscheinungen des Lebens sind, und die man in dignified and time-honoured – but old-fashioned London fast nirgends antrifft, falls man nicht über ein Einkommen von sagen wir "von Pfd. 800 an aufwärts" verfügt!! Hier geniesst jeder Arbeiter (selbst die wenigen Arbeitslosen) diese Vorteile.

[Seite 2:]

Es herrscht eine geradezu erstaunliche sociale Ausgeglichenheit hier vor, die ich noch nirgends in diesem Maße erlebt habe und die, gerade nach einem Einblick in die englischen Verhältnisse, hocherfreulich und zukunftsträchtig wirkt: Man sieht, selbst bei so ungesunden Weltzuständen kann ein kleines Agrarland mit nur wenig Industrie das erreichen – was wäre bei einiger Vernunft dann sonst in der Welt möglich….. Es gibt gewiss keinen solchen Reichtum wie ~~Dänemark~~ England, aber entschieden weniger krasse Armut und der grosse Durchschnitt der Bevölkerung lebt <u>zufrieden</u> auf einem ganz erstaunlich hohen allgemeinen Lebensstandard! Welch herrliche moderne Wohnsiedlungen rings um die prachtvoll gebaute city! Es gibt nur ganz wenige wirkliche Armutswohnstrassen älterer Bauart in der Stadt. Jeder kann sich bis zu einem gewissen Grad moderne technische Hygiene und gesundes Wohnen in gut gebauten Massensiedlungen im Grünen leisten. (Kopenhagen hat nahezu 1 Millionen Einwohner). Geradezu unglaublich ist der Aufwand, den sich das Ländchen an sog. kulturellen Leistungen öffentlicher Art noch nebenher leistet. Zwei Universitäten, Galerien u. Museen wie Sand am Meer, und wissenschaftliche Stiftungen die dem Gemeinsinn der Industriellen alle Ehre machen! Besonders das dänische Bier trägt dazu bei. Z.B. fliessen a l l e Einkünfte der grossen Carlsberg-Brauerei heute nur noch in die Wissenschaft, und der Rask-Ørsted Fondet, von dem ich ja lebe, und der z.B. dem weltberühmten Atomzertrümmerer, Prof. Niels Bohr, ein ganzes modernes Experimental-physikalisches Institut hingestellt hat, ist auch nicht von schlechten Eltern. _ So könnte ich noch viel Lobenswertes erzählen. Aber ich höre Sie schon – vielleicht mit einigem Recht – sagen "der Mensch ist ein Produkt seiner Lebensumstände: geht's einem gut, sieht man leicht alles zu rosig, gehts einem schlecht noch leichter alles zu grau an…."

Meine Arbeit hat einen befriedigenden Anfang genommen. Das Nationalmuseum ist ein höchst modern und gut

geleitetes Institut und die Münzsammlung im Besonderen hat einen reizenden Abteilungsdirektor und prachtvolle grosse Räume, complette Fachbibliothek, alle Zeitschriften etc. Ganz nahe davon ist Prof. Johansens archäolog. Universitätsinstitut (im gleichen Haus!) mit ebenfalls guter Bibliothek und 5 Minuten weiter gleich die NY-Carlsberg Glyptothek mit Ihren geradezu herrlichen Schätzen an antiker Plastik und moderner Malerei (samt einer weiteren archäolog. Fachbibliothek!). Und was man dort nicht hat, findet man bestimmt dann in der ausgezeichneten Kgl. Bibliothek! – Ich habe nicht weniger wie ca. 25 000 griech. Münzen zu bearbeiten, die z. Teil seit der Renaissance hier eine Art Dornröschenschlaf schlafen, aber wohlbehütet, und zuletzt von einem Eckhel-Schüler, Ramus, (1816) in einem lateinischen Katalog behandelt wurden! In diese Arbeit teile ich mich – nach den Vorschriften des Rask-Ørsted Fondets – mit einem dänischen Mitarbeiter, der aber als Kustos an dem antiken department des Museums auch sonst noch mit reichlich viel Arbeit gesegnet ist… Wie bei jeder Katalogisierung (es soll in der von der British Academy herausgegebenen, von E.S.G. Robinson editierten "Sylloge"-Reihe erscheinen) fallen nebenher natürlich reichlich Probleme und Aufsatzspäne ab. Shortly – it is the ~~work~~ kind of work I like to do!

Nun aber noch schnell zurück zu Ihrem Brief! Hinks hat seine Position am BM. natürlich erst dann endgültig aufgegeben, als er bereits eine ihn reizende und ehrende neue an der Warburg-Library in London in der Tasche hatte! Also ist es mit <u>dieser</u> Idee nichts. Dagegen lege

[Seite 3:]

ich Ihnen hier "particulars" eines ausserordentlich sympathischen höchst befähigten und, wie Sie sehen, von autoritativsten englischen Stellen rekommandierten jungen deutschen Leidensgenossen vor, mit dem ich in London oft zusammen war. Zudem kenne ich die Familie von München und Augsburg her und weiss daher, welch Geistes Kind der Mann ist: Kurz, alles wie gemacht, um die von Ihnen angedeuteten Bedingungen zu erfüllen. Er schreibt mir zudem, dass sein Name erst kürzlich bei den Bliss's genannt und daher gewiss noch in Erinnerung sein müsse: Sein Freund Albi Rosenthal (Sohn von Erwin R.) hätte dort einen Besuch gemacht, und auf ähnliche Fragen nach einem koptischen Specialisten etc. den seinen genannt und seinen "Ruhm gesungen"…..Kitzinger hat ausgezeichnete, jetzt durchaus englische Manieren, beherrscht die Sprache fliessend ohne jeden Accent – hingegen müsste er den amerikanischen erst erlernen!

45

Die Sache hat, wie sie gleichfalls sehen, keine sonderliche Eile, da K. zur Zeit ja einen sehr ehrenden und jetzt sogar etwas einkömmlichen job am BM. [British Museum] hat – aber das wird ja kaum was Dauerhaftes werden, und wie jeder strebt auch er weg und betrachtet das BM., mit Recht natürlich, als das beste Sprungbrett. Es ist geradezu erstaunlich, wie er dort "hereingekommen" ist und in der führenden clique als d e r charmante blonde junge Deutsche gilt, dem man wegen seiner menschlichen Qualitäten und fachlichen Befähigung – so weit man sie dort zur Zeit benutzen und gebrauchen kann! – den Weg ebnen müsse. – Also sehen Sie 'mal zu, was man machen kann; Sie werden mit Ihrem besonderen Geschick in solchen Dingen, mit Ihrem Takt und Ihrer Discretion vielleicht wirklich etwas erreichen! Um die letztere bittet Sie K. natürlich ganz besonders, schon wegen seiner momentanen Stellung am BM., auf die durch Entrierung dieser Sache natürlich kein Schatten fallen darf…

Hoffentlich haben Sie sich nun inzwischen doch gut in W. eingelebt. Ich kann mir kaum vorstellen, dass Sie nicht an jedem Ort der Welt nach kurzer Zeit Ihre eigene Art und Ihren privaten "Stil" doch wieder durchsetzen und dann die Befriedigung haben, ein eigenes gesellschaftliches und geistiges Centrum, Ihres individuellen Gepräges, zu bilden! Hören Sie eigentlich noch etwas von den gemeinsamen in der Welt verstreuten Freunden? Am eifrigsten stehe ich eigentlich mit Frln. Philippson in Verbindung. Hat sie Ihnen ihr neues schönes opus "Griechische Gottheiten in ihren Landschaften", Symbolae Osloenses Fasc.Supplet.IX, geschickt? Sonst herrscht die

Verbindung mit den englischen Freunden vor. Vagn Poulsen war grade in Athen und brachte mir Grüsse von vielen dortigen – er musste jedoch, auf Anraten Young's, seine Reise infolge der drohenden Kriegsgefahr plötzlich abbrechen u. reiste plötzlich mit seiner jungen Frau Hals über Kopf heim. Von den Amerikanern (Homer Th. and Lucie T.) erzählte er Erfreuliches, wenn sie auch alle reichlich nervös seien…. Kunze fand er besonders reizend in Olympia – und schweigsam über die weniger erbaulichen Dinge! Welter hat er diesmal nicht gesehen. – Von Petros hör' ich kein Sterbenswörtchen….. Und von Guiol etc. erwarte ich nichts! Wedeking schreibt mir brav aus Rom – es geht ihnen allen jetzt im Grunde innerlich schlechter wie uns….

Nun hoffe ich, recht bald ' 'mal wieder von Ihnen zu hören. Verzeihen Sie den überlangen Brief – "ich hatte keine Zeit für einen kürzeren", um klassisch zu schliessen!

Ihr Willy Schwabacher

[handschriftlich am linken Blattrand:]
Wie steht es mit Ihren Geschwistern in D.?? M. Mutter u. Schwester können nun – endlich! – in diesem Monat nach London ziehen, unter Drangabe alles *Besitzes…..*

DR. ALEXANDRA KANKELEIT
Deutsches Archäologisches Institut
Abteilung Athen
Fidiou 1 | GR–10678 Athen
kontakt@alexandra-kankeleit.de

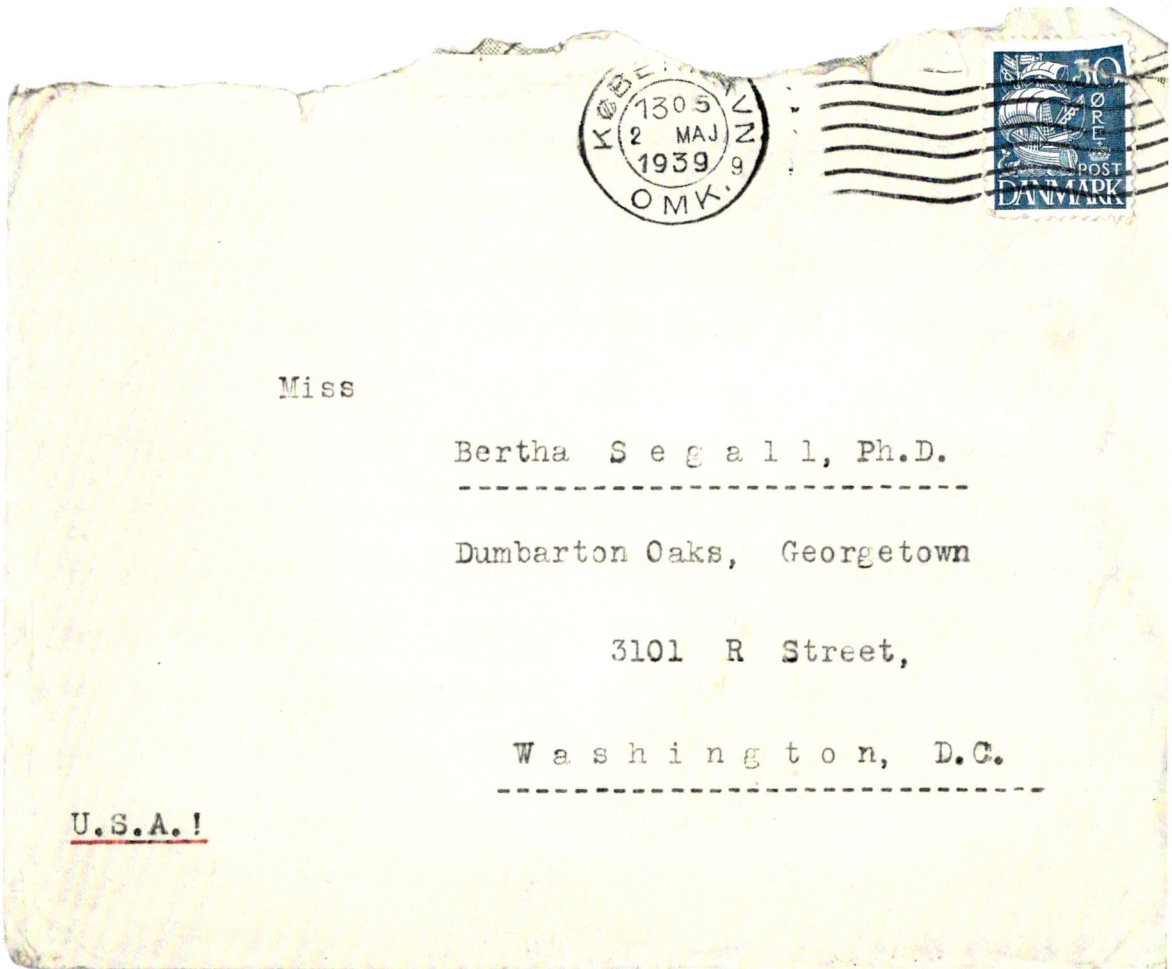

Miss

Bertha S e g a l l , Ph.D.

Dumbarton Oaks, Georgetown

3101 R Street,

W a s h i n g t o n, D.C.

U.S.A.!

Fig. 4. *Letter from Willy Schwabacher to Berta Segall (Source: Berta Segall archive at the Antikensammlung Basel und Sammlung Ludwig).*

Copenhagen, 1.Mai 1939.
Aaboulevard 3, Pension "Solborg"

Liebes Fräulein Segall,

es hat leider sehr lange gedauert, bis man mir Ihren Brief vom
12.März hierher nachsandte, sodass ich ihn erst gegen den 20.April
erhielt. Und dann verursachte sein Inhalt erst einige Nachfragen
in London, die nun heute eintrafen.

Ich freute mich sehr mit allen Ihren Nachrichten und halte die
paar weniger erfreulichen Schilderungen für die überall im Leben
mitauftretenden Complementärerscheinungen zu im Ganzen doch sicher
erträglichen,wenn nicht zufriedenstellenden Umständen! Vor allem
Ihr Triumph in Baltimore und Ihre private reception dort haben mich
gefreut. Ich kann mir gut vorstellen, mit welchem Geschick Sie das
alles arranged hatten. Haben Sie noch eines der leaflets übrig ?
Dann würde es mich natürlich s e h r interessieren. Ich hoffe mich
baldigst mit dem reprint eines grösseren Aufsatzes revanchieren zu
können, der kürzlich an der Spitze des 100 sten Jahrganges des "Numismatic Chronicle" erschien, zugleich der erste grössere in Englisch. Das Heft ist schon 1 Monat heraus und ich hatte schon eine
Reihe von Briefen mit interessierten Anfragen und Complimenten --
aber ich erhielt noch immer keine copies, sodass Sie noch etwas warten
warten müssen. Zwei andere kommen demnächst ebendort heraus.

Ja, seit 5 Wochen bin ich nun hier sehr glücklich installiert.
I feel really very happy here and prefer the rather continental style
of life, as you know, to the "Chinese" ceremonies of Old-England!
Aber ich will gewiss nicht undankbar sein : die englischen 10 Monate
und besonders die befreundeten englischen Menschen haben mir unendlich viel gegeben. Es war im Ganzen eine äusserst wichtige Zeit für
mich dort drüben und ich bin um unendlich viele Lebenserfahrungen-
Einsichten und Eindrücke reicher. Dafür - aber gewiss nur dafür! -
will ich sogar "unserm" Führer danken, vorausgesetzt dass er nun doch
bald sein Sterbchen macht, ohne vorher die Welt ins Verderben gestürzt zu haben......

Copenhagen is a lovely town. People are rather quiet and less excited in this country, knowing that their fate entirely depends on
decisions taken elsewhere! Zudem haben die Dänen durchschnittlich ein
von Natur heiteres Temperament und Copenhagen amüsiert sich, wie wohl
stets, auch am Rand des Abgrunds. Was will es auch machen ? Ich wohne sehr hübsch in einer Pension, in der es gut schliessende Fenster,
eine Erfindung des 20.Jahrhunderts genannt Centralheizung, moderne
und stets funktionierende Badeeinrichtung etc.etc. alles für verhältnismässig erschwingliches Geld gibt - alles Dinge, die zwar noch lange
keine Kultur, aber doch erfreuliche Begleiterscheinungen des Lebens
sind, und die man in dignified and time-honoured - but old-fashioned
London fast nirgends antrifft, falls man nicht über ein Einkommen
von sagen wir "von Pfd. 300- an aufwärts" verfügt!! Hier geniesst jeder Arbeiter (selbst die wenigen Arbeitslosen) diese Vorteile.

Es herrscht eine geradezu erstaunliche sociale Ausgeglichenheit
hier vor, die ich noch nirgends in diesem Maße erlebt habe und die,
gerade nach einem Einblick in die englischen Verhältnisse, hocherfreulich und zukunftsträchtig wirkt : Man sieht, selbst bei so ungesunden
Weltzuständen kann ein kleines Agrarland mit nur wenig Industrie das
erreichen - was wäre bei einiger Vernunft dann sonst in der Welt möglich..... Es gibt gewiss keinen solchen Reichtum wie in Dänemarkxx
England, aber entschieden weniger krasse Armut und der grosse Durchschnitt der Bevölkerung lebt zufrieden auf einem ganz erstaunlich
hohen allgemeinen Lebensstandard! Welch herrliche moderne Wohnsiedlungen rings umd die prachtvoll gebaute city! Es gibt nur ganz wenige wirkliche Armutswohnstrassen älterer Bauart in der Stadt. Jeder
kann sich bis zu einem gewissen Grad moderne technische Hygiene und
gesundes Wohnen in gut gebauten Massensiedlungen im Grünen leisten.
(Kopenhagen hat nahezu 1 Million Einwohner). Geradezu unglaublich ist
der Aufwand, den sich das Ländchen an sog. kulturellen Leistungen öffentlicher Art noch nebenher leistet. Zwei Universitäten, Galerien u.
Museen wie Sand am Meer, und wissenschaftliche Stiftungen die dem Gemeinsinn der Industriellen alle Ehre machen! Besonders das dänische
Bier trägt dazu bei. Z.B. fliessen a l l e Einkünfte der grossen
Carlsberg-Brauerei heute nur noch in die Wissenschaft, und der Rask-
Ørsted Fondet, von dem ich ja lebe, und der z.B. dem weltberühmten Atomzertrümmerer, Prof. Niels Bohr, ein ganzes modernes Experimental-physikalisches Institut hingestellt hat, ist auch nicht von schlechten El-
tern. So könnte ich noch viel des Lobenswerten erzählen. Aber ich hör
Sie schon - vielleicht mit einigem Recht - sagen "der Mensch ist ein
Produkt seiner Lebensumstände : geht's einem gut, sieht man leicht alles zu rosig, gehts einem schlecht noch leichter alles zu grau an...!

Meine Arbeit hat einen ganz befriedigenden Anfang genommen. Das
Nationalmuseum ist ein höchst modern und gut geleitetes Institut und
die Münzsammlung im Besonderen hat einen reizenden Abteilungsdirektor
und prachtvolle grosse Räume, complette Fachbibliothek, alle Zeitschriften etc. Ganz nahe davon ist Prof. Johansens archäolog. Universitätsinstitut (im gleichen Haus!) mit ebenfalls guter Bibliothek und
5 Minuten weiter gleich die Ny-Carlsberg Glyptothek mit Ihren geradezu
herrlichen Schätzen an antiker Plastik und moderner Malerei (samt einer weiteren archäolog. Fachbibliothek!). Und was man dort nicht hat,
findet man bestimmt dann in der ausgezeichneten Kgl. Bibliothek! Ich
habe nicht weniger wie ca. 25 000 griech. Münzen zu bearbeiten, die
z. Teil seit der Renaissance hier eine Art Dornröschenschlaf schlafen,
aber wohlbehütet, und zuletzt von einem Eckhel-Schüler, Ramus, (1816) in
einem lateinischen Katalog behandelt wurden! In diese Arbeit teile
ich mich - nach den Vorschriften des Rask-Ørsted Fondets - mit einem
dänischen Mitarbeiter, der aber als Kustos an dem antiken department
des Museums auch sonst noch mit reichlich viel Arbeit gesegnet ist...
Wie bei jeder Katalogisierung (es soll in der von der British Academy
herausgegebenen, von E.S.G. Robinson edierten "Sylloge"-Reihe erscheinen) fallen nebenher natürlich auch reichlich Probleme und Aufsatzspäne ab. Shortly - it is the kind of work I like to do!

Nun aber noch schnell zurück zu Ihrem Brief! Hinks hat seine Position am BM. natürlich erst dann endgültig aufgegeben, als er bereits
eine ihn reizende und ehrende neue an der Warburg-Library in London
in der Tasche hatte! Also ist es mit dieser Idee nichts. Dagegen lege

49

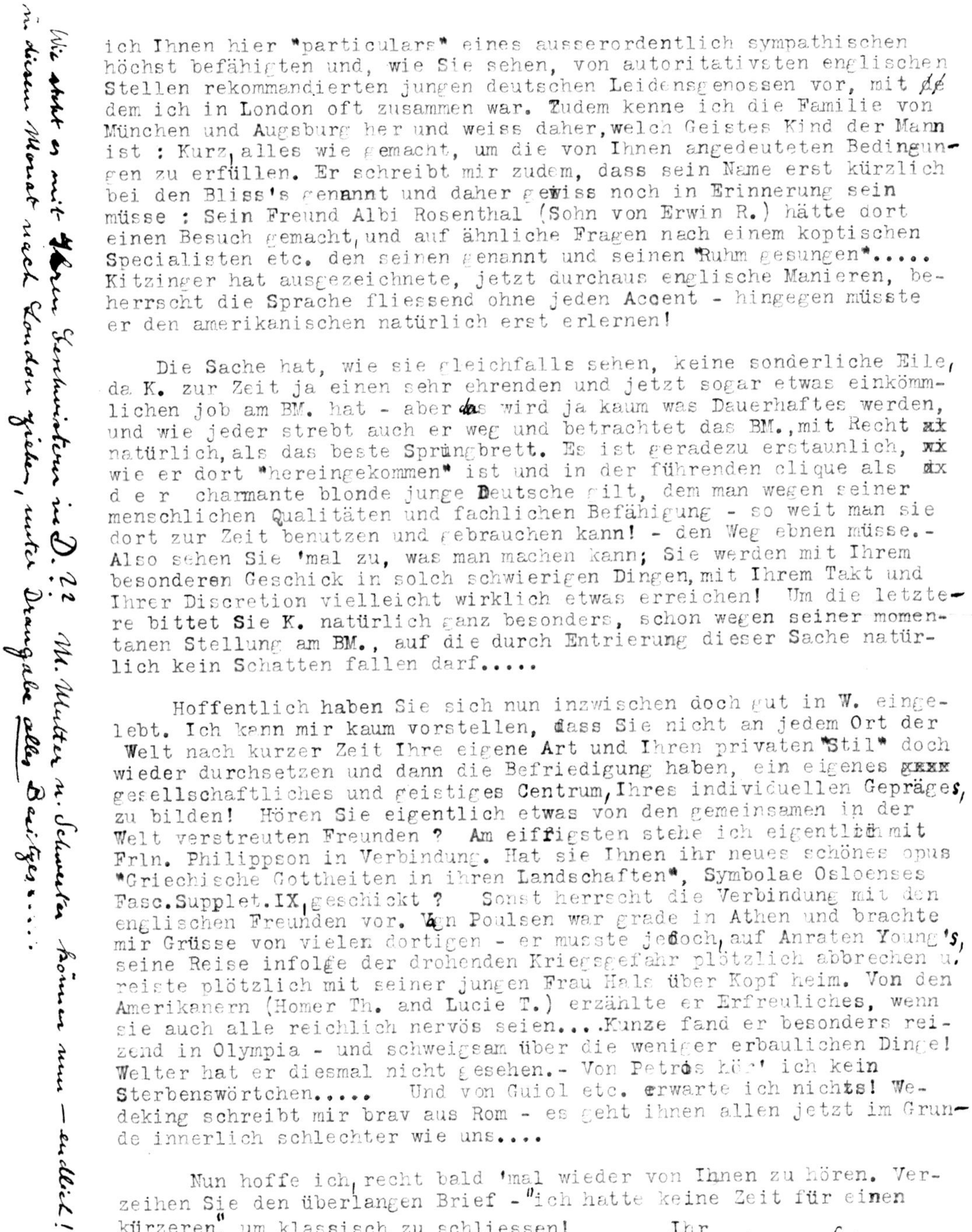

ich Ihnen hier "particulars" eines ausserordentlich sympathischen höchst befähigten und, wie Sie sehen, von autoritativsten englischen Stellen rekommandierten jungen deutschen Leidensgenossen vor, mit dem ich in London oft zusammen war. Zudem kenne ich die Familie von München und Augsburg her und weiss daher, welch Geistes Kind der Mann ist : Kurz, alles wie gemacht, um die von Ihnen angedeuteten Bedingungen zu erfüllen. Er schreibt mir zudem, dass sein Name erst kürzlich bei den Bliss's genannt und daher gewiss noch in Erinnerung sein müsse : Sein Freund Albi Rosenthal (Sohn von Erwin R.) hätte dort einen Besuch gemacht, und auf ähnliche Fragen nach einem koptischen Specialisten etc. den seinen genannt und seinen "Ruhm gesungen"..... Kitzinger hat ausgezeichnete, jetzt durchaus englische Manieren, beherrscht die Sprache fliessend ohne jeden Accent - hingegen müsste er den amerikanischen natürlich erst erlernen!

Die Sache hat, wie sie gleichfalls sehen, keine sonderliche Eile, da K. zur Zeit ja einen sehr ehrenden und jetzt sogar etwas einkömmlichen job am BM. hat - aber das wird ja kaum was Dauerhaftes werden, und wie jeder strebt auch er weg und betrachtet das BM., mit Recht natürlich, als das beste Sprungbrett. Es ist geradezu erstaunlich, wie er dort "hereingekommen" ist und in der führenden clique als d e r charmante blonde junge Deutsche gilt, dem man wegen seiner menschlichen Qualitäten und fachlichen Befähigung - so weit man sie dort zur Zeit benutzen und gebrauchen kann! - den Weg ebnen müsse.- Also sehen Sie 'mal zu, was man machen kann; Sie werden mit Ihrem besonderen Geschick in solch schwierigen Dingen, mit Ihrem Takt und Ihrer Discretion vielleicht wirklich etwas erreichen! Um die letztere bittet Sie K. natürlich ganz besonders, schon wegen seiner momentanen Stellung am BM., auf die durch Entrierung dieser Sache natürlich kein Schatten fallen darf.....

Hoffentlich haben Sie sich nun inzwischen doch gut in W. eingelebt. Ich kann mir kaum vorstellen, dass Sie nicht an jedem Ort der Welt nach kurzer Zeit Ihre eigene Art und Ihren privaten "Stil" doch wieder durchsetzen und dann die Befriedigung haben, ein eigenes gesellschaftliches und geistiges Centrum, Ihres individuellen Gepräges, zu bilden! Hören Sie eigentlich etwas von den gemeinsamen in der Welt verstreuten Freunden ? Am eifrigsten stehe ich eigentlich mit Frln. Philippson in Verbindung. Hat sie Ihnen ihr neues schönes opus "Griechische Gottheiten in ihren Landschaften", Symbolae Osloenses Fasc.Supplet.IX, geschickt ? Sonst herrscht die Verbindung mit den englischen Freunden vor. Van Poulsen war grade in Athen und brachte mir Grüsse von vielen dortigen - er musste jedoch, auf Anraten Young's, seine Reise infolge der drohenden Kriegsgefahr plötzlich abbrechen u. reiste plötzlich mit seiner jungen Frau Hals über Kopf heim. Von den Amerikanern (Homer Th. and Lucie T.) erzählte er Erfreuliches, wenn sie auch alle reichlich nervös seien....Kunze fand er besonders reizend in Olympia - und schweigsam über die weniger erbaulichen Dinge! Welter hat er diesmal nicht gesehen.- Von Petros hör' ich kein Sterbenswörtchen..... Und von Guiol etc. erwarte ich nichts! Wedeking schreibt mir brav aus Rom - es geht ihnen allen jetzt im Grunde innerlich schlechter wie uns....

Nun hoffe ich, recht bald 'mal wieder von Ihnen zu hören. Verzeihen Sie den überlangen Brief - "ich hatte keine Zeit für einen kürzeren", um klassisch zu schliessen! Ihr

Willy Schwabacher

Wie steht es mit Ihren Geschwistern in D.?? M. Mutter u. Schwester können nun – endlich! – in diesem Monat nach London ziehen, unter Drangabe alles Besitzes.....

Fig. 5. *Letter from Willy Schwabacher to Berta Segall (Source: Berta Segall archive at the Antikensammlung Basel und Sammlung Ludwig).*

Bibliography

Arendt, H. 2017
'Wie ich einmal ohne Dich leben soll, mag ich mir nicht vorstellen: Brief-wechsel mit den Freundinnen Char-lotte Beradt, Rose Feitelson, Hilde Fränkel, Anne Weil und Helen Wolff', in missing book title, U. Ludz & I. Nordmann (eds), München, page no.

Altekamp, S. 2008
'Klassische Archäologie und National-sozialismus', *Kulturwissenschaften und Nationalsozialismus*, J. Elvert & J. Niels-en-Sikora (eds), Stuttgart, 167-209.

Altekamp, S. 2014 2016/17?
'Klassische Archäologie und National-sozialismus: Vorlesung Sommersemes-ter 2014', *Zweitveröffentlichungen* vol. no., page no.

Berghaus, P. 1972
'Willy Schwabacher, 22. Juli 1897-30. August 1972', *Hamburger Beiträge zur Numismatik* 24, 7-8.

Boehringer, C. 1973
'Willy Schwabacher, 22. Juli 1897-30. August 1972', *Schweizerische numisma-tische Rundschau* 52, 155-61.

Boehringer, C. 2014
'Willy Schwabacher 1897-1972. Versuch eines Porträts', *Jahrbuch für Numismatik und Geldgeschichte* 64, 301-22.

Brands, G. 2012
'Archäologen und die deutsche Ver-gangenheit', in *Lebensbilder. Klassische Archäologen und der Nationalsozialismus* (Band 1), G. Brands & M. Maischberg-er (eds), Rahden, 1-34.

Brands, G. & M. Maischberger (eds) 2012
Lebensbilder. Klassische Archäologen und der Nationalsozialismus (Band 1), Rahden.

Brands, G. & M. Maischberger (eds) 2016
Lebensbilder. Klassische Archäologen und der Nationalsozialismus (Band 2), Rahden.

Broch, H. 2010
'Briefe an Erich von Kahler (1940-1951)', in missing title/journal and no., P. Lützeler (ed.), Berlin, page no.

Chapoutot, J. 2014
Der Nationalsozialismus und die Antike, Darmstadt.

Freyberger, R. & E. Rochau-Shalem, 2013
'Volontäre an den Staatlichen Museen zu Berlin 1933-1945', in *Zwischen Politik und Kunst. Die Staatlichen Museen zu Berlin in der Zeit des Nationalsozialis-mus*, J. Grabowski & P. Winter (eds), Köln, 67-82.

Hochwarter, E. 2008
'Berta Segall', *Wiener Kunstgeschichte gesichtet*, accessed July 2018.

Hofter, M. 2012
'Ernst Buschor (1886-1945)', in *Leb-ensbilder. Klassische Archäologen und der Nationalsozialismus* (Band 1), G. Brands & M. Maischberger (eds), Rah-den, 129-40.

Jantzen, U. 1986
Einhundert Jahre Athener Institut, 1874-1974, (Das Deutsche Archäologische Institut. Geschichte und Dokumente 10), Mainz.

Junker, K. 1997
Das Archäologische Institut des Deutschen Reiches zwischen Forschung und Politik: die Jahre 1929 bis 1945, Mainz.

Krumme, M. 2012
'Walther Wrede (1893-1990)', in *Leb-ensbilder. Klassische Archäologen und der Nationalsozialismus* (Band 1), G. Brands & M. Maischberger (eds), Rah-den, 159-76.

Krumme, M. & V, Vigener, 2016
'Carl Weickert (1883-1947)', in *Leb-ensbilder. Klassische Archäologen und der Nationalsozialismus* (Band 2), G. Brands & M. Maischberger (eds), Rah-den, 203-22.

Kyrieleis, H. 1979
'Abteilung Athen', in *Beiträge zur Geschichte des Deutschen Archäologis-chen Instituts 1929 bis 1979* (Teil 1), K. Bittel, W. Deichmann, W. Grünhagen, W. Kaiser, T. Kraus & H. Kyrieleis (eds), Mainz, 41-64.

Lindenlauf, A. 2015
'Georg Heinrich Karo. "Gelehrter und Verteidiger deutschen Geistes"', *Jahrbuch des Deutschen Archäologischen Instituts* 130, 259-354.

Lindenlauf, A. 2016
'Georg Heinrich Karo (1872-1963)', in *Lebensbilder. Klassische Archäologen*

51

und der Nationalsozialismus (Band 2), G. Brands & M. Maischberger (eds), Rahden, 55-78.

Lullies, R. & W. Schiering (eds) 1988
Archäologenbildnisse. Porträts und Kurzbiographien von Klassischen Archäologen deutscher Sprache, Mainz.

Maischberger, M. 2002
'German archaeology during the Third Reich, 1933-45: a case study based on archival evidence', *Antiquity* 76, 209-18.

Manderscheid, H. 2010
'Opfer – Täter – schweigende Mehrheit: Anmerkungen zur deutschen Klassischen Archäologie während des Nationalsozialismus', *Hephaistos* 27, 41-69.

Marx, K. 1859
Zur Kritik der Politischen Ökonomie, Berlin.

Marx, K. 1979
A Contribution to the Critique of Political Economy, London.

Miller, H. 1941
The Colossus of Maroussi, San Francisco.

Möbius, H. 1949
'Paula Philippson', *Gnomon* 21, 279.

Obermayer, H. 2014
Deutsche Altertumswissenschaftler im amerikanischen Exil. Eine Rekonstruktion. Berlin.

Philippson, P. 1939
Griechische Gottheiten in ihren Landschaften, Oslo.

Sailer, G. 2015

Monsignorina. Die deutsche Jüdin Hermine Speier im Vatikan, Münster.

Schauer, C. 1998
'Die "Sekretäre" des Sekretariats Athen und ihre Tätigkeit. Otto Walter (1910/11-1945)', in *Hundert Jahre Österreichisches Archäologisches Institut Athen 1898-1998*, V. Mitsopoulos-Leon (ed.), Athens, 51-3.

Schmidt, M. 1977
'Berta Segall zum Gedenken', *Antike Kunst* 20, 121-2.

Segall, B. 1938
Museum Benaki. Katalog der Goldschmiede-Arbeiten, Athen.

Vigener, M. 2012
"Ein wichtiger kulturpolitischer Faktor". Das Deutsche Archäologische Institut zwischen Wissenschaft, Politik und Öffentlichkeit, 1918-1954, Rahden.

Wegeler, C. 1996
"… wir sagen ab der internationalen Gelehrtenrepublik". Altertumswissenschaft und Nationalsozialismus: Das Göttinger Institut für Altertumskunde 1921-1962, Wien.

Wendland, U. 1999
Biographisches Handbuch deutschsprachiger Kunsthistoriker im Exil, München.

Wlach, G. 1998
'Otto Walter', in *Hundert Jahre Österreichisches Archäologisches Institut Athen 1898-1998*, V. Mitsopoulos-Leon (ed.), 113-114.

Selected Bibliography of Willy Schwabacher

Schwabacher, W. 1925
Die Tetradrachmenprägung von Selinunt, München.

Schwabacher, W. 1933a
Die Voit von Salzburg'sche Münz- und Medaillensammlung der Universitätsbibliothek Erlangen, München.

Schwabacher, W. 1933b
'Zu den Münzen von Katana', *Römische Mitteilungen* 48, 121-6.

Schwabacher, W. 1937
'Pelinna. An early Thessalian Mint', *Numismatic Chronicle* 17, 102-6.

Schwabacher, W. 1938
'Die Münzen der Olynthos-Grabung. Zu Hugo Gaebler's "Fälschungen makedonischer Münzen II"', *American Journal of Archaeology* 42, 70-76.

Schwabacher, W. 1939a
'Contribution to Greek Numismatics', *Numismatic Chronicle* 19, 1-20.

Schwabacher, W. 1939b
'A Find from the Piraeus', *Numismatic Chronicle* 19, 162-6.

Schwabacher, W. 1939c
'A hoard of drachms of Elis', *Numismatic Chronicle* 19, 239-65.

Schwabacher, W. 1939d
'Some Coins of Metapontum in the Royal Collection at Copenhagen', *Acta Archaeologica* 10, 120-31.

Schwabacher, W. 1941
'Hellenistische Reliefkeramik des Ker-

ameikos', *American Journal of Archaeology* 45, 182-228.

Schwabacher, W. 1942
Sylloge nummorum Graecorum. The royal collection of coins and medals, Danish National Museum, Kopenhagen.

Schwabacher, W. 1944
'Carl Gustav Tessin and the great Brescello Gold Hoard of 1714', *Nordisk Numismatisk Årsskrift* vol no., 231-43.

Schwabacher, W. 1953
'Zur Technik der Stempelherstellung in griechischen Münzwerkstätten klassischer Zeit', *Congrès international de numismatique. Paris 611 juillet 1953* (2. Actes), 521-28.

Schwabacher, W. 1957a
'Ein Silberstater der Stadt Tlos in Lykien', *Schweizer Münzblätter* 7, 3-6.

Schwabacher, W. 1957b
'Satrapenbildnisse. Zum neuen Münzporträt des Tissaphernes', in *Charites. Studien zur Altertumswissenschaft. Festschrift Ernst Langlotz*, K. Schauenburg (ed.), Bonn, 27-32.

Schwabacher, W. 1958a
Das Demareteion, Bremen.

Schwabacher, W. 1958b
'Zu den Herstellungsmethoden der griechischen Münzstempel', *Schweizer Münzblätter* 8, 57-63.

Schwabacher, W. 1961a
'The Olympian Zeus before Phidias', *Archaeology* 14, 104-9.

Schwabacher, W. 1961b

'Zur Prägetechnik und Deutung der inkusen Münzen Grossgriechenlands', *Congresso internazionale di numismatica. Roma 11-16 settembre 1961. Atti*, 107-16.

Schwabacher, W. 1962a
Grekiska mynt ur Konung Gustaf VI Adolfs samling, Malmö.

Schwabacher, W. 1962b
'Olympischer Blitzschwinger', *Antike Kunst* 5, 9-17.

Schwabacher, W. 1962c
'Die Azoren und die Seefahrt der Alten', *Schweizer Münzblätter* 12, 22-6.

Schwabacher, W. 1964
Neue Methoden in der griechischen Münzforschung, Lund.

Schwabacher, W. 1965
'Nochmals der olympische Blitzschwinger', *Römische Mitteilungen* 72, 209-12.

Schwabacher, W. 1966a
'The production of hubs reconsidered', *The Numismatic Chronicle and The Journal of the Royal Numismatic Society* vol no., 41-5.

Schwabacher, W. 1966b
'Altrömische Münzbezeichnungen in einem Gedichtfragment des 5. Jahrhunderts n. Chr.', *Schweizer Münzblätter* 16, 89-90.

Schwabacher, W. 1968a
'Nils-Gustaf Palin. Nachträge zu einem schwedischen Sammler- und Forscherschicksal im Süden', *Opuscula Atheniensis* 8, 203-11.

Schwabacher, W. 1968b
'Lycian coin-portraits', in *Essays in Greek coinage, presented to Stanley Robinson*, C. M. Kraay and G. K. Jenkins (eds), Oxford, 111-24.

Schwabacher, W. 1968c
'Pythagoras auf griechischen Münzbildern', *Opuscula. Carolo Kerenyi dedicata*, Stockholm, 59-63.

Schwabacher, W. 1974
Griechische Münzkunst. Kurze Kunstgeschichte an Beispielen aus der Sammlung S.M. Gustaf VI. Adolf, König von Schweden, Mainz.

Schwabacher, W. 1975
'Zur Münzprägung der Samier in Zankle-Messana', in *Wandlungen. Studien zur antiken und neueren Kunst. Ernst Homann-Wedeking gewidmet*, Waldsassen, 107-11.

Selected Bibliography of Berta Segall

Segall, B. 1929
'Ein Paduaner Codex von 1399 im Kupferstichkabinett zu Berlin', *Amtliche Berichte aus den Staatlichen Kunstsammlungen Berlin*, 133-6.

Segall, B. 1938
Katalog der Goldschmiede-Arbeiten im Benaki Museum, Athen.

Segall, B. 1939
'A rock-crystal Statuette of Heracles', *The Journal of the Walters Art Gallery* 2, 113-7.

Segall, B. 1941a
'Dumbarton Oaks collection', *American Journal of Archaeology* 45, 7-17.

53

Segall, B. 1941b

'Two gold pins in the Classical Collection', *Bulletin of the Museum of Fine Arts* 39, 54-8.

Segall, B. 1942

'The earring with winged charioteer in the classical department', *Bulletin of the Museum of Fine Arts* 40, 50-4.

Segall, B. 1943a

'Some sources of early Greek jewelry', *Bulletin of the Museum of Fine Arts* 41, 42-6.

Segall, B. 1943b

'Greece and Luristan', *Bulletin of the Museum of Fine Arts* 41, 72-6.

Segall, B. 1945

'Two hellenistic gold medallions from Thessaly', *Record of the Museum of Historic Art, Princeton University* 4, 2-21.

Segall, B. 1946a

'The problem of Phoenician artisans in Egypt. An early hellenistic earring', *The Journal of the Walters Art Gallery* 9, 97-101.

Segall, B. 1946b

'Realistic portraiture in Greece and Egypt. A portrait bust of Ptolemy I', *The Journal of the Walters Art Gallery* 9, 52-67.

Segall, B. 1955a

'Sculptures from Arabia Felix. The Hellenistic period', *American Journal of Archaeology* 59, 207-14.

Segall, B. 1955b

'The arts and King Nabonidus', *American Journal of Archaeology* 59, 315-8.

Segall, B. 1956a

'Notes on the iconography of cosmic kingship', *The Art Bulletin* 38, 75-80.

Segall, B. 1956b

'Problems of copy and adaption in the second quarter of the first millenium B.C. Some Syrian and "Syro-Hittite" elements in the art of Arabia and of the West', *American Journal of Archaeology* 60, 165-70.

Segall, B. 1957

Sculpture from Arabia Felix. The earliest phase, Washington.

Segall, B. 1958

'The lion-riders from Timna', *Archaeological discoveries in South Arabia*, 155-82.

Segall, B. 1959

'Zum Hamburger Zeus. Der Typus in der antiken Apotheose', *Festschrift für Erich Meyer zum 60. Geburtstag am 19. Oktober 1957*, Hamburg, 7-24.

Segall, B. (ed.) 1964

Festschrift Eugen v. Mercklin, E. Homann-Wedeking & B. Segal (eds), Waldassen.

Segall, B. 1966a

Tradition und Neuschöpfung in der frühalexandrinischen Kleinkunst, Berlin.

Segall, B. 1966b

Zur griechischen Goldschmiedekunst des vierten Jahrhunderts v. Chr. Eine griechische Schmuckgruppe im Schmuckmuseum Pforzheim, Wiesbaden.

Sources

Antikenmuseum Basel und Sammlung Ludwig, Archiv
[Archive of the Basel Museum of Ancient Art and Ludwig Collection]

Deutsches Archäologisches Institut Berlin, Archiv der Zentrale
[Deutsches Archäologisches Institut Berlin, Central Archive]

Deutsches Archäologisches Institut Athen, Archiv
[Deutsches Archäologisches Institut Athen, Archive]

Entschädigungsbehörde des Landes Berlin
[Compensation Authority Berlin]

Museums für Kunst und Gewerbe Hamburg, Archiv
[Museum of Art and Design Hamburg, Archive]

Staatsarchiv des Kantons Basel-Stadt
[State Archives Basel-Stadt]

Stadtarchiv Wuppertal
[City Archives Wuppertal]

Universität Leipzig, Ägyptologisches Institut / Ägyptisches Museum, Archiv
[Archive at the University of Leipzig, Egyptology Museum]

Zentralarchiv Staatliche Museen zu Berlin
[Central Archive Berlin State Museums]

Simplicity and Essentiality:
Carl Nielsen's Idea of Ancient Greek Music

PAOLO MUNTONI

Abstract

Taking its point of departure in Nielsen's talk about Ancient Greek Music presented at the Greek Society in Copenhagen in 1907, this essay reflects on how the features of the Greek music exposed by Nielsen mirror his aesthetic beliefs of simplicity and essentiality, as revealed by some of his writings and exemplified by one of his later works for piano.

At the same time the cultural influence of Ancient Greek culture in Northern Europe at the turn of the century is evident in some of Nielsen's major works from the 1910s and 1920s, where emphasis is put on values such as the unity between man and nature and the importance of the bodily element, whose musical representation, sound, thus becomes an object of study and exploration.

Greek culture has been a model and cultural reference for artists from countless generations. In ancient times, the Romans were the first to imitate the Greek artists, taking their aesthetics as a model. Later, Ancient Greece was rediscovered after the Middle Ages, inspiring the Renaissance's occupation with harmonious balance, symmetry and clarity. In recent times, the fascination of antiquity has continued, especially through Neoclassicism and Romanticism – the former with its ideal of perfection, harmony, clarity, purity and stylised beauty, the latter with its fondness for ancient history and landscapes where the remains of the past, in the form of ruins, played a major role.

In the early 1900s, especially in the countries of Northern Europe, Greek culture was also considered in a different way, having less to do with abstract ideals, and more with physical values, in the most literal sense of the word. The first Olympic Games of modern times, which were held, symbolically, in Athens at the turn of the century – 1896 – ushered in a preoccupation with the bodily element, the physical beside the spiritual, i.e. the idea of harmony between body and mind that belonged to the Greek worldview and was reinterpreted in the first decades of the twentieth century by movements such as vitalism and naturism.

This was the cultural climate that surrounded many of the artists from the early 20th century, a picture that emerges clearly in the chapter "Hellenics" in Daniel Grimley's monograph *Carl Nielsen and the idea of Modernism*.[1] Grimley observes that in this period Northern Europe was characterised by ideological trends that promoted a more Southern or Mediterranean way of living and mak-

---

ing art: "Nietzsche's decisive anti-Romantic turn and famous call for the 'Mediterraneanisation of music' in *The Case of Wagner*, promoted energetically in Copenhagen in the 1890s by Georg Brandes"[2] became "an antidote to the perceived moral and aesthetic decay of modern society".[3] The Northern Neo-Hellenic movement, as noted by Grimley, is indivisible from an insistence on bodily health. For these artists the idea of harmony between body, spirit and mind was essential, as they aspired to observe the balance derived from the Greek ideal of communion between inner and outer qualities, meaning that men ought to take equal care of their body and of their soul.

In Denmark some groups adhering to these principles were formed in the same decade. In the essay "Den sunde natur" by Gertrud Oelsner,[4] special emphasis is put on the first Danish example of these groups, that of the Hellenists (*Hellenerne*), centred on the figure of Gunnar Sadolin.[5] Their basic references were the work of Nietzsche, Ancient Greek sources and French *en plein air* painting. They met near Kalundborg around the middle of 1890 and were characterised by an essential lifestyle: they dressed in simple clothes and even practised naturism, engaged in sports and winter swimming, and promoted a primarily masculine model of youth, strength and vigorous physical activity, both as artistic inspiration and as a life example.[6]

Grimley reports on some of the letters[7] between Anne-Marie and Carl Nielsen in which they mention a manual containing a training method[8] with exercises like those practised by the Hellenists. While irony is not absent in these comments, the Nielsens were not too far from this model, both in their lifestyle and in their artistic interests, which Grimley associates with their countryside background, where the lifestyle is more physical and outdoor activities are more common than in the city: "Like the Hellenists, Nielsen imaginatively transposed an idealised notion of an antique Classical landscape onto his home soil".[9] It is also well known that Anne-Marie in particular was interested in the description of the body in motion, as testified by her studies of Ancient Greek works, as well as by the sculptures that portray Nielsen as a young Greek god, where references to the god Pan are evident.

It is therefore no surprise that Anne-Marie applied for a six-month stay in Athens in 1903, where she was granted the *Anckerske Legat* and got permission to copy some of the sculptures in the Acropolis. She was later joined by her husband, who was treated with great respect and was provided with a grand piano during his stay at the Music Conservatory of the Greek capital.[10] The landscape and atmosphere inspired him to compose an orchestral work, the *Helios Overture*, which traces the sun's journey across the Aegean Sea. But beyond this, this composition was also considered a tribute to the sun as a divine symbol of energy and vitality, an interpretation that is expressed by various commentators; it is thus suggested that the piece engages with the vitalistic philosophy of the time, a connection that has been proposed and discussed on several occasions.[11]

We do not know whether Nielsen's interest in Ancient Greek music developed in this period, but it is certain that he visited some archaeological areas, where he had access to a few original sources. It is nevertheless certain that the subject appealed to him to such an extent that he began himself that he began studying some of the features of Ancient Greek music, which years later, as a member of the Greek Society, he was to present to the Danish public.[12]

My point of departure in this essay is the transcription of this talk, given in Copenhagen in October 1907, with Michelsen's article "Carl Nielsen and Greek music" and the abovementioned chapter from Grimley's monograph

---

2   Grimley 2010, 64.

3   Grimley 2010, 68.

4   Oelsner 2008, 159-97.

5   Danish artist and entrepreneur.

6   Grimley 2010, 68.

7   Letter to Anne-Marie 6/2/1905, in Fellow (ed.) 2005-13, 43.

8   Müller 1904, later also published for women (1924). Müller was a gymnast and his manual became a paradigm for many works of the kind.

9   Grimley 2010, 71.

10   Fjeldsøe 2010, 36.

11   See for example Jensen 1994, 58-77; Fjeldsøe 2009, 26-42; Dam 2010; Fjeldsøe 2010, 33-55.

12   Carl Nielsen writes: "When I was in Delphi, some years ago, I saw this interesting piece [a hymn to Apollo] and was allowed to take a picture of it", 'Græsk Musik', in Fellow (ed.) 1999, 110. Another significant musical source mentioned in his talk is the so-called 'Song of Seikilos' (on page 130 of

as constant references. Michelsen reflects on how the features of the Greek music exposed by Nielsen mirror his aesthetic beliefs by comparing them to some of his later writings, while Grimley links Nielsen's speech with the cultural influence of 'The Hellenics', showing how they share the same aesthetic beliefs and how this can be perceived in Nielsen's music.

The ideal of a Hellenic spirit is notable in Carl Nielsen's music even after this decade, and is not limited to the *Helios Overture* and the *Sinfonia Espansiva*, the two pieces examined under this light by Grimley. I will argue that the most enduring ideals Nielsen takes from the Hellenics are the unity between man and nature and the insistence on the bodily element as something worth cherishing. In Nielsen's music these values are represented respectively by a sonic landscape capable of evoking the feeling of harmony between man and nature and by a study of what can be considered the body of music, sound. I will briefly take into consideration two works in which these tendencies are particularly evident, the Fourth Symphony and the Flute Concerto.

Finally, I will insist on Michelsen's point that the talk on Greek music was for Nielsen a first exposition of some aesthetic principles that he was to develop further in his later writings. I believe that ideas such as the return to simplicity, in the sense of going back to what is essential in music, and the need for clarity and purity in melodic discourse, can not only be found in his later writings but also in his works. *Klavermusik for smaa og store*, in particular, offers us an example of these principles applied to the praxis of the musical composition.

The idea of ancient Greek Music

One of the most obvious manifestations of the interest in Ancient Greek culture in Northern Europe at the turn of the century was the creation in 1905 of a 'Greek society', founded in Copenhagen by, among others, the philologists Johan Ludvig Heiberg and Anders Bjørn Drachmann, the philosopher Harald Høffding and the critic Georg Brandes.[13] Carl Nielsen and his wife Anne-Marie joined it almost at the beginning, although the composer himself claims that he was a founding member.[14] The purpose of the society was the promotion of Hellenic culture through a spectrum of activities, most notably through the arts. This was the context for Nielsen's preparation and delivery of a talk on Ancient Greek music. A transcription of the speech is published in John Fellow's anthology, *Carl Nielsen til sin samtid*; additional sources that bear witness to Nielsen's interest in Ancient Greek music include two notebooks, the first containing musical transcriptions of Ancient Greek melodies as well as material for the presentation, the second also containing preliminary work for the writing of the two essays[15] 'Mozart and our time' and 'Words, Music and Programme Music'. An examination of the transcript of the talk reveals a commonality of aesthetic intent with the two abovementioned articles that were in fact published in the same decade (1906 and 1909 respectively) and later included, together with other material, in Nielsen's anthology from 1925, *Living Music*.[16]

Among the topics Nielsen deals with in his presentation we find some consideration, often of a polemical nature, of contemporary tendencies and musical practices. The music-theoretical discussion also covers topics such as the relationship between harmonics and numerical proportions, the ethos of Ancient Greek musical scales and the homophonic nature of melody.

This last point, the primacy of the melodic element in music, is probably the most important for Nielsen, and in fact most of his polemic considerations arise against the use of a certain type of polyphony, vertical polyphony, which he believed was the most common in contempo-

his essay, Michelsen, in fact, reports that he played excerpts from the hymn to Apollo, from Euripides' Orestes, as well as the melody defined by the composer as "the prettiest of them all" (Nielsen 1907, 110), the song of Seikilos, now at the National Museum of Copenhagen). It is without doubt that Nielsen was especially fascinated and probably inspired by the simplicity of this melody. Michelsen even claims that there is a similarity in the musical scale used in Seikilos (the modern Mixolydian) and the beginning of Helios (pp. 220-1). I believe that the use of the flattened sixth, as well as the continuous shift from minor to major third, are characteristics of Nielsen's style that are independent from this fascination, as demonstrated by the fact that he already used them in his First Symphony, a work that precedes Nielsen's visit to Greece by half a decade.

13   Schousboe (e.d) 1983, 181.
14   Michelsen 1998, 221.
15   Michelsen 1998, 222.
16   I will refer here to the English translation of the book, Nielsen 1925 (transl. Spink 1953), 13-24; 25-40; 41-53.

rary music writing. The ideals of organic polyphony and monophonic melody can be found in *Living Music* as well as in several letters written to fellow composers, such as Julius Röntgen and Knud Harder.[17]

The basic idea outlined by Nielsen is that of a distinction between 'good' and 'bad' polyphony. In good polyphony a melodic line organically generates other melodic lines, and, as such, its contrapuntal development appears as a natural evolution of the melody. It is therefore important for polyphonic composers to keep a close adherence to the original melodic material. Only a few contemporary composers were interested in this kind of polyphony, one of them being the German Max Reger, who Nielsen praises highly. Still following Michelsen,[18] we encounter a letter Nielsen wrote to the composer Knud Harder about Reger:

He is a man who can do everything that has almost fallen into disgrace because of these unfavourable times. I mean the real polyphony, which through Wagner and especially his followers, is reflected in a characterless counterpoint, which does not express anything other then muggy sentimentality or empty, stormy passion. This art must be reverted to its basic principles, yes, all the way back to its monophonic origin.[19]

Most of the composers of the time, however, used polyphony in a harmonic, vertical way, without considering the necessity of the melody. This "degenerated" polyphonic style simply aims to create sound effects that have the harmonic vertical element as justification. In this sense, the polemical vein present in some of the statements in Nielsen's talk is also an aesthetic manifesto. Composers such as Wagner and Strauss have forced polyphony into their composition, while a good polyphonic composer knows how to capture and express the melody's essence: when the melody has the urgency to develop polyphoni-

cally, he/she can interpret this potential and let it grow it according to its nature. A similar thought was expressed by the Italian (but Germany-based) composer Ferruccio Busoni when developing his concept of Young Classicism:

With Young Classicism I include the definite departure from what is thematic and the return to melody again as the ruler of all voices and all emotions (not in the sense of a pleasing motive) and as the bearer of the idea and the begetter of harmony, in short, the most highly developed (not the most complicated) polyphony.[20]

This polemic against the polyphonic music of the time goes hand in hand with the critique of those who attributed to Ancient Greek music a polyphonic character.[21] Nielsen fights this thesis from an aesthetic point of view (because the homophonic melody has greater strength and clarity, and is used by the greatest composers when they want to acquire meaningful expression),[22] but also from a philological one. He mentions Aristoteles, who in the *Politics* underlines the presence of the octave interval as the only diversion from choral singing to unison, and Plato, a favourite of the composer's, who writes about the ethos of the Ancient Greek musical scales.[23]

Following the Greek philosophers, Nielsen asks himself rhetorically: how can a melody based on a specific scale have a certain ethos if another melody is superimposed on it? The ethos of a melody was determined by the *harmonia*, or *tropos*,[24] meaning that it had to do both with the succession of the intervals in the scale, with its note of departure and with the way in which the intervals followed one another.[25] When the vertical dimension is added, the sense of this last element is lost.

Nielsen's considerations on the ethos of Greek scales are therefore instrumental to his theory that Greek music was homophonic, and as such could be used as an ex-

---

17 Michelsen 1998, 225-6.
18 Michelsen 1998, 226.
19 Letter to Knud Harder dated 13 February 1907, quoted in Michelsen 1998, 226.
20 Busoni 1922 (transl. Ley 1957), 21.
21 Michelsen 1998, 223-4.
22 Nielsen 1907, 105.
23 Nielsen 1907, 100, 107.
24 The two terms, depending on the different periods and sources, were used to indicate the series and type of intervals that make up a musical scale, as well as the first note of this scale. See for example Monro 1894, 1-2.
25 Nielsen 1907, 100.

ample for a new contemporary music that was called to observe rules dictated by the characteristics of its essence. The ideals of vigour and energy from one side and of healthiness and harmony from the other are at the core of Nielsen's argument. This, as Grimley observes,[26] is also in line with the aesthetic beliefs of the Hellenics, who promoted a lifestyle based on simplicity, healthiness, exercise and outdoor activities that bring man closer to harmony with nature, and, overall, with the basic idea of Ancient Greek music, where the different scales were used for educational or even therapeutic purposes.

A peaceful strength: Nielsen's Fourth Symphony

It is important to note that the connection between the values expressed in Nielsen's music and the broader cultural environment that promoted the same set of values led to an association between Nielsen and the vitalistic movement in art and culture.[27] This point is also significant in Grimley's analysis of some of Nielsen's works, where he sees a continuity between the paradigm of Nielsen's Hellenic phase, i.e. *Helios Overture*, and one of the major works of the next decade, the Third Symphony *Espansiva*,[28] which is also seen as the climax of Nielsen's optimistic vitalism.[29] Both works are emblematic of the idea of strength and energy possessed by the melodic line. This quality underlies the validity of the equation force = simplicity, where by simplicity we do not mean lack of complexity, but recourse to the elementary level – in this case the constitutive elements of music, which for Nielsen are the intervals and the rhythm. This equation also makes it possible to reflect on another element that is always present in his music, next to the vitalism: the return to the origin, understood not as an invitation to archaism, but as a principle of purity.[30]

As Michelsen also observes, similar considerations are expressed in the essay 'Musical Problems', first published in 1922 and later included in *Living Music*, where the author stresses the importance of intervals as the constituent elements of music and strives for a return to the original, homophonic character of the melody, thus showing that the ideals of clarity and simplicity formulated in the context of a talk about Ancient Greek music are not limited to the first decade of the century, but crucial to Nielsen's aesthetical thought as a whole.

In 'Musical Problems', the alpha and omega of music – "pure, clear, firm, natural intervals and virile, robust, assured, organic rhythm" –[31] are discussed along with the natural characteristic of the melody that, as a necessity, also needs to rest or pause.[32] It is obvious that Nielsen here is speaking at a theoretical level, but the contrast between energetic movement and rest is nonetheless very evident in his music. Even in the works that are considered the *acme* of his vitalistic phase, energetic and assertive musical episodes are always followed (or preceded) by nocturne-like, contemplative moments, in which action gives way to reflection, often opening a window to a new musical landscape. This happens as early as *Helios*, and continues in some of his significant later works (the andante of the *Espansiva*, some parts of the Fourth Symphony and the *Proposta Seria* of the Sixth Symphony), where Nielsen offers us, as noted by Grimley, glimpses of naturalistic landscapes, in the form not of a description but of an imagination.[33] The idea of the body in activity offered in *Helios* and in *Espansiva*, especially in the symphony's finale, is therefore closely connected to the idea of cohesion between man and nature in a way that reminds us strongly of the cultural movement of Arcadia; just as the idea of health (the consequence of the correct activity of the body) is connected to the idea of equilibrium (understood both as a harmonious

---

26 Grimley is not the only one to note these values in Nielsen's music from the Third Symphony onwards, where he exhibits "a certain predilection for the early twentieth-century motives of naturism, athleticism and energy cult", Martinotti 2010, 216.

27 See for example Jensen 1994, 58-77; Fjeldsøe 2009, 26-42; Dam 2010; Fjeldsøe 2010, 33-55.

28 Grimley 2010, 96-131.

29 Fjeldsøe 2010, 39-43.

30 Neill 1965, 11-5.

31 Nielsen 1925, 53.

32 Nielsen 1925, 50-2.

33 The naturalistic side of Nielsen has been a popular subject among commentators. See for example Grimley 2010, 65-7; Neill 1968, 154-60; Martinotti 2010, 211-2; Muntoni 2012, 187-90.

relationship between body and spirit and as a harmonious relationship between microcosm and macrocosm, man and nature).

Traditionally in Nielsen criticism the Fourth Symphony has been associated with two main ideas: vitalism and conflict. According to many interpretations the vitalism of the Fourth begins to be different from that of previous works, as life, represented by the musical flow, seems to be endangered. Several commentators have nevertheless inscribed the Fourth Symphony in the orbit of Nielsen's Mediterraneanising vitalism, which has many points in common with the values perceived as Hellenic at the turn of the century, without forgetting the problems that will become acute in the Fifth, where the idea of conflict is radicalised and the vitalistic instance is reduced to vital impulse and struggle for survival.[34]

The very title of the symphony, 'The Inextinguishable', seems to presuppose a fundamental optimism, a feature that has often been considered as one of the most recognisable traits of Nielsen's personality. Today, thanks to an extensive knowledge of written sources, especially letters and essays, we know that this is a simplistic reduction. Nielsen has demonstrated in his work that there is never only one side, but everything is related, can be compared to or is in contrast with something else.

That Nielsen appreciated nuances, flexibility and the ability to express an unexpected feeling is evident from his opinions about Mozart, as expressed in his article 'Mozart and Our Time'. His admiration can also be explained in terms of personal affinity: he not only praises Mozart's lightness (even as a stylistic figure) but also the presence of contrasts in his music. In his best works

beauty leads to reflection, and the smiling and laughter cease. That marvellous magic beauty which pervades, for example, *Le nozze di Figaro*, is so entrancing because it brings tears to our eyes when we want to laugh, and makes us smile when the music is most moving.[35]

It is impossible not to see that this contrast is also one of the major characteristics of Nielsen's works.

The 'optimism' of the Fourth Symphony is not total and cannot be one-sided. The use of the timpani, in particular, has often been identified with a hostile, negative and obstructive element, opposed to the positive force expressed by the rest of the orchestra, which represents music and its vital flow. The thing that is inextinguishable, which is the best translation of the title of the Fourth ('The Inextinguishable' suggests that it is an 'inextinguishable symphony', while the Danish word is neutral, not 'den uudslukkelige [symfoni]', but 'det uudslukkelige', or 'what is inextinguishable'), refers to a double reference implied in the equation presented by the author as the motto of the work: "Music is life, like it inextinguishable".[36]

The idea of trust expressed in relation to life, and the idea of a flow destined never to cease even if hindered, is here celebrated musically to an extent never yet reached by the Danish composer up to this point. As is well known, this is the first time Nielsen uses an open form, in the sense that the individual movements of the usual symphonic form, here still clearly identifiable, are chained together in a single continuous, constant flow. The continuity is also granted by a cyclical formal pattern, according to which the second theme of the 'first movement' returns in the last thematic section of the work in a reminiscence of the cyclic structure in *Helios*, which shares with the symphony the idea of celebration of life as energy and movement.[37] But the linearity and the progressive character that were an essential part of *Helios*, next to the circularity of the form, are here questioned, and the musical and narrative discourse becomes more complex. It is precisely because of this complexity that we can still consider the symphony as a step inside that world defined by the Hellenics, in which the strength of the body in movement and the harmony between men and nature were the major goals, which in the symphony appear as two polarised elements: movement and energy on one hand, rest and contemplation on the other.

34 Fjeldsøe 2010, 43-7.
35 Nielsen 1925, 19.
36 From Nielsen's programme note for the premiere of the Fourth Symphony, Fellow (ed.) 1999, 194-95.
37 Progress is represented by the dynamic course of the piece, in which an initial simplicity progressively grows. The trajectory of the Sun from dawn to sunset is accompanied by the linear progression proper of the melodic element.

The contrast of these two forces is represented by the dialectic between the first and the second theme typical of the sonata form, still discernible in the first part of the symphony. A restless and unstable melodic idea, which cannot even be defined as a real theme, is based on rhythm and energy and represents movement;[38] a second, cantabile theme, is based on melody and reflection, representing rest. This later thematic opens up an imaginary landscape, not only in virtue of the melodic character, but also because of the symbolic association with wind instruments, which are well represented in this section.

The first real melodic idea of the work will eventually be the 'winner' of the fight. Here it is no longer a simple melody played by the humble wind instruments, but loaded with musical and narrative weight thanks to the contribution of the entire orchestra. The triumph represented here would therefore be that of music and life: the music that survives those who tried to obstruct it and make it simply noise (the timpani), the life that survives by celebrating itself just when it seemed most threatened.

We must therefore conclude that in the Fourth Symphony the apparently polarised forces and opposed values of movement and rest are united in the ideal of a communion between man and nature celebrated by the Hellenists. This is a visionary and revolutionary ideal, the ideal of a strength that is inner, harmonic and not destructive, but constructive. A strength that is the natural consequence of the communion between man and nature: a peaceful strength. From this point of view, the very Nielsenian *topos* of man living in communion with nature (evident in his other works, as well as in *My Childhood in Funen*)[39] becomes both an ideal way of living and a means of conquering peace.

This is why, after the Fourth and the Fifth Symphony, the conflict or contrast is never again associated with military images, but becomes a sort of ludic interplay between sonic elements. In almost all of Nielsen's mature works humouristic sketches are present together with more serious episodes, building up a series of contrasts in the musical narrative, and proposing once again the nuances and variety within a feeling that he so much admired in Mozart. At the same time, the game is reinforced by the frequent use of dialogic sections, in which a solo instrument converses, even quarrels, with one or more other instruments in the orchestra. In the next chapter I will therefore discuss how the conflict loses the characteristic of struggle for survival and becomes a musical game, and how this allows Nielsen to explore the sonic body in the voices of individual instruments. The interest in the body in movement that we see in other figurative arts is therefore translated into interest in sound as the 'body' of music, described in a rich range of moods and varieties.

Sonic embodiment: Nielsen's Flute Concerto

After the thoroughly dramatic Fifth Symphony, Nielsen became more and more concerned with the need to express his musical discourse with simplicity and essentiality, concepts that he also expresses in the essay 'Musical Problems', first published in 1922,[40] the year he composed the Wind Quintet. The struggle for survival gives way to a musical conversation between two or more players, while the orchestral weight is also diminished, assuming the dimensions of a chamber music ensemble, in works such as *Sinfonia Semplice* and the two concertos, one for flute and the other for clarinet. At the same time Nielsen became more absorbed with the study of sound, through the exploration of the ranges and timbres of individual instruments.

These two elements, the reduction of orchestral weight and the study of the sound object, are related to each other. By reducing the orchestra Nielsen can more easily concentrate on the solo instrument; at the same time, the latter's peculiarity is expressed not only through its musical range, but also through comparisons with other instruments, creating a humourous, sometimes ironic, even at times sarcastic interplay.

This new phase was inaugurated by the Wind Quintet, a work that was hailed by many as the starting point for a neoclassical period in Nielsen's music. What is certain is that the composer saw many possibilities both in the use

---

38 In stressing the importance of the rhythmic element in his essay 'Musical Problems', Nielsen uses adjectives that are typical of the first thematic group of the sonata form: "virile, robust, assured, organic rhythm", Nielsen 1925, 53.

39 Nielsen 1927.

40 Michelsen 1998, 225.

of wind instruments and in the players of Copenhagen's Wind Quintet, even thinking about writing five concertos, one for each of them. Eventually he only wrote two, but there is no doubt that they fully represent Nielsen's aspiration to convey a musical message with the maximum simplicity of means.

The interest in the sonic body of music is not limited to Nielsen's mature years, though it is here that it finds its most cogent expression. On the contrary, his childhood and adolescence in the countryside, together with an innate curiosity, made him very sensitive to sounds: "as a small child, Carl noted the sounds of insects, animals, humans and machines with keen interest", sounds that could be not only heard but also seen, as when Carl saw a piano for the first time:

This was something quite different. Here the notes lay in a long shining row before my eyes. Not only could I hear them; I could see them. And I made one great discovery after another. First of all that the deep notes went to the left and the high ones the other way.[41]

Before the Wind Quintet and the two wind concertos, this study of the sound is already present in some of his compositions. In *Helios*, as Grimley observes, there is "a description of the sound object, or *Klang*",[42] while several of the piano works are focused on the instrument's sonic possibilities as a percussive medium.[43] In his Ph.D. dissertation *Den fortrængte modernisme: den ny musik i dansk musikliv 1920-40*, Michael Fjeldsøe analysed this aspect with specific reference to Nielsen's use of percussion instruments, which are, beginning with the Fourth Symphony, fully dignified members of the composer's orchestra, even being given solo parts. Moreover, the use of these instruments on equal terms with the more canonical ones shows the composer's interest in their specific sonic quality, one that is very close to noise.[44] In this way the artist fully justifies his claim "Music is sound".[45]

All these elements are present in the Flute Concerto. The imaginary landscape, often defined as Arcadian[46] by stereotypical associations of the solo instrument with the pastoral mood and landscape, is not a union between man and nature that is endangered by extraneous forces, as we saw in the Fourth Symphony in particular, but rather a reminder of the modern coexistence of countryside and city life. The dreamy atmosphere present in some passages is never at ease

because the bucolic proposals of the flute are echoed in the trumpeting of the bass trombone and impatient rain of strokes of the timpani, so these interventions are seen as digressions in the difficult field of musical humour.[47]

The Arcadian state that had been gained through struggle in the Fourth Symphony is here once again presented but never endangered – if anything it is opposed by trivial routine, expressed especially by the glissando on the trombone. At the same time the interplay between the drums and the orchestra, which in the Fourth was presented as a matter of survival (and even more so in the Fifth), is here represented in a ludic and humoristic dimension, not a larger-than-life drama, but a more down-to-earth musical dialogue.

The two movements that make up the concerto are full of examples where this dialogue, as if between characters in a kind of musical drama, takes place. At the same time the sonic quality of the flute is represented in many possible varieties, in the parts in which the instrument has the leading role, accompanied by the orchestra, in its cadenzas, where Nielsen forces the flautist to exhibit an unlimited range of moods, and finally in the parts where the sound of the flute interacts with a co-protagonist (the bassoon and the trombone in the first movement, the trombone and the timpani in the second).

The discourse of the first movement does not lack profundity, especially in parts of the solo cadenza and

41 Lawson 1997, 19.

42 Grimley 2010, 61.

43 Neill 1968, 158.

44 Fjeldsøe 1999, 158-60.

45 Fjeldsøe 1999, 160; the statement is taken from an interview with Carl Nielsen by Andreas Vinding from the Danish newspaper *Politiken*, reproduced in Fellow (ed.) 1999, 378-9.

46 Neill 1970, 8.

47 Neill 1970, 10.

the lyrical theme at the heart of the piece. The singing of the flute, at times lyrical and at times whimsical, moves through unpredictable changes of mood: sometimes opening up to imaginary landscapes, other times, especially in its dialogue with the orchestra, the bassoon and the trombone, shedding its traditional Arcadian character, instead screaming out to reclaim its role as the concerto's *primadonna*. The atmosphere of indefiniteness, even of mystery, present in the cadenza and in the final passage of the movement confirms once again the elusiveness of this piece, in which we find ourselves at turns charmed and puzzled by the flute's voice.

The much shorter second movement starts in a more pastoral mood, as the solo instrument's melody seems innocent and unproblematic. Even the second theme, of a more mysterious character, suggests the illusion of a distant landscape. After a central part in which various musical motives and moods are displayed, the final episode is built on a simple march, a modification of the flute's first theme, which the orchestra tries to make its own. What strikes us most at this point is the yawning of the trombone, that with its glissando implies not only that the flute's singing bores him/her but also that this is after all a trivial matter. Perhaps Nielsen simply wants to remind us that we should not take things too seriously, and what remains is the music, this kaleidoscope of sounds that he has just finished portraying.

Klavermusik for smaa og store: Nielsen's approach to essentiality

It is an old experience that when an everyday object gradually loses its form owing to over-embellishment, there is often a sudden return to the original, to the plain and simple, the purpose of which is abundantly clear.[48]

This is how Nielsen articulates the essential and elementary values of music, intervals and rhythm, in his 1922

essay 'Musical Problems', at the beginning of his mature years. But it is not only in his writings that we find these ideas: one of Nielsen's latest works is a perfect practical demonstration of this interest.

The miniatures in *Klavermusik for smaa og store*, written in 1930, are the clearest example of Nielsen musically dealing with the values that he had first defined in the talk about Greek music and the contemporary essays 'Mozart and Our Time' and 'Words, Music and Programme Music', and later demonstrated to some extents in his musical works. The fact that these piano pieces were composed in 1930 shows the enduring importance of these principles in his life.

In this work, thanks to the dimensions of the pieces and the use of a single instrument instead of an orchestra, Nielsen's poetic intentions are expressed in their purest form. The idea that the piano is a suitable medium for conveying the composer's musical message is expressed by several commentators. David Fanning, in the preface to the volume of the Carl Nielsen Edition dedicated to the piano and organ works, writes:

the piano works are more revealing than any other genre of the essential Nielsen, thanks partly to the colouristic limitations of the medium, which throw greater musical weight onto the notes themselves, and partly to the fact that he did not approach the instrument with the preformed instincts of a professionally adept exponent.[49]

A similar point is expressed by Edward Neill, who was particularly fond of Nielsen's piano music,[50] which he saw as a clear example of his artistic patterns from 1890, the date of his first piano composition, to 1930, the year in which *Piano Music for Young and Old* was published.[51]

His final contribution to this literature is particularly significant in its emphasis on "the primary sources of the music itself: diatonicism and modal pentatonicism".[52] When asking himself what the essence of Nielsen's music is, Neill mentions Nielsen's comment about intervals[53]

---

48   Nielsen 1925, 41.

49   Fanning 2006, xi. Fanning mentions this point of view, referring to the pianist's Arne Skjold Rasmussen's introduction to his *Carl Nielsens samlede klaverværker*, Copenhagen, 1987.

50   See for example Neill 1965, 15 and Neill 1968, 157-8.

51   Neill does not mention Nielsen's piano piece in C from 1931. It may be that he did not know it.

52   Neill 1970, 7.

53   "The glutted must be taught to regard a melodic third as a gift of God, a fourth as an experience, and a fifth as the supreme bliss ... We thus see how necessary it is to preserve contact with the simple original.", Nielsen 1925, 45.

and then answers with another question: "A return back to the origins? An invitation to archaism? Or both?".[54]

Ultimately, "even if chromaticism often peeks out in Nielsen's compositions to underline certain musical situations, it is the same diatonic writing that reveals the simplicity of Nielsen's discourse and its primitive clarity".[55] And if Neill, describing Nielsen's musical discourse, also states that his musical discourse rarely exceeds the range of a melodic fifth, this becomes the rule for his new piano compositions. The composer himself writes:

I've been composing each day a little piano piece in a new tonality, because I want to get up to 24 (up to B major/G sharp minor and G flat major/E flat minor), and it interests me like nothing before, because the task is so circumscribed that it's very difficult. These are five-note pieces; and naturally that means that for example in C major I use within the range C–G both D flat and C sharp, E flat and D sharp, F sharp and G flat. But look: you can move your hand or hands in many ways within the tonality, e.g. in the right hand (e.g. in B minor) G–D and the left B–F sharp or (right) E–B (left) F sharp–C sharp etc. in many ways without thumb-crossing and still get variety. The old piano methods (so far as I know) only have the basic range in both hands; so for G major: G–D, G–D. So I regard it as something new to work in this way, and as I've said, it has my greatest devotion in this little form.[56]

These pieces were conceived with a pedagogic intent, but it would be wrong to consider them merely as didactic material. The most important feature of the series is the range of a fifth that both hands observe. But, as Nielsen himself notes, this range was the same in all the similar studies that were composed until that time, while in his pieces "variety" was granted by the presence of two different ranges, one for the left and one for the right hand.

Each of the pieces is set in a tonal range, following the circle of the fifths, but the tonality of G major is represented twice, so the total count is 25, instead of 24. The first book contains the tonalities on the sharp side for a total of 13 pieces (nr. III, in G major, is divided into IIIa and IIIb), while the second book explores the flat regions. The pieces are not thematically connected; on the contrary,

each can be played as an independent musical work, but some similarities and patterns can be observed. In this way, while the first ones illustrate in an exemplary way Nielsen's emphasis on intervals and notes, the compositions become successively more and more complex once we reach the second series.

The short pieces are presented in pairs, the first element in a major key, and the second in the minor relative. A short analysis of some of them will allow us to reveal the elements that characterise the work as a whole. In this respect I believe that the first pieces are the most representative. An analysis of the first pair will therefore be sufficient as an introduction to the poetical world the composer creates with these musical miniatures.

Nielsen mentions in his description the possible presence of flat and sharp notes even within the range of the C major tonality. In the first piece the melodic alternation between major and minor third is already evident, an element that is also typical of works built on a larger scale.

The extremely simple melody in the left hand proposes all the notes of the pentatonic scale, which are successively developed by the right hand. The melodic figure of the first two bars is then repeated in bars 3 and 4, in which the melody is inverted and dilated. In the subsequent measures the pattern of the first 4 is repeated with a single but significant element of novelty: the flattened E that leads to C minor.

Bars 13–16 repeat bars 5–8, again with the third degree of the scale on the flat side, and propose a chromatic play in which the descending segment is replaced by a rhythmically and chromatically intensified group, F – E – E flat – C, in which emphasis is placed on the chromatic element (apparently as opposed to the diatonic) in the first three notes, and on the minor third that separates the last two elements of the scale, characteristic of the second part of the piece.

In bar 14 we encounter a new alteration, this time present at the second degree of the scale, where the D flat is in chromatic tension with the first, while bar 16 also insists on this new element, *tenuto* and *ritardando*. The last bars of the piece bring us back to C major, but by now the mixture has taken place, and the two scales coexist in

54 Neill 1970, 7.
55 Neill 1970, 7.
56 Fanning 2006, xxxix, quoted from Anon. 1932, 'Af to Carl Nielsen-breve', *Dansk Musiktidsskrift* 7, 2-3.

Fig. 1 *Allegretto, 149.*

Fig. 2 *Allegretto, 150.*

the same melodic pattern. Thus, while the left hand plays a natural third, the right touches the flattened degree of the scale. These are the first signs of Nielsen's free or expanded diatonicism, which he advances throughout the entire work. In the final bars, the right hand also returns to the major mode, so that the E flat of the penultimate bar (n. 20) is sharpened before the final C major chord.

In the second piece, which shares with the first the tempo indication Allegretto, the melody is presented first in A minor and then in its major relative. In addition, while in the first piece we encountered an alteration of the second degree, which was flattened to generate chromatic tension with the tonic, here the altered element is the fourth degree of the scale. In this way, the dominant grade is also stressed in the scale.

From these first two pieces, Nielsen constructs a dialectical discourse in which identity and contrast coexist on various levels. Both compositions alternate between major and minor tonalities, and they do so in a specular manner (C major–C minor in the first, A minor–A major in the second); both present a chromatic alteration aimed at highlighting a key element of the melody (even here, specularly, the first and the fifth degree are charged with tension by the alteration of the second and fourth degree respectively); finally, both pieces present the typical flex-

ion of many works by Nielsen between the major third and the minor, which often coexist in the same melodic segment. All these dialectic elements are added to the macrostructural dualism that is in place not only in the first, but in each set of two pieces, according to which a major tonality is followed by its minor relative.

In the following pieces Nielsen gradually introduces us to the basic idea of this collection, i.e. that we should refrain from regarding tonality as a fixed element, stressing the various possibilities that it offers. This is the meaning of his initial statement "for example in C major I use within the range C–G both D flat and C sharp, E flat and D sharp, F sharp and G flat". We have seen how Nielsen did this in the first two pieces, where he altered all the possible degrees of the scale, behaviour that is also expressed by the next couple of pieces, III and IV, in which Nielsen fights to make us conceive of the flattened and sharp notes as a part of the natural environment of the scale, and not as alterations.

The first four pieces are the only ones in which the range of the fifth is located in the same values for both the left and right hand. Starting with piece V, the ranges of the two hands begin to vary, so that a greater variety can be encompassed in the melodic discourse, which in fact becomes more complex as we progress towards the sharp-

65

Fig. 3 *XIV, Molto Adagio, 174.*

Fig. 4 *XIV, Allegretto commodo, 175.*

er regions during the first book. By the time we reach the second book, the pieces fully reveal that a limited melodic range does not necessarily equate with limited expressiveness and pregnancy. Chromaticism becomes fully integrated in the melodic discourse, not as an element that has harmonic significance, though at times it is still the most obvious means to reach enharmonic tonalities. Such is the extent of the chromatic element that even the term in itself loses its original meaning (as something that is extraneous to diatonicism); Nielsen wants us to consider it a part of his expanded diatonic environment, as happens in a very convincing manner in piece XVIII, Prelude in C minor, the composer's favourite.[57]

In the final piece the movement by half tones is evident from the start, when the left hand's bordone in the first bar is imitated by the right hand in the successive measure, with the first two notes being identical in the two figures (see example). By the third bar, we are so far from the initial tonality of E flat minor that it seems the melody is written on an enharmonically disguised E major, while the left hand continues moving by half

tones. In the next bar we are already back in the initial tonic environment thanks to the cadenza on the dominant chord.

The melody is then presented in the major relative C flat, before leading to an episode in which the tension is enhanced by elements that even in this expanded diatonicism we perceive as chromatic, until we return to the dominant chord as in bar 4, taking us back to the repetition of the first measure. A rhapsodic phrase, as if in a solo cadenza, introduces us to a chromatic environment that is ultimately made tonally familiar when the complexity that had characterised the piece up to this point unexpectedly evanesces, replaced by one of the "clear and firm melodies" that Nielsen cherished. He chooses, having reached the maximum degree of complexity, to end this work with an E flat motive that is as diatonic as possible, until an F sharp in bar 25 creates a dissonance that for some reason is less puzzling for the listener than an F natural, just to remind us that he has not changed his mind: he still believes in expanded diatonicism and in complexity within simplicity.

57   Fanning 2006, xxxix, Letter from Carl Nielsen to Anne-Marie, dated 15 January 1930.

The way Nielsen ends this collection of miniatures is consequent of the aesthetic principles he maintained throughout his career. By using the miniature and reducing the range, he was able to follow the aesthetic principles he had exposed in his writings and write music that was based on its basic elements, intervals. Simplicity cannot exist, however, without complexity and variety, so that even the concept of diatonicism can be reinterpreted. This is the final lesson of Nielsen: freedom exists even when rules are established, and a musical discourse based on essentiality does not necessarily lack variety or complexity.

Paolo Muntoni
muntonip@gmail.com

Bibliography

Busoni, F. 1922 (transl. R. Ley 1957)
The essence of music and other papers,
New York.

Dam, A.E. 2010
Den vitalistiske strømning: i dansk litteratur omkring år 1900, Århus.

Fanning, D. 2006
'Preface' to 'Piano Works', *Carl Nielsen Works Edition II* (vol. 12), D. Fanning & N. Foltmann (eds), Copenhagen, ix-xli.

Fanning, D. & N.B. Foltmann (eds) 2006
Carl Nielsen Works Edition II (vol. 12), *Piano and Organ Works*, Copenhagen

Fellow, J. (ed.) 200513
Carl Nielsens Brevudgaven, Copenhagen.

Fjeldsøe, M. 1999
Den fortrængte modernisme: den ny musik i dansk musikliv 1920-1940, Copenhagen.

Fjeldsøe, M. 2009
'Carl Nielsen and the Current of Vitalism in Art', *Carl Nielsen Studies* 4, 26-42.

Fjeldsøe, M. 2010
'Vitalisme i Carl Nielsens Musik', *Dansk Musikforskning Online* 1, 33-55.

Flensborg Petersen, K. (eds) 2005
'Preface' to 'Concerto for Flute and Orchestra', in, *Carl Nielsen Works Edition II* (vol. 9), Copenhagen, vii-xix.

Grimley, D. 2010
Carl Nielsen and the idea of modernism, Oxford.

Jensen, J.I. 1994
'Carl Nielsen: Artistic Milieu and Tradition: Cultural–Historical Perspectives', *The Nielsen Companion*, M. Miller (ed.), London, 58-77.

Lawson, J. 1997
Carl Nielsen, London.

Martinotti, S. 2010
'Carl Nielsen. I quattro temperamenti in Danimarca', *Dietro l'angolo. Saggi musicali*, Bologna, 206-19.

Michelsen, T. 1998
'Carl Nielsen og den Græske Musik – nogle Kilder til Belysning af den musikæstetiske Konflikt mellem Komponisten og hans Samtid i Begyndelsen af Århundredet', *Fund og Forskning* 37, Copenhagen, page nos.

Monro, D.B. 1894
The modes of ancient Greek Music, London.

Müller, J.P. 1904
Mit system – 15 minutters daglit arbejde for sundhedens skyld, Copenhagen.

Muntoni, P. 2012
'Nielsen in the United Kingdom', *Carl Nielsen Studies* (vol. 5), 165-95.

Neill, E. 1965
'Carl Nielsen nel centenario della nascita (1865-1965) – Introduzione ad un sinfonista originale', *Disclub – rivista bimestrale di critica musicale e informazione discografica* 15, 11-5.

Neill, E. 1968
'Moti e atteggiamenti umani nella musica di Carl Nielsen', *Rassegna Musicale Curci* 21, 154-60.

Neill, E. 1970
'Carl Nielsen', *Musicalia* 1, 4-13.

Nielsen, C. 1907
'Græsk Musik', in *Carl Nielsen til sin samtid – Artikler, foredrag, interview, presseindlæg, værknoter og manuskripter*, J. Fellow (ed.), Copenhagen, 99-110.

Nielsen, C., 1925
'Carl Nielsen og instrumenternes sjæl', in *Politiken*, J. Fellow (ed.), 378-9.

Nielsen, C. 1927
Min fynske barndom, Copenhagen.

Nielsen, C. 1925 (transl. R. Spink 1953)
'Mozart and Our Time', *Living Music*, London, 13-24.

Nielsen, C. 1925 (transl. R. Spink 1953)
'Words, Music and Program Music', *Living Music*, London, 25-40.

Nielsen, C. 1925 (transl. R. Spink 1953)
'Musical Problems', *Living Music*, London, 41-53.

Oelsner, G. 2008
'Den sunde natur', *Livslyst. Sundhed, skønhed, styrke i dansk kunst 18901940*, G. Hvidberg-Hansen & G. Oelsner (eds), Odense, 159-97.

Røllum-Larsen, C. 2000
'Symphony no. 4 op. 29 – The Inextinguishable', *Carl Nielsen Works Edition II*, Copenhagen, 4.

Schousboe, T. (ed.) 1983
Carl Nielsen – Dagbøger og brevveksling med Anne Marie Carl-Nielsen, Copenhagen.

Modernity and Legacies:
Representations of Greco-Roman Antiquity in Star Trek, 1966-9*

EVANTHIS HATZIVASSILIOU

Abstract

The article discusses receptions of Classical antiquity in Star Trek: The Original Series *(TOS), from 1966-9, based on analysis of the episodes and the archive of the creator, Gene Roddenberry, as well as the archive of scriptwriter Paul Schneider. TOS allows scholars to trace aspects of the perceptions of Classical antiquity during a time when American society was undergoing important transformations; as it slowly entered the post-industrial era, it naturally rethought its legacies. Although respect for Classical antiquity was clear, TOS appeared ambivalent towards its legacies, which it connected with isolationism or conservatism. This is a characteristic of the discourse of novel worldviews during the time of their growth, when they have to establish their distinction from older concepts. In contrast, TOS's sequel from the 1980s,* The Next Generation, *was created at a time when the move to the post-industrial era had been completed, and it tended to insist on the value of intellectual legacies as a necessary ingredient of a conscious modernity.*

Introduction

A major American cultural phenomenon, *Star Trek: The Original Series* (TOS) addressed a number of crucial problems of contemporary societies, including foreign policy and the use of force, relations with the Other (either within societies or in international affairs), race, gender, religion, psychology and legacies. This article examines TOS's perceptions of Greek and Roman antiquity as a political and intellectual point of reference of contemporary Western societies. TOS had a special relationship with Classical antiquity, regularly addressing its themes in episodes. Still, TOS appeared ambivalent towards Classical tradition. Although respect for its legacies was clear, it was usually connected with isolationism or conservatism, which *Star Trek* strongly rejected. TOS is an interesting case study, since it was made at a time when American society was undergoing important transformations, and thus rethinking its legacies.

The relationship between Classical tradition, popular culture and science fiction has been extensively discussed, mostly by Classicists. These scholars focus almost exclu-

---

* The author wishes to thank Dr. *Thomas M. Brogan*, the Director of the Institute for Aegean Prehistory, Study Center for East Crete, Dr Natalia Vogeikoff-Brogan, Doreen Canaday Spitzer Archivist of the American School of Classical Studies at Athens, and Professor Jack L. Davis of the University of Cincinnati, as well as the Director of the Danish Institute at Athens, Dr Kristina Winther-Jacobsen for organising a lecture on this topic on 14 February 2017. This article is dedicated to the memory of Nikos Birgalias, Professor of Ancient Greek history at the University of Athens, whose youthful spirit could go where no one had gone before.

sively on receptions of ancient myth. They generously note that ancient myth is "deployed superficially", but it is precisely this looseness that allows creators to approach wider audiences, establish continuity between the past and the future and function didactically.[1] Myth is an important element in the Western tradition, and the technologically advanced societies that created modern science fiction carried it in their intellectual baggage. Analyses of the reception of Classical antiquity in *Star Trek* mostly address myth, the notion of immortality and the image of gods,[2] refraining from drawing conclusions about the wider political and social connotations of TOS' negotiation of Classical legacies. Moreover, these analyses are not based on archival evidence. They examine *Star Trek* episodes, in the excellent phrase of Martin Winkler, as "visual texts",[3] but do not apply the archive-oriented methodology of historians.

The present article discusses TOS from the point of view of contemporary history, and attempts to trace perceptions of Greco-Roman antiquity during the late 1960s, an era characterised by a tense and dense evolution of political and social value systems. The end product – the episodes themselves – are examined both as "visual texts" and as a "revealing popular culture document of American social and political actions and attitudes of the 1960s",[4] namely, as primary sources. In addition, extensive use is made of archival sources, in particular the collections of Gene Roddenberry, the creator of *Star Trek*, and of scriptwriter Paul Schneider.

As is the case in any study of contemporary history, archival research presents significant opportunities: it offers a clear, almost definite, picture of what the creators intended to say, and of their understanding about the possible reception of these messages by the public.[5] Moreover, although Roddenberry undoubtedly had a pivotal role, the archival material shows that the production of TOS episodes was a collective effort of scriptwriters, producers, De Forest Research (TOS' scientific advisors) and the National Broadcasting Company (NBC); thus,

the process involved interactions of their knowledge and worldviews. The discussions among the creative team shed new light on the dilemmas that the receptions of Antiquity raised for contemporary societies. In short, this material is crucial in allowing scholars to place TOS' negotiation of Classical antiquity in its historical context.

On the other hand, it is equally important to have in mind the limits of the archive, especially in a study of popular culture. First, perceptions evolve rapidly (especially in the contemporary era) and thus form a moving target, while notions of Classical legacies involve fundamental (and often unspoken) assumptions. These call for great care on the part of the historian, who needs to avoid the traps of hindsight or cultural arrogance towards an older generation. Second, it is important to remember that the archival material refers to the intentions of the members of *the creative team*; it does not – or does not necessarily – reveal the episodes' full impact on popular opinion. As happens with all cultural products, once the TOS episodes were broadcast, they tended to acquire a dynamic of their own, and this could be different from the one the creators had originally intended. This is a constant challenge when studying popular culture.

The Moment of Relevance: The American 1960s, the Starship *Enterprise* and the Reception of the Past

In a discussion of the negotiation of Antiquity in science fiction, three dates are important: Antiquity itself, the time of production and the imaginary future. It may not be surprising that a student of contemporary history would point to the importance of the era (and the society) that created the particular work. This is a well-established conclusion of recent scholarship: "In the popular media of today, both the recreations of the past and the imaginative creations of the future necessarily reveal the moment of their making";[6] by placing its "story" in a distant future, science fiction "provides a space and a language for con-

---

1   See, among others, Fredericks 1980; Winkler 2007; Winkler 2009; Rogers & Stevens 2015.
2   Pearson 1999; Asa 1999; Baker 2010; Tomasso 2015; Kovacs 2015; Gordon 2016.
3   Winkler 2009, 20-50.
4   Worland 1988, 116-7.
5   On the importance of the use of archival sources in the study of *Star Trek*, see the groundbreaking work of Sarantakes (2005).
6   Winkler 2001, 289.

temporary issues to be addressed".[7] And if these are scholarly representations of the intellectual dilemma, it is worth noting how a prominent practitioner, Gene Roddenberry himself, presented his perspective in one of his early guidance documents for the scriptwriters, which later grew to become the celebrated *Star Trek* writers' guides:

Remember, the only Westerns which failed miserably were those which *authentically* portrayed the men, values, and morals of 1870. The audience applauds John Wayne playing what is essentially a 1966 man.[8]

Starting, then, from the working hypothesis that the moment of relevance is the second half of the 1960s, it is important to place *Star Trek* in its historical perspective. In contemporary discussions of the 1960s, the focus is usually on the notion of 'revolt', Vietnam and the civil rights movement, which sparked national soul-searching that gave rise to serious tensions.[9] However, recent scholarship has pointed to additional currents that were running beneath the surface. The US, the most advanced country in the world, was beginning to enter the post-industrial era, in which perspectives began to change, sometimes significantly. To give a few telling examples, in this new era the expansion of human rights, equal opportunities, the rights of smaller groups, the integration of science into the decision-making process and the protection of the environment would all play a crucial role in determining the quality of a Western democracy. Access to technology and popular participation would be enhanced. Social legitimisation presupposed this elevated participation, especially during the Cold War, which defined the antagonism between radically different proposals about the organisation of human societies.[10] Of course, this move into the post-industrial era is a process that we now recognise with the benefit of hindsight; the people of the late 1960s would not have described themselves as entering a 'post-industrial' phase. This particular term

was not used before the second half of the 1970s, when it was introduced by the Jimmy Carter administration in the US. However, the beginning of the new era can be identified in the late 1960s.[11]

There were additional points of reference for the creators of TOS. Despite Roddenberry's early guidance to scriptwriters to avoid scenarios based solely on "intellectual conflict" ("It's hard to get a good story out of philosophical conflicts"),[12] TOS episodes usually centered on a moral/political dilemma, alongside the action. Roddenberry and his team (mostly people like Gene L. Coon, Robert Justman, John Meredyth Lucas and Dorothy C. Fontana) intended to 'educate' the public, and to project a liberal understanding of the world. In this juncture, the term 'liberal' denotes a tradition of American political culture with origins in Franklin D. Roosevelt's New Deal, which evolved to become the political agenda of the Democrat presidents of the 1960s. The notion of the 'final frontier', so prominent in the narrative of *Star Trek*'s title sequence, drew on John F. Kennedy's New Frontier. Lyndon B. Johnson's notion of the Great Society – the vision of a new social inclusiveness – also heavily influenced the creators.[13]

The liberalism of the creative team appeared on the bridge of the *Enterprise* as a version of the future. The vessel belongs to a state initially called United Earth and then United Federation of Planets (UFP), in which no segregation exists on the basis of race, gender or religion – a major issue in US society in the 1960s. As a federation (not an 'empire'), the UFP is able to respect the identities of both its member-states and its citizens (thus, both collective identities and human rights).[14] The *Enterprise* officers include the Captain, James T. Kirk (William Shatner) and the Chief Medical Officer, Dr Leonard 'Bones' McCoy (DeForest Kelley), but also Sulu, of Asian descent (George Takei), the Russian Pavel Chekov (Walter Koenig) – pointing to the overcoming of Cold War enmities – the Scotsman Montgomery Scott

7   Chapman & Cull 2013, 220.
8   UCLA/Schneider Collection, Box 10, 'Star Trek: Writer-Director Information', 15 March 1966. Emphasis in the original.
9   See, among others, Suri 2003; Fink, Gassert & Junker 1998.
10 See, among others, Ferguson 2010.
11 See, for example, Leggewie 1998.
12 UCLA/Schneider Collection, Box 10, 'Supplementary Pages: Writer-Director Information', n.d. [1966].
13 See, among others, Worland 1994; Sarantakes 2005; O'Connor 2012.
14 Neumann 2001.

('Scotty' – James Doohan) and even an extraterrestrial, or at least a half-Vulcan, Mr Spock (Leonard Nimoy), a member of a people who have suppressed emotion and follow pure logic. Prominent among the *Enterprise* bridge officers is an African woman, Lt Uhura (no first name is mentioned; she is played by Nichelle Nichols). It was a priority of Roddenberry to radiate this message of inclusiveness.[15] Thus, the *Enterprise* is a vanguard in many respects. The starship is the ultimate explorer, operating at the 'final frontier' of space. At the same time, it mirrors a society going through important social transformations, thus getting into uncharted waters of a different kind. *Star Trek* "encourages humanity's need to grow and explore".[16]

This forward-looking notion had to renegotiate fundamental concepts and attitudes. In his early guidance to scriptwriters, Roddenberry expressly noted that the human past would be a theme of the series: "our format envisions a great number of 'parallel worlds'. We will find planets similar to many parts of our own – and with societies duplicating or intermixing almost any era in man's development".[17] This raised an additional set of intellectual dilemmas. The liberal West that the *Enterprise* and the UFP incarnate saw its roots as going back to Greco-Roman antiquity, the rediscovery of which during the Renaissance formed the basis for the gradual emergence of the notion of the West.[18] The US itself was a product of the Enlightenment. The US Constitution found a political and intellectual reference in the institutions of Republican Rome, with its admirable austere attitudes, stern patriotism and reliance on the rule of the law; official Washington was built on the model of a Greco-Roman city.[19] Few would doubt that Classical antiquity formed one of the intellectual bases of modern American and Western societies.

In this context, it was natural that references to Classical antiquity, sometimes oblique and sometimes direct,

would appear in TOS. Thus, in his early analysis of *Star Trek* characters, Roddenberry noted that the background of Spock's culture is "stoic, possibly akin to the direction which was being taken at one time by our own Greek civilization", although the Vulcans developed some elements further, mostly the suppression of emotion.[20] It is a matter of debate whether, by using the word "stoic", Roddenberry meant exactly what an expert of the Classics would have meant, but the reference to "our own Greek civilization" is telling, pointing to the relevance of the Classical tradition for modern American society.

On the other hand, social developments during the 1960s also raised important questions about attitudes towards the past. American society always prided itself, not without reason, on its ability to free itself from the oppressive bonds of history (or nationalism) in the search for novel solutions to problems. In the second half of the 1960s, it was becoming clear that a new version of modernity was appearing, which *Star Trek* was eager to represent. These two contexts created a dilemma in the creative team's attitudes towards legacies. What needed to be underlined, continuity or break?

"We've outgrown you": Representations of Greek Antiquity

The first episode that dealt with a subject from Antiquity was aired on 22 September 1967, and depicts the *Enterprise* crew meeting the Ancient Greek god Apollo in a distant part of the Galaxy.[21] The initial title was 'Olympus Revisited'. The eventual one, 'Who Mourns for Adonais', was a reference to the poem by Percy Bysshe Shelley, written in 1821 on the death of Keats.[22] The *Enterprise* is captured by the god Apollo. An away team consisting of Kirk, McCoy, Chekov, Scotty and Lt Carolyn Palamas, the *Enterprise* expert on archaeology, anthropology and ancient civili-

---

15 Hark 2008, 15-7.

16 Kovacs 2015, 209.

17 UCLA/Schneider Collection, Box 10, 'Star Trek: Writer-Director Information', 15 March 1966. This guideline was repeated in the more definite version of the Star Trek guide: '*Star Trek* Writers/Directors Guide', third revision, 17 April 1967, at https://www.bu.edu/clarion/guides/Star_Trek_Writers_Guide.pdf, accessed 20 August 2016.

18 See McNeill 1963.

19 See for more, Richard 1994.

20 UCLA/Schneider Collection, Box 10, Roddenberry to writers/directors, 'Character Analysis: Mister Spock'.

21 'Who Mourns for Adonais?' *Star Trek: TOS* (1966).

22 Kovacs 2015, 204; Cushman 2014b, 95-6, 105, 112.

sations, transfer to the surface; although it is not readily apparent what an expert of 'archaeology, *anthropology* and ancient civilizations' is doing on a spaceship operating in deep space. Apparently, it is important to legitimise Lt Palamas' presence on board the *Enterprise*, but her official duties remain less than convincing. Apollo prohibits Spock, "the one with the pointed ears", from coming to the planet, because he reminds him of the god Pan. This is an interesting discrimination against Spock that will be explained below. It is soon shown that the Ancient Greek 'gods' were in fact super-beings travelling in space, whom the simplistic Ancient Greek shepherds mistook for gods. The incredulity of the protagonists' advanced technological culture towards deities is prominent, and when Apollo dramatically reveals himself ("I am Apollo"), the young and inexperienced Chekov brushes aside the claim with little regard for diplomatic (or 'first contact') niceties: "And I am the Czar of all the Russias". Apollo tells them that he intends to keep the *Enterprise* crew on the planet to worship him, since a god cannot survive without worship; indeed, the other 'gods' have been reduced to a non-corporeal existence without it. In exchange for their devotion, he offers them life in the planet's "paradise". He also falls in love with Lt Palamas and offers to deify her. Thus, temptation is introduced into the plot: will the young officer, who is also clearly attracted to the vibrant Apollo, accept the offer? But bigger dilemmas also appear. Apollo projects a distinctly conservative, if not reactionary, worldview:

Man thinks he's progressed. They're wrong. He's merely forgotten those things which gave life meaning. You'll all be provided for, cared for, happy. There's an order of things in this universe. Your species has denied it.

This is a violent intrusion into the lives of the crew, based on the denial of the pivotal notion of progress. A tense argument soon develops between the 'god' and Kirk. In a famous exchange, the captain rejects Apollo's demand to collect laurel leaves:

Apollo: I can give life or death. What else does mankind demand of its gods?
Kirk: Mankind has no need for gods. We find the One quite adequate.

We will revisit the blurred notion of the One, but at this stage it is important to note that Apollo is clearly pointing *backwards*. As Kirk says to his officers, it is unthinkable to end up "spending an eternity bending knee and tending sheep". Kirk asks Lt Palamas to discard Apollo, thus weakening him. After some soul-searching, she agrees, and rejects the 'god', putting forward the ultimate argument of modernity – "I am a scientist" – meaning she cannot accept the arguments of a pre-modern god, although this point is not made in the episode in so many words. Stricken, Apollo loses control, allowing the *Enterprise* to fire her phasers and destroy his temple, which is also his power source. The 'god' has now been defeated, and Kirk explains to him: "We've outgrown you. You have asked for something we could no longer give". The 'god' then vanishes: "The time has passed. There is no room for gods". Following their victory, the members of the crew have second thoughts. Dr McCoy says that "I wish we hadn't had to do this", receiving a melancholic reply from Kirk:

So do I. They gave us so much. Greek civilization, so much of our culture and philosophy came from a worship of those beings. In a way they began the Golden Age. Would it have hurt us, I wonder, to have gathered a few laurel leaves?

This episode has attracted much scholarly attention. Ancient Greek gods were certainly presented as profoundly egotistical,[23] although the Apollo character's behaviour is also characterised as "totalitarian", since he recognises no private sphere or rights for his "subjects".[24] Moreover, it has been said that the story presents Apollo as recognising in the *Enterprise* crew the descendants of Agamemnon, Hector and Odysseus, and thus "retells its mythic subject matter to both renounce the past and yet embody its heroic nature".[25] Last but not least, it has been argued that the episode reflected Roddenberry's distrust of organised

23   Kovacs 2015, 208-10.
24   Winkler 2009, 86-90.
25   Baker 2010, 82.

religion, and the secularism prevalent in Western culture in the 1960s.[26]

The study of the archival material shows that the concerns of the productive team and the main message that they wanted to radiate were slightly different. The problem was 'believability', a major consideration in science fiction, and one to which the attention of the writers was drawn in the *Star Trek* guide.[27] In this case, however, the problem manifested itself with greater intensity, because of the challenge of combining myth with the future. In fact, myth was seen as a potentially embarrassing element. As Stanley Robertson of the NBC indicated to Roddenberry, the Greek gods were "pure mythology", and *Star Trek* intended to depict the *realities* of the future in 200 years' time; it should not become "fantasy".[28] Roddenberry solved the problem by furthering the idea that the Ancient Greek gods were super-beings mistaken by an ancient people for deities. Moreover, realising that not all members of the audience were familiar with archaeology, Roddenberry decided against his first idea for the character's name, 'Apollo Belvedere' (pointing to the famous statue discovered in Italy), and a reference in the early scripts to Delphi was finally omitted.[29] The need for believability also led the creative team to decide to leave Spock on the *Enterprise* (in early scripts he was a member of the away team), as it would have been difficult to assimilate a character who followed pure logic into a story from mythology[30] – another indication of the tense relation between myth and science fiction. In the early scripts, the name of the female crew member who would be romantically involved with Apollo was Carolyn Basset, but producer Robert Justman suggested giving her "a different first name in order to help the situation between her and Apollo. Perhaps a name which is in some way related to the Ancient Greeks, such as Helen or Diana".[31] 'Helen' was to be used in other episodes, and 'Diana' is, of course, Latin, so eventually it was the surname of the

character that was changed to make the link. It was not possible to trace in the archival sources the reason for the selection of 'Palamas'. Costis Palamas was a towering figure among Greek poets in the twentieth century, but no evidence points to an association between him and the choice of the surname.

The archival evidence regarding Kirk's famous statement that humanity has "no need for gods" and that it finds the "One" adequate is even more interesting. The treatment of religion in a popular television series was a delicate matter: in his initial approval of the story outline, Jean Messerschmidt of the NBC asked Roddenberry that "the religious aspects be treated with dignity and good taste".[32] However, this was a rather vague guideline, and during the development of the script new dilemmas appeared. In earlier versions of the script there was a clearer reference to Christianity that provoked some reactions among the productive team. Justman noted to Coon that the episode should not indicate that "our future civilization is to have a Christianity-dominated type of culture", thus offending other religions or agnostics.[33] Thus, the reference to the 'One', with its constructive ambiguity, is deliberately inclusive: an early example of the move to the multicultural society.

More importantly, however, the creators intended to give a clear central message. Apollo's offer to the *Enterprise* crew would entail the abandonment of their exploration and their quest for progress, as well as ultimately isolation. In his instructions to the scriptwriter, Gilbert Ralston, Coon stressed that the main conflict should be between Apollo's demand for "things to be as they were before", and the *Enterprise*'s progressive scientific logic: "Apollo is addressing them on very primitive terms and Kirk represents a highly sophisticated culture, science and technology".[34] Roddenberry also stressed to Coon that rational thought and science offer the solution for the *Enterprise* crew, allowing them to evade the *entrap-*

26 Pearson 1999; Asa 1999; Kovacs 2015, 206-7.
27 'Star Trek Writers/Directors Guide', 17 April 1967.
28 UCLA/Roddenberry Collection, Box 13, Folder 1, Robertson to Roddenberry, 23 March 1967, and Coon to Ralston, 14 April 1967.
29 UCLA/Roddenberry Collection, Box 13, Folder 1, Roddenberry to Coon, 18 May 1967.
30 UCLA/Roddenberry Collection, Box 13, Folder 1, Justman to Coon, 12 April, and Coon to Ralston, 14 April 1967.
31 UCLA/Roddenberry Collection, Box 13, Folder 1, Justman to Coon, 18 May 1967.
32 UCLA/Roddenberry Collection, Box 13, Folder 1, Messerschmidt to Roddenberry, 15 March 1967.
33 UCLA/Roddenberry Collection, Box 13, Folder 1, Justman to Coon, 18 May 1967.
34 UCLA/Roddenberry Collection, Box 13, Folder 1, Coon to Ralston, 14 April 1967.

ment of the arrogant Apollo: this, Roddenberry stressed, "is inherent in what they are doing".[35] According to the creators, the conflict between conservatism and progress is one of the central themes of the episode, with Apollo (ironically, for the god of light) representing the former.

Isolationism and the threat of entrapment is also the theme of the second episode that has a strong flavour of Ancient Greece. 'Plato's Stepchildren' was aired on 22 November 1968. It has remained in popular memory as the one with the first interracial kiss in the history of American television, between Kirk and Uhura. The title is significant: Plato's '*grand*children' could be taken to mean the modern Greeks, whereas his stepchildren could be anyone. The episode is thus relevant to all modern societies. The initial working title was 'The Sons of Socrates'.[36]

The *Enterprise* encounters a highly-developed people, the Platonians. They are the products of a mass eugenics programme, which De Forest Research, the scientific advisors of TOS, described as a programme of "selective breeding",[37] a menacing concept. The Platonians travelled in space, came to Earth at the time of Classical Athens, and embraced Ancient Greek civilisation. They subsequently reached their present home, where they set up their Plato-based 'Republic'. The Platonians are the ultimate elitist and isolationist society: the population is only 38 people, hidden from the rest of the galaxy. They are an advanced people who have developed longevity and telekinetic abilities, but as often happens with advanced and isolationist cultures in *Star Trek*, they prove to be extremely backward in other aspects. For example, because of their longevity, they have not developed medicinal sciences, and the slightest wound may prove fatal for them. This is why they ask for the help of the *Enterprise*: their leader, Parmen – who describes himself with the Platonic term "philosopher-king" – has suffered a wound, and his life is in danger. Dr McCoy heals the wound.

Soon it becomes apparent that something is wrong with this society. The servant of the Platonians, the dwarf Alexander, is constantly humiliated by them, and is mocked for his size. He is effectively a slave; at any rate his character points to social inequalities, reflecting the

concerns of the American civil rights movement of the 1960s. Kirk explains to the terrified Alexander that "where I come from, size, shape or color makes no difference". But things get even worse. Parmen, an arrogant figure lacking any sense of measure, decides to keep McCoy, against his will, as a healer in the community. He offers him longevity in exchange (once more, the temptation), which McCoy rejects. Then, however, the members of the away team find that they cannot move of their own volition; their movements are controlled by Parmen's telekinetic abilities. Spock protests that Parmen violates Plato's teachings, to which the Platonians say they have made some "adaptations" to Plato's ideas, but have created the true "democratic" society. In *Star Trek*, the Other's critique of the UFP's Western values is always presented strongly, allowing for a climax in the conflict on a moral dilemma, and Parmen spares no words:

In your culture justice is the will of the stronger. It is forced upon people by means of weapons, starships. Our justice is the will of the stronger mind, a vast improvement.

In the end, scientific observation once again allows the team to trace the source of their tormentors' power and overcome them. The Platonians are defeated and Alexander is freed from their tyranny. Even Parmen now admits the value of what Western political theory has known as checks and balances: "Uncontrolled, power will turn even saints into savages".

Once more in this episode, there was a problem with 'believability' in the idea of meeting an imitation of a Terran culture of the past in deep space.[38] De Forest Research protected the creative team from some historical mistakes; for example, they suggested the term 'Platonic Republic', instead of 'Utopia', coined by Thomas More in the sixteenth century AD, which the Platonians would not have known, since they left Earth 2,000 years earlier; still, the word 'Utopia' is mentioned in the episode. Similarly, De Forest Research made sure that no 'mousse chocolat' or 'coffee' would be served in the Ancient Greek symposium. There were other cases where the scientific

---

35   UCLA/Roddenberry Collection, Box 13, Folder 1, Roddenberry to Coon, 18 May 1967.

36   'Plato's Stepchildren', *Star Trek: TOS* (1968); Cushman 2014b, 349-67.

37   UCLA/Roddenberry Collection, Box 20, Folder 2, De Forest Research comments, 26 July 1968.

38   UCLA/Roddenberry Collection, Box 20, Folder 3, Roddenberry to Freiberger (Paramount Studio), 8 October 1968.

advisors arguably were less successful: thus, at their suggestion, the Platonians offer as a gift to Kirk the 'shield of Pericles', though the historical figure did not go around the Athenian Assembly carrying a shield.[39] Moreover, there is a notable oversimplification of Platonic ideas. Plato's 'philosopher-king' refers to excellence and virtue, not to inequality based on eugenic enhancement (nor to "essential Fascism" as De Forest Research noted in its comments – another case of a historically controversial use of a 20th-century term in the context of Antiquity). On the other hand, neither is Plato's Republic a "democracy", as Parmen boasts. The result is rather confusing:

The Platonians' application of Plato's teaching is an example of distortion through reception: it would be very difficult, if not impossible, to properly reconstruct the philosophy of Plato through analysis of the Platonians' own actions.[40]

However, the main theme of the episode is the denunciation of elitism and isolationism, both represented by the Platonians. The scriptwriter, Meyer Dolinsky, "had an agenda to attack intellectual snobbery and social class structure".[41] The *Enterprise* officers resist the Platonians, expressing the impatience of a modern society accustomed to the ideas of participation, professionalism, inclusiveness, meritocracy and efficiency. As Robertson of the NBC put it to Fred Freiberger of Paramount Studio, the episode is "a story of entrapment of our heroes".[42]

The third episode with an Ancient Greek flavour was aired on 20 December 1968. Its references to Antiquity are not visualised in terms of clothes or buildings, but remain indirect. The episode bears the title 'Elaan of Troyius', a corruption of 'Helen of Troy', although from the start Roddenberry also intended to include elements from Shakespeare's *The Taming of the Shrew*. In Roddenberry's original idea (of 1966) and in the first drafts of spring 1968,

the name was 'Helen'.[43] In his instructions to scriptwriter John Meredyth Lucas, Roddenberry also made repeated references to the 1964 film *My Fair Lady*, telling the story of the transformation of an uneducated girl into a person acceptable to society; Roddenberry noted that the *My Fair Lady* model "*is our basic tale*".[44] In other words, in this episode the references, parallels and models are oblique and multifaceted.

Elaan is the sovereign of the planet Elas (which is, phonetically, the official name of Greece – Hellas), who has to marry the leader of the planet Troyius to bring peace. In the initial story outlines the name of Elaan's planet was 'Hellias', which is even more reminiscent of Greece. These changed at Roddenberry's suggestion to Lucas to avoid direct parallels in the pursuit of believability:

Although we must keep the name Troyius, we do wonder if we want to go as smack on the nose as calling the other planet Hellias, calling the woman Helen, and so on. Probably all the way through in names as well as customs, hardware, etc., we need more S.F. and a little less of the Earth parallel.[45]

The *Enterprise* has undertaken a mission of mediation. The planets Elas and Troyius have reached an impasse in their long antagonism, and now seek reconciliation. They are not as advanced as the UFP (they have not developed interstellar travel or weapons more sophisticated than 'dirty' nuclear missiles), and in many respects they remind the viewer of 20th-century Earth. The *Enterprise* must transport Elaan and her entourage for the marriage, as well as a Troyian Ambassador who will teach her Troyian ways. The Elasians are depicted as violent and aggressive. Spock, the voice of logic, notes that "all the Elasians seem highly irrational". In his guidance, Roddenberry characterised them as "savage", noting that this term accurately describes a late twentieth century Terran civilization.[46]

39 For the guidance by DeForest Research, see UCLA/Roddenberry Collection, Box 20, Folder 2, De Forest Research comments, 26 July 1968.
40 Kovacs 2015, 210-1.
41 Cushman 2014b, 350.
42 UCLA/Roddenberry Collection, Box 20, Folder 3, Robertson (NBC) to Freiberger, 25 June 1968.
43 'Elaan of Troyius', *Star Trek: TOS* (1968); Cushman 2014b, 83-102; Baker 2010, 82.
44 UCLA/Roddenberry Collection, Box 22, Folder 13, Roddenberry to Lucas, 13 March 1968, and Roddenberry to Freiberger, 20 May 1968. Emphasis in the original.
45 UCLA/Roddenberry Collection, Box 22, Folder 13, Roddenberry to Lucas, 1 April 1968.
46 UCLA/Roddenberry Collection, Box 22, Folder 13, Roddenberry to Coon, 5 June 1966; Box 22, Folder 12, De Forest Research comments, 21 May 1968.

Moreover, Roddenberry made sure that the Elasians would have additional idiosyncratic characteristics: "an arrogant race such as that on the planet Hellias would tend to be highly conservative and retain numerous messages of the past as a matter of pride"[47] – again the thread connecting static adherence to the past with conservatism or backwardness. Elaan herself is an epitome of irrationality: spoilt, bad-mannered and violent. According to a telling comment in *TV Guide* of mid-December 1968, she "has the hauteur of a Chinese empress – and the manners of Henry VIII".[48] Roddenberry described her as an "impossible barbarian", and De Forest Research referred to her "provincialism".[49] Still, the creative team ensured that the she was not a hollow character: she has a moral fabric, as she is ready to sacrifice herself for peace.[50]

In contrast to the near-barbaric Elasians, the Troyians are more refined and reasonable. This, of course, is not an invention of *Star Trek*. Euripides had made the point in his *Troades* in the fifth century BC. This also touches upon one of our own well-established contemporary perceptions regarding the Trojan War. A prominent scholar of International Relations reminds us that Achilles is "a person who is seriously dysfunctional, but still magnificent at the same time, a man so many soldiers over the ages have wished to be, but also feared they might become". On the contrary, he writes, Homer depicts Hector as "the warrior with whom we most identify today … Hector is the greater man, although Achilles is the greater warrior". The students of the US Naval War Academy studying the *Iliad* "confess that they would rather be 'a Hector who wins'".[51]

Elaan, supported by her bodyguard Kryton (another Greek-sounding name), insults everybody, torments the Troyian Ambassador, and finally stabs him, fortunately with no fatal results. Kirk then undertakes the daunting task of showing Elaan civilised manners. This is the opportunity for a flirting game, at which time we learn that Elasian women have a strange biochemical substance in their tears, which, if touched by a man, make him fall desperately in love with them. Kirk confronts Elaan, vainly calling for reason. She warns him not to touch her, and an impatient Kirk indicates that "[i]f I touch you again, Your Glory, it will be to administer an ancient Earth custom called a spanking, a form of punishment administered to spoiled brats". However, eventually Kirk touches Elaan's tears and falls in love with her, whereupon the Elasian sovereign displays a sudden interest in the ancient Earth custom of spanking. Sexism apart (blatant as it is in TOS of the 1960s), she proposes Kirk use the *Enterprise* to destroy Troyius and marry her. Thus, this time the danger is one of *voluntary* confinement for Kirk, but one that would still end his quest for exploration. Meanwhile, a vessel of the Klingons, the UFP's adversary, appears and threatens the diplomatic process. Finally, Kirk manages to overcome his affection for the spoilt queen, because his real love is the *Enterprise* herself. The *Enterprise* defeats the Klingons and delivers Elaan to Troyius. It is Kirk, this time, who has overcome a more earthly temptation. In his early directions to Coon in December 1966, Roddenberry detailed this dilemma for both Kirk and Elaan: "the story between Kirk and Helen develops into a vital and almost barbaric love affair which at the end both of them realize they must break off because for each of them there are duties and stakes much more important".[52]

The awe of Roman legacies

References to Roman antiquity are qualitatively different. The creators of TOS had a fascination with gladiators. In the 1967 episode 'Arena', a race of super-beings intervene to stop a battle between the *Enterprise* and an alien vessel, then send Kirk and the alien captain to a planet to fight it out while they observe.[53] In another instance, the advanced 'Providers' enslave members of the *Enterprise* crew, and force them to fight as gladiators. However, in that episode there are no visual Roman references, and

---

47   UCLA/Roddenberry Collection, Box 22, Folder 13, Roddenberry to Lucas, 1 April 1968.
48   Quoted in Cushman 2014b, 82.
49   UCLA/Roddenberry Collection, Box 22, Folder 13, Roddenberry to Lucas, 13 March 1968; Box 22, Folder 12, De Forest Research comments, 21 May 1968.
50   UCLA/Roddenberry Collection, Box 22, Folder 13, Justman to Roddenberry, 11 March 1968.
51   Coker 2014, 16-37.
52   UCLA/Roddenberry Collection, Box 22, Folder 13, Roddenberry to Coon, 5 December 1966.
53   'Arena', *Star Trek: TOS* (1967).

even the weapons are not Roman; indeed, one of them looks less like a spear and more like a can opener.[54]

In 1968, the episode 'Bread and Circuses' dealt directly with Roman legacies.[55] The *Enterprise* finds the remains of a Terran commercial vessel in an uncharted area of the galaxy. They reach the closest habitable planet and discover that this is a replica of Earth, where Rome has survived until the equivalent of the 20th century: the planet has television, cars (the sport model Jupiter Eight) and even miniskirts, a feature on which TOS steadily insisted. This 'Rome' is not ancient. Consequently, important notional problems occurred in the preparation of the episode, and the coexistence of the ancient and the modern sometimes created a confusing picture. The greatest problem involved the extent of the Roman parallel. The creative team advised that this should involve 'external' aspects, such as wardrobe, hairstyles or weaponry, but the episode would not give "a Roman flavor to every piece of modern equipment", because in that case "we shall be getting ourselves into a rather sticky wicket".[56] Yet, this general rule could not provide an answer to all questions, and in some respects it was more honoured in the breach. Thus, it is not readily apparent how this modern industrial society could base its economy on slavery or be attracted to fights of Roman gladiators. Roddenberry himself conceded that a society using combustion engines would hardly need slaves for "horsepower", but perhaps people could exploit them to better their everyday lives, much like how Americans of the 20th century used their housekeepers – an indirect critique of modern class structure.[57] On its part, De Forest Research once more corrected mistakes: for example, "General Sextus" would not do, as this was a Latin first name, while "Antonius" was a family name and should not be used as a forename. Moreover, the scientific advisors noted that Dr McCoy should not wonder about "ancient" treatment of disease, as this 'Rome' was not ancient.[58] Still, perhaps inevitably, not all notional

problems could be solved. In due time, Roman legionnaires, complete with helmets and cuirasses and armed with 20th-century machine guns, appear on the stage; in the love scene, illumination is provided by a Roman lamp, although this is a society with electricity.

Despite its inevitable problems, the episode poses two important moral and political dilemmas. The first involves the limits of interference in the affairs of an alien planet, namely Starfleet's "Prime Directive", which is that the *Enterprise* crew should not interfere in the natural development of an alien culture. The Prime Directive has been interpreted by experts of the Classics as the concern of the *Enterprise* crew that they do not "play god",[59] but other scholars have pointed to its obvious relevance in the debate over contemporary power politics and US interventions in the developing world, especially in Vietnam.[60] The second theme refers, once more, to the association of isolationism with an 'ancient' culture.

An away team beams down to the planet and meets a group of runaway slaves, former gladiators (the Spartacus parallel is strong). The slaves are sun worshippers, and preach brotherhood and love. McCoy makes the (mistaken) observation that this is strange, as there were no sun worshippers in Rome.[61] Kirk and the away team soon discover that the captain of the lost commercial vessel survived and has become the "first citizen" of the province, but also the puppet of the pro-consul, a cunning local politician who intends to lure in the *Enterprise* crew and keep them on the planet. Indeed, the inhabitants of the planet are not permitted to learn about space civilisations. Thus, the *Enterprise* people are once more threatened by isolationists who intend to confine them. The compromised captain of the commercial vessel explains the advantages of isolation to Kirk:

This is an ordered world, Jim. A conservative world based on time-honored Roman strengths and virtues … There's been

54 'The Gamesters of Triskellion', *Star Trek: TOS* (1967).
55 'Bread and Circuses', *Star Trek: TOS* (1968).
56 UCLA/Roddenberry Collection, Box 14, Folder 13, Staff comments on story outline, 27 March 1967.
57 UCLA/Roddenberry Collection, Box 14, Folder 14, Roddenberry to Kneubuhl, 14 March 1967. See also Cushman 2014a, 332
58 UCLA/Roddenberry Collection, Box 14, Folder 13, De Forest Research comments, 10 May, 7 & 15 September 1967.
59 Kovacs 2015, 213-5.
60 Lagon 1993; Franklin 1994; O'Connor 2012; Worland 1988; Sarantakes 2005; Hatzivassiliou forthcoming.
61 The inaccuracy had been noted by the scientific advisers, but their advice was ignored: UCLA/Roddenberry Collection, Box 14, Folder 13, De Forest Research comments, 15 September 1967.

no war for 400 years here. Could your land of that same era [the 20th century] make that same boast? I think you can see why they don't want to have their stability contaminated by dangerous ideas of other ways and other places.

This returns the narrative to a wider question. Spock considers whether a *conservative empire* that has evaded Earth's "three world wars" is an acceptable alternative to the UFP's *progressive federation*. But the answer is clear: losing both freedom and the ability to progress is too high a price to pay. The climax of the episode takes place in a 'Roman' television studio, broadcasting a live glad-iator fight between Kirk and Spock and two locals. The scene was intended as satire of American television of that period, and presents the opportunity for some acid innuendos.[62] As we enter the studio, we hear the speaker announcing that the show is "brought to you by your Jupiter Eight [the car] dealers *from coast to coast*" – which is an American, not a Roman allusion. However, in the end the *Enterprise* crew escape this time-prison. They also find out that the survival of this Rome was based on a misunderstanding: the oppressed slaves made a mistake, worshipping the *sun*, instead of the Son of God. But now that they know, they are ready to change the face of their world. The *Enterprise* is thus free to continue her quest for knowledge and progress.

The Roman world also appears in a lower profile and yet as a more central theme in TOS. One of the UFP's adversaries, the Romulan Empire, is clearly modeled on Ancient Rome. The immediate context is not Antiquity but the Cold War. Indeed, the title of the first episode is a Cold War term ('Balance of Terror'), while the second ('The Enterprise Incident'), written by a major figure of the *Star Trek* team, D. C. Fontana, was inspired by the capture of a US surveillance vessel by the North Koreans.[63] Still, the Roman references are clear. The Romulan Empire is centered on the twin star system of Romulus and Remus. Romulan costumes are vaguely reminiscent

of Roman legionnaires' uniforms, while their names and military ranks are Roman-like (for example, "Decius" and "centurion"). The head of their state is the "praetor". They are a dedicated people, reminding the viewer of the legendary discipline of Roman legions. At the same time, they are xenophobic and isolationist.[64] All these, of course, were representations in a popular television series which faced its own practical challenges. Thus, rather in-gloriously for the grandiose aspirations of a scholar eager to find clear intellectual references, the archival material also points to the more practical aspects of the making of the episodes: the Romulan helmets are reminiscent of those of Roman legionnaires, but they were used, at Justman's insistence, to cover the Romulan officers' heads and thus avoid the need to show their pointed ears, which at that time required very expensive makeup.[65]

What is so frightful about Ancient Rome, to make it a suitable model for a major enemy of the UFP? The structure of the Roman Empire, so often losing perspec-tive under the leadership of omnipotent emperors, might be expected to provide the inspiration. The association of Roman emperors with authoritarianism or even mental instability seems to be a widely accepted theme in con-temporary Western culture. In 1935, Robert Graves had his Claudius say exactly that: "Yes, we are all mad, we Emperors. We begin sanely, like Augustus and Tiberius and even Caligula … and monarchy turns our wits".[66] Scholars have noted "the negative view of imperial Rome generally present in popular culture".[67] *Star Trek* shared this attitude. Thus, in 'Bread and Circuses', the Roman Empire has survived until the equivalent of the 20th cen-tury, and Kirk informs the viewer that this is "a world ruled by emperors who can trace their line back 2,000 years to their own Julius and Augustus Ceasars". Preparing the same episode, the script consultant, D. C. Fontana, noted that the character of the pro-consul displays "some of the madness of the Caesars".[68] The earlier episode 'Mirror, Mirror' presents an alternative universe where

---

62   Cushman 2014a, 330.

63   Sarantakes 2005, 97-9.

64   'Balance of Terror', *Star Trek: TOS* (1966) 'The Enterprise Incident', *Star Trek: TOS* (1968).

65   UCLA/Schneider Collection, Box 10, Justman to Black, 26 April & 24 May 1966. See also UCLA/Roddenberry Collection, Box 21, Folder 7, Just-man to Freiberger, 2 April 1968.

66   Graves 1989, 504.

67   Winkler 2001, 273.

68   Cushman 2014a, 334.

the *Enterprise* herself belongs to a repressive, violent and cruel 'empire' (not the progressive 'federation'), led by a "Caesar".[69]

However, things are not that simple with the Romulans. Their state is an 'empire', but not a monarchy.[70] In the case of the Romulans, there is little distinction between the Roman Republic and the Empire. But there were other aspects of Ancient Rome that were appropriate for picturing an enemy: its highly militaristic values, and its slave-based social system. More significantly, there is a thinly-concealed awe of Roman legacies. The Romulans are depicted as a respectable, intellectually strong enemy, if also arrogant and aristocratic. As the scriptwriter of the first Romulan episode, Paul Schneider, noted: "It was a matter of developing a good Romanesque set of admirable antagonists that were worthy of Kirk. The Romulans [were] an extension of the Roman civilization to the point of space travel".[71] Producer Justman described them as "formidable" and "quite ruthless opponents".[72] These Roman elements play a pivotal role in presenting the opponents as respectable and fearsome. As the compromised captain tells Kirk in 'Bread and Circuses': "Maybe now you understand why I gave in, Jim. The Romans have always been the strongest".

Conclusions

There is another angle to all this. In a Greek motion picture of the late 1960s, a university professor of Ancient History, weary of his poverty and seeking to earn some money, agrees to write Antiquity-related scenarios for an American 'photo romance' magazine. But once he starts giving in to unscientific temptation, he is soon ready (presumably, at the encouragement of his American patrons) to introduce 2,000 American Indians into the siege of Troy.[73] This is a critique of the lack of historicity in many motion pictures, but also a manifestation of the shallow stereotype of the "uneducated Americans", so often projected in postwar Europe. In other words, there is the question of how other people with a claim to the Classical tradition perceived American popular culture oversimplifications, but also their attractions which were not only material. These perceptions, of course, bore their own oversimplifications. If nothing else, photo romance was a European (Italian), rather than an American phenomenon.[74] Mistakenly associating American culture with this particular kind of entertainment (which had also become quite prominent in Greek popular magazines of that time) is an interesting manifestation of Greek parochialism, rather than an accurate critique of American popular culture.

Popular culture is a difficult field of study, because it involves the convergence and interaction of many societal and intellectual processes. This article, focusing on TOS as a case study, has argued that, in this endeavour, access to the archival material of the creators is of pivotal importance, since it offers a clear picture of their intentions and attitudes. On the other hand, even archival material cannot automatically offer all the answers, especially in a study of perceptions and assumptions about major points of reference of contemporary Western societies. Sometimes, as is often the case with the use of archival evidence, a certain degree of deconstruction may occur (for example when the constantly recurring problem of 'believability' surfaced, or when the scientific advisors pointed to factual mistakes of the creators), but even these point to real problems that the makers of *Star Trek* faced, on both conceptual and practical levels. Thus, the archival material is an indispensable tool for the scholar seeking interpretations, and it confirms the relevance of Classical legacies for our post-industrial societies.

This mixture of sources – the episodes and the archival evidence – has revealed a complicated process. *Star Trek* was a popular television series; scholarly accuracy

---

69   'Mirror, Mirror', *Star Trek: TOS* (1967).

70   In subsequent *Star Trek* series, the Romulans' political system is republican, with a Senate and a government based on procedure. See, among others, 'Unification', two parts, *Star Trek: The Next Generation* (1991). Interestingly, in 1966 Roddenberry asked Schneider to find alternatives to the "archaic earth words" such as "praetor" and "Caesar", but this evidently proved impossible. See UCLA/Schneider Collection, Box 10, Roddenberry to Schneider, 18 April 1966.

71   Quoted in Cushman 2013, 238.

72   UCLA/Roddenberry Collection, Box 21, Folder 7, Justman to Freiberger, 5 June 1968.

73   *O Stratis Parastratise* (1969). This film describes the photo romance as 'worse' than comics.

74   See for example, Small 2009, 24-6.

was not a primary concern of the creators,[75] but they did intend to raise wider moral/political issues, including the dilemmas involving legacies. In this context, TOS refused to glorify Antiquity, as so often happened in the Western literary tradition. TOS also partially disassociated itself from the positive representations of Greek and Roman antiquity in Hollywood motion pictures, for example *Quo Vadis* (1951), *The Robe* (1953), *Alexander the Great* (1956), *Ben-Hur* (1959), *Spartacus* (1960), *Cleopatra* (1963) and others. TOS used Antiquity as a pivot upon which to hang a dilemma, as a crucial part of the political and social messages that it wanted to radiate. It did not reject Classical legacies: the members of the *Enterprise* crew "mourn for Adonais"; they protest against the Platonians' *corruption* of the Platonic ideal; they are charmed by the bad-mannered Elaan/Helen; and they accept Rome's impact. But TOS suggests that Antiquity was *valuable as a stage* of the development of mankind, who now need to go forward. The "Golden Age", in Kirk's words, is today, not in the days of Pericles.

However, this is not the whole story. TOS associated Classical antiquity (or its contemporary uses) with conservatism. Apollo's immortality and the Platonians' longevity are representative of a key preoccupation in *Star Trek*, with absolute power that corrupts absolutely. TOS "associates immortality with stagnation and a depletion of moral fiber".[76] Moreover, all 'ancient' worlds are isolationist, and demand the *Enterprise* crew give up their claim to freedom and progress. This is exactly, in Kirk's words to Apollo, what "we could no longer give". In all the series of *Star Trek*, the worlds opting for isolation "are portrayed as morally deficient or at best dubious".[77] The archival material makes it clear that in these episodes the creators persistently tried to bring out a fundamental conflict between conservatism and the demand for "things to be as they were before" on the one hand, and liberal

professionalism, scientific knowledge and forward-looking attitudes on the other.

In this respect, it is important to trace what Classical tradition, rightly or wrongly, represented for many people in the 1960s. An interesting problem of perspective was becoming manifest: TOS was a work of popular culture (although a work of popular culture can also be one of high quality, as was *Star Trek*), but Antiquity was associated with the high culture of the West. The reserved attitudes towards Antiquity, to some extent, mirror the climate of the Western 1960s, with the Classics, as a salient feature of the worldview of the 'establishment', representing elitism. Most officials in Europe were men from the upper classes, graduates of mainstream Universities, usually from the fields of the classics.[78] In other words, a challenge to the contemporary uses of Antiquity was part of the ongoing social reconfigurations of the era, with the ascending new social forces questioning the restrictions and certainties of the 'old order'. Indeed, there were other TOS episodes in which even Early Modern Western high culture was associated with conservatism and isolationism.[79]

This is not to say that *Star Trek* represented a 'revolt' of popular against high culture; that would be to read too much into it. Social processes and the shaping of worldviews are not the products of a laboratory, and can be confused, even contradictory phenomena. However, during the shift into the post-industrial era, it was natural to pose questions about legacies. During this process, TOS had a tendency to place its emphasis on the breaks, rather than on continuities.

It is interesting that the 1980s series, *Star Trek: The Next Generation* (TNG), adopted a different attitude towards legacies. Antiquity was not a salient theme, but TNG insisted on the value of intellectual tradition as a necessary ingredient of a conscious modernity, mostly using Shakespeare as a point of reference.[80] The Captain,

---

75   Roddenberry cautioned script writers that '[w]e don't need essays, however brilliant'. See '*Star Trek* Writers/Directors Guide', 17 April 1967, 5.

76   Kovacs 2015, 205.

77   Neumann 2001, 619.

78   For example, this pattern remained in the British Foreign Service: Hughes & Platt 2015. Even in West Germany, a visible break with the past was evident and a new policy (oriented to the European project) was pursued; social inertia could not be avoided. Members of the upper middle classes were admitted to the West German Foreign Service, but this happened gradually and the dominance of "Protestant wealthy members of the nobility and the bourgeois upper class" remained well into the 1960s: see Wiegeshoff 2018.

79   See 'The Squire of Gothos' (1967); 'Requiem for Methuselah' (1969).

80   'Hide and Q', *Star Trek: The Next Generation* (1987). Shakespeare was a source of inspiration for TOS episodes as well: see Kreitzer 1996. However, in TNG Shakespeare is projected as a model for the contemporary human.

Jean-Luc Picard (played by Sir Patrick Stewart, a Shakespearean actor), reads Homer in ancient Greek, and is noted for his respect for old books, his scholarly interest in archaeology (alien, rather than Terran) and his ability to combine forward-looking attitudes with tradition. He is portrayed as "an exemplary figure of western humanism".[81] Indeed, to some extent at least, the allegories are reversed, and Picard's old archaeology professor makes an interesting parallel: "You're like some Roman centurion out patrolling the provinces, maintaining a dull and bloated Empire". In the same episode, Picard comments: "the past is a very insistent voice inside me".[82] But TNG was a product of a society where the move to the post-industrial era had been completed, and thus many of the dilemmas regarding the burdens of legacies no longer assumed existential proportions. Therefore, TNG was much more ready to stress continuities, and indirectly *lamented* the loss of the emphasis on Classical culture in the mature West of the 1980s. TNG expressed a certainty that elevated consciousness (for which a Classical tradi-

tion is indispensable) would enrich, rather than threaten, its modernity.

Thus, it is important to view *Star Trek: TOS* and its various sequels within their historical context. The series radiated messages that were relevant to their era. In the 1960s, when the 'new' had yet to establish itself, the creators tended to insist on breaks. But even the ambiguous relationship with the Classics projected in TOS confirms the centrality of the Classical tradition, and its relevance to modern societies.

EVANTHIS HATZIVASSILIOU
Department of History and Archaeology
National and Kapodistrian University of Athens
School of Philosophy, University Campus,
GR-15784 Athens
xevanthis@arch.uoa.gr

---

81 Pearson and Messenger-Davies 2003.
82 'The Chase', *Star Trek: The Next Generation* (1993).

Bibliography

Primary Sources

A. ARCHIVAL SOURCES

'*Star Trek* Writers/Directors Guide', third revision, 17 April 1967, at https://www.bu.edu/clarion/guides/Star_Trek_Writers_Guide.pdf, *Norway Productions*, accessed 20 August 2016.

University of California at Los Angeles Library, Performing Arts Special Collections, Gene Roddenberry Star Trek Television Series Collection (referred to as UCLA/Roddenberry Collection).

University of California at Los Angeles Library Special Collections, Charles E. Young Research Library, Paul & Margaret Schneider Papers (referred to as UCLA/Schneider Collection).

B. TELEVISION/FILM

'Arena', dir. Joseph Pevney, in *Star Trek: TOS*, DVD (1967; Hollywood, CA: Paramount Pictures, 2004).

'Balance of Terror', dir. Vincent McEveety, in *Star Trek: TOS*, DVD (1966; Hollywood, CA: Paramount Pictures, 2004).

'Bread and Circuses', dir. Ralph Senensky, in *Star Trek: TOS*, DVD (1968; Hollywood, CA: Paramount Pictures, 2004).

'Elaan of Troyius', dir. John Meredyth Lucas, in *Star Trek: TOS*, DVD (1968; Hollywood, CA: Paramount Pictures, 2004).

'Hide and Q', dir. Cliff Bole, in *Star Trek: TNG*, DVD (1991; Hollywood, CA: CBS Studios, 2006).

'Mirror, Mirror', dir. Marc Daniels, in *Star Trek: TOS*, DVD (1967; Hollywood, CA: Paramount Pictures, 2004).

O Stratis Parastratise [Stratis went astray], dir. Costas Karagiannis (Athens: Karagiannis-Karatzopoulos, 1969).

'Plato's Stepchildren', dir. David Alexander, in *Star Trek: TOS*, DVD (1968; Hollywood, CA: Paramount Pictures, 2004).

'Requiem for Methuselah', dir. Murray Golden, in *Star Trek: TOS*, DVD (1969; Hollywood, CA: Paramount Pictures, 2004).

'The Chase', dir. Jonathan Frakes, in *Star Trek: TNG*, DVD (1993; Hollywood, CA: Paramount Pictures, 2002).

'The Enterprise Incident', dir. John Meredyth Lucas, in *Star Trek: TOS*, DVD (1968; Hollywood, CA: Paramount Pictures, 2004).

'The Gamesters of Triskellion', dir. Gene Nelson, in *Star Trek: TOS*, DVD (1967; Hollywood, CA: Paramount Pictures, 2004).

'The Squire of Gothos', dir. Don McDougall, in *Star Trek: TOS*, DVD (1967; Hollywood, CA: Paramount Pictures, 2004).

'Unification', two parts, dir. Les Landau and Cliff Bole respectively, in *Star Trek: TNG*, DVD (1991; Hollywood, CA: Paramount Pictures, 2002).

'Who Mourns for Adonais?', dir. Marc Daniels, in *Star Trek: TOS*, DVD (1966; Hollywood, CA: Paramount Pictures, 2004).

Works cited

Asa, R. 1999
'Classic *Star Trek* and the Death of God: A Case Study of "Who Mourns for Adonais?"', in *Star Trek and Sacred Ground: Explorations of Star Trek, Religion, and American Culture*, J. Porter & D. McLaren (eds), Albany, NY, 33-60.

Baker, D. 2010
'"Every Old Trick is New Again": Myth in Quotations and the *Star Trek* Franchise', in *Star Trek as Myth: Essays on Symbol and Archetype at the Final Frontier*, M. Kapell (ed.), Jefferson, NC, 80-90.

Chapman J. & N. J. Cull 2013
Projecting Tomorrow: Science Fiction in Popular Cinema, London.

Coker, C. 2014
Men at War: What Fiction Tells us about Conflict, from the Iliad to Catch-22, London.

Cushman, M. (with S. Osborn) 2013
These are the Voyages: TOS (vol. 1), San Diego, CA.

Cushman, M. (with S. Osborn) 2014a
These are the Voyages: TOS (vol. 2), San Diego, CA.

Cushman, M. (with S. Osborn) 2014b
These are the Voyages: TOS (vol. 3), San Diego, CA.

Ferguson, N. 2010
'Crisis, What Crisis? The 1970s and the Shock of the Global', in *The Shock of the Global: the 1970s in Perspective*, N. Ferguson, C. Maier, E. Manela & D. Sargent (eds), Cambridge, MA, 1-21.

Fink, C., P. Gassert & D. Junker (eds) 1998
1968: The World Transformed, New York.

Franklin, H. B. 1994
'*Star Trek* in the Vietnam Era', *Science-Fiction Studies* 21, 24-34.

Fredericks, S. 1980
'Greek Mythology in Modern Science Fiction: Vision and Cognition', in *Classical Mythology in Twentieth-Century Thought Literature*, W. Aycock & T. Klein (eds), Lubbock, TX, 89-106.

Gordon, J. 2016
'When Superman Smote Zeus: Analysing Violent Deicide in Popular Culture', *Classical Receptions Journal* 9.2 (2017), 211-36.

Graves, R. 1989
Claudius the God and his Wife Messalina, New York.

Hark, I. R. 2008
Star Trek, Basingstoke.

Hatzivassiliou, E. forthcoming
'Images of the International System and the Cold War in *Star Trek*, 1966-91', *Journal of Cold War Studies*.

Hughes, M. & R. Platt 2015
'Far Apart but Close Together: A Quantitative and Qualitative Analysis of the Career Structure and Organisational Culture of the Post-war British Diplomatic Service', *Diplomacy and Statecraft* 26.2, 266-93.

Kovacs, G. 2015
'Moral and Mortal in *Star Trek: The Original Series*', in *Classical Traditions in Science Fiction*, B. Rogers & B. Stevens (eds), Oxford, 199-216.

Kreitzer, L. 1996
'The Cultural Veneer of *Star Trek*', *Journal of Popular Culture* 30.2, 1-28.

Lagon, M. 1993
'"We Owe It to Them to Interfere": *Star Trek* and U.S. Statecraft in the 1960s and the 1990s', *Extrapolation* 34.3, 251-64.

Leggewie, C. 1998
'A Laboratory of Postindustrial Society: Reassessing the 1960s in Germany', in *1968: The World Transformed*, C. Fink, P. Gassert & D. Junker (eds), New York, 277-94.

McNeill, W. 1963
The Rise of the West: History of the Human Community, Chicago.

Neumann, I. 2001
'"Grab a Phaser Ambassador": Diplomacy in *Star Trek*', *Millennium: Journal of International Studies* 30.3, 603-24.

O'Connor, M. 2012
'Liberals in Space: the 1960s Politics of *Star Trek*', *The Sixties* 5.2, 185-203.

Pearson, A. 1999
'From the Thwarted God to Reclaimed Mystery? An Overview of the Depiction of Religion in *Star Trek*', in *Star Trek and Sacred Ground: Explorations of Star Trek, Religion, and American Culture*, J. Porter & D. McLaren (eds), Albany, NY, 13-32.

Pearson R. & M. Messenger-Davies 2003
'"You're Not Going to See That on TV": *Star Trek: The Next Generation* in Film and Television', in *Quality Popular Television: Cult TV, the Industry and Fans*, M. Jancovich & J. Lyons (eds), Basingstoke, 103-17.

Richard, C. J. 1994
The Founders and the Classics: Greece, Rome, and the American Enlightenment, Cambridge, MA.

Rogers B. & B. Stevens 2015
'Introduction: the Past Is an Undiscovered Country', in *Classical Traditions in Science Fiction*, B. Rogers & B. Stevens (eds), Oxford, 1-24.

Sarantakes, N. 2005
'Cold War Pop Culture and the Image of US Foreign Policy: The Perspective of the Original *Star Trek* Series', *Journal of Cold War Studies* 7.4, 74-103.

Small, P. 2009
Sophia Loren: Moulding the Star, Bristol.

Suri, J. 2003
Power and Protest: Global Revolution and the Rise of Détente, Cambridge, Mass.

Tomasso, V. 2015
'The Twilight of Olympus: Deicide and the End of the Greek Gods', in *Classical Myth on Screen*, M. Cyrino & M. Safran (eds), New York, 147-57.

Wiegeshoff, A. 2018
'The "New Look" of German Diplomacy: The West German Foreign Service after the Second World War', *Diplomacy and Statecraft* 29.2, 187-207.

Winkler, M. 2001
'Star Wars and the Roman Empire', in *Classical Myth and Culture in the Cinema*, Martin M. Winkler (ed.), Oxford, 272-90.

Winkler, M. 2007
'Greek Myth on the Screen', in *The Cambridge Companion to Greek Mythology*, R. Woodard (ed.), Cambridge, 454-80.

Winkler, M. 2009
Cinema and Classical Texts: Apollo's New Light, Cambridge.

Worland, R. 1988
'Captain Kirk: Cold Warrior', *Journal of Popular Film and Television* 16.3, 109-17.

Worland, R. 1994
'From the New Frontier to the Final Frontier: *Star Trek* from Kennedy to Gorbachev', *Film and History* 24.12, 19-35.

Classical Reception in a New Key:
Contemporary Hellenic Polytheism in Modern Greece

TAO THYKIER MAKEEFF

Abstract

This article deals with the reception of Greek antiquity among religious groups in Modern Greece, a phenomenon referred to as contemporary Hellenic polytheism. After a brief historical introduction to some of these groups and their activities, the author discusses their uses of ancient Greek religious history as cases of reception. The author underlines how such receptions themselves are in part influenced by scholarly accounts of antiquity, and suggests that the field of Classical Reception Studies could benefit from including the practices of religious groups who interpret antiquity in their scope of interest. This, the author suggests could be done in interdisciplinary projects, which combine studies of textual and material culture with ethnographic fieldwork.

Introduction

Over the past four decades, a number of new religious communities have emerged that find inspiration in pre-Christian Greek polytheism. Most of these groups share nationalist or national-romantic sentiments, a critical stance towards Christianity and a combination of a focus on Ancient culture with innovative ritual behaviour and social interaction. This new religious development, which I refer to as contemporary Hellenic polytheism, is a predominantly urban phenomenon that began in Athens in the 1980s, but, aided by the internet and increasing transnational mobility, today it has become a well-consolidated and growing religious phenomenon with ties to the wider international religious phenomenon known as contemporary Paganism. My aim with this article is twofold; to introduce the reader to the contemporary Hellenic polytheism and to suggest that the field of Classical Reception Studies would be enriched by expanding the scope to include the study of references to Antiquity by religious groups (using both ethnographic methods and textual analysis).[1] I imagine that this could involve interdisciplinary projects, combining the expertise and distinct methodological and theoretical perspectives of

---

1   The following text is based on my ongoing PhD project at the Centre for Theology and Religious Studies, Lund University, which deals with the social, textual and ritual aspects of contemporary Hellenic Neopaganism. The aim of the project, more specifically, is to investigate the background, context, formation and social organisation of contemporary Hellenic polytheist communities in Greece, and the way their negotiation between the textual and archaeological remains of Greek antiquity and their innovative approaches to ritual practice takes place in the context of (and sometimes in opposition to) contemporary Greek and European society. The project is based on a total of approximately one year of fieldwork in Athens undertaken during the years 2013-2017.

disciplines such as archaeology, art history, textual studies, ethnography and the (comparative) history of religion in the study of new religious receptions of the Greek (and Roman) past.

Contemporary Hellenic polytheism is a subcategory of the wider religious phenomenon known as contemporary Paganism. This has been studied extensively in the past decades, primarily by Pagan Studies scholars,[2] and while I find that much of the work that has been done has been rigorous and highly commendable, I have come to the conclusion that the future study of such phenomena in the context of modern interpretations of pre-Christian Greek religion (or Roman for that matter) would benefit greatly from the linguistic and historical expertise found in Classical Reception Studies. Classical Reception Studies has gradually been expanding the concept of text, from words and visual culture to performances, including theatre and most recently films[3] and computer games.[4] If the study of actors, audiences and gamers has become a legitimate scientific area of focus, why not study people and their practices? In other words, why not study Pagans? Studying people's practices could be the next logical next step in the process of expanding the concept of text[5] in Classical Reception Studies. However, before I discuss this any further, I shall provide the reader with an introduction to the subject matter: the re-appropriation, re-interpretation and reception of Greek antiquity in the religious practices of contemporary Hellenic polytheists.

The scope, methods and background of my study

In 2013, I became aware that there were a number of religious groups in Greece that looked to Greek antiquity for inspiration for their practices. At the time, I was an independent scholar, but I saw research potential in this phenomenon, particularly since it had only been discussed by a handful of scholars at the time. I contacted a number of these groups in order to see if they would be willing to participate in a study, and help me establish a wider network in Greece. After meeting with representatives from the groups YSEE and Labrys in the summer of 2013 I worked on my application for a PhD, which was subsequently accepted by the University of Lund in the summer of 2014. During this period, I had already begun working on my project, collecting data, expanding my network of informants and conducting a 3month period of fieldwork in Athens in February-April of 2014, supported by the Danish Institute at Athens. Since 2014, I have returned twice (for periods of approximately three months each time), in 2015 and 2017, to collect data. The core method of my research is ethnographic fieldwork. Beyond fieldwork I have conducted textual studies, and an extensive cyber-ethnographic study of the communication of contemporary Hellenic polytheists on websites, discussion boards and social media. The main part of my fieldwork has been done in Athens within one group (Labrys), but I have also researched a number of other groups.

Terminology

In Greece, a number of terms are used to refer to contemporary religious groups that base their activities on Ancient Greece. Most Greeks usually use the terms *Dodekatheismos* (worship of the twelve gods), *Olympianismos* (Olympianism) or *Neopaganismos* (Neopaganism). However, these terms are usually not used by the Greek practitioners themselves, since the Greek Orthodox Church uses them in a derogatory manner. Some international contemporary Pagan groups and solitary practitioners do use them, however.[6] Greek groups and individuals

---

2   For recent studies on contemporary Paganism (and the related phenomenon of native faith movements) in central and eastern Europe, see: Aitamurto & Simpson (eds) 2013.

3   Winkler 2001, 2009; Blanshard & Shahabudin 2011; Apostol & Bakogianni 2018. For an overview of the study of Classical reception in films before 2010, see Paul 2010.

4   Lowe in Lowe & Shahabudin 2009; Bishop 2018.

5   I understand 'text' in an open sense as any object or cultural product or practice that can be 'read' – that is, interpreted. This open definition of 'text' is not alien to literary theory, from which Classical Reception Studies is inspired.

6   In particular, the international contemporary Hellenic polytheist organisation Elaion seems to accept *dodekatheism* as one of a number of a number of self-definitions (see http://elaion.org/about/). However, the most popular term used by international Hellenic polytheists is *Hellenismos* (Hellenism).

prefer terms like *Elleniki Ethniki Thriskeia* (Hellenic Ethnic Religion), *Elliniki Thriskeia* (Hellenic Religion) and *Ellinikos Polytheismos* (Hellenic Polytheism). Finally, the term *Archaiolatreia*[7] (worship of Antiquity) is often used both by the Greek Orthodox Church to refer to individuals and groups who in their view are too interested in the pre-Christian history of Greece, and by contemporary Hellenic polytheists in Greece to imply that other contemporary Pagans are not sincerely religiously motivated in their love of Ancient Greece.

The modern history of contemporary Hellenic polytheism in Greece

Since its inception, contemporary Hellenic polytheism has been met with criticism and contempt by the Greek Orthodox Church. In particular the words of Father Efstathios Kollas[8] who in 2007 described this novel Greek religious minority as "a handful of miserable resuscitators of a degenerate dead religion who wish to return to the monstrous dark delusions of the past" have been quoted often by journalists as well as by contemporary Pagans.[9] Another, much more nuanced analysis of the Contemporary Hellenic polytheist phenomenon in Greece has come from Zissis Papadimitriou (1939-2015), a sociologist at the University of Thessaloniki, who in 2004 argued that this new religious development was a symptom of socio-economic circumstances, and an example of a intrinsically cosmopolitan wish to create a new positive identity:

Because of globalization, because of the European Union, the Greek people are in a period of transformation. So they are seeking a new identity – a Greek identity. (…) As a country, as a people, we are too small to be important economically. We have to play a cultural role in the world, and to play this role we have to have a very strong identity.[10]

Although there are certainly many nationalist, as opposed to cosmopolitan, examples of contemporary Paganism, as well as a myriad of variations within that spectrum of approaches, it is certain that Papadimitriou's analysis is more on point than that of Father Kollas. As I have seen repeatedly in my research, despite the assumptions of clergy, laymen and some scholars, contemporary Hellenic polytheists are generally not interested in returning to the past or reviving it in its entirety. Rather, they are interested in certain elements of the (religious) past and how these may be used in the present, often in order to make the future better, according to their individual or community-based perceptions of what is good.

Contemporary Hellenic polytheism

The contemporary re-appropriation and reception of Greek Antiquity by contemporary Hellenic polytheists in Greece has in part been shaped by a number of historical factors, such as the role of Antiquity in different periods of modern Greek history – from the time before the founding of the Greek nation state, through the shifting national narratives, such as the notion of the Hellenic-Christian synthesis[11] developed by Zambelios and Paparrigopoulos, or the idea of the "Third Hellenic Civilization"[12] promoted by the Metaxas-regime or the Delphic festivals of Angelos Sikelianos and Eva Palmer – and the role of Ancient Greek religion (or religious locations at least) in the branding of Greece in tourism, both past[13] and present.[14] However, although Greece's majority narratives about the role of Antiquity are an important perspective, the direct origins of the current religious groups can be located in the 1980s and 1990s, when a number of individuals founded small communities, predominantly in Athens.

The current Hellenic Polytheist milieu in Greece is comprised of a number of religious organisations as well as more loosely organised communities, study groups, sol-

---

7   For a discussion of the use of the term *archaiolatreia* in the Romantic period, see Esterhammer (ed.) 2002, 271-2.
8   Kollas was President of Greek Clergymen at the time.
9   Brabant 2007.
10   Miller 2004.
11   Grigoriadis 2013.
12   http://metaxas-project.com/third-hellenic-civilization/
13   Zacharia 2014, 186-8.
14   Andriotis 2009; Gill 2013, 233-2.

itary practitioners and fringe social phenomena, a number of which have been around since the late 1980s.[15] The year 1987 marked a turning point of great importance for the development of contemporary Hellenic polytheism in Greece, as two of the key figures in the milieu began their public religious activities. After a number of years as associate professor[16] at the University of Stockholm (Stockholm Business School), a Greek named Tryphon Kostopoulos[17] had moved back to his native country and in 1987 he founded the religious community *Ellinon Epistrofi* (Return of the Hellenes). Kostopoulos, who is now known by his new Hellenic religious name Tryphon Olympios, is still a key figure in the contemporary Hellenic polytheist milieu and the organiser of the largest contemporary Hellenic polytheist festival in Greece, *Prometheia*, which takes place in July each year on the slopes of Mount Olympos and has been held annually for the past 23 years. 1987 was also the year when Vlassis Rassias[18] – another well-known religious leader in Greece – began arranging rituals. Rassias had moved to the United States in the 1980s and engaged in civil rights work with Native Americans; in 1986 during a divination he was allegedly told by a Mohawk shaman to return to Greece and "fight for the religious rights of his own native people".[19] Rassias has also described his Native American impetus in an interview with a contemporary Pagan website:

For almost a decade, I also explored the spirituality of the native people of the Americas, the "First Nations" as they define themselves. And in the mid-eighties I received from a Mohawk old man that brilliant response to my question raised on how I could become perfect partaker of the native wisdom: "In the language that you are dreaming in, there you'll definitely find the truth that you seek". Since then, I focused mainly in the Hellenic spiritual path.[20]

A few years after arranging his first rituals in Greece, he founded the polytheist journal *Diipetes* (1991-2012),[21] and the following year he published his first book on the topic of polytheism. After allegedly having been contacted in 1993-94 by a group of people who claimed that they had knowledge of an uninterrupted tradition of pre-Christian Greek religion, Rassias began incorporating new elements into his practices, such as texts by the neo-Platonic scholar George Gemistos Plethon. Shortly after, in July 1997, he founded the religious organisation Ypato Symboulio ton Hellenon Ethnikon, usually simply referred to as YSEE.[22]

YSEE is one of the largest, most well-known and studied groups in Greece.[23] It is a non-profit organisation that has members and international chapters in the US and other countries, and members refer to it as an umbrella organisation. However, despite this claim, this group seems to be primarily headed by Vlassis Rassias, who also often functions as the main representative and spokesperson. In 2008, on the winter solstice,[24] Labrys Latreutiki Koinotita (Labrys Religious Community)[25] was founded in Athens.[26] Among the founders were a number of

15 In order fully to understand the patchwork of religious receptions of Greek pre-Christian history, sociologist Colin Campbell's famous term "the cultic milieu" may be useful. Campbell describes this as a milieu which includes "all deviant belief systems and their associated practices" as well as the "collectivities, institutions, individuals, and media of communication associated with these beliefs". Campbell in Kaplan & Lööw 2002, 14.
16 Although he refers to himself as "former associate professor" on social media, the website for his annual festival *Prometheia* describes him as: "the Stockholm University Professor of Philosophy, dr. Tryphon Olympios". https://prometheia.wordpress.com/.
17 Kostopoulos earned his PhD in Business Economics (Swedish *företagsekonomi*) from Stockholm University with his dissertation *The Decline of the Market: the ruin of capitalism and anti-capitalism*, published in 1987. A review of the dissertation is available at http://nationalekonomi.se/filer/pdf/155joa.pdf accessed 11 May 2018.
18 See https://www.rassias.gr
19 Vlassis Rassias, personal communication, June, 2013.
20 "Voice of Olympus Interviews: Hercules Invictus Interviews Vlassis Rassias". http://herculesinvictus.net/voiceofolympusinterviews/Vlassis_Rassias.html accessed 11 May 2018.
21 The title *Diipetes*, which means "Sent by Zeus", was subtitled "In Defense of the Ancient Psyche".
22 Leading up to the foundation of YSEE, Rassias had established ties with other contemporary Hellenic polytheist groups in Sparta and Thessaly in 1993, leading to a temporary coalition of groups in 1995-96.
23 Fotiou 2014; Voulgarakis 2014.
24 Labrys and other contemporary Hellenic polytheists perform rituals at solstices and equinoxes, as well as new and full moons. Although some claim that this is based on ancient Greek traditions, it seems more likely to be an inspiration from contemporary Anglo-Saxon paganism or Wicca.
25 Henceforth simply referred to as 'Labrys'.
26 See: http://www.labrys.gr/en/about.html

former members of YSEE, including Christos Pandion Panopoulos, who had been a protegé of Vlassis Rassias, and whom Rassias had hoped would at some point take over the reins of YSEE.[27] These former members had become dissatisfied with the organisational structure and what they viewed as lack of autonomy in YSEE, as well as a polemical tendency in public communication, and had decided to break away and start a new, more egalitarian and open religious community that did not engage in the same level of public debate, but would still perform rituals open to the public.

Apart from YSEE and Labrys there are a number of other groups in Greece, many of which are centred around Athens. However, since my own fieldwork has mainly focused on Labrys and to a lesser extent on YSEE, and since the present article only attempts to provide a cursory view of the wider milieu, I shall just mention the more significant groups.[28] The Helliniki Hetaireia Archaiophilon,[29] which also refers to itself as the Societas Hellenica Antiquariorum and Dodecatheon. is a group[30] led by Panayiotis Marinis.[31] This community, often referred to by the contemporary Hellenic polytheists I have talked to simply as the "Marinis group", is based in Athens; it has been around since the 1990s and is still active, performing public and private rituals and publishing books. This group received some Greek and international media attention in the years leading up to the 2004 Summer Olympic Games in Athens, when they (alongside a number of other contemporary Hellenic polytheists, including members of the group Heliodromion) objected to the commercial use (and the specific design) of Athena and Apollo as the official mascots of the 2004 Summer Olympics. The objection took the form of a petition, signed by 378 Greek citizens with their names, addresses and professions,[32] and supposedly also a €3 million lawsuit.[33]

Another Greek contemporary Hellenic polytheist group is The Heliodromion Society,[34] who describe their activities as "the research, study and application of the cultural elements that can turn today's mechanical and submitted to alien forces man, into an enlightened being, worthy to be called Human (Anthropos)".[35] For a number of years, Heliodromion published the magazine *Romfaia*,[36] which was described as "one of the activated 'rays' in Heliodromion's field of action". Like a number of other contemporary Hellenic polytheist groups in Greece, they also publish books through their own publishing company Heliodromion Publications. While some of these are by Ancient Greek authors such as Proclus, Apollonius the Sophist, Porphyry of Tyre and even the Christian grammarian Stephanos of Byzantium, others are modern works on topics that include women's emancipation, Gaia theory and the (hyper-)diffusionist theory of "the Hellenic origin of the Araucans of Chile".[37] In their description of the role of the reception of the past in the present as a "reconstruction" combined with a new elements and responses to "the new needs of our time", The Heliodromion Society combine a pessimistic view of the present with an optimistic view of how the virtues of the past may be used to shape the future:

Living in today's age and overcoming all kinds of difficulties as we go along, we are called as modern Hellenes (Greeks)

27 Vlassis Rassias, personal communication, June 2013.

28 In my research I have identified more than 10 active groups in Greece, most of which are based in Athens. There are no statistics on the number of members, but my estimate based on my knowledge of some groups, interviews with group founders and information about the number of participants in larger collective events such as festivals is that there are at least one thousand (and perhaps many more) active contemporary Hellenic polytheists in Athens, and several thousand more around the country. Beyond this, there is a much larger milieu of people with little or no group affiliation.

29 The name could be translated as "Greek Society of the Friends of Ancient Things" or "Greek Society of the Friends of the Ancients".

30 Officially recognised as a non-profit company (*Mi Kerdoskopiki Etaireia*).

31 See http://dodecatheon.blogspot.se/ accessed 12 May 2018.

32 www.heliodromion.gr/palaio/e_nea1.htm accessed 12 May 2018.

33 *Ekathemerini*, 19 June 2002.

34 Old website: http://www.heliodromion.gr/palaio/index.htm New website: http://www.heliodromion.gr/index.shtml. Both accessed 12 May 2018.

35 http://www.heliodromion.gr/palaio/e-skopoi.html accessed 17 May 2018.

36 *Romfaia* is the term used in a number of Ancient Greek sources to refer to either a type of spear or sword. The now discontinued magazine of the Heliodromion Society should not be confused with another Greek web-based magazine of the same name, http://www.romfea.gr/, which is an Orthodox Christian church news site active since 2007.

37 http://www.heliodromion.gr/palaio/e_araoukanoi.html accessed 12 May 2018.

to recollect our Ancient Knowledge and open a New Way for the Spiritual Renaissance of Hellas (Greece) and all healthy Mankind.[38]

It should be noted that in this combination of pessimism and hope, criticism of the present and idealisation of the potential role of the past in the transformation of the future, The Heliodromion Society echoes sentiments that seem to be prevalent in a number of the Greek contemporary Hellenic polytheist groups.

The last contemporary Hellenic polytheist group I shall introduce is ELLIN.A.I.S.[39] This group, which was founded in 2005, is still very active and has arranged a number of public rituals in order to direct attention to their demands for recognition from the state, which they have obtained to a limited extent.[40] In 2007 they performed a lengthy ritual spectacle at the temple of Olympian Zeus in downtown Athens, which resulted in massive media coverage and criticism from Orthodox clergy, including the words of Father Efstathios Kollas quoted above. This group has several times ignored the prohibition against holding rituals in Ancient temples or at archaeological sites, and even performed a ritual on the Acropolis in September 2008.[41] One of the group's most famous spokespersons is the former advertising executive, now High Priestess Doretta Peppa, who during the same period as the controversial rituals at the Acropolis and the Temple of the Olympian Zeus was the (self-exposed) protagonist of much media attention due to her claim to be in possession of some early sketches by Vincent van Gogh.[42]

Finally, it should be noted that beyond the many groups (some more well consolidated than others) that in some way or another re-interpret pre-Christian Greek religion, there is a much larger and less organised reli-gious milieu, which includes study groups who meet in local restaurants and cafés or in private homes to discuss religious or philosophical topics, and a large number of cultural organisations that reinterpret Ancient Greek music, theatre[43] and dance, as well as alternative medicine and martial arts. Apart from the organised communities, study groups, cultural re-interpreters and re-enactors and social events such as festivals, the religious reception of pre-Christian Greece in contemporary contexts is also present in a number of fringe right-wing political radicalist groups that award Antiquity a special place in their worldview. One religiously oriented fringe reception of Greek antiquity that seems to be particularly popular in extreme right-wing political circles is the conspiracy theory about the so-called Epsilon Omada (Epsilon Team), an imagined anti-Semitic secret society with roots in both Ancient Greece and outer space. The Epsilon Omada theories have been around since the late 1970s. Another much more recent but somewhat related phenomenon is the personal cult centred around Artemis Sorras[44] and his organisation the Ellinon Syneleusis (the Assembly of Greeks). Some of Sorras' theories seem to have been taken directly from the mythological substratum of the Epsilon Team conspiracy theories. For example, his notion that Greeks are the only true humans and the rest of humanity are aliens who want to dilute Greek DNA as a part of some nefarious master plan[45] is very reminiscent of some of the fundamental tropes of Epsilon conspiracy theories, where "true Greeks" possess a so-called *Ichor* gene, and are the only real humans, who are at war with "the Jews" (and in some versions of the theory also the Chinese), who are referred to in dehumanising terms, such as "draconians" or creatures made of condensed methane.[46] Although it is perhaps not at the core of the group's practices, the Ellinon Syneleusis have been ob-

---

38   http://www.heliodromion.gr/palaio/e-skopoi.html accessed 12 May 2018.

39   *Ellinon Archaiothriskon Ieron Somateion* (The Holy Association of Greek Ancient Religion). http://ellinais.gr/

40   Voulgarakis 2014, 93.

41   Nellas 2008.

42   McElroy 2008.

43   In Athens, perhaps the most influential theatrically oriented religious/philosophical organisation is the Ideotheatron (founded by Radamanthy Anastasaki in 1991), which offers a number of courses and lectures on topics such as Orphicism, Pythagoreanism, Platonism and mysticism and publishes books on the topic of Ancient Greece. See: https://www.ideotheatron.gr/ accessed 12 May 2018.

44   See: http://www.artemis-sorras.gr/

45   Chondrogiannos 2017.

46   Makeeff 2018

served performing ceremonial prayers to Zeus at public rallies.[47]

The reception of places, objects and texts

As illustrated by the rituals performed by ELLIN.A.I.S. at the Acropolis and the temple of the Olympian Zeus, locations considered to have special historical value are of great importance to contemporary Hellenic polytheist groups in Greece. The religious community Labrys regularly use the *Museion* on Philippappou Hill in Athens, and it is a common practice in many groups to visit archaeological sites or natural sites such as caves for special ritual occasions. The role of places viewed as significant for religious practice may be viewed as a case of embedding historical narrative in the physical environment, which although particularly relevant in the context of contemporary Hellenic polytheism in contemporary Greece has been a recurring practice throughout the history of modern Greece.[48] Among contemporary Hellenic polytheists, this tendency reflects a wish to build a culture of recurring ritual practice where time and space weave together, as calendrical rituals are connected to their Ancient counterparts.

Whereas places are often employed in ritual contexts as focal points of stability, objects tend to have multifunctional roles. Most groups have a large collection of paraphernalia, such as statues, ceramics, masks, clothing, thyrsos-staffs and musical instruments (including obviously exotic artefacts such as South American percussion instruments and Tibetan singing bowls), which are often employed for a variety of purposes. Many of these are bought in tourist shops or museums (which does not seem to pose any problems of authenticity, but are rather viewed pragmatically as affordable and entirely acceptable ways of engaging with material culture), while other artefacts such as masks, clothing and musical instruments are frequently made by specialised artisans in the contemporary Hellenic polytheist milieu. In some instances, items (as well as performative elements of rituals) are borrowed from existing Greek traditional

festivals. One example of this culture of "borrowing" is found in the Phallephoria, a Phallic procession which has taken place in Athens in February each year since 2014, co-arranged by the groups Labrys and ELLIN.A.I.S. for a few years and in the past two years performed separately by these groups with a week's interval. Although loosely inspired by sources from Antiquity, this ritual procession includes costumes from the Skyros Goat Festival and music, songs and some paraphernalia from the Bourani festival in Tyrnavos, and temporally located in the carnival week, all of which indicate a strategic and negotiated re-inscription of meaning upon the elements borrowed from both Antiquity and contemporary rural and national traditions. In the case of texts, we see a combination of the stability sought after in places and the malleability and re-inscription of meaning found in material culture. The textual reception of contemporary Hellenic polytheist groups includes the uses of Homeric hymns, Classical drama, Roman texts, Hellenistic texts and texts from late Antiquity (such as the hymns of Proclus), as well as the late Byzantine hymns of George Gemisto Plethon. In addition, social media and academic studies play a significant role in the textual cultures of contemporary Hellenic polytheists.

Among contemporary Hellenic polytheists in Greece, places, objects and texts all function as palimpsests upon which new meaning and new contexts are inscribed, as ideas about authenticity and chronology are fluid and constantly negotiated. In the context of reception studies, studying the negotiation of such aspects may shed light on issues of identity, social organisation and distribution of power, as well as a sense of freedom, autonomy and even playfulness that my research indicates has attracted many who were discontent with the lack of personal freedom of interpretation in their previous lives as Orthodox Christians.

---

47 Chrysopoulos 2017. For a performance of the oath, see 'Artemis Sorras – orkomosia sta dervenakia argolidas', 11 March 2015, YouTube. https://www.youtube.com/watch?time_continue=676&v=1NO4To9ilHo accessed 17 May 2018.
48 The Delphic Festivals of Angelos Sikelianos and Eva Palmer could be viewed as a similar phenomenon.

An Ethnographic Approach to Reception Studies?[49]

As pointed out by Herzfeld, "ancient Greece is the idealized spiritual and intellectual ancestor of Europe".[50] As researchers of Antiquity know, this idealisation has taken many forms throughout history. It would be tempting to read Herzfeld's division of spiritual and intellectual as a distinction between a tendency to mythologise the origins of nations and the meaning of individuals of one hand, and the history and lineages of Western philosophical thought on the other. However, in the category 'intellectual' we should also include scientific thought, which warrants an investigation and open discussion of the potential risk of idealisations of Antiquity by the very same scholars that study it. In its inception, reception studies represented a new way of analysing texts, which marked a clear break from the prevalent scientific paradigm at the time. However, although still a dynamic discipline that is constantly evolving and challenging its own fundamental assumptions, it seems to me that the combined elements of the revolutionary aspect of Reception Studies and the somewhat custodian elements of Classical Studies may have contributed to a certain degree of conservative protectionism in the guise of open-minded innovation and self-scrutiny in Classical Reception Studies.

As scholars (and as human beings) we all occasionally project our pre-conceived notions of authenticity, relevance or aesthetic value upon the people, things and phenomena we interact with. Nevertheless, I believe that it is our duty as scholars to be as aware of such value judgements as possible, and to bring them to the attention of ourselves and each other constantly. Choosing a topic for research inevitably means ignoring other topics. It is an expression of distinction, of taste, of idiosyncrasies, ultimately of power and potentially even of epistemological hegemony. In 2006 Professor Charles Martindale described Classical Reception Studies as encompassing "all

work concerned with postclassical material" (Martindale 2006, 1), a definition so all-encompassing that one would expect it to include even ethnographic studies. However, less than a decade later[51] Martindale distinguished more discriminatingly:

Classics is more alive to my thinking in Joyce's *Ulysses* or the poetry of Seamus Heaney than in Gladiator (2000: Ridley Scott). And does Gladiator or Alexander (2004: Oliver Stone) initiate us into a serious or profound dialogue with antiquity? (of course a film *could* achieve this — Agora (2009: Alejandro Amenábar) comes closer). To avoid misunderstanding I say again that what is wrong with Gladiator in terms of its suitability for a Classics syllabus is not that it is a popular film but that it does not present a thoroughly imagined classical world. Ancient subject matter on its own should not confer such suitability.[52]

Martindale's rejection of some films, but not others, depending on their level of imagination, or the degree of seriousness or profundity of the dialogue we may engage in with them, seems to me a highly subjective and un-scientific method of selection, but raises a number of questions that I believe we need to address in the open, rather than through more or less transparent implicit choices in our work. What should we study or not study? Are seriousness, beauty or authenticity relevant criteria for selecting or discarding data? Are there people, things or phenomena that are not relevant (or worthy) objects or topics of study? Similarly to Martindale's distinction between different films, some classical scholars discard the reception of antiquity in new religious movements as inauthentic and therefore irrelevant. One example of this stance is Mary Beard, who in the *Times Literary Supplement* concluded that "until these eager neo-pagans get real and slaughter a bull or two in central Athens, I shan't worry that they have much to do with ancient religion at all".[53] Meanwhile, others have argued that Classics schol-

---

49 This section is based in part on my conference paper 'Remembrance, Reception and Re-canonisation Among Greek Neopagans; An ethnographic approach to classical reception studies', presented at the conference *Classical Antiquity & Memory*, 28-30 September 2017 at the University of Bonn, Germany.

50 Herzfeld 1987, 1.

51 Although Martindale's 2013 text was addressing the basis for establishing a Classics syllabus and not parameters for a hierarchy of material worthy of study, I would argue that even in the context of a syllabus for teaching Classics and reception, Martindale's distinction between "good" and "bad" types of reception was highly subjective and unconvincing.

52 Martindale 2013, 176. Emphasis added.

53 Beard 2007.

ars should take an interest in contemporary Paganism; Sarah Iles Johnston notes that the bricolage and re-imaginings of contemporary Pagans is not entirely different from that of ancient Greek religious culture, and that even Classical scholars "inevitably re-imagine the gods as we do our work".[54] The difference between Johnston, Beard and Martindale is not whether or not they imagination in their work, but the degree to which they are aware and cautious of it. While Johnston seems very aware of the role of imagination in historical studies and Beard on the other hand seems to have a much more fixed, selective[55] and un-reflexive view of authenticity when it comes to the past, Martindale (of 2013) is somewhere between the two, aware of his subjectivity, but perhaps not reflexive about the role of imagination in his judgements of what is relevant and what is not.

In a recent interview by A. Bakogianni, Professor Lorna Hardwick addressed the question of methods and delineations of the field of Classical Reception in a way that seemed to resonate more with Martindale's 2006 definition than with his 2013 text quoted above:

It is such a wide field that presents so many possibilities. I would actually be quite cautious about saying: "this is what the field is. This is what the methods are". It's exploratory and will continue to be so, and I think actually that is part of the rationale. That there is this continuing re-examination, re-formulation, and really just an open-ended debate.[56]

Hardwick's point about the open-endedness and exploratory nature of Classical Studies mirrors points made by her interviewer A. Bakogianni, who advocated the adoption of concepts such as juxtaposition or simulacra as alternatives to notions of a hierarchical relationship between present and past (found in traditional theories of reception), and that reception "is about our dialogue with the classical past, whatever form that takes, and as a two-way conversation rather than as a monologue prioritizing one over the other".[57] Discarding any example

of a reference to Antiquity categorically, based on idiosyncrasies, is doing a disservice to the discipline, since it limits our view of what is actually happening around us. Any cultural product or practice that claims inspiration from the Greek or Roman past should be examined as an example of a reception of Antiquity, no matter whether it be thoroughly imagined or not. Therefore I find more inspiration in the open approaches of Hardwick, Bakogianni and Martindale's 2006 definition than the more idiosyncratic approaches of Beard (2007) and Martindale (2013).

Depending on our individual educational backgrounds and expertise, we study different types of sources using different methods and base our analyses on specifically selected theories relevant to our academic disciplines. But, the reality of Classical Reception Studies is that it is both a specialised and an interdisciplinary field that shares some theoretical perspectives but differs in methods depending on the sources, which is perhaps why no-one has taken up ethnographic studies yet, although the study of receptions of Antiquity beyond the sphere of art, performance and literature seems to be a possible (and prudent) next step. Popular culture is being studied as well as theatrical performances, so studies of both living, breathing human beings and marginal and perhaps academically "un-informed" receptions are already present in Classical Reception Studies. But why are there no studies of religious groups? Some possible reasons may be that in an interdisciplinary perspective, apart from the Classical scholars, those studying popular culture come from media studies, gaming studies, film studies and literary studies, whereas those studying theatrical studies are typically from theatre studies. None of these disciplines tend to employ ethnographic work. Furthermore, religion is often perceived as something special, and hence perhaps avoided as scholars who are not specialists may see it as somebody else's topic. Finally, I suspect that many scholars working on Classical reception are not aware that there are religious movements

---

54 Johnston 2011, 133.

55 Although bull sacrifice was an important type of sacrifice it was certainly not the only one, and should not be emphasised as the reason why modern interpretations of Ancient Greek rituals should be disregarded. It is clear that the ritual activities of contemporary Hellenic polytheists are innovative and only loosely based on historic practices, but they engage with Antiquity and as such should be researched as a type of reception.

56 My transcript of an interview with Lorna Hardwick by Anastasia Bakogianni 'Classical Reception, Past, Present and Future, with Lorna Hardwick', published 14 March 2014. https://www.youtube.com/watch?v=h_jTT_RfNl8 accessed 12 May 2018.

57 Bakogianni 2016.

that are relevant to the reception of Antiquity, or they know they exist but either find them irrelevant (because they seem inauthentic to them) or view them as a threat to their (intellectual or even emotional) ownership of Antiquity.[58] As Mary Beard says, the great thing about studying Antiquity is that they're all dead, and hence one is not accountable to anyone except one's colleagues and academic critics. But whether we like it or not, contemporary Pagan receptions of Antiquity are intricately connected to the academic study and dissemination of Antiquity. As Stefanie von Schnurbein has recently pointed out in her study of Scandinavian and Germanic contemporary Paganism:

Museums, folklorists, and archeologists themselves participate actively in popularizing the past, often in order to garner public acceptance and thus funding for their research. Evidently, the ideals behind such popularizations change according to the respective contemporary values through which the past is perceived.[59]

Consider for example the role of museums as participants in the making or kindling of the modern mythological imagination. In what I have elsewhere referred to as "the semiotics of strategic gardening",[60] a number of Greek archaeological museums/sites actively engage in staging the imaginative reception of their material by planting trees associated with Ancient gods connected to their location. At the Acropolis there is an olive tree, reminding the spectator of the sacred *Moria* of Classical antiquity; at Delphi laurel trees grow, underlining the connection to Apollo; there is a great oak at Dodona, reminding the spectator of the divinatory practices connected to Zeus; and there are palm trees in the "oasis" at Delos, as an *aide memoire* of the myth of the birth of Apollo.

Referring to points made by Erika Sandström in the case of Swedish museums, von Schnurbein has recently argued that "while a hundred years ago encounters with a venerable history were meant to incite patriotism, today they are meant to nurture empathy, engagement, and equality". However, von Schnurbein adds that they "at times revive older holistic (national-)Romantic identity projects in the process".[61] The presence of religiously entangled trees are but one such example, and as von Schnurbein concludes the contemporary Pagan imagination exists in the context of an "entangled web of scholarship, creative arts, pop culture, esotericism, religion, and politics", where:

Scientific reconstructive attempts and aesthetic appropriation of sources, ideas, and images of the past intersect in a multitude of ways. They are suspended in a field of tension between the transference of tainted or dated knowledge, its rejection where it is recognized, and the enjoyment of the freedom to imaginatively (re-)create.[62]

This (religious) use of academic work in the process of reception, re-construction and re-imagination among individual and social movements has been studied by a number of scholars and is commonly referred to as "readbacks".[63] The phenomenon of readbacks underlines the dynamic relationship between academic work and the contemporary Pagan imagination, and is an additional reason to study contemporary Hellenic polytheism from the perspective of reception studies, as the reception of scholarship and public outreach initiatives evidently plays an important role in the religious innovations of contemporary Pagans. Like Sarah Iles Johnston's argument about the role of the imagination in the interplay between scholarship and contemporary Paganism, that we as scholars

58 I am reminded of an episode which happened some years ago, when I asked a Greek historian who studied receptions of Antiquity if he had looked into contemporary Hellenic polytheists. He replied in a less than calm voice: "Those crazy people? No. I know nothing about them!" I am entirely certain that he knew something about them, since they are discussed in the Greek media every so often, and I have never before encountered a Greek who did not know at least that the phenomenon existed. It was clear from our brief conversation that the historian in question did not want to know, because he found the polytheists ridiculous. Although this is a valid opinion as a private person, I find it questionable as a scientific position if one is a scholar of the reception of Antiquity.
59 von Schnurbein 2016, 295-6.
60 Makeeff 2017.
61 von Schnurbein 2016, 295-7.
62 von Schnurbein 2016, 295-7.
63 Hornborg 2009, 61-77.

of antiquity or reception "inevitably re-imagine the gods as we do our work", von Schnurbein has pointed out that:

Scholarly constructions of wholeness and coherence are themselves dependent on operations which belong to the realm of the aesthetic: imaginations of a whole, a Gestalt, and experiential intuition, through which the fragments are held together and the gaps between them filled.[64]

The main obstacle in the development of a research endeavour of ethnographic work informed and aided by Classical studies at the moment seems to be the existence of contesting views of authenticity. Contemporary Hellenic polytheists base their innovative practices in part on the work of scholars (although sometimes on outdated findings), but their practices are often perceived as being inauthentic and hence irrelevant. Let me here return to the objections made by Mary Beard, that "until these eager neo-pagans get real and slaughter a bull or two in central Athens, I shan't worry that they have much to do with ancient religion at all". Besides the fact that sacrificing bulls could in no way be justifiably argued to be *the only* type of ancient (Greek) religion, it seems that Mary Beard ignores another very important point. Contemporary Hellenic polytheists are rarely interested in a complete return to Ancient practices or life. On the contrary, they are keenly aware that they live in the 21st century. They drive cars, wear jeans, use cell phones and in general tend to view the role of their chosen Ancient traditions as something that connects them to the past of their country or ethnicity, and which must be creatively and selectively re-imagined and brought into the modern context of (urban) life. Regarding the example Beard uses – animal sacrifice – most of the contemporary Hellenic polytheists I have interviewed do not seem to consider this a necessary part of what they view as a modern authentic reception of Ancient Greek religion. As one Athenian contemporary Hellenic polytheist told me, "personally, I'm against animal sacrifices, maybe in the past it had a meaning but situations have changed and as the Hellenic religion is evolved through the ages such practices should also evolve".[65] Although they sometimes

romanticise the past, the vast majority of contemporary Hellenic polytheists I have talked to feel that just as religion changed over time before the Christianisation of Greece, so should its modern reception be moulded to suit the challenges and circumstances of the present.

The need for collaboration

As Bakogianni has pointed out, "reception involves so many different perspectives that no single person can ever hope to master it all". This is certainly true in the case of contemporary Pagan receptions of ancient historical cultures. In my own work I have benefited greatly from discussions with scholars from other disciplines, such as archaeology, Classical studies and modern Greek studies, and while I have encountered rejection and ridicule of my subject matter, I have been fortunate enough to have been welcomed by a number of experts in Greek antiquity who seemed interested in the contemporary Pagan phenomenon and were aware that neither myself nor the contemporary Hellenic polytheists claimed that they wanted to replicate the past in its entirety. Bakogianni concludes her observation that the plethora of perspectives involved in reception studies means that "we must work together in order to produce research that maintains its integrity and is truly inclusive and interdisciplinary".[66] As is probably clear from the previous pages, I agree wholeheartedly with this observation. There is a great potential outcome from interdisciplinary approaches, in particular in the case of the contemporary Pagan receptions of Ancient Greece and Rome. Firstly, there is almost no research on contemporary Hellenic or Roman polytheists, and even less written in the English language. Secondly, philological angles are often lacking in ethnographic studies on contemporary Pagans (including my own study, I must admit). Expertise in Ancient or Modern Greek could provide critical perspectives on the reception and translation of Ancient texts by contemporary Pagans. The same is naturally the case when it comes to the reception of material culture and places. Here archaeologists could contribute greatly to the nuanced study of contemporary Hellenic polytheist practices. Furthermore, beyond the study of how contem-

---

64   von Schnurbein 2016, 297.
65   Interview, 25 April 2017.
66   Bakogianni 2016.

porary Pagans interact with textual and material culture, I believe that an interdisciplinary study of contemporary Pagan receptions of Antiquity could lead to new theoretical and methodological developments in the field of reception studies. Finally, rigorous scholarship in this understudied area would lead to increased awareness of the role of reception in shaping contemporary social movements and in turn could lead to improvements in the freedom of practice and belief of such religious minorities. While this is perhaps not a primary objective for any scholar, it should be borne in mind that although a number of international charters[67] guarantee both religious freedom and the right to manifest one's beliefs through practice without persecution, the ambition for state recognition for religious minorities is an ongoing struggle for many in a number of countries across the world, and although we as scholars may not want to become involved in such conflicts, our work may be used by both advocates and opponents of the rights and recognition of minority groups. However, the absence of scholarly studies also plays a role in the same quests for recognition. In this light, choosing not to study the phenomenon is as important and consequential a choice as choosing to do so.

Conclusion

Contemporary Paganism is a global phenomenon, which takes distinct forms depending on the regional contexts in which it develops. The contemporary Hellenic polytheist phenomenon in modern Greece has a history of a little more than three decades. In this time, many groups have reinterpreted the ancient past in a number of ways, some involving radical political views, while others focus more on personal transformation. Contemporary Hellenic polytheist groups and individuals engage with places such as archaeological sites, museums and natural structures such as caves, lakes and rivers, often in order to establish recurring ritual practices where time (history) and place intersect. They engage with the material and textual culture of antiquity in creative ways, and in their creative re-interpretations and re-configurations, the rituals (and ritual objects) of contemporary Hellenic polytheists may

be viewed as palimpsests. Many contemporary Hellenic polytheists are very aware of their selective and anachronistic uses of the past, and furthermore do not want to reconstruct any particular period in its entirety. Rather, they view their practices as modern transformations of Ancient Greek religion, accommodated to suit life in the 21st century. While some scholars reject the contemporary Hellenic polytheist phenomenon as inauthentic, others take a self-reflexive stance and argue that contemporary Paganism and scholarship are intricately connected, and that contemporary Paganism is worthy of study. I agree with this second position, and have argued for the development of interdisciplinary research initiatives involving experts on Antiquity as well as scholars with ethnographic experience and knowledge of the contemporary development of religious and social movements.

To conclude, I am not arguing that there is a need for some all-encompassing re-evaluation of the foundations of Classical Reception Studies. Rather, I find that Classical Reception Studies is a vibrant and rigorous field with great courage and interest in new phenomena. I am not criticising the ways Classical Reception Studies are already being conducted, but the limits of the materials chosen for study. Within the accepted areas of study, such as literature, drama and film, the scope is wide, but the religious lives of living people seem to be missing entirely. I suggest that the next natural step for Classical Reception Studies is to study living people and their practices. This could be done ethnographically, but also by combining textual and ethnographic studies in cyber-ethnographies. My own PhD project is an attempt to combine ethnography and Classical Reception Studies and it is my hope that others will be inspired to do similar work, either as individual researchers or in the context of interdisciplinary projects.

TAO THYKIER MAKEEFF
History of Religions and Religious Behavioural Science
Centre for Theology and Religious Studies
Lund University
Box 192, S-221 00 Lund, Internpost hämtställe 30
tao.thykier_makeeff@ctr.lu.se

---

67   For example, the Universal Declaration of Human Rights (UDHR) and the International Covenant on Civil and Political Rights (ICCPR) (which should be interpreted in the light of the UN Human Rights Committee's General Comment no. 22), as well as the EU Guidelines on the promotion and protection of freedom of religion or belief.

Bibliography

Aitamurto, K. & S. Simpson (eds) 2013
Modern Pagan and Native Faith movements in central and eastern Europe, Durham.

Andriotis, K. 2009
'Early Travellers to Greece and their Modern Counterparts', paper presented at *Tourist Experiences: Meanings, Motivations, Behaviours*, 1 April 2009, University of Central Lancashire, Preston., UK.

Apostol, R. & A. Bakogianni (eds) 2018
Locating Classical Receptions on Screen: Masks, Echoes, New York.

Bakogianni, A. 2016
'What is so "classical" about Classical Reception? Theories, Methodologies and Future Prospects', *Codex – Revista de Estudos Clássicos* 4, 96-113.

Beard, M. 2007
'Paganism without the blood', *A Don's Life, The Times Literary Supplement*, 26 January.

Bishop, C. 2018
'Reading Antiquity in Metro Redux', *Games and Culture* vol no., 1-20.

Blanshard, A. & K. Shahabudin 2011
Classics on Screen: Ancient Greece and Rome on Film, Bristol.

Brabant, M. 2007
'Ancient Greek gods' new believers', *BBC News*, 21 January, http://news.bbc.co.uk/2/hi/europe/6285397.stm accessed 7 January 2019.

Campbell, C. 2002
'The Cult, the Cultic Milieu and Secularization', in *The Cultic Milieu: Oppositional Subcultures in an Age of Globalization*, J. Kaplan & H. Lööw (eds), Oxford, page nos.

Chondrogiannos, T. 2018
'I Spent Two Months with a Cult That Believes it Can Solve Greece's Debt', *Vice*, accessed 11 May 2018, https://www.vice.com/en_uk/article/ypeza7/i-spent-two-months-with-a-cult-that-believes-it-can-solve-greeces-debt accessed 11 May 2018.

Chrysopoulos, P. 2017
'Greeks Gather at Acropolis Foothill to Declare their Faith to Zeus', *Greek Reporter*, http://greece.greekreporter.com/2017/02/21/greeks-gather-at-acropolis-foothill-to-declare-their-faith-to-zeus-video/ accessed 17 May 2018.

Ekathemerini, 2004
'2004 mascots "parody" gods', *Ekathemerini*, 19 June 2002. http://www.ekathimerini.com/6531/article/ekathimerini/news/2004mascots-parody-gods accessed 12 May 2018.

Esterhammer, A. (ed.) 2002
Romantic Poetry, Amsterdam.

Fotiou, E. 2014
'"We are the Indians of Greece": Indigeneity and Religious Revitalization in Modern Greece', *Crosscurrents* 64.2, 219-35.

Gill, D. W. J. 2013
'Cultural Tourism in Greece at a Time of Economic Crisis', *Journal of Eastern Mediterranean Archaeology & Heritage Studies* 1.3, 233-42.

Grigoriadis, I. 2013
Instilling Religion in Greek and Turkish Nationalism: A "Sacred Synthesis", London, New York & Shanghai.

Herzfeld, M. 1987
Anthropology through the Looking-Glass: Critical Ethnography in the Margins of Europe, Cambridge.

Hornborg, A. 2009
'Owners of the Past: Readbacks or Tradition in Mi'kmaq Narratives', in *Native American Performance and Representation*, S. E. Wilmer (ed.), Arizona, 61-77.

Johnston, S. I. 2011
'Whose Gods are These? A Classicist Looks at Neopaganism', in *Dans le laboratoire de l'historien des religions: Mélanges offerts à Philippe Borgeaud*, F. P. Rescendi & Y. V. Olokhine (eds), Genève, page nos.

Lowe, D. 2009
'Playing With Antiquity: Videogame Receptions of the Classical World', in *Classics for All: Reworking Antiquity in Mass Culture*, L. Dunstan & K. Shahabudin (eds), Newcastle upon Tyne, page nos.

Martindale, C. 2006
'Introduction: Thinking Through Reception', in *Classics and the Uses of Reception*, C. Martindale & R. F. Thomas (eds), Maldon and Oxford, 1-13.

101

Martindale, C. 2013
'Reception – "a new humanism"? Receptivity, pedagogy, the transhistorical', *Classical Receptions Journal* 5.2, 169-83.

Paul, J. 2010
'Cinematic receptions of antiquity: the current state of play', *Classical Receptions Journal* 2.1, 136-55.

Makeeff, T. T. 2017
'Remembrance, Reception and Re-canonisation Among Greek Neopagans; An ethnographic approach to Classical reception studies', paper presented at *Classical Antiquity & Memory*, 2830 September 2017 at the University of Bonn, Germany.

Makeeff, T. T. 2018
'Was Aristotle an anti-Semitic alien? Conspiracy Theory, Ufology, and the Colonization of the Past in Contemporary Greece', in *Brill Handbook of Conspiracy Theory and Religion*, Leiden, page nos.

McElroy, D. 2018
'Family claims back seized "Van Gogh notebook"', *The Telegraph*, 1 January 2008. https://www.telegraph.co.uk/news/worldnews/1574238/Family-claims-back-seized-Van-Gogh-notebook.html accessed 17 May 2018.

Miller, J. 2004
'Return of the Hellenes', *Worlds of Difference,*. http://homelands.org/stories/return-of-the-hellenes/ accessed 17 May 2018.

Nellas, D. 2018
'Pagans pray for protection of Acropolis', *Associated Press*, 1 September 2008, https://www.deseretnews.com/article/700255437/Pagans-pray-for-protection-of-Acropolis.html accessed 17 May 2018.

von Schnurbein, S. 2016
Norse Revival: Transformations of Germanic Neopaganism, Leiden.

Voulgarakis, E. 2014
'Mary, Athena, and Guanyin: What the Church, the Demos, and the Sangha Can Teach Us about Religious Pluralism and Doctrinal Conformity to Socio-cultural Standards', in *Experiencing Globalizations*, D. Nault, B. Dawei, E. Voulgarakis, R. Paterson & C. Suva (eds), London, New York, Melbourne & Delhi, page nos.

Winkler, M. M. 2001
Classical Myth & Culture in the Cinema, Oxford.

Winkler, M. M. 2009
Cinema and Classical Texts: Apollo's New Light, Cambridge.

Zacharia, K. 2014
'Postcards from Metaxas' Greece: The Uses of Classical Antiquity in Tourism Photography', in *Re-imagining the Past: Antiquity and Modern Greek Culture*, D. Tziovas (ed.), *Oxford Scholarship Online*, 186-208.

The Classical in Contemporary Sculpture:
A Global View

BENTE KIILERICH

Abstract

The early 21st century has witnessed a growing interest in revisiting ancient sculpted images: the Venus de Milo, the Nike of Samothrace, the Apollo Belvedere and many other renowned antique statues have served as points of departure for the creation of new works by artists of very different cultural backgrounds. This article presents examples of classical borrowings in contemporary European, African, American and Asian sculpture. It also addresses the concept of modern Classicisms and tries to identify why Greek and Roman antiquity continues to fascinate artists in the 21st century.

Introduction

Several recent exhibitions have focused on the interaction between Classical and contemporary art. In 2014, 'A Thousand Doors', at the American School of Classical Studies in Athens, showed the works of a dozen contemporary artists, several of whom revisited ancient forms. One example was the British artist Daniel Silver (b. 1972) whose installation 'Dig', from 2013, brought the viewer into contact with purported finds from a pseudo–archaeological excavation (Fig. 1). Athens also hosted the 'Liquid Antiquity' exhibition held at the Benaki Museum in spring 2017, 'liquid' suggesting the fluid quality of the idea, as well as playing on Zygmunt Bauman's concept of "liquid modernity".[1] 'Modern Classicisms' was the title of a conference held in London in November 2017, with the ensuing exhibition, 'The Classical Now', on show from March to April 2018.[2]

Solo exhibitions have similarly embraced the classical sphere. At the Venice Biennale in 2017, British artist Damien Hirst staged a show entitled 'The Wreck of the Unbelievable'. It consisted of large installations of sculptures with crusted surfaces, giving the impression of having been found in the sea and reminiscent of finds from the Antikythera shipwreck.[3] Although more baroque than classical in taste, the Damian Hirst exhibition is an eloquent example of the general fascination with sunken treasure, mythology, Antiquity and the Classical world.

The problematic concepts 'classical' and 'classicism'

The term 'classical' can be understood on many levels: a) it can indicate a discrete historical period, namely the

---

1   Holmes & Marta (eds) 2017; Baumann 2000, "liquid modernity" concerns the late modern emphasis on shift and movement, the constant changing of places, jobs, etc.
2   Squire, Cahill & Allen 2018; cf. the review of the exhibition by Besnard 2018.
3   Greene & Leidwanger 2017.

Fig. 1. *Daniel Silver, 'Dig', 2013. Installation exhibited in the American School of Classical Studies, Athens, 2014. (Photo: author).*

one known as the Classical period in Greece, 480-323 BC; b) it can designate the style of this period; c) it can be expanded to stand for Greco-Roman Antiquity in a wider chronological frame, roughly encompassing the late Archaic to the late Antique era; d) it can refer to works of later periods made in a style that recalls that of Greece and Rome; e) it can be used as an aesthetic category in a broad sense that indicates qualities such as symmetry and harmony; and f) it can denote value, with a similar meaning to the term 'first-class'.[4] It is clear that 'classical' can be used with a wide range of meanings and in very different contexts.

As the British philosopher Thomas Hulme noted in 1912, words like 'classical' tend to go through three phases: at first they carry a precise meaning, then they acquire a dozen meanings, and finally they have three hundred meanings.[5] That is, one can use the concept quite freely with regard to both form and content. As early as the 18th century, Joshua Reynolds aptly defined 'the classical' as a store of common property from which each person could take the materials he or she wanted.[6] By now, 'the classical' and its various derived 'classicisms' have seemingly acquired an endless potential of meanings. This can be witnessed in the so-called modern classicisms.

---

4   Tatarkiewicz 1958 limits its uses to four categories. For a thorough discussion of the concepts of 'classical' and 'classicism' and their applications, see Settis 2006.

5   Hulme 1912; Morley 1988, 61; Kiilerich 2006, 263.

6   Reynolds 1778, VI, 1, 464-8.

Modern Classicisms

The last quarter of the 20th century saw an upsurge of 'classicisms' in the visual arts. These have been variously referred to as 'new', 'modern' or 'contemporary classicisms', or 'classical sensibilities' (all rather imprecise terms used for want of an alternative).[7] Many of the artists associated with such classicisms are, unsurprisingly, Italian. Classical elements are present in paintings (*pittura colta*),[8] but it is in sculpture that artists make the most direct references to archaeological artefacts, some modern works copying antique statues exactly. One example of this trend is Giulio Paolini (b. 1940). His 'Mimesi' compositions consist of either two identical plaster casts of the Venus de'Medici or two identical plaster casts of Praxiteles' Hermes (1975-76). One of his 'L'altra figura' installations (1984-86) takes its departure point in the Marathon Boy, again reproduced in plaster.[9] In a different vein, in the early 1980s Mario Ceroli (b. 1938) reformulated the Artemision Zeus and the Riace bronzes as three-dimensional sculptures in wood and in reliefs and painted panels.[10]

Again in the 1980s, the British artist Edward Allington (1951-2017), one of the names represented in the 'A Thousand Doors' exhibition in Athens in 2014, revisited antique architectural elements and antique statues. Reproduced in painted resin cast, the images are often multiplied; for instance, there are two red Apollo Belvedere busts, three Discoboloi in red, white and green, nine Capitoline Venuses, also in red, white and green, with the bases similarly painted, while 'Victory Boxed' counts no less than 99 small Nike of Samothrace figures (1987).[11] Allington's sculptures epitomise many of the characteristics of late 20th-century classicism: the material has changed from expensive to cheap; the colours are changed; the size is reduced; the image is multiplied; and it is differently titled. Allington's 'Tame Time/Venus ad infinitum' (1986) includes 15 small plaster casts of the Venus de Milo, a recurrent figure in modern and contemporary classicism.

No other ancient image has been reused and abused to the same extent as the Venus de Milo. Found accidentally by a farmer in 1820, the statue arrived in Paris the following year.[12] Now known to be Hellenistic, the statue was believed then to be a Classical work, either by Phidias, or stylistically more likely by Praxiteles. Having been forced to return to Italy a great number of ancient art works that had been brought to Paris by Napoleon, the French were desperately in need of antique statues. Venus came to serve the purpose. Throughout the 19th century, the image of Venus de Milo was proliferated through the new photographic medium, and plaster copies in reduced sizes were also fabricated, making it possible to have one's own version of the famous icon.[13] Thus the Venus de Milo became the first truly hyped artwork. While the earliest representations depicted Venus in white and respected her outer form, the attitude changed dramatically in the course of the 20th century as modern artists made surrealist and deconstructionist versions. The image that was to gain the greatest following and have an enduring impact on the arts of the following decades was Salvador Dalí's 'Venus au tirroirs' ('Venus with drawers'), a plaster cast in reduced size – with drawers – from 1936.[14] Since then, numerous artists have referenced the statue and, like Dalí, returned to it on several occasions and revised the image in endless ways. The Venus de Milo remains a focal point in early 21st-century sculpture.

A global classicism in the early 21st century

An interesting aspect of contemporary references to Antiquity is the fact that they are not limited to European artists. European artists of African descent and American

---

7   See, e.g., Sanguinetti, Fochessati & Sborgi 1995; Di Stefano (ed.) 1998; Cuzin *et al.* 2000; Jensen & Wieczorek (eds) 2002. For the interplay of modern art and prehistoric archaeology, see Renfrew 2003.

8   The most prolific of the painters working in a figurative classical style is Carlo Maria Mariani (b. 1931), who is still active. Other 'classical' late 20th-century painters include Alberto Abate and Stefano di Stasio; see Kaiser 2003.

9   Di Stefano (ed.) 1998, 1623; Kiilerich 2006, 246-50.

10   Kiilerich 2006, 258-60.

11   Decter 1988; Kiilerich 2006, 256-7, 262-3; Vout 2018.

12   For the story behind the acquisition, see Curtis 2005.

13   A large number of Venus versions from the 19th through the 20th centuries are discussed by Cuzin, Gaborit & Pasquier 2000, 457-99. See further Salmon 2002; Prettejohn 2006; 2012.

14   Cuzin, Gaborit & Pasquier 2000, 464-5, no. 259; for other Dalí Venuses, *ibid.*, 462-7 (R. Descharnes).

Fig. 2. *Bjørn Nørgaard, 'Hommage à Yves Klein', from the 'Venus spejler – spejler Venus' series, 2005. Statens Museum for Kunst, Copenhagen (photo: author).*

comprises seven compositions: Auto Portrait, Hommage à Yves Klein, The Siberian Brothers, Venus Modification, Burnt Venus, Hidden Sides of Venus and The Promised Land. Except for the burnt Venus, the Venuses are mostly plaster casts, one gilded (Fig. 2).[17] In the gilded Venus, Klein's signature blue colour is splashed on the sculpture's surface, gold being yet another characteristic of Klein's works. While these multimedia compositions are quite complex and rich in associations, 'Recycling Art (Venus de Milo)', from 2009, is deceptively simple: a plaster Venus thrown into a recycling bin. As may be expected, since then, the Venus de Milo has been recycled by several artists, including Nørgaard himself in the installation 'Fake – som i et spejl' ('Fake – as in a Mirror') from 2012. As we shall see, other statues, like the Nike of Samothrace, the Hercules Farnese and the Apollo Belvedere, have also had their share of reuse within the last decade.[18]

One protagonist of the 'Classical Now' exhibition, the Frenchman Léo Caillard (b. 1985), dresses up ancient statues in contemporary clothes. He does not always actually clothe a given sculpture, but primarily manipulates images photographically, so that his photos present the statues in contemporary guise. The Apollo Belvedere, for instance, wears sunglasses and a T-shirt and holds in his outstretched hand a mobile phone, with which he is taking a selfie. Other sculptures are similarly presented wearing blue jeans and other modern clothing.[19] Caillard's series 'Hipster in Stone I–III' (2012-16) depicts, among others, the Hercules Farnese in jeans and a dying warrior from the east pediment of the Athena Aphaia temple at Aegina in a chequered shirt. This was followed by the 'Hipster in Bronze' series (2016-17), which includes shiny busts of the Hercules Farnese and the Apollo Belvedere, both endowed with caps and spectacles.[20]

Apollo Belvedere is also featured in the work of the Italian Francesco Vezzoli (b. 1971). In one image, Vezzoli enters into a dialogue with Antiquity by making his own physique present in the ancient image: 'Self-Portrait as

and Asian artists have also revisited these works – the Classical has become a 'global' visual language shared by all.[15] The point all such works have in common is the reimagining of famous icons of the past.[16]

The Venus de Milo plays an important part in recent works by the Danish sculptor Bjørn Nørgaard (b. 1947). 'Helga from Holte meets Venus from Milo' (2004) consists of plaster casts of a living woman and of Venus dissected and combined in a novel way. The following year Nørgaard presented a more ambitious series: 'Venus spejler – spejler Venus' ('Venus Mirrors – Mirrors Venus'). It

---

15 For globalisation and art, see, e.g., Ratnam 2004.
16 Since many of the works discussed here are of very recent date, relevant publications are mainly confined to short reviews and internet references, including the artists' homepages.
17 Kiilerich 2009, esp. 244-47.
18 For the Nike of Samothrake in contemporary art, see Kiilerich 2018.
19 One may compare the Danish–Norwegian duo Elmgreen & Dragset, who in 'The Thorvaldsen Series' from 2011 presented large photographs of nine of the Neoclassical sculptor's statues dressed in socks, briefs, etc.
20 Squire, Cahill & Allen 2018, 112-22, interview with Caillard.

Fig. 3. *Yinka Shonibare, 'Discus Thrower (after Myron)',
2016. (Yinka Shonibare MBE. All Rights Reserved, DACS/
Artimage 2018. Image courtesy Stephen Friedman Gallery.
Photo: Mark Blower/BONO 2018).*

Apollo Belvedere' from 2015 combines the body of Apollo and the head of Vezzoli, reminding us of the Roman
practice of placing a portrait head on an idealised body.
'Self-Portrait as Apollo Belvedere's Lover' juxtaposes an
Apollo bust and a Vezzoli bust, both executed in white
marble. Another take on Antiquity is seen in the artist's
'Teatro Romano' project, 2014-15, in which he re-in-
terprets the lost polychromy of some ancient sculpted
heads.[21]

One of the more eye-catching recent Italian sculptures is by Francesco Rubino (b. 1960). His 'Vittoria alata'

(Winged Nike) is based on the Nike of Samothrace.[22] In
a short text accompanying the work, the process of constructing the statue, which took place between 2010 and
2013, is documented in words and images.[23] Rubino first
took photos of the statue in the Louvre and subsequently
made sketches based on these. The next stage consisted
of building a new model of the goddess in which part of
the belly and part of the drapery were modelled on the
antique Nike. The main part of the body was made of
horizontal wooden elements attached to a metal arma-
ture.

We reencounter the Nike of Samothrace in 'Splash
Nike' (2011), a work by the Italian-Egyptian artist Omar
Hassan (b. 1987 in Milan). This plaster cast of the Nike is
covered in pink, red, purple, violet and blue paint splash-
es. Venus de Milo appears in both full length and bust
form in works from 2014-2016, similarly sprinkled with
paint running down the white plaster. Hassan's recent
exhibition 'Do Ut Des' took place in the Chiesetta della
Misericordia in Venice in 2017. Using the church space
both as a vehicle for display and as a conceptual part of
the 'Give To Get' installations, the Belvedere torso, seated
on the ground, looks deserted and vulnerable, while the
female figures of Nike, Venus de Milo and the Capitoline
Venus, placed in niches with their backs to the wall, seem
more at ease.[24]

The British-Nigerian Yinka Shonibare MBE (b. 1962)
is known for his colourful sculptures in which ornamen-
tal textiles play an important part. In 2016 he presented
the 'Venus de Milo (after Alexandros)', the 'Capitoline
Venus', the 'Winged Victory of Samothrace', the 'Apollo of the Belvedere (after Leochares)' and the 'Discus
Thrower (after Myron)' (Fig. 3), as well as 'David (after
Michelangelo)' in fibreglass painted with batik patterns
and with globes for heads. Originating in India and In-
donesia, the batik technique involves applying molten
wax as a dye resist directly onto the fabric. Batik cloth
was later mass-fabricated by the Dutch and sold to the
colonies in West Africa. Shonibare points to the material
as a sign of African identity.[25] From the neck down, the

21   http://momaps1.org/exhibitions/view/392 (accessed 25 April 2018).

22   For the antique statue, see most recently Stewart 2016.

23   Iacometti n.d.

24   For the 'Do Ut Des' exhibition, see https://www.continiartuk.com/omar–hassan (accessed 10 March 2018); Kiilerich 2018, 78, fig. 9.

25   http://www.yinkashonibarembe.com (accessed 18 April 2018)

Fig. 4. *Xu Zhen, 'Eternity-Poseidon-Pigeons', 2014. De Haan, Belgium. (Photo: Wikimedia Commons/Art work in the public domain).*

surfaces of the statues are totally covered with decorations in strong colours – yellow, orange, red, violet, blue and green. There is a profound difference between the white surface of the ancient statues (their original colours having disappeared) and their revisited multi-coloured appearance. By associating the decorative patterns with the antique 'icons' of Western art, Shonibare invites viewers to reconsider the conventional priority given to 'fine' art over decorative art.

In contrast with Shonibare's hallmark of colourful compositions, other contemporary artists keep the sculptures white. In the USA, the notorious Jeff Koons (b. 1955) has exploited Antiquity in various ways. Among his recent works, 'Gazing Ball', from 2013, is a series of plaster casts of famous statues – Sleeping Ariadne, the Belvedere Torso, Hercules Farnese, Crouching Aphrodite, a centaur and Lapith woman from the Temple of Zeus at Olympia, the Barberini Faun, in addition to some everyday objects: garden gnomes and letter boxes. All are endowed with a blue glass ball, placed on top of or next to the figure. As

plaster casts – like the earlier works of Giulio Paolini – the images are mass produced, as they have been over the centuries for cast collections. Their basic purpose, then, would be for study rather than art. However, by adding the ball, the artist moves the ready-mades into a different sphere.[26]

Koons' contemporary Barry X Ball (b. 1955) is also concerned with replicas. His approach, however, is totally different. Being interested in the physical crafting of the object, Ball uses computer technology to present new versions of old works. The sculpture is first scanned with a 3D digital scanner and then carved in stone with the aid of a computer program. The chosen stone usually differs from that in which the original was carved. One example is the 'Sleeping Hermaphrodite' (2008-2010), carved in Belgian black marble. Although the hermaphrodite is identical in form to its ancient counterpart, and still resting on Bernini's mattress, the change from white to black has a profound effect on our perception of the sculpture. The playful innocence of the white reclining

26 Holzwarth 2015, 87-90; Holmes & Marta (eds) 2017, 204-16, interview with Jeff Koons.

figure gives way to a slightly uncanny blackness that is open to various interpretations.[27]

Among contemporary Asian artists who draw on classical precursors, it is worth singling out two Chinese artists, Li Hongbo (b. 1974) and Xu Zhen (b. 1977). Although the bust of the Apollo Belvedere initially appears quite conventional in Li Hongbo's version from 2014, it is actually the result of a very special technique. Li Hongbo layers thousands of white sheets of paper, one by one, attaching each with glue at special points to create a honeycomb pattern. He then uses a saw to cut out the preliminary form from the paper stack. For the shaping, he uses scissors or an angle grinder, and as a final step polishes the sculpture with sandpaper. When seen from a distance, and perhaps even close up, the result looks deceptively like marble. By means of this technique, which derives from traditional Chinese paper art, the seemingly static image becomes expandable and can stretch like an accordion into an elongated shape. Another example is 'Roman Youth', made in 2013.[28]

The unusual material used to create Xu Zhen's 'Venus de Milo' bust (2010) certainly drew attention. It was modelled out of panda excrement by 8year-old schoolchildren. This subversive move implies that rather than a great artist fashioning a statue in expensive marble, the same image may be fashioned in cheap material and even by young children. Since then, Xu has made other works that draw on the classical tradition in various ways. The statue 'Eternity-Poseidon-Pigeons' (2014) shows a replica of the Artemision Zeus with red pigeons perched on his head and arms, now set up on the shore at De Haan in Belgium (Fig. 4). 'New (Marathon Boy)', 'New (Marsyas)' and 'New (Hercules)' from 2016 are made of fibreglass and marble grains, to which are glued oil paintings on canvas. The sculptures' surfaces display landscape paintings of woods, mountains and sunsets. They give the impression of being completely covered with multi-coloured Japanese yakuza tattoos. Like many of Xu's other works, these are produced by his MadeIn Company (a reference to Made in China).[29]

A significant aspect of Xu's installations is the pairing of Eastern and Western sculptural forms. In one installation, made of fibreglass, steel and cement, a Bodhisattva carries an upside-down Nike of Samothrace including the ship-base (2013). A larger composition, 'Eternity-Parthenon' (2014), shows a reproduction of the Parthenon east pediment with upside-down Buddhist sculptures atop some of the pediment figures in place of their missing heads. In the very recent 'Eternity-Buddha in Nirvana', commissioned in 2017 by the National Gallery of Victoria in Australia, white-surfaced casts of the Dying Gaul, Hercules Farnese and many other Antique, Renaissance and Neoclassical sculptures inhabit the gigantic body of the reclining Buddha, a replica of an 8th-century Tang Dynasty Buddha. The 18 m-long base is decorated with Chinese paintings.[30] The Mediterranean sculptures here become subservient to the totally dominant Eastern sculpture, and the combination challenges viewers to ask why images of Greek divinities and heroes have become staples of art historical surveys, whereas Buddhist images are sidestepped, regarded as art on the edge. The combination of Greek and Chinese antiquities into new contemporary works may also be seen as a satirical play on the idea of the East meeting the West.[31]

Discussion

As the above survey makes clear, in the last decade, artists from different continents and with different aims have revisited Classical sculpture in very different ways. Whether Chinese, American, Nigerian or French, the point they have in common is that their new works rephrase famous antique statues. Within the last decade, the Nike of Samothrace has been presented in painted plaster and in a combination of wood and steel, and even been placed upside-down on top of a Bodhisattva. The Discobolus has been given a globe for a head and covered in colourful patterns. The Apollo Belvedere has sported sunglasses and been turned into an expandable paper sculpture. The transformations are manifold, and more contemporary

---

27   Adlmann 2011; for a presentation of the artist and his working process, see www.barryxball.com/files/process/18.pdf (accessed 7 February 2018).
28   https://theculturetrip.com/asia/china/articles/li–hongbo– (accessed 20 April 2018)
29   Moore, Trantow, Pölzl & Tinari 2016; for an overview of Xu Zhen's works, see Pollack 2018, 37-54.
30   McDowall 2017 shows images of the construction and assembly process.
31   Pollack 2018, 39.

artists than those presented here have revisited the statues in still other ways. But why do these statues, created some two millennia ago, still hold such a fascination?

It may seem surprising that artists continue to revisit ancient art works and that the public still takes an interest in the revised subjects. One may of course refer to the *auctoritas* of the ancient models and the notion of Greek art as a universal visual language. For the Greeks today, in a period of economic and political crisis, a nostalgic pull towards the glorious past may give some kind of comfort.[32] Still, in the early 21st century, Classical references prevail in many other places. For artists with non-European cultural backgrounds, there may be several reasons for drawing on the classical tradition. The appropriation of ancient symbols may in some instances be understood as a questioning of the canons of Western art. This applies to Xu Zhen's combination of Chinese and Greek images and, more provocatively, his fashioning of a Venus de Milo from the excrement of China's national symbol, the giant panda. The combination of elements from Greek Antiquity in Asian art is also a mocking expression of cultural globalisation.[33] It may be noted that as early as 1964, when the (original) Venus de Milo was exhibited in Japan, nearly 1.5 million people came to see it.[34] But the actual physical presence of a given work is perhaps less important than the spreading of images through the Internet. It is telling that Xu Zhen has never been outside China, and therefore has never experienced first-hand the Parthenon sculptures or the other Greek antiquities he incorporates into his new compositions. But today images are no longer physical entities confined within strict geographical boundaries, like statues in a museum; they belong to a global culture – as the globes replacing heads in Shonibare's sculptures perhaps ironically suggest. Classical art has become a universal visual language that is as easily embraced by Asian and African as well as by American and European artists.

But why do artists focus on very specific statues, the foremost being the Venus de Milo, the Nike of Samo-thrace, the Apollo Belvedere, the Discobolus and a few others, rather than on some of the many lesser-known sculptures that have been preserved from Antiquity?[35] The continual popularity of specific works may be explained by the circumstance that popularity leads to more popularity. In this connection, the so-called processing fluency theory is of interest.[36] The theory holds that the more often we have been exposed to an image, the more easily the visual information is processed. Since we have been exposed to the Venus de Milo many times, the familiarity of this image facilitates identification of images that can be associated with it, such as the various revisited forms. Being familiar with famous antique statues such as the Venus de Milo and the Discobolus, we will have less difficulty with processing or 'grasping' new works based on these images. The recreations by very different artists from very different cultural backgrounds therefore seem familiar to us because they are already familiar in their ancient forms and, accordingly, become easier to reprocess in their novel form. A revisited form only requires a few clues to be recognisable.

The contemporary artwork has a double identity: through the contemporary image we see the ancient one, and seeing the ancient one, we switch back to the contemporary work, and new aspects of both emerge. It may, however, seem that the antique–modern interaction is complex and involves more than a dialogue between an old and a new image. In fact, when an artist in the 21st century makes a new work based on the Venus de Milo, he or she is not necessarily referring to Antiquity. In 'Venus Recycled', Bjørn Nørgaard references his own 'Venus Mirrors – Mirrors Venus' and 'Helga from Holte meets Venus from Milo'. The 'Venus Mirrors' compositions present references to other artists such as Yves Klein, Joseph Beuys and Salvador Dalí. The Venus is thus a means and not an end. Indeed, it may be claimed that when Dalí chose this particular statue, making numerous copies and variations in all sizes, shapes and materials, the statue became trivialised to the point where it lost most of its original

---

32   For classical references in Greek paintings of the later 20th century, see Lambraki Plaka (ed.) 2000. For the cultural symbolism of Greek sculpture, see Plantzos 2012; 2017.

33   Xu Zhen points out that "to be called a global artist is an insult, but to be called a Chinese artist is an even bigger insult", quoted in Pollack 2018, 40.

34   Salmon 2002, 6.

35   The antique statues included in Bonazzoli & Robecchi 2013, 22-37, are the Discobolus, the Nike of Samothrace, the Venus de Milo and the Laoc-oon. The latter seems to have fallen out of favour among 21st-century artists.

36   Chenier & Winkielman 2009.

appeal. One can even claim that the Venus de Milo is no longer an ancient but a modern image.[37] To a large extent this applies to all the revisited works: they have lost their status as archaeological artefacts and become part of a contemporary visual culture.[38] Depending on one's point of view the statues can be seen as empty symbols or as open symbols to be filled with new meaning.

Conclusion

While the ancient statues in their new guises, in spite of changes in material and colour, are recognisable to the modern viewer, it may be questioned whether these works should rightfully be branded 'modern classicism'. When Thomas Hulme pointed to 'the classical' changing from having one specific meaning to 300 meanings, he would hardly have imagined the point where it has become close to meaningless. As in Jeff Koons' 'Gazing Ball' series, it matters but little whether the image provided with a glass ball is a plaster cast of Hercules Farnese or of a garden gnome. In Joshua Reynold's store of common property, marble statues and plastic objects are now stored side by side.

The adjective 'classical' is generally associated with concepts such as symmetry, harmony, beauty and grandeur. By contrast, the superficially classical works that so far have been produced in the 21st century are often asymmetrical, disharmonious and lacking in grandeur, the new materials presenting quite different and often distorted images. This so-called modern classicism may even be understood as a kind of anti-classicism. Nevertheless, by reinterpreting antique sculptures, these contemporary artists have revisited the past and, through witty reinterpretations, caused the ancient images to become part of contemporary culture. This should make us consider the fact that the sculptures made some two millennia ago were themselves once contemporary.

BENTE KIILERICH
University of Bergen
Department of Linguistic, Literary and Aesthetic studies
Pb 7805
N–5020 Bergen
Bente.kiilerich@uib.no

---

37   It is noticeable that art history students are more familiar with Dalí's 'Venus with drawers' than with the original Hellenistic statue in the Louvre.

38   A related tendency can be observed with regard to recycled Neoclassical images, such as Pistoletto's 'Venus of the Rags' (variations from 1967 to 2013 and possibly later), a work of variable forms and dimensions based on Bertel Thorvaldsen's 'Venus'; Trione 2013, 148-51; Kiilerich 2015.

Bibliography

Adlmann, J. E. 2011
'The Theatrum Mundi of Barry X Ball', *Sculpture* 30:9, 30-5.

Bauman, Z. 2000
Liquid Modernity, Cambridge.

Besnard, T.-A. 2018
'Compte rendu de l'exposition Londonienne "The Classical Now" (Mars–Avril 2018)', https://antiquipop.hypotheses.org.

Bonazzoli, F. & M. Robecchi 2013
Io sono un mito. I capolavori dell'arte che sono diventati icone del nostro tempo, Milan.

Chenier, T. & P. Winkielman 2009
'The origins of aesthetic pleasure: processing fluency and affect in judgment, body and the brain', in *Neuroaesthetics*, M. Skov & O. Vartanian (eds), New York, 275-89.

Curtis, G. 2005
Disarmed. The Story of the Venus de Milo, Stroud.

Cuzin, J.-P., J.-R. Gaborit & A. Pasquier (eds) 2000
D'après l'antique, Paris.

Decter, J. 1998
'Edward Allington: allegorical inventories, artifactual narratives', *The Classical Sensibility in Contemporary Painting and Sculpture, Art & Design* 4, 6-16.

Di Stefano, E. (ed.) 1998
L'ombra degli dei. Mito Greco e arte contemporanea, Naples.

Greene, E. S. & J. Leidwanger 2018
'Damien Hirst's tale of shipwreck and salvaged treasure', *AJA* 122, 1. www.ajaonline.org/online-museum-review/3581.

Holmes, B. & K. Marta (eds) 2017
Liquid Antiquity, Geneva & Athens.

Holzwarth, H. W. (ed.) 2015
Jeff Koons, Cologne.

Hulme, Th. 1912
A Tory Philosophy, London.

Iacometti, G., n.d.
La Nike di Francesco Rubino, Rome.

Jensen, I. & A. Wieczorek (eds) 2002
Dino, Zeus und Asterix. Zeitzeuge Archäologie in Werbung, Kunst und Alltag heute, Mannheim.

Kaiser, L. 2003
L'anacronismo e il ritorno alla pittura. L'origine è la meta, Milan.

Kiilerich, B. 2006
'From Greek original to modern pastiche: the reformulation of the classical statue in contemporary art', *ActaAArtHist* 20, 241-65.

Kiilerich, B. 2009
'Gamle statuer i nye værker', in *Antikken i ettertiden*, M. Skoie & G. Vestrheim (eds), Oslo, 240-50.

Kiilerich, B. 2015
'Michelangelo Pistolettos *Venere degli stracci*', *Kunst og Kultur* 98, 84-93.

Kiilerich, B. 2018
'Nike – fra Samothrake til Shanghai', *Klassisk Forum* 2, 70-83.

Lambraki Plaka, M. (ed.) 2000
Classical Memories in Modern Greek Art, New York.

Lambraki Plaka, M. (ed.) 2007
Classical Memories in Modern Greek Art, Athens & Peking.

McDowall, C. 2017
'NGV triennial-artist Xu Zhen, knocking our socks off!', http://www.thecultureconcept.com/ngv.

Moore, C., K. Trantow, P. Pölzl & P. Tinari 2016
Xu Zhen: Corporate. Produced by MadeIn Company, New York.

Morley, S. 1988

'What is classicism?' *The Classical Sensibility in Contemporary Painting and Sculpture, Art & Design* 4, 61-4.

Plantzos, D. 2012

'The *kouros* of Keratea: constructing subaltern pasts in contemporary Greece', *Journal of Social Archaeology* 12, 220-44.

Plantzos, D. 2017

'Caryatids lost and regained: rebranding the classical body in contemporary Greece', *Journal of Greek Media & Culture* 3, 3-29.

Pollack, B. 2018

Brand New Art from China, London & New York.

Prettejohn, E. 2006

'Reception and ancient Art: the case of the Venus de Milo', in *Classics and the Uses of Reception*, C. Martindale & R.F. Thomas (eds), Malden, 227-49.

Prettejohn, E. 2012

The Modernity of Ancient Sculpture. Greek Sculpture and Modern Art from Winckelmann to Picasso, London & New York.

Ratnam, N. 2004

'Art and globalisation', in *Themes in Contemporary Art*, G. Perry & P. Wood (eds), New Haven & London, 277-313.

Renfrew, C. 2003

Figuring It Out. What are We? Where do We come from? The Parallel Visions of Artists and Archaeologists, London.

Reynolds, J. 1778

Discourses on Art (Vol. 1-7), London

Salmon, D. 2002

La Vénus de Milo – un mythe, Paris.

Sanguinetti, C., M. Fochessati & F. Sborgi 1995

Il mito e il classico nell'arte contemporanea italiana 1960-1990, Milan.

Settis, S. 2006

The Future of the 'Classical', Cambridge.

Squire, M., J. Cahill & R. Allen (eds) 2018

The Classical Now, London.

Stewart, A. 2016

'The Nike of Samothrace: another view', *AJA* 120, 399-410.

Tatarkiewicz, W. 1958

'Les quatre significations du mot *classique*', *Revue internationale de philosophie* 12, 5-22.

Trione, V. (ed.) 2013

Post-classici. La ripresa dell'antico nell'arte contemporanea italiana, Milan.

Vout, C. 2018

'Venus ad infinitum', in *The Classical Now*, M. Squire, J. Cahill & R. Allen (eds), London, 97-113.

The Snake who Became a Prince, or The Girl with Two Husbands:

An Analysis of the Fairytale (AT *433B) Based on Hatzi-Yavrouda's Version from Kos

BIRGIT OLSEN

Abstract

The classic version of this tale is well known in the southern and southeastern parts of Europe, as well as in Scandinavia. In the Danish tradition it is known as Kong Lindorm (King Lindworm) and, as indicated by the first of the above titles, it is a story about a kind of a snake (or worm) who turns out to be a prince in disguise. In the East Mediterranean area the story has its own so-called oikotype, which is different from most of the Scandinavian versions. In the second part, where the heroine, after having rescued and married the snake-prince, is driven away from her home, she attaches herself to a second man in order to survive. The second part of the story is common in Greece and Asia Minor, which is why the Greek Folktale Catalogue gives two titles to the story.

In this paper I analyse and discuss the version of this oikotype of the tale by Koan storyteller Hatzi-Yavrouda, collected at the beginning of the 20th century by Iakovos Zarraftis and published in Richard M. Dawkins Forty-five Stories from the Dodekanese in 1950. I use Danish folktale scholar Bengt Holbek's synthetic model to analyse the tale. Thus the plot is divided into moves, the protagonists are placed according to the scheme of roles, their development from Y(oung) to A(dult) is followed, while the change – or not – in their social positions as H(igh) and L(ow) respectively is defined and the gender of the tale is established. This is a female tale with a persecuted heroine. Furthermore, Holbek's model means including analyses of variant versions. Hatzi-Yavrouda's version is compared to other versions of the tale from the Greek area. This has proved a very fruitful approach because it helps shed light on the interpretation of the story, not least the intriguing second part. Finally, as is essential for Holbek's approach to tales, the relationship between tale and surrounding society is discussed.

Introduction

In this paper, it is my intention to give an example of how the late Danish folktale scholar Bengt Holbek's model of analysis works on a specific Greek fairytale.

The tale in question originates from the island of Kos and was collected by Iakovos Zarraftis in his native village of Asfendiou. We do not know when it was recorded, but Zarraftis sent it to Cambridge in 1908. It was published as no. 36 in *Forty-Five Stories from the Dodekanese* by Richard M. Dawkins in 1950.[1] It has the title Yavrouda and is a version of the Greek-East Mediterranean oikotype of AT *433B.

The reasons for presenting this particular tale are various: I believe that it had a special importance to the narrator, Hatzi-Yavrouda.[2] A Danish version of it, though rather different apart from the central story, was analysed as one of Holbek's application examples.[3]

The second part, the story about the second husband, which is distinctively different from the Danish versions, but a common part of the Greek tradition, has always intrigued me, and therefore I would like to venture my own interpretation.

The narrator

While we cannot be a hundred percent certain that it was actually Hatzi-Yavrouda of Asfendiou who told this tale to Zarraftis, since he did not state the name of his source, I have thus far taken this for granted,[4] and my further analysis of the tale's narrative technique, style, and language supports this assumption. This tale is told by the same narrator who told no. 33 in Dawkins' edition, entitled Myrmidonia and Pharonia and attributed to Hatzi-Yavrouda by Zarraftis.[5] Yet another argument for Hatzi-Yavrouda as the narrator is the name of the female protagonist and thus the title of tale: it is her own name without the prefix. The fact that she chose to give the heroine her own name also makes me believe that this tale had a special place close to her heart and probably to her experiences and views of the (female) world. She was probably an old woman by the time she told Zarraftis the tale, but she could relate to this young girl who had to face so many trials of womanhood before she could triumph in the end.

Holbek's method

Bringing together earlier approaches to fairytale research, such as the geographico-historical, cataloguing method of Arne-Thompson, the structural, morphological method of Propp and later structuralists, the craftsmanship viewpoint and the psychoanalytical approach,[6] Holbek creates a synthetic method for analysing and interpreting fairytales. The geographico-historical approach renders the vital means of comparing various versions of a given tale from the same and different cultures. Propp and later elaborations of his approach is an essential tool for analysing the narrative structure of the tale. The craftmanship approach brings the circumstances of the surrounding society of narrator and audience into the analysis, and finally the psychoanalytical approach offers important clues for the interpretation of the tales and not least their marvelous elements.

The first premise of Holbek's method is that it is "exclusively concerned with tales, which end with a wedding or with the triumph of the couple who were cast out earlier in the tale because their marriage was a misalliance".[7] The second premise is that the social setting of the communities where tales were told is regarded as "a basic fact without which no understanding of fairy tales is possible", and furthermore that connections exist between the contents of the tales and the living conditions of the narrators;[8] in this connection Holbek sees the marvelous elements of the tales as

expressions of what the storytellers and their audiences themselves feel and think about their own lives. The 'marvelous' elements are traditional expressions, i.e. they have been in use for centuries, perhaps millennia, but they are only retained because they are still meaningful to their users.[9]

---

1   Olsen 1997; 1999a.

2   I shall return to this point below.

3   Holbek 1987, 457-98.

4   Olsen 1999a, 30-1.

5   I have treated this aspect in the paper *Hatzi-Yavrouda and the craft of storytelling*, read at the conference *From Homer to Hatzi-Yavrouda. Aspects of oral narration in the Greek tradition* (Athens, September 2018).

6   Holbek 1987, 219-401. On these pages Holbek discusses and evaluates in detail previous fairytale research. I am aware of the criticism Holbek's work has met from Vaz da Silva 2000 and Lindow 1989 among others, but I still find that, used with care, it provides a very useful tool for analysing tales; their points of criticism are not relevant to the current study.

7   Holbek 1987, 404.

8   Holbek 1987, 405.

9   Holbek 1987, 406.

Here Holbek is in accordance with Dundes, who in his article Projection in Folklore: A Plea for Psychoanalytic Semiotics expresses the same views in an attempt to understand the meaning of fairytales and explain the supernatural or marvellous elements, which were for a long time neglected by folklorists.[10]

In defining the structure of tales, Holbek operates with a number of "moves" based on the structure of functions, first defined by Vladimir Propp. Propp, like Holbek, paid more attention to the result of a given act than to the act itself. This means that superficially identical actions may represent different functions if they produce different results and *vice versa*.[11] Holbek's five moves are thus defined by their results. A move ends when a new situation has been created. This is a very productive way to grasp the structure of a tale.

In the kind of tales he analyses, i.e. the ones ending with a wedding, Holbek argues that there is not one protagonist but two – a male and a female, a hero and a heroine (M/F).[12] They both have to undergo a process of maturation and one of them also has to undergo a process of social mobility. In the beginning of the tale they are both young (Y), but they come from different social strata, hence the aforementioned "misalliance". One is of a low social status (L) and the other high (H). By the end of the tale they both will have passed to adult status (A), and the one of low social status will also have risen to high (H). So they end up as HAM and HAF respectively. According to the gender of the protagonist of low social status, the gender of the tale can be defined as either masculine (LYM) or feminine (LYF). These three-dimensional tale roles represent the three semantic oppositions present in the tale: that of social status (high *vs* low), that of the sexes (male *vs* female) and that of generations (young *vs* adult).[13]

The group of fairytales Holbek treats (AT 300-749) all concern the breaking up of an old family and creation of a new one, hence the wedding or the triumph of the

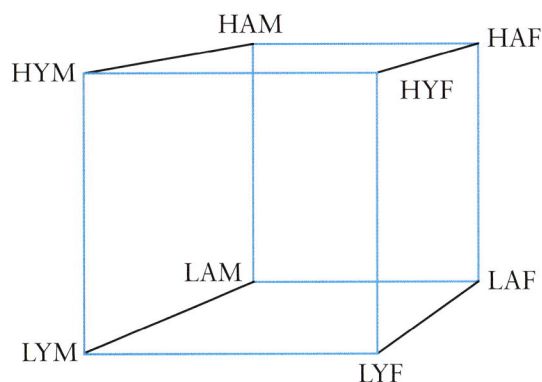

Fig. 1. *A simplified representation of the three-dimensional model.*

young couple in the end. A generational shift has taken place. The young hero and heroine have replaced the old king and queen who at the beginning of the tale occupied the positions of HAM and HAF.

Structural analysis of the tale

After this short introduction to Holbek's method of analysis, it is time to apply the model to the Greek tale. As mentioned in the beginning, for my analysis of this tale type I have chosen the version from Kos told by Hatzi-Yavrouda.[14] One of this brilliant storyteller's characteristics is that she tells long tales. This is also the case here. Hatzi-Yarouda's version is 40 percent longer than the longest of the other variants (*Tsirogles*, no. 9).[15] It is too long to quote in full, so a résumé is needed.

Plot résumé

The tale starts with a very detailed description of an embroidery teacher and the handicraft of her female pupils (Introduction).[16]

---

10   Dundes 1976.

11   Propp 1968, 25-70.

12   Note the two titles given to this tale type in the Greek Catalogue of Tale Types (Angellopoulou & Brouskou 1999, 787). They refer to the hero and the heroine respectively.

13   For paradigmatic models of the positions and transformations of hero and heroine, see Köngäs Maranda & Maranda 1997, 23, and Holbek's moderations, Holbek 1987, 432-3. For Holbek's entire discussion of the "system of tale roles", see Holbek 1987, 416-34.

14   Olsen 2002.

15   See below.

16   Olsen 1999b, 1.

The teacher desires the father of one of her pupils, the heroine, Yavrouda, and therefore causes the girl to kill her own mother accidentally, by dropping the lid of the walnut chest on her neck. Afterwards the girl persuades her father to marry the teacher. Having achieved her goals, the former teacher turns into a wicked stepmother (Move I).

The queen of the country is giving birth, but no midwife is able to deliver the child because it eats their hands. The stepmother secretly makes the king send for the heroine. She visits her mother's grave in despair, receives advice and delivers the child using iron hands. The child is a snake. The girl is richly rewarded and returns home. The snake needs a nurse, but it eats their breasts. Again, the stepmother offers the heroine for the job. The girl once more visits her mother's grave, is given advice, and manages to feed the snake using iron breasts and milk. Again, she is richly rewarded, much to the vexation of her stepmother. The third task is to marry the snake, and the chain of events repeats itself once more. Everybody feels sorry for the beautiful young heroine who is going to be eaten in her wedding bed, like the snake's previous brides (Move II).

On the night of the wedding the snake demands she take off her clothes, but she reverses the demand and acts just as firmly as him. This procedure of alternate "undressing" goes on seven times, and in the end the snake is naked but has become a beautiful youth, while the girl still has one more shift to take off. She quickly burns his seven skins, and thus he must surrender and admit that she has won him and is worthy of him.

Everybody expected to hear of the girl's being eaten, but the next morning the king and queen get the message that the young couple is awake. They rush into the bridal chamber and at first cannot believe what they see, but the heroine assures them that the young man is their son, and he on his part also tells them that he is the snake who the heroine has won by her worthiness. An even greater wedding feast is held (Move III).

At this point the tale could easily finish with the happy ending, but it does not. A retarding move, as Holbek calls it, follows, with new persecutions of the heroine. This part functions as move IV in the tale, and the structure of this inserted story may again be broken up into moves: The snake prince goes off to war. His wife's stepmother manages to falsify the letters to and from his parents. In the false letters the parents are commanded to expel their

Fig. 2. *Niels Skovgaard. Statens Museum for Kunst, Copenhagen. The text says "King Lindorm shed a skin".* Lindorm *is the Danish word for the snake, and also the title of many of the tale variants.*

daughter-in-law because she has proved to be a whore. Reluctantly, they send her to the mountains, where she is left pregnant and entirely on her own, far from her mother's grave (Move Ia).

While lamenting her fate the heroine sees a youth coming out of a tomb. On his request, she tells him her story, and he promises to help her. Afterwards he in his turn tells his story. His name is Neros, and he used to be a man, but of ill deeds. He would wed a girl in the evening and demand her death in the morning. Then one night he was enchanted by twelve fairies and since then has been half dead, only allowed to walk around in the evenings, but by midnight the fairies will come for him to dance with them all night. He takes Yavrouda to his mother, the queen of the country, where she seeks shelter by using his name (Move IIa).

Yavrouda gives birth to a boy. The following evening, Neros visits her and he treats the child as if it were his own. He instructs her to sing a certain lullaby to the baby, which reveals it as Neros' offspring. To her reluctance to lie in this way, he answers that from now on both she and the child are his, and that they must struggle to save one another. Yavrouda does as Neros demands, and his mother, the queen, overhears the lullaby. She starts questioning the young girl about where she met Neros, who has been dead for years now. The girl refuses to answer. This procedure of Neros' visit in the evening, Yavrouda's singing and the queen's overhearing the lullaby is repeated, and in the end the queen gets very angry with the girl and threatens to kick her out together with the child. At the same time, a spy reports to her that her son is visiting the mother and child, and that he asks explicitly about the lullaby. The queen then sends all kinds of gifts to Yavrouda and pays her a visit in order to find out more. The heroine breaks down and reveals the whole truth. On his next visit Neros instructs Yavrouda to demand from his mother a cloth woven of one thread and in one day, and to use it to wrap up the whole tower so that not even the tiniest speck of dust can get through. Every fold and every crack should be closed by a red cross on the outside and a green on the inside. When the fairies come to get him, they cannot get in, and he cannot get out, and thus he is redeemed. Forty days pass. The palace is unwrapped and the wedding of the heroine with Neros is celebrated (Move IIIa).

We now return to the main story:

The snake-prince returns from war to find his wife gone. The fraud is revealed, and the prince takes off to seek his wife. He finds her and the child and claims them for his. Neros for his part also claims them. They decide to put their fate in the hands of a judge. The woman and the two husbands are to walk up a mountain, the one man carrying the child, the other a jug of water. The woman, who knows nothing of the scheme, will ask for either the child or the water, and whoever carries the item she asks for will keep her for his wife. The snake-prince, who carries the water, wins, and Neros is resigned, saying that what belongs to another, always belongs to another. The snake-prince and the heroine return home. Yavrouda is asked to decide the punishment of the stepmother. She wants to pardon her so that she may understand that good is returned for evil. But when she gets this message, the stepmother explodes in her jealousy (Move V).

Important deviations from the plot pattern in the variants

An important element in Holbek's method of analysis is based on Dundes's suggestion of comparing different versions of the same story in order to disclose the various 'allomotifs'. This term was coined by Dundes to describe interchangeable motifs that give the same result. With this method,

we may gain access to implicit native formulations of symbolic equivalence. If A and B fulfill the same motifeme [i.e. function], then in some sense is it not reasonable to assume that the folk are equating A and B? In other words allomotifs are both functionally and symbolically equivalent.[17]

I have thus examined the 14 variants of this tale type listed in the Greek Catalogue of Tale Types,[18] as well as one that is not included in the catalogue (see note 19). In the following I will note major differences between these variants and our main tale *Yavrouda*.[19] This may help shed light on the interpretation and disclose the meaning of some of the marvellous or symbolic elements.

Tale no. 9 is named *Tsirogles* and comes from Skyros. The opening (transition) episode is not a description of the teacher but of the heroine's parents, an exemplary couple. When the girl wants her father to marry the teacher, after having killed her own mother, he warns her about getting a stepmother.

The stepmother has a child of her own. She sends off her stepdaughter to do all the hard labour with very little food. The girl does not dare complain to her father. As the heroine grows older, she understands her guilt and visits her mother's grave. The mother tells her that she will suffer agonies because of her sin (κρίμα), but that she has to be patient, and then maybe God will forgive in the end. The mother also advises her daughter, if she is ever in trouble, to seek her grave to get her blessing. In this variant another tale type is incorporated, a common phenomenon in the Greek tradition of the tale type. When the girl is beaten up by her stepmother, she seeks comfort at her mother's grave. The mother once more

---

17   Dundes 1980, 92.

18   Angellopoulou & Brouskou 1999, 794-7.

19   I use the numbering of the catalogue. I take the published versions (nos 9, 5, 3) first and then the mss versions. I do not discuss all 15 variants here, but only the ones that show major differences. Some of the variants are incomplete or very short.

admonishes her to be patient "until you have paid off your sin, you still have time".

The tale then returns to the main story. The queen of the country begs for a child "be it even a snake". The story continues along the lines of *Yavrouda*, but then the young wife gives birth before she is told to leave the palace. She meets Tsirogles, a shadow, who sends her to his mother and comes to lie with her every night.

The two husbands' armies meet at a spring. A wise man advises them not to fight and perhaps cause the deaths of many men, including themselves, but to let the queen decide for herself. She is to ask for water of the man she wants. Her answer is that she has loved the snake and made him a human being, but he poisoned her when he drove her out. On the other hand, Tsirogles became a human because of his love for her. He picked her up from the street and made her queen, and in verse she concludes: "I love Ofis (the snake) and want Tsirogles. Tsirogles, fetch me water for I'm dying". And that she does.

Tale no. 5 is called The Three-fold Cursed, and is from Thrace. The plot follows the same patterns as Tsirogles, but in this version the heroine goes to the priest and makes a confession. He tells her that she has committed a major sin (αμάρτημα) and that nobody can give her absolution. She is to seek advice at her mother's grave. The mother agrees to guide her because after all she is her child, and she feels sorry for her, but nevertheless she is three-fold cursed (τρισκαταραμένη).

When the fake letters begin to arrive, the king and queen do not want their daughter-in-law to know how her husband has turned on her, and therefore hide them. Eventually she finds them and by her own initiative leaves the castle. The heroine works for some shepherds and in the field sees a buried man (Rigas), and the nymphs coming to amuse themselves with him.

The snake-prince seeks his wife dressed as a peddler, seeing her as she is sending her maid to buy a toy for the child. He insists on dealing with the mistress. They meet. She tells him that it is all over, and that she now has a child.

This time a judge is involved in solving the problem of the two husbands. He demands the two men give the heroine a sleeping drug, and whoever gives her water when she wakes up will be her rightful husband. When she finally wakes up days later, both men are asleep. In verse, she says that she wants and loves the snake, and asks him to fetch water for she is dying. She dies, and so do both men when they wake up to see her dead.

The Teacher, from Asia Minor, is another variant.[20] The girl herself explicitly wishes the teacher to become her mother. She even tells her father, but he answers that she has a mother. The girl is instructed to drop the lid of the chest when her mother is bending over it. The stepmother makes her do all the hard work. The girl seeks her mother's grave to beg forgiveness. The mother puts all the blame on the teacher. The girl does not dare tell her father about the stepmother.

While the snake-prince is away, the king is asked to kill the heroine in the false letters. He refuses to do so, but sends her to her fate, loaded with money.

From this point on, the story becomes so different from our main story that a comparison is of no interest up until the point when the snake-prince returns.

He sets out to find his wife by her special mark (at that time, we learn, golden teeth were not usual, but the prince had given his wife one). He sells flowers for smiles and thus finds her.

The law is to decide which is the rightful husband. The court's verdict is that the three of them must eat sardines and in the heat of summer walk up a mountain, and whoever the girl asks for water shall keep her.

On the way up both men drink, but the heroine refrains because she does not want to hurt either of the men. When at the top she finally cannot take any more, and, again in verse, says that she loves the snake and will die for him, she again asks her second husband, called Peristeras, to fetch water for she is dying. Both men run for water, but before they are back her soul has left.

Tale no. 3 from Ipiros only exists in a German translation and is called *Das Schlangekind*. The motif of the teacher is lacking, and the heroine does not kill her own mother. She is just a stepdaughter whose stepmother tries to get rid of her.

The motifs of delivering and nursing the snake are not present. The girl only has to marry him, and she is told

20 This version, from Mousaiou-Bougioukou 1976, is not listed in the Greek catalogue of Angellopoulou and Brouskou (Angellopoulou & Brouskou 1999), and it does differ in motifs, but still I find enough similarities to our tale to include it in my analysis.

in advance by her mother that he is a youth. At night the snake is a man, and he is redeemed by the collaboration of his wife and mother (they burn his slough).

While the snake is away, the stepmother replaces his wife with her own daughter. On his return from the war the snake finds out and wants his wife back.

In the meantime, she has married another man, Kyrikos, who was buried alive but called back to life by her tears. A judge makes the two men race down a mountain, and whoever comes first shall keep the woman for his wife. The snake wins and Kyriakos "returns to where he was before".

Tale no. 4 has the title *Rodoula, the Dragon, and kir-Giorgis*, and it is from Thrace. The dragon's mother gave birth to a dragon instead of a child because she became pregnant by a dragon.

The heroine's mother holds her responsible for her death, and therefore she will suffer. "Unfairly you have slain me, and you will meet an unfair end," she repeats four times.

The stepmother forces the girl to deliver the child/dragon and subsequently nurse, teach and marry the dragon by asking "you who were able to kill your own mother, you cannot help the queen give birth?" etc.

Instead of using iron gloves, the girl lures the dragon out of his mother's womb with bowls of milk and honey.

The heroine brings kir-Giorgis back to life by her tears, and she has a child by him.

The dragon recognises his wife by a golden tooth he gave her after having knocked out the original one when she was teaching him.

In the end the heroine says that she loves both her husbands and asks for water because she is dying, and then she dies.

Tale no. 14 has the title *A Mother's Curse* and is from Mainland Greece. Before she dies, the girl's mother curses her by asking God and The Holy Virgin to see to that "you who killed me shall be seeking my grave for my advice …. because of what you did to me you'll pass great torments". And when the girl does come to her grave, she says that she will have to suffer this and a great deal more.

The snake's mother asks God for a child – even a snake. The snake is a youth at night. He prohibits the heroine from telling anybody, but she does and thus has to seek him and in doing so goes to the underworld where she meets the second husband, Grigoris. He has been taken by

nymphs and every night plays the violin while they dance. She becomes pregnant by him and is sent to his mother, who saves him once she has accepted that the child is his.

The heroine cannot make up her mind and dies.

Tale no. 16 is titled *Asvantis and the Snake* and comes from Cyprus. The girl blames herself for the killing of her mother – "my dear wrongly killed mother … who wrongly I killed" – and the mother answers "what you wished for you got … and now you are crying".

The snake's mother goes directly against his admonitions to take good care of his wife while he is away, and expels her daughter-in-law.

The heroine meets Asvantis, who has been taken by dragons. She becomes pregnant by him and is sent to his parents. His father knows what to do and using fire tricks the dragons to give up his son. The girl cannot make up her mind and dies.

Tale no. 11 has the beginning line as its title: *I will tell you about*. It is from Ithaka. The king asks for a child, "be it even a snake".

The mother forgives the daughter: "you killed me, but it doesn't matter".

The girl is to lure out the snake with 7 bowls of milk and honey, and again at their wedding night she is to place 7 bowls beside the bed for 7 nights, and afterwards the snake crawls into bed as a beautiful youth.

Tale no. 7 is called *The Snake who Became a Prince* and is from Mitilini. The only interesting difference here is that the queen eats an onion without peeling it and therefore gives birth to a snake.

Discussion of the variants

The comparison of variants has shown to be very rewarding in the case of this tale. In the following I shall list the main differences and similarities.

1) First of all, the opening scene in *Yavrouda* is much more elaborate than in any other version. The audience is transported very subtly from a reality-like narrative into the world of the fairytale by the means of a detailed description of the girls' various embroideries. Embroideries on linen were widely used by the islanders and probably surrounded the audience while they were listening to the tale. As the collector Iakovos Zarraftis informs us in a letter, the village of

121

Asfendiou, where he collected the tale, had a tradition of fine embroidery (Letter of October 20, 1905).[21] This kind of transitory introduction we do not find in any of the other versions. *Das Schlangekind* and the other less elaborate mss variants even lack the motif of the envious teacher, which places them closer to the Danish tradition. Only one of the Danish versions of the tale has this motif (no. 13).[22]

2) The degree of the heroine's active part in the killing of her mother is an interesting difference. In *Yavrouda* the poor girl is entirely free of guilt. She acts as the passive tool for the teacher's ambitions. In *The Three-fold Cursed* and *The Teacher*, on the other hand, she deliberately kills her mother. In *The Teacher* she even takes the initiative herself by expressing her wish that the teacher may be her mother instead of the one she has. Accordingly, the mothers blame their daughters or fail to do so. In *Yavrouda* the mother does not mention guilt, but the girl herself is aware both of her fault (λάθος) and of the fact that she bears a mother's curse and therefore is persecuted by her stepmother. Daughter and mother address each other as "hapless" (πικρο(μάνα) – πικρο(κόρη)). In *The Three-fold* a priest, who does not occur in any other version, makes it clear that the girl has committed a sin (αμάρτημα), and the mother calls her τρισκαταραμένη (three-fold cursed). In *The Teacher* the mother only blames the teacher. In *Tsirogles* the girl, as she grows older, herself becomes aware of her sin (κρίμα). As the title also indicates, *A Mother's Curse* is the variant with the strongest element of the mother blaming her child and even cursing her, but nonetheless she helps her. In *Asvantis* the girl expressively blames herself, and the mother foresees a dire end for her. The essence is that, whether or not the heroine has deliberately killed her own mother, and whether or not the mother blames her, she has committed a sin (κρίμα/αμάρτημα) and as a result bears a mother's curse and must endure the consequences of this. To be cursed by a parent is,

according to Greek folklore, one of the worst things that may happen to a person; on the other hand, with a parent's blessing you are capable of anything. Note e.g. how the mother in *Tsirogles* advises the daughter to seek her grave for her blessing. However, it is also clear that, no matter what, the mother will be the girl's helper in the trials she will face. It is this conflict that is the point of departure of the tale, and it is also this that makes it a feminine tale with a persecuted heroine. Apart from her mother's help and advice, the virtue the heroine must call upon to bear her trials and, in the end, succeed is explicitly stated in *Tsirogles* when the mother tells the heroine "not to speak and be patient". Then God may forgive her just as she herself has forgiven her. It is also stated, although in a different manner, in *The Teacher*; in the second half of the story, which has a different theme from our main story, the girl orders "the stone of patience" and several times asks it if she should kill herself or be patient. She chooses the latter and thus in the end wins what is rightfully hers. As I have argued elsewhere, we are getting at some central values here.[23] Not complaining and being patient are the virtues that will enable the heroine to endure all the stepmother's attacks on her life, and as ethnological studies have repeatedly demonstrated, these are also core attributes for women in rural Greece and a woman's means of securing success in married life.[24]

3) Not all the versions give a reason for the snake being born in this shape, but when given, the most frequent reason is that the queen – and once the king – wishes for a child, be it even a snake/dragon.[25] However, in the Danish versions of this tale the reason is almost always that the snake's mother has failed to carry out instructions as they were given to her by a helper/donor who advised her in her distress over her childlessness. This is also the case in at least one Greek version, no. 7, *The Snake who Became a Prince*. The queen does not peel the onion she has been told to eat. Finally, in one version, no. 4, *Rodoula*, the queen

---

21   The mss of the letters are kept at the library of the Department of Classics, Cambridge University. See also Olsen 1999b.

22   Holbek 1987, 473-5.

23   Olsen 2002, 70.

24   See e.g. du Boulay 1976, 134-5; Hirschorn 1978, 67, 89, 151-3; Stewart 1990, 73.

25   Nos 1, 5, 6, 14.

slept with a dragon. This is a very good example of how a function may be fulfilled in different ways but with the same result – an example of allo-episodes.[26]

4) The method of delivering the queen of the child seems to be either by the use of iron gloves/hands or by luring the snake out with bowls of milk and honey, but the result is the same, which means that these are allomotifs.

5) For the final encounter with the snake, in most versions the girl has been told by her mother to put on many (7/9/40) shifts. In other words, she has been advised to "dress well for her wedding night", as Lindow puts it,[27] and in this scene the young heroine shows just as much courage and firmness as any male dragon-slayer.

6) The father of the heroine's child in most versions is her second husband, but in *Yavrouda* and *Tsirogles* it is her first husband. However, this does not make any difference to the story. The second husband always passes the child off as his own.

7) The ending is another point where the variants differ. There seem to be two solutions to the intricate problem of one woman having two husbands: either the girl cannot make up her mind and therefore dies, or, even though she also cares for the second husband, she chooses the first, the snake-prince. According to Holbek, tragic endings of fairytales may be due to literary influence from e.g. chapbooks.[28] If this is the case here, this influence must have come at an early stage of the development of the oikotype, since so many variants from all over the Greek area and from different periods have this motif.

8) In all versions water plays a role, even when it is entirely meaningless, as in *Tsirogles*. In *The Teacher* a reason for the water is given in that the three protagonists are to eat salted fish and climb a mountain in the heat of summer. In the Danish versions the reason for the girl's wanting water is always that she has eaten something salty. But apart from that, water is essential to life and in Greece particularly valued, as the lovely expression "beautiful like the cold water" shows. The expression is used in *Tsirogles* but generally known in Greek folklore. Another example is the healing effect of the αθάνατο νερό (the immortal water), also a well-known motif from Greek folklore.

Interpreting the Yavrouda tale

This tale is the quintessential female tale with a persecuted heroine. It is about the trials of womanhood, about mother-daughter ties and oppositions, about childcare, marriage and violent male sexuality, and finally it shows how to overcome these trials. As we have seen in comparing the variants, the moral message is that by the virtue of patience the heroine can endure the various persecutions she is exposed to and in the end secure happiness in marriage.

At the beginning of the tale the young girl does not want to grow up and learn the task of womanhood from her mother. She therefore "kills" her. But when she gets something that is worse, a persecuting stepmother, she realises that only by seeking the help of her mother (listening to her/learning from her) can she overcome the challenges set before her and thus in the end free the snake from his enchantment. We may interpret the mother and stepmother as a psychological split of one and the same person.[29] It is a maturing girl's way of dealing with conflicting feelings towards her mother and her own approaching womanhood. She splits the mother figure into two opposites: the caring, helping, dead mother and the cruel, living stepmother.

It is interesting that in the Greek versions of the tale the girl has to deliver the snake and nurse him before she has to marry him. In the Danish versions the nursing element comes during the wedding night, after the confrontation between the two protagonists.[30] When the snake has shed all his sloughs and the girl has one undergarment remaining, she bathes him in milk and swaddles him in either her undergarment or some linen cloth, and then sleeps with him in her arms. But the result is the same in both traditions. She has made him a human being by nursing him, either before or after confronting him.

---

26 Holbek 1987, 355.
27 Lindow 1993, 64.
28 Holbek 1987, 404.
29 For the use of such splits in connection with fairytales, see e.g. Bettelheim 1976, 67.
30 For the Danish versions, see Holbek 1987, 457-98.

A puzzling question as regards the Greek-East Mediterranean oikotype of this tale is the meaning of its second part. Why does the tale not stop after the happy rescue of the snake? Hatzi-Yavrouda is the only one of our narrators who offers some kind of explanation. When the heroine is expelled by her in-laws, she is left pregnant and entirely on her own, far from her mother's grave. In this second part of the story she has to manage without her mother's help.

The two protagonists have had their sexual encounter – the child is the obvious evidence – but neither of them are yet ready for a mature relationship. They have not yet passed the "sexual conflict" to use Holbek's terms: they are still at the YH stage in the model. The hero may still be too attached to a mother who is probably the reason for his deformation. Because of her actions, which again in some of the variants have sexual connotations, he has a problem of untamed sexuality, physically expressed by his being born as a snake/dragon. As Holbek remarks, he may just as well have been named King Phallus.[31] His mother has violated some prohibitions either by wishing for too much or by eating too much (the peel of the onion or more than one). Eating and sex are allomotifs in traditional folklore. But it is interesting to note that in one case her fault is explicitly connected to sex. In *Rodoula*, no. 4, the queen becomes pregnant by a dragon, and to quote Holbek, "Very often one version may express in 'clear speech' what is veiled in symbols in another version".[32]

Now the hero's turn has come for the maturity test. He disappears literally and metaphorically because he does not want to take responsibility as a husband and a father, and he is not yet free of his mother.

Yavrouda, on the other hand, also has to cut herself loose from her mother and form a reciprocal relationship with a man. Thus, to her reluctance to lie about the child being his, Neros answers that from now on both she and the child are his, and that they must struggle to "save one another". Furthermore, she also has to gain her position as new queen and replace the old, the mother of her husband. This she is obviously not yet mature enough to do, and therefore she is literally or metaphorically cast out to undergo new trials. The person who instigates this development is her old persecutor, her stepmother, who

this time we may take to be a split not for her own mother but for her mother-in-law. The young girl's redeeming the snake may have allowed her to pass the conflict of maturity at the low level – she has passed from LYF to LAF; it may also have allowed her to pass the social conflict – she has risen to HYF; but to rise to HAF she has to resist the attacks of the old queen, her mother-in-law, and in order for her to do so, her husband has to free himself from his ties to his mother.

But who is the second husband? What does he represent? For we should not forget that according to Holbek's approach, "It is a basic assumption that apparently supernatural beings, phenomena and events are expressions of natural beings, phenomena and events".[33] My suggestion is that Neros in fact represents Yavrouda's first husband, the snake. He is the husband as he should be. Let me offer some arguments for this interpretation. First of all, the snake's and Neros' guilt psychologically could be interpreted as the same, i.e. exaggerated sexual behaviour. They both "kill" women. But when Neros meets Yavrouda, he has realised that in his former life he has acted immorally (έκαμα άδικα... έκαμα κακά, "I acted wrongly...I did bad things"), and as we saw above, he is ready to be released from the enchantment by saving her. He is ready to undertake the responsibility that the snake refused. In the end, Yavrouda says that she loves the snake, but Neros loves her. If this interpretation is accepted, it means that both protagonists have to learn to love as well as to accept love. Yavrouda accepts Neros' love and care for her in the same way she herself has cared for the snake. The snake does not realise his love for his wife until she is gone, but then he sets out to regain her. He shows strength of character, and passes the maturity test.

Secondly, the way in which Neros acts as a husband and father is a good indication. He insists that both Yavrouda and the child are his. He even deceives his own mother to get her help. And as we saw, in most of the versions the second husband is actually the child's father, but both variations meet the same end. It makes no difference to the story.

If we accept that Neros and the snake are two sides of the same person, the ending is rather logical. Yavrou-

31 Holbek 1987, 481.
32 Holbek 1987, 496
33 Holbek 1987, 485.

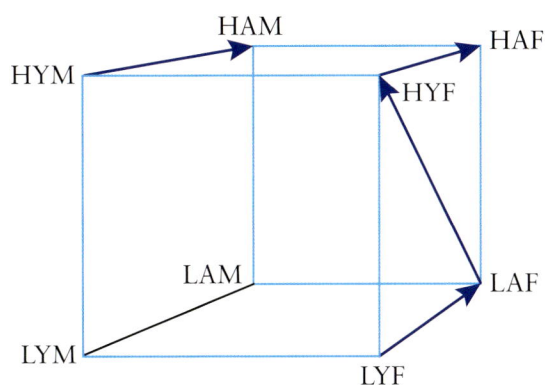

Fig. 3. *A simplified three-dimensional model of the two protagonists' developments in AT *433B.*

da "returns" to a much more mature husband who has learned not only to behave sexually but also to take the responsibility that marriage and parenthood demand, and to put his mother in the right place. It is interesting in this connection that Neros himself knows exactly what to do to break the enchantment, but he needs his mother to do it. Afterwards he vanishes out of the story. He is not needed any more, and as it is expressed in *Das Schlangekind* "he goes back to where he was before".

Yavrouda for her part has learned to manage without the help of her mother but to rely on her husband instead and to accept his love for her, and with his help she has won the power struggle with the old queen, her mother-in-law.

As we saw, the first mother-in-law, the snake's mother, by way of split, was probably the reason why the young queen was expelled; in one version this is actually expressed in "clear speech" (*Arvantis*, no. 16). The old queen sees the young heroine as her replacement both in power and in her relationship with her son. She is not ready to give up her position. So she keeps her ties with her son and expels his wife. Accordingly, if we take Neros to represent the snake, Neros' mother must represent the snake's mother. At first she is suspicious of the young woman who comes to her and seeks help in the name of her dead son, but once she realises that only by yielding and accepting this young woman as her son's wife and mother of his child can she save him from the dead, she

turns from adversary to helper and thus accepts the inevitable development of things.

Seen in this way, the young couple has now risen to the status HA in Holbek's model, and after this retarding interval they may live happily ever after.

In traditional society conflicts like those treated in this tale were present but could not be spoken of directly, and therefore the narration of fairytales offered a way of dealing with these taboos in an oblique way. To quote Holbek:

The symbolic elements of fairy tales convey emotional impressions of beings, phenomena and events in the real world, organized in the form of fictional narrative sequences, which allow the narrator to speak of problems, hopes and ideals of the community.[34]

Hatzi-Yavrouda and her fellow villagers of Asfendiou probably recognised the issues dealt with directly or indirectly in the tale of *Yavrouda*. In their surroundings there may have been examples of ties between a parent and a child that were too close; growing girls may not have wanted to follow their mothers' examples and thus positioned themselves in opposition to their mothers; first encounters with the opposite sex may have seemed scary and demanded a lot of courage; young brides may not have found it easy to live in the same house as their in-laws; the older generation may have found it difficult to give way to the younger, etc., etc. We may assume that both narrator and audience knew the "grammar" of the narration,[35] and, without suggesting that they could make a psychoanalytic analysis of the tale, we may also assume that the marvellous elements were meaningful to them. Once the fairytales ceased to carry a meaningful message, the craft of narration ceased to exist.

Birgit Olsen
The Danish Institute at Athens
Herefondos 14 GR-10558-Athens
birgit.olsen@diathens.gr

---

34   Holbek 1987, 435.
35   Holbek 1987, 407.

Bibliography

Αγγελοπούλου, Α. & Αι. Μπρούσκου 1999
Επεξεργασία Παραμυθιακών Τύπων και Παραλλαγών ΑΤ 300-499 (Α και Β). Γεωργίου Α. Μέγα/Κατάλογος Ελληνικών Παραμυθιών 3, Athens.

Bettelheim, B. 1976
The Uses of Enchantment: The Meaning and Importance of Fairy Tales, New York.

Dawkins, R. M. 1950
Forty-Five Stories from the Dodekanese, Cambridge.

Dundes, A. 1976
'Projection in Folklore: A Plea for Psychoanalytic Semiotics', MLN 91, No. 6 Comparative Literature, 1500-1533.

Dundes, A. 1980
'The Symbolic Equivalence of Allomotivs in the Rabbit Herd (AT 570)', Arv 36, 91-8.

Holbek, B. 1987
Interpretation of Fairy Tales: Danish folklore in a European perspective (vol. CIII no. 239), Helsinki.

du Boulay, J. 1974
Portrait of a Greek Mountain Village, Oxford.

Hirschorn, R. 1978
'Open body/Closed Spaces: The Transformation of Female Sexuality', in Defining Females. The Nature of Women in Society, S. Ardener (ed.), New York, 66-88.

Köngäs Maranda, E & P. Maranda 1971
Structural Models in Folklore and transformational Essays (Approaches to Semiotics 10), The Hague/Paris.

Lindow, J. 1989
'A Quest for Meaning in Fairy Tales', Scandinavian Studies 61, 404-9.

Lindow, J. 1993
'Transforming the Monster. Notes on Bengt Holbek's Interpretation of Kong Lindorm', in Telling Reality. Folklore Studies in Memory of Bengt Holbek (Copenhagen Folklore Studies Vol. 1), M. Chesnutt (ed.), Copenhagen & Turku, page nos.

Μουσαίου-Μπουγιούκου, Κ. 1976
Παραμύθια του Λιβισιού και της Μάκρης, Athens.

Olsen, B. 1997
'Women and Gender Roles in Modern Greek Folk Tales', Copenhagen Folklore Notes 3-4, 3-12.

Olsen, B. 1999a
'Women and Gender Roles in Modern Greek Folk Tales', Κάμπος: Cambridge Papers in Modern Greek 7, 21-42.

Olsen, B. 1999b
'And they embroidered all kinds of embroidery', Copenhagen Folklore Notes 4, 1-6.

Olsen B. 2002
'The exception that proves the rule? A female storyteller from Kos', Scandinavian Journal of Modern Greek Studies 1, 61-74.

Πέρδικα, Ν. Λ. 1943
ΣΚΥΡΟΣ ΙΙ Μνημεία του Λόγου του Λαού, Athens.

Propp, V. 1968
Morphology of the Folktale (second edition of the English translation), Austin, TX.

Σαραντή, Ε. Σ. 1941
'Παραμύθια της Θράκης', Θρακικά 15, 343-55.

Stewart, C. 1991
Demons and the Devil, Princeton.

Vaz da Silva, F. 2000
'Bengt Holbek and the Study of Meanings in Fairy Tales', Cultural Analysis 1, 3-11.

von Hahn, J. G. 1864
Griechische und albanesische Märchen (Vol. 1-2), Leipzig.

The Nine Lives of Adam Friedel, the Portrayer of the Protagonists of the Greek Revolution*

JOHN LUND

Abstract

The Danish Philhellene Adam Friedel is mainly remembered today for his lithographic portraits of some of the protagonists of the Greek Revolution (Figs 1-3). His role in the Greek Revolution was poorly understood until 2007, when Dimitra Koukíou-Mitropoúlou published his biography (with an updated second edition in 2014). A German by birth, Friedel enlisted in the Danish army in 1803, obtained Danish citizenship in 1811 and married in 1812. After military service and having tried his hand at various occupations, he left his family for Russia, where he allegedly came into contact with the Philikí Etairía, arriving in Greece by the end of 1821. Masquerading as a baron, he gained the trust of leading Greek figures like Alexandros Mavrokordatos and Ioannis Kolettis, who employed him as a commissar. Friedel's role, however, was poorly understood by his fellow Philhellenes, and his claim to be a baron was called into question by another Danish Philhellene in the spring of 1822. This suspicion was apparently not widely circulated at first, allowing Friedel to continue to carry out assignments for the Greek authorities. He obtained a letter of recommendation from Lord Byron at Missolonghi shortly before the latter's death on 19 April 1824, but left Greece under a cloud shortly afterwards. Friedel next settled in Great Britain, where he published the lithographic portraits of the protagonists of the Greek Revolution. He re-married (bigamously) and established a new life, but left England and his new family for good in 1847, turning up later in Greece, where he tried to obtain a state pension due to services rendered during the Greek Revolution. He subsequently lived for some years in Smyrna and Constantinople before returning to Greece in 1866 or 1868, where he made a new attempt at obtaining a state pension. By way of conclusion, this article attempts to define some recurring patterns of behaviour of the highly gifted yet deeply flawed character of the man who called himself Adam Friedel (as well as Fridel, von Friedel, or de Friedel).

---

* I extend my warm thanks to Hanna Lassen and Nikolaos Roussos for helping me gain access to archival material in Athens. I am grateful, also, to Mogens Pelt for having drawn my attention to the thesis of Huseyin Sukru Ilicak (2011) and to Anne Haslund Hansen for attempting to locate Friedel's tomb in the Feriköy Protestant Cemetery in Istanbul.

Introduction

In 2008 Roderick Beaton observed with reference to the Greek War of Liberation that "we still await a history of that conflict, one that will draw on material now available only in Greek … A whole further dimension, as yet unexplored as far as I know, is the Ottoman perspective on events".[1] This situation is already changing for the better, and other sources are emerging as well.[2] The purpose of this article is to add a Danish perspective.

Danish involvement in the Greek war of Independence has not been forgotten by international scholarship,[3] but the subject attracted little scholarly interest in Denmark until Ellen Vibeke Krarup's thesis of 1985.[4] Twenty years later, Marina Friis Ghazaleh treated the Danish Philhellenic Movement in another thesis,[5] and Aristea Papanikoláou-Kristensen published a study of the same topic in 2010.[6] These three scholars discussed the dozen or so Danes who went to fight in Greece within the broader context of Danish Philhellenism.[7] The present article, in contrast, focuses on one of the active Danish Philhellenes, Adam Friedel (who also called himself Fridel, von Friedel and de Friedel). He arguably played a more important role than the others, but it was a role that has been poorly understood.

Our knowledge of Friedel was until recently mainly based on his oft-reproduced lithographic portraits of 24 of the protagonists of the Greek Revolution (Figs 1-3),[8] and on reminiscences by other Philhellenes,[9] whose accounts led to the caricature of him sketched by William St Clair.[10] Recent publications by two Greek scholars, however, have presented a more balanced picture: Charikleia G. Dima-

kopoulou's account of Friedel's life from 2003 and Dimitra Koukíou-Mitropoúlou's monograph from 2007.[11] Both are to a considerable degree based on previously untapped archival material in Greece, of which the most important is an autobiography Friedel submitted to the authorities at the age of 82 in support of his claim for a remuneration from the Greek nation that was due to him as a combatant in the War of Independence.[12]

This article was originally written in 2013. Its aim was to provide a more rounded picture of the man than Koukíou-Mitropoúlou had done in 2007 by adding new evidence from Danish and British archives on Friedel's youth in Denmark and on his later life. In 2014, Koukíou-Mitropoúlou published an expanded second edition of her book, which incorporated many of the same additional sources, and this volume stands as the definitive biography of Friedel. The modest aim of the present article is to introduce non-Greek speakers to the fascinating life of an enigmatic Danish artist and Philhellene, who remains to this day almost completely unknown in Denmark – one of his home countries.

1. Early years (1786/1788 to 1803)

The parish register of the Church of the Army Garrison in Copenhagen informs us that "Adam Fridel" converted from Judaism to the Lutheran faith on 16 September 1811.[13] He had obtained Danish citizenship by a law of 2 August 1811, quoting Germany as his country of birth,[14] and on the eve of his marriage in November 1812 he solemnly declared that he was unable to produce a birth certificate

---

1   Beaton 2008, xx.

2   Cf. Erdem 2009; Ilicak 2009, 2011.

3   See for instance Barth & Kerhrig-Korn 1960 and St Clair 2009, of which the first edition appeared in 1972.

4   Krarup 1985, 49-62.

5   Ghazaleh 2005.

6   Papanikoláou-Krístensen 2010 and 2009; also Pelt 2000.

7   For a definition of "Philhellenism", see Landfester & Lessenich 2002; many aspects of the concept are treated in the anthology by Mandilará *et al.* (eds) 2015.

8   Tsigakou 1981, 56-7, 196-7.

9   Lessing 1823, 67, 83-4; Byern 1833, 144-5; Striebeck 1834, 161-2.

10   St. Clair 2008, 89-90, 175 echoed by Richardson 2013, 103 note 148. For more balanced accounts see Krarup 1985, 50-1; Haugsted 1996, 86 note 1 (where he is confused with Waldemar von Qualen); Ghazaleh 2005, 48-9; Papanikoláou-Krístensen 2010, 74-83.

11   Dimakopoúlou 2003; Koukíou-Mitropoúlou 2007.

12   Dimakopoúlou 2003, 230-3; Koukíou-Mitropoúlou 2007, 263-4 no. 26; 2014, 296-8 no. 60. On the law, see Gallant 2001, 35-7.

13   Kirkebøger, Københavns Amt, Sokkelund Herred, Garnisons Sogn, birth register for 1810 to 1814 (<http://www.sa.dk/content/dk/ao-forside/find_kirkeboger#> accessed April 2014). Such conversions were not unheard of in those days, cf. Lausten 2002, 375-589.

14   <http://www.ddd.dda.dk/immibas/immibas2.asp> accessed September 2018.

Fig. 1 *Demetrios Ypsilantis. Lithography, "drawn from life" and published by Adam Friedel in London and Paris, 1827, after Koukíou-Mitropoúlou 2007, 144 fig. 69.*

or any other documentation relating to his age, despite having travelled to Königsberg in Prussia – now Kaliningrad – in an attempt to obtain them.[15] The city was indeed home to a Jewish community in the 18th century,[16] but

Friedel's story about the missing documentation is suspicious. Still, it may explain the uncertainty that surrounds the date of his birth. In the aforementioned solemn declaration, he swore his birth date was 15 January 1788, but his autobiography implies that he was born two years earlier,[17] and 1786 was also recorded as the year of his birth in the Census of England, Wales and Scotland of 1841.[18]

2. Denmark (1803-19)

According to his autobiography, Friedel joined the "Seelandischen Jäger Corps" in 1803. He was still a German citizen, but it was a common enough practice for Germans to enlist in the Danish army at the time. He states that he studied in 1807 at the "Militärische College" in Copenhagen, emerging with the rank of second lieutenant in 1808. He went on to serve in the "Holsteinischen leichten Infanterie Battalion", stationed in Kiel, but his conversion to the Lutheran faith took place in Copenhagen in September 1811, and in 1812 he was second lieutenant in the Corps of Jutland Sharpshooters, stationed at Kastellet in the Danish capital.[19] He made lieutenant the next year.[20]

Friedel married Georgine Mauritzelle Frisch on 6 November 1812, and a daughter, Sofie Magdalene, was born to the couple on 25 August 1813. He was appointed military judge a year after the abolishment of the Corps of Jutland Sharpshooters in 1816,[21] and his first son, Christian Ditlev, was born on 17 June 1817.[22] The date of birth of his second daughter, Dorothea Wilhelmine Friedel, is unknown.[23] According to his autobiography, Friedel was employed on 20 December 1816 at the Customs house at Horsens,

---

15 He wrote the statement when taking out an obligatory policy for his future wife at "Enkekassen", a pension system for widows of state employees. I am grateful to Børge Fogsgaard, who kindly answered my questions concerning the "Enkekassen". Cf. Rigsarkivet, Den Almindelige Enkekasse, Indskudssager, Policenummer 10150. (http://www.fogsgaard.org/index.php/2013-11-01-14-49-57/sogindskyder> accessed September 2018). He signed as Adam Friedel, but other documents in the file refer to him as "Adam v. Friedel". Striebeck (1834, 162) claims that his original name was Friederich Adam, but this assertion is unsupported by any evidence and seems unlikely.

16 Jolowicz 1867.

17 Koukíou-Mitropoúlou 2007, 263-4 no. 26; 2014, 296-8 no. 60.

18 <http://www.nationalarchives.gov.uk/records/census-records.htm> accessed September 2018.

19 Rigsarkivet, Den Almindelige Enkekasse, Indskudssager, Policenummer 10150 (http://www.fogsgaard.org/index.php/2013-11-01-14-49-57/sogindskyder> accessed September 2018).

20 S. Nygaard, Jysk Personalarkiv. <http://nygaards-sedler.dk/viewpage.php?page_id=72&nr. =101668&sort=e&vis=2> accessed in October 2013 but no longer online in September 2018.

21 In 1815 Friedel had applied (unsuccessfully) for a position in the Chamber of Customs ("General Toldkammer"), Rigsarkivet, Generaltoldkammeret, Toldkammerkancelli og Sekretariat Arkivserie: Fortegnelse over ansøgninger om embeder under Generaltoldkammeret 1787-1848.

22 See *supra* note 18.

23 In a letter to J. G. Adler on 4 August 1835 or 1837, Wilhelmine Dorothea Friedel wrote below her signature "daughter of the deceased captain von Friedel", Rigsarkivet, Privat Arkiv no. 5008, J.G. Adler 1784-1852 AI.4.

129

where his father-in-law was inspector.[24] The employment probably came to an end when his father-in-law died on 3 August 1817. Friedel was appointed undertaker in Horsens on 30 January 1819, but he did not find the work congenial and was released from the post soon afterwards, leaving Horsens for good in June 1819. In so doing he abandoned his children and pregnant wife, who gave birth to a son, Ove Ferdinand, on 20 August 1819.[25]

3. The road to Greece (1819-21)

According to his autobiography, Friedel went to Russia in the summer of 1819 to visit his brother, "Baron Eduard Friedel", a doctor at the court of Czar Alexander I. In 1820, he allegedly came into contact with the Philikí Etairía (The Society of Friends) in St Petersburg and Moscow, the clandestine organisation that paved the way for the Greek Revolution.[26] The leader of the Society, Alexander Ypsilantis,[27] dispatched his brother, Prince Demetrios Ypsilantis (Fig. 1), to the Peloponnese,[28] and Friedel was supposed to accompany him to Argos, but he claimed that arthritis and rheumatism prevented him from doing so. Instead he visited various spas and cities in Russia before reaching Odessa in February 1821.[29] The Russian Greek Committee there charged him to go to Greece as "Comissaire", and by way of Constantinople and Kea, Friedel duly turned up at Ypsilantis' camp in Argos.

The reminiscences of Eugen von Byern, a Prussian captain, give quite a different account.[30] He states that Friedel sailed to Greece from Marseille, where he had turned up carrying nothing but a rucksack containing a lithographic hand press,[31] his drawing requisites and a spare pair of glasses.[32] The German Philhellene Carl Theodor Striebeck published a third version: "*Als Unterofficier in dänischen Diensten … 1815 unter der Dienerschaft eines angesehenen Mannes von Kopenhagen nach Konstantinopel gereist, von dort nach Zanthe gegangen und im Jahre 1821 nach Morea gekommen*".[33] This is demonstrably mistaken, because we know that Friedel remained in Denmark until 1819, but von Byern's story is on the face of it not implausible given that the majority of Philhellenes embarked for Greece from Marseille.[34] Still, Friedel's own account in the autobiography would seem to come closest to the truth. The Philikí Etairía was extremely active in Russia,[35] and Demetrios Ypsilantis did indeed travel from Russia to Greece, where he arrived on 8 June 1821.[36] A month or so later, he was at Tripolis (now Tripoli),[37] which fell to the Greeks on 23 September, and he moved on to Argos a month later, finally reaching Corinth on 14 December.[38] If Friedel met Ypsilantis at Argos as he claims, then this must have happened between the end of October and the middle of December 1821.[39]

---

24 V. Richter, Den Danske Toldetat 1750-1896, Det kgl. Bibliotek, Håndskriftafd. Ny kgl. Saml. 2685, 4°, 76: Christian Ditlev Frisch.

25 See *supra* note 18.

26 Frangos 1973; Hatzopoulos 2009; Beaton 2013, 74-6.

27 Clogg (ed.) 1973, 192-4.

28 Woodhouse 1973, 222-31; Clogg (ed.) 1973, 198.

29 Cf. Dimakopoúlou 2003, 231 note 13; Koukíou-Mitropoúlou 2007, 17-8; 2014, 24.

30 On von Byern, see Barth & Kehrig-Korn 1960, 88; Quack-Eustathiades 1984 *passim*; Quack-Eustathiades 2008, 194, 196; Koukíou-Mitropoúlou 2007, 19 note 23; St Clair 2008, 287-8; Koukíou-Mitropoúlou 2014, 25 note 42.

31 If this piece of information can be given credit, it was probably an example of the portable press invented by Alois Senefelder in 1818, cf. Twyman 1967, 37-9 pl. 3 and figs 47-8. The press was 17 inches wide (43.2 cm) and 23 inches long (58.4 cm).

32 Byern 1833, 144-5; Koukíou-Mitropoúlou 2007, 244-6 no. 64; 2014, 267-8 no. 2.

33 Striebeck 1828, 162. For Striebeck, see Barth & Kehring-Korn 1960, 237-9; Koukíou-Mitropoúlou 2014, 24-5.

34 St Clair 2008, 66-77; only three departures from Marseille in 1821 are listed *ibid*., p. 357: in July, August and October, but the information with regard to that year is very incomplete. Friedel is not mentioned among the Philhellenes who arrived at Kalamata on 20 November 1821, cf. Raybaud 1824, 23-4.

35 Frangos 1973, 87, 94; Woodhouse 1973, 118-9; 174 and *passim*; Jewsbury 1999, 752-3; Ars 2011; Beaton 2013, 74-5.

36 Dakin 1973, 163; Ars 2011, 438.

37 Brewer 2001, 113-23.

38 St Clair 2008, 49.

39 There was hardly time for Friedel to meet up with Ypsilantis in July, since the Prince had already reached Aspros by June, cf. Kolokotronis 1892, 150. See further Koukíou-Mitropoúlou 2007, 18 note 17; 2014, 24 note 32.

Fig. 2 *Alexandros Mavrokordatos. Lithography published by Friedel in London in 1826, after Koukíou-Mitropoúlou 2007, 102 fig. 29.*

Fig. 3 *Ioannis Kolettis, lithography published by Friedel in London, August 1826, after Koukíou-Mitropoúlou 2007, 116 fig. 43.*

4. In Piáda, Corinth and Tripolis (1822)

According to the autobiography, Friedel went to Piada at Epidauros for the First Greek National Assembly, which was held between December 1821 and January 1822. Here he proposed to members of the Senate that the new national flag of Greece should have a white cross like the Danish flag, but on a blue instead of a red background.[40] There is no independent proof of this assertion, but the resemblance is striking and this scheme was indeed accepted by Alexandros Mavrokordatos (Fig. 2), the president of the Executive (the Provisional Government), in a decree signed on 15 March 1822. It served as the Greek national flag between 1822 and 1969 and from 1975 to 1978.[41]

In a letter written in Corinth on 23 March 1822, Ioannis Kolettis (Fig. 3), the Minister of the Interior, assigned "Baron Mr. Adam de Friedel" to oversee the making of the seals of the new administration in Tripolis, and to bring them back to Corinth together with the lithographs (perhaps designs made by Friedel from which the seals were cut).[42] It was probably while carrying out this task that he encountered von Byern in a coffeehouse in Tripolis.[43] The German described him thus:

ein sehr langer, dürrer, bebrillter, alternder Mann,[44] mit überaus feiner durchdringender Stimme … Unbekümmert um die zahlreichen Gäste fand ich ihn beschäftigt, einen nicht unbedeutenden

---

40 Dimakopoúlou 2003, 231 note 11; Koukíou-Mitropoúlou 2007, 263; 2014, 297.

41 Mazarákis-Ainían 1996, xxxiii–xxxv; Khatzilíras 2003 and Koukíou-Mitropoúlou 2007, 18 note 19; 2014, 27 note 46.

42 Koukíou-Mitropoúlou 2007, 20-1 and 247-8 nos 4-5; 2014, 31-4, 271 no. 12.

43 Barth & Kehrig-Korn 1960, 88; Quack-Eustathiades 2008, 194, 196; St Clair 2008, 287-8. Henrik Krøyer, who sailed to Greece from Marseille on the same ship as von Byern, paints an unflattering picture of him (Krøyer 1870, 52).

44 Friedel was either 34 or 36 years old at the time, considerably older than most of the other Philhellenes.

Defekt an seiner Kleidung aufzubessern, die bereits unzählige Spuren einer solchen Arbeit an sich trug. Er unterhielt sich … sehr eifrig mit einem jungen Menschen, dem er vergeblich zuzureden schien, bei ihm zu bleiben, bis sie gemeinschaftlich die Wanderung nach Korinth antreten könnten, an der er für jetzt noch durch sehr wichtige Geschäfte verhindert. Auf den ersten Blick in ihnen Phil-hellenen erkennend, und durch ihre Unterhaltung in meiner Mut-tersprache in dieser Meinung bestärkt, war es mir durchaus neu, einen dieser vernachlässigten und zurückgesetzten Fremdlinge in der Residenz der Landesdeputierten des Peloponnes von Geschäften reden zu hören, die in Beziehung zu den stolzen Namen Ypsilantis, Pietro Bey und Kolokotronis unterschied. Neugierig trat ich näher hinzu und begrüßte meinen Mann als Landsmann und Leidens-gefährten. Ohne seine Arbeit zu unterbrechen, erwiderte er mir, er wisse nicht in wie fern er sich diese Ehre aneignen könne, er sei Däne von Geburt, der Baron Friedel von Friedelsburg, und was seine jetzige Stellung betreffe, geheimer Sekretär im Bureau des Fürsten Ypsilanti.[45]

Von Byern adds that another Danish Philhellene, Walde-mar von Qualen,[46] questioned Friedel's claim to be a bar-on, observing quite rightly that no manor house called Friedelsburg is to be found in Denmark.[47] But the sus-picions raised by von Qualen were apparently not wide-ly circulated at first.[48] Quite the reverse, "*Fertig met der Feder*", Friedel was – according to Byern – for a time em-ployed (as secretary?) by a commission established by the Philhellenes,[49] presumably the one set up to "look into the claims of the volunteers and grade them by rank".[50]

5. Athens, Argos, Egypt and the Aegean (1822-24)

Friedel presented himself as "Regierungs-Commissar" when Byern met him again in Corinth and Athens,[51] but after an unsuccessful attempt to capture the Acropolis, "*an dem er natürlich keinen Antheil nahm entfernte er sich jedoch auch von hier*".[52] This may be a reference to the un-successful attempt to capture the Turkish Garrison of the Acropolis that took place in March or April 1822.[53] But on 14 May, in advance of a planned transfer of the Senate and the Executive from Corinth to Argos, Mavrokordatos no-tified Kolettis that Friedel was to organise the housing of the administration in Argos.[54] This is where the German Philhellenist Friedrich August Lessen met him:

Den Tag nach meiner Ankunft in Argos kam ein Mann in eu-ropäischer Kleidung auf die Kanzlei, und kündigte sich mit einer Protectionsmiene als Baron Adam Friedel, früher Oberstlieutenant in Dänischen Diensten, jetzt Griechischen General-Commissair, an; als solcher sei er jetzt in Argos, um Quartier für den Senat zu machen.[55]

---

45 Byern 1833, 148-9.

46 According to Raybaud 1824, 23-4, Von Qualen arrived at Kalamata on 20 November 1821, and he is known to have been in Athens on 5 March 1822 thinking about going to Delphi (see Papanikoláou-Krístensen 2010, 36-9). But he went to Lamia instead, where he was killed in action at Hagia Ma-rina, cf. Ross 1848, 85. An inscription in his memory can be seen in the *plateia* of Agia Marina: http://amfictyon.blogspot.com/2014/06/1799-1822. html. In 1897, the Danish journalist Henrik Cavling saw Von Qualen's eight-foot-high tombstone close to Thermoplylae, with an inscription saying that he died on 4 April 1822, cf. *Politiken* 25 May 1897 and Kaarsted 1960, 159. See further Clausen & Rist (eds) 1912, 75 note 1, where his death is said to have occurred on 17 April. The discrepancy may be due to the difference between the Julian calendar used in Greece until 1923 and the Gregorian calendar introduced in Denmark in 1700. Others have quoted 3 July as the day of his death, cf. Barth & Kehrig-Korn 1960, 202-3; Krarup 1985, 52.

47 However, von Qualen was wrong in believing that Friedel was born in Holsten and had been in turn a student, actor and gambler, cf. Byern 1833, 150-1.

48 According to Striebeck 1828, 162, Friedel was in Argos: "als er von einem Philhellenen aus Dänemark erkannt und auf der Stelle entlarvt wurde. Darauf ward er nach vorhergegangener Untersuchung cassirt, ihm der Sabel zerbrochen, und er für ehrlos erklärt". But this is almost certainly un-true. Friedel wore civilian clothes during his stay in Greece, and the Greek authorities never lost their trust in him. Moreover, Striebeck implies that he was unmasked in the second half of 1823, but by then von Qualen had been dead for at least a year.

49 Byern 1833, 153.

50 Striebeck 1828, 208; St Clair 2008, 89-90.

51 Byern 1833, 150.

52 Byern 1833, 153-4.

53 Brewer 2001, 169-75; St Clair 2008, 86-7.

54 Dimakopoúlou 2003, 228 notes 3-4; Koukíou-Mitropoúlou 2007, 21-2 and 249 no. 8; 2014, 35-7 and 276 no. 44; see p. 277 no. 27, a letter written in Argos by Ioannis Varvatis and Adam de Fridel.

55 Lessen 1823, 67.

Another German Philhellene, C. W. Danneberg, ran into him in Argos at about the same time:

Von dem Senate war nun kein Mitglied gegenwärtig, die andern hielten ihre Sieste. Man wies uns zu den Ephoren, wo wir einen Mann in fränkischer Kleidung verwanden, welcher deutsch sprach, und sich mit einer vornehmen Wichtigkeit als General-Commissair von Griechenland, darstellte, und der hier als Quartiermacher fungierte. Man gab uns ein Haus zur Wohnung, und, statt der Lebensmittel ein Geldequivalent von 26 Paradis.[56]

A few days later, Friedel, "*der quasi General-Commissair*", was responsible for interrogating a supposedly deaf and dumb prince from Argos who claimed that he was called Alepso. He had travelled from Marseille to Navarino in May 1822 on the same ship as the Danish Philhellene Carl Wederkinch,[57] who had this to say about him:

Besides those mentioned, a pretended deaf and dumb was in our company, he was supposed to be a son of a Greek Prince in Argos. He had arrived with von Seeman from Stutgard. The Society for Greek Assistance there had handed him over to von Seemann's care, who should lead him to Argos. The Society had supplied him with ample money and decent clothing, yet being an unfortunate prince he had even been presented to the King of Würtemberg and His majesty had graced him with a considerable gift. No one dreamt that he was – as it later turned out – an imposter, because he knew masterly how to play his role.

Ironically, Friedel – himself an imposter – was responsible for unmasking him.[58] Letters in Greek archives show that the Dane next embarked on a long journey on behalf of the Greek authorities.[59] On 15 October we find him in Tenos,[60] on 10 November in Naxos[61] and on 28 December in Siphnos.[62] On 21 August 1823, Friedel arrived at Alexandria in Egypt,[63] where he also visited Cairo. From there he went to Crete,[64] and (probably by way of Kythera)[65] reached Zanthe (Zakynthos),[66] then Missolonghi by the beginning of 1824.[67]

6. Friedel and Lord Byron

On 21 February, Mavrokordatos in Missolonghi supplied Friedel with a letter of recommendation, referring to his great zeal for the Greek cause and explaining that he has returning to Denmark to take care of some family business and intended to go to England afterwards.[68] And on 4 March, Friedel obtained a letter of introduction to the London Greek Committee from Lord Byron in Missolonghi:[69]

Gentlemen, I am desirous to introduce to your notice the bearer of this Baron Adam Friedell who appears (from his well authenticated papers & the knowledge he possesses of the present state of the affairs in Greece having lately returned from the Morea) to be an individual who may be usefully consulted by your Honourable Committee. I have at his particular request

---

56   Danneberg 1823, 111-2.

57   Wederkinch 1822, quoted from Krarup 1985, Bilag II, 4.

58   Lessen 1823, 83-4; Dannenberg 1823, 112-3: *"Der sogennante General-Commissair hatte eine Untersuchung gegen den Pseudo-Prinzen eingeleitet, deren Resultat Anfangs sehr schreckend schien, da man sogar von Aufknüpfen sprach, späterhin auf Rücksendung nach Stuttgart zu decretiren Willens schien, zuletzt aber die Freigebung des angeklagten Betrügers"*; Barth & Kehring-Korn 1960, 119; Quack-Eustathiades 1984, 59; Koukíou-Mitropoúlou 2007, 22; St Clair 2008, 72; Koukíou-Mitropoúlou 2014, 36-7.

59   Koukíou-Mitropoúlou 2007, 263 no. 26; 2014, 296-8 no. 60.

60   Koukíou-Mitropoúlou 2007, 22 and 250 no. 10; 2014, 39, 281 no. 36: a letter from Adam Fridel to Mavromichalis and Kolettis.

61   Koukíou-Mitropoúlou 2007, 23 and 251 nos 11-2; 2014, 39-40, 281-2 nos 37-8.

62   Koukíou-Mitropoúlou 2007, 23 and 252-3 no. 13; 2014, 42-3, 282-3 no. 39: a letter from Adam Fridel to Mavromichalis and Kolettis.

63   Dimakopoúlou 2003, 229 note 6; Koukíou-Mitropoúlou 2007, 253-4 no. 14; 2014, 43-4, 283-4 no. 40.

64   Koukíou-Mitropoúlou 2007, 254 no. 15; 2014, 285 no. 43.

65   J. St. M. Macphail (1928) refers to a letter written by Baron Friedel in March 1824 to "a gentleman holding an official position in one of the Ionian Islands, in which he mentions amongst other matters, that he has had conferences with Byron and Mavrocordato". The gentleman in question may have been John Macphail, who was British resident at Cerigo (=Kythera) from 1823 to 1831, cf. Harlan 2011, 334 note 5.

66   Koukíou-Mitropoúlou 2007, 24 and 255 no. 16; 2014, 44, 284 no. 41: written by "Adam de Fridel" to Ioannis Kolettis Zakynthos on 10 February 1824.

67   Koukíou-Mitropoúlou 2007, 255 no. 17; 2014, 284-5 no. 42: letter of recommendation by Lord Byron written in Missolonghi on 4 March 1824.

68   Koukíou-Mitropoúlou 2007, 262 no. 24 β); 2014, 290-1 no. 50 β). In his autobiography, Friedel quotes health problems as a second reason for leaving Greece.

69   On the London Greek Committee, see Dimaras 1973, 204-19; Beaton 2013, 124-6 and *passim* on Byron's relations with the Committee.

furnished him with this letter to avail himself herewith for that purpose—& I am Gentlemen yours most sincerely &c. NOEL BYRON.[70]

On 21 March 1824, Friedel was in Kephallonia informing the Senate of his impending departure,[71] but he had a nasty surprise later the same day when he read an article in the *Greek Chronicle* (Ελληνική Χρονικά),[72] warning Philhellenic societies in Switzerland, Germany and elsewhere in Europe against the Danish Baron Adam Friedel.[73] He immediately sent Lord Byron a long rebuttal,[74] which prompted the latter two days later to write to the *Greek Chronicle*:

Sirs – I have read for the first time yesterday an article in the Chronica Greca – denouncing the Danish Baron Adam Friedel – who is not here to respond. – I do not know if this is just but it does not appear to me to be generous. Baron Friedel came here with the strongest recommendations of the Greek Government in general and of several distinguished Greeks in particular. – He requested an introduction to the English Committee – and I have given it to him – His Excellency Prince Mavrocordato has done the same. B[aron] A[dam] F[riedel] has served the Government and the Nation – and they have thanked him for his services – certainly the Nation must know better than you or me – they have been his most zealous defenders. – I do not know the B.A.F. as a compatriot and scarcely as a person – but he is alone – a foreigner – oppressed – and now far away – and for these reasons I take up his defense – until I see evidence that would discredit him. – If after all he is an ad-

venturer worthy of being denounced in a public paper – which pretends to the most liberal sentiments – I have nothing more to say – except neither Baron Kolbe – nor the Marchese Bellier de Launay – nor Dr. Meyer – nor the German and Swiss [distressed ones?] can scorn those with false titles – intentional trickery – dubious intrigues – or equivocal conduct toward the public of whatever kind are not to be believed of him more than them.[75]

Johann Jakob Mayer, the editor of the *Greek Chronicle*, later tearfully apologised to Byron in person and the latter forgave him.[76]

Before his departure, Friedel also sent letters refuting the allegations to Mavrokordatos,[77] and to the Senate,[78] and he obtained a certificate of identity from Count Lunzi, the Danish Consul at Zanthe on 3/15 April:[79] "*il presente certificate onde attestare: che risulta dai suoi passport a carte ben regulate esser egli quale si nomina Baron Adam de Fridel Nobile native di Danimarca*".[80] By an odd coincidence, Friedel travelled to England on "Florida", the ship carrying Lord Byron's embalmed body, which left Zanthe on 25 May.[81]

7. A new life in England (1824-47)

Friedel was so well received in England that he decided to extend his stay and in 1825 he began publishing the 'Twenty-Four Portraits … of the Principal Leaders and Personages who have made themselves most conspicuous in the Greek Revolution', of which many were drawn from life.[82]

---

70 Marchand (ed.) 1981, 127-8; Koukíou-Mitropoúlou 2007, 255 no. 17; 2014, 284-5 no. 42.

71 Koukíou-Mitropoúlou 2007, 254 no. 15; 2014, 285 no. 43: written by "Adam Fridel" at Kephallonia on 21 March 1824; 255-8 no. 18; 2014, 285-7 no. 44: written by Adam Fridel to Lord Byron at Kephallonia on 21 March.

72 Beaton 2013, 220, 222-5.

73 Dimakopoúlou 2003, 229 note 8; Koukíou-Mitropoúlou 2007, 24 note 35; 2014, 45 note 153.

74 In the archive of the Πολεμικό Μουσείο, αρ. 4428. A Greek translation can be found in Koukíou-Mitropoúlou 2007, 255-8 no. 18; 2014, 285-7 no. 44.

75 The letter was written in Italian; it is quoted from the translation by Daniela Noè in Marchand (ed.) 1994, 83-4; Koukíou-Mitropoúlou 2007, 259 no. 20; 2014, 288-9 no. 46 (translated into Greek).

76 Kennedy 1830, 308-9. Meyer later claimed that Byron had died in his arms, cf. Beaton 2013, 269.

77 Koukíou-Mitropoúlou 2007, 259-60 no. 21; 2014, 288-9 no. 47.

78 Koukíou-Mitropoúlou 2007, 260-1 no. 22; 2014, 289-90 no. 48.

79 Nørgaard 2000.

80 Koukíou-Mitropoúlou 2007, 26 and 261 no. 23; 2014, 290 no. 49.

81 Parry 1825, 146-7; see further Hobhouse 1910, 56, 64-6. Erdman 1960, 582 cites from an autograph album collected by William Upcott: "ADAM FRIEDEL, as frind [sic] of the late Lord Byron, and resided with him at Messalonga and accompanied his remains in July 1824 to England. The 12 August. 1824."

82 Tsigakou 1981, 56-7, 196-7; Macphail 1928, 27 refers to a letter in his possession written by General Thomas Gordon at Cariness in September 1827: "During my absence Baron Friedel has been in England, trying to persuade people to buy a set of engraved portraits from originals done by him in Greece".

Their popularity is reflected by the fact that a sixth edition came out in 1832 in Paris as well as London,[83] and *The British Magazine* referred to him in 1830 as *"the distinguished foreigner Baron Adam Friedel".*[84] In the same year he published an essay on 'Drawing on Stone. With the necessary Instructions for Lithography … Materials for Drawing Printing etc. etc. to be had at A. Friedel's Office' at 24, Greek Street Soho".[85] By 1835, the Lithographic Establishment had moved to 15, Southampton Street. It was located at 252, Tottenham Court Road from 1838 to 1842, and at 3, Charlotte Street, Bloomsbury in 1844 and 1845.[86] Friedel reportedly travelled extensively in England and Scotland,[87] and claims in the autobiography to have become a member of the Philanthropic Society and co-founder of the "Adelleide Gallery", i.e. the Adelaide Gallery, also known as the Gallery of Practical Science, which opened in London in 1832.[88] He was also a member of the Royal Polytechnic Society, and one of his lithographs shows visitors in the great hall of the Polytechnic Institution.[89] In 1844, the Polytechnic Society published a pamphlet (?) by Friedel entitled 'The New Royal Exchange'.[90]

Around 1826, Friedel had married Susanna, the daughter of John Monins Hodges of the Greek Committee, and sister of Hodges, "one of the artificers at Missolonghi".[91] A daughter, Sarah, was born to the couple in 1827, and about this time word reached his family in Denmark that "Colonel Friedel … fell during the battle of Navarino [20 October 1827] while in English service".[92] The rumour of

his death was exaggerated, and in the census of England, Wales and Scotland conducted in 1841 the family is listed in the recording district St Giles & St George in Middlesex. By contrast, only Susanna and Sarah are listed in the census of 1851.[93] Friedel had by then left England, giving as a reason – according to his autobiography – that the climate was not beneficial to his health. He travelled to Nice via Paris and Marseille, using a passport issued by Frederik Ditlev Reventlow, Danish Ambassador at the Court of St. James.

8. Genoa, Athens, Smyrna, Constantinople and Bucharest (1847-61)

Friedel must have left England in 1847, because he informs us that he stayed for two winters in Genoa before embarking from Naples on a ship bound for Athens in 1849.[94] Friedel was kindly received in Athens, where he attended two audiences with King Otho and was decorated with the Royal Order of the Redeemer in silver and the Cross for the War of Independence.[95] But he left the hot climate of Athens and settled down in Smyrna for two years, establishing a Drawing Academy at the "Greek Gymnasium".[96] The son of an American missionary in Smyrna later recalled meeting him there:

a German baron, who soon requested the favor of a small loan, with apologies that his drafts had been unexpectedly delayed.

---

83 The artistic output of Friedel is exhaustively treated by Koukíou-Mitropoúlou 2007, 29-40; 2014, 48-55 and 61-265.

84 *The British Magazine: A Monthly Journal of Literature, Science, and Art* 1 (1830), 240: "Some beautiful specimens in coloured lithography have been laid before us. They are productions of the distinguished foreigner Baron Adam Friedel, and consist of a series of copies of old masters, and of portraits of the most celebrated of the Greeks, who distinguished themselves in the late Revolutionary War in the East. The prints possess considerable merit … The baron is evidently an accomplished artist."

85 Koukíou-Mitropoúlou 2007, 27 and 268; 2014, 49-50.

86 Twyman 1974/1975, 33.

87 Graham 1915.

88 Cf. Altick 1978, 377-81; Wade 2012, 153 pl. 32.

89 Wade 2012, 153 pl. 33. Moreover, in 1840, three lithographs of fossils were published. 'Retransferred from the Daguerreotype Plate. On stone by A. Friedel at the Polytechnic Institution', cf. Thackray 1985, 179 fig. 2 189 nos 37-9.

90 Friedel 1844. I have not been able to find a copy of this publication.

91 Dimakopoúlou 2003, 229 note 9; St Clair 2008, 385 note 18; Koukíou-Mitropoúlou 2014, 48.

92 This emerges from a biography of Sophie Magdalene Friedel's husband, Jonas Christoffer Leonhard Hjelte, Zeuthen 1893, 468; Koukíou-Mitropoúlou 2014, 48 note 171. In 1834 his Danish wife lived in Copenhagen with a new husband, with whom she had a four year old son, census available online <http://ddd.dda.dk/kiplink1.htm>.

93 http://www.nationalarchives.gov.uk/records/census-records.htm.

94 Koukíou-Mitropoúlou 2007, 264; 2014, 297.

95 Koukíou-Mitropoúlou 2007, 28 note 72; 2014, 56 note 209 quotes a newspaper account dated 31 August 1849 citing the reasons why he was decorated. For the Royal Order of the Redeemer, see Romanoff 1987, 42-5 and 120-1.

96 Augustinos 1992, 158.

Baron Friedel had shown a number of his drawings, indicating a good artist in black and white, or pencil drawing, and my father with some shrewdness suggested a way to relieve the Baron's embarrassment, by his giving to the children of the family bi-weekly drawing lessons in return for his board. Thus began my first education in art. Everything was rosy for a while, we children took hold with zeal and our instructor seemed interested, but this soon waned, as time elapsed, and the so-called baron failed to fulfill obligations, and my father was obliged to decline longer to entertain him … the first lesson I took with Baron Friedel acted as decisively as the first chapter of Peter Parley's history which I read, as already stated, at Trebizond. From that day to this I have been passionately fond of my brush and pencil, a passion that has sometimes slumbered only to awake with renewed vigor.[97]

By his own account, Friedel next moved to Constantinople, where he set up a lithographic press, with which he published portraits of the Grand Vezir, the Sultan and various ambassadors at the *Porte*,[98] and he allegedly found employment there during the Crimean War (1853 to 1856).[99] On 13 January 1858, Friedel wrote from Bucharest to Henry Lytton Bulwer, who was British Ambassador at Constantinople from 1858 to 1865, in order to direct his attention to two estates for sale in the principality of Wallachia. He signed the letter as "Baron Adam Friedel". The recipient seems to have asked for more information, because Friedel sent him a second letter dated 23 January 1858, in which he acknowledged that he "scarcely [had] the honour of being known to Your Excellency" and that "For a long time I have sought for an employment without success, and my present situation forces me to solicit confidently your Excellency's protection". He proposes to raise capital for buying estates in Moldavia and Wallachia "by means of shares in England", adding that "To execute my plan, I am forced to go to London, & for that reason I request from Your Excellency the favour of an introduction to persons in London, who may forward my enterprise".[100] It is unlikely that anything came out of this scheme, and Friedel was probably not all that eager to undertake a journey to England at this point, because according to a family tradition "after being at Constantinople during the Crimean War [he] crossed to the Balkans and was heard of no more".[101] He had evidently performed the same vanishing act on his English family as he had done on his Danish wife and children some twenty years earlier.[102] Friedel does not refer to any of this in his autobiography, of course, where it is simply stated that he left Constantinople in favour of the spas in Bohemia and Baden Baden.

9. Athens and Constantinople (1861 to after 1868/1870)

In 1861, Friedel was in Athens again hoping to obtain a pension due to him because of his active involvement in the Greek War of Independence. In this he was unsuccessful, and he claims to have returned to Constantinople because of internal unrest in Greece from 1863 to 1865.[103] Still, he went to Athens again in 1868 or 1870 to make a new attempt at obtaining his pension, and it was for this purpose that he wrote his autobiography at the age of 82.

This is the last we hear of Adam Friedel. He was probably never awarded the pension from the Greek state, and the place and time of his death are also unknown. He is not among the relatively few Danes buried in the Protestant Cemetery in Athens, so it seems likely that he returned to Constantinople with (or more likely with-

---

97 Benjamin 1914, 70-1.

98 Cf. Graham 1915: "He published some coloured engravings of Turkish characters."

99 Oliver Graham was in possession of "some of his letters from the East in the years 1853-5", cf. Graham 1915.

100 Norfolk Record Office, Bulwer of Heydon Family Papers: Friedel, Baron Adam 138/39-40. Correspondence of HLB BUL 1/138/1-40 565 x 9 1856-1858. Koukíou-Mitropoúlou 2014, 58-9, 294-5 nos. 57-8.

101 <http://archiver.rootsweb.ancestry.com/th/read/GENBRIT/199806/0896925330> accessed October 2013, but no longer online in September 2018.

102 According to Graham 1915: "*He was a Dane, and an officer in the Danish army, and is reported to have been killed in battle. Afterwards his estates were confiscated. Whether this occurred at the time of the annexation of Schleswig-Holstein or not, I cannot say, as he suddenly disappeared, and nothing was heard of him. A few letters were received from him, written on the battle-field, but the letters have been lost, and owing to the death of his daughter (to whom the letters were written) a few years ago, I am unable to obtain any clue to his decease.*"

103 See Friedel's autobiography and Koukíou-Mitropoúlou 2014, 59-60.

out) his Greek pension. Perhaps he died there, but he is not among those laid to rest in the Danish section of the Feriköy Protestant Cemetery in Istanbul.

Conclusion

When Friedel departed from Germany and signed up for the Danish army in 1803, he seems to have established a pattern of behaviour, which he repeated sixteen years later, when he left Denmark and his Danish family, and again in 1847, when he abandoned his English wife, whom he had married bigamously. Moreover, Friedel habitually exaggerated his position in life: he left the Danish army as a lieutenant, but claimed to be a lieutenant colonel in Argos in 1821, and in the message conveyed to his Danish family informing them of his supposed death at Navarino he is referred to as a colonel. At least from the time of his arrival in Greece he presented himself as a baron, living the part so convincingly that he fooled everyone – except his compatriot von Qualen, who alerted some of the Philhellenes in Greece to the fraud. Nonetheless, Friedel continued to play the role successfully even after the *Greek Chronicle* warned Philhellenes in Europe against him in 1824. He still used the title in his letters to Henry Lytton Bulwer in 1858.

Friedel is mostly silent about his personal life in the autobiography he wrote towards the end of his life, but the information in this document that can be verified by other sources seems to be correct. Perhaps significantly, the text does not refer to his claim to be a baron, and he signs it "Adam Friedel". He was regularly beset by financial problems and claimed to be of poor health, which did not, however, prevent him from living into his 80s. At the same time, Friedel was not short of talents. He spoke and wrote German and Danish fluently and was adept at Modern Greek and English.[104] He was in addition an able artist, who was among the first to grasp the potential of the newly invented lithographic technique,[105] and his involvement in the Adelaide Gallery in London is testimony to his continued interest in scientific inventions.

Friedel was the odd man out among the Philhellenes due to his relatively advanced age, civilian dress and abstention from taking an active part in the fighting. He rather associated himself with some of the leading Greek politicians and military men of the day: Demetrios Ypsilantis at first, and beginning in 1822 he carried out assignments at various places given by Mavrokordats and Kolettis, the leading figures in the "modernising, internationalist tendency within the Revolution [that] would win over the locally based power-structures represented by the warlords".[106] The regular Philhellenes were perhaps understandably confused by his behaviour, and some of them moreover were so suspicious of Friedel due to his fake claim to be a baron that they failed to grasp that he was in fact a commissar acting on behalf of the Greek authorities.[107] But the decorations bestowed on him in later life show that his efforts were recognised and indeed appreciated by the authorities in Greece.[108]

JOHN LUND

Collection of Classical and Near Eastern Antiquities
Ancient Cultures of Denmark and the Mediterranean
The National Museum of Denmark
Frederiksholms Kanal 12
DK-1220 Copenhagen K
John.Lund@natmus.dk

---

104 The Greek letters written by Friedel (Koukíou-Mitropoúlou 2007, 250 nos 9-10, 252 no. 13, 254-5 nos 15-6, 259-62 nos. 21, 22, 24; 2014, 269 no. 5, 270 nos 8-9, 275 no. 22, 277 no. 27, 281 no. 36, 282-3 no. 39, 284 no. 41, 285 no. 43, 288-90 nos 47-8, 292 no. 52, 293-4 no. 56, 295 no. 59) show that Byern (1833, 144-145) is mistaken in stating that he was "Unbekannt mit der Landssprache".

105 The lithographic technique was invented by Alois Senefelder in 1796, cf. Senefelder 1818; Twyman 1967. The technique was introduced in Denmark by Wilhelm Heinrich Wenzler in 1812, cf. Schmidt Hansen 2013, 28-30.

106 Beaton 2013, 270-271; 147-157.

107 Thus also Koukíou-Mitropoúlou 2007, 17.

108 Portraits of the protagonists played an important part in the promulgation of images of the in the war in France, cf. Kastríti 2006, 51. The French edition of Friedel's series is mentioned *ibidem*, 56 note 14.

Bibliography

Altick, R. D. 1978
The shows of London, Harvard.

Ars, G. L. 2011
Η Φιλική Εταιρία στη Ρωσία, Αθήνα.

Augustinos, G. 1992
The Greeks of Asia Minor: Confession, Community, and Ethnicity in the Nineteenth Century, Kent, Ohio & London.

Barth, W. & M. Kehrig-Korn 1960
Die Philhellenenzeit von der Mitte des 18. Jahrhunderts bis zur Ermordung Kapodistrias' am 9. Oktober 1831, München.

Beaton, R. 2009
'Introduction', in Beaton & Ricks (eds) 2009, 1-18.

Beaton, R. 2013.
Byron's War. Romantic Rebellion, Greek Revolution, Cambridge.

Beaton, R. & D. Ricks (eds) 2009
The Making of Modern Greece, Farnham & Burlington, Vt.

Benjamin, S. G. W. 1914
The Life and Adventures of a Free Lance, Burlington, Vt.

Brewer, D. 2001
The Flame of Freedom: The Greek War of Independence 1821-1833, London.

Byern, E.v. 1833
Bilder aus Griechenland und der Levante, Berlin.

Clausen, J. & P. F. Rist (eds) 1912
Oberst Jakob Thore Ræders Barne- og Ungdomserindringer, (Memoirer og Breve 16), Kjøbenhavn.

Clogg, R. (ed.) 1973
The Movement for Greek Independence 1770-1821: Essays to mark the 150th anniversary of the Greek War of Independence, London & Basingstoke.

Dakin, D. 1973
'The Formation of the Greek State, 1821-33', in Clogg (ed.) 1973, 156-81.

Dannenberg, C. W. 1823
Harmlose Betrachtungen gesammelt auf einer Reise von Hamburg nach Griechenland, Constantinopel und dem schwarzen Meere im Jahre 1822, Hamburg.

Dimakopoúlou, Ch. G. 2003
'Ο Adam Friedel αυτοβιογραφούμενος', Ο *Ερανιστής* 24, 227-33.

Dimaras, A. 1973
'The Other British Philhellenes', in Clogg (ed.) 1973, 200-23.

Echinard, P. 1973
Grecs et Philhellènes à Marseille, de la Révolution française à l'Indépendance de la Grèce, Marseille.

Erdem, Y. H. 2009
'The Greek Revolt and the end of the Old Ottoman Order', in Pizánias (ed.) 2009, 281-88.

Erdman, D. V. 1960
'Reliques of the Contemporaries of William Upcott, "Emperor of Autographs"', *Bulletin of the New York Public Library* 64, 581-87.

Frangos, G. D. 1973
'The Philiki Etairia: A Premature National Coalition', in Clogg (ed.) 1973, 87-103.

Friedel, A. 1844
The New Royal Exchange, London.

Gallant, T. W. 2001
Modern Greece, London.

Ghazaleh, M. F. 2005
Danmark og den Græske Frihedskrig: Den dansk philhellenistiske bevægelse i 1820erne, Thesis, University of Copenhagen.

Graham, O. 1915
'Baron Adam Friedel', *Notes and Queries* 40, 433.

Harlan, D. 2011
'British Lancastrian schools of nineteenth-century Kythera', *Annual of the British School at Athens* 106, 325-74.

Hatzopoulos, M. 2009
'From resurrection to insurrection: "sacred" myths, motifs, and symbols in the Greek War of Independence', in Beaton & Ricks (eds), 81-93.

Haugsted, I. 1996
Dream and Reality: Danish antiquaries, architects and artists in Greece, London.

Hobhouse, J. C. 1910
Recollections of a Long Life. With Additional Extracts from his Private Diaries (Vol. 3), London.

Ilicak, H. S. 2009
'The revolt of Alexandros Ipsilantis and the fate of the Fanariots in ottoman documents', in Pizánias (ed.), 320-33.

Ilicak, H. S. 2011
A Radical Rethinking of Empire: Ottoman State and Society during the

Greek War of Independence (1821-1826), PhD thesis, Harvard. University.

Jewsbury, G.F. 1999
'The Greek Question. The view from Odessa 1815-1822', *Cahiers du Monde russe* 40, 751-62.

Jolowicz, H. 1867
Geschichte der Juden in Königsberg i. Pr., ein Beitrag zur Sittengeschichte des Preussischen Staates, nach urkundlichen Quellen bearbeitet, Posen.

Kaarsted, T. 1960
Henrik Cavling som krigskorrespondent, Aarhus.

Kakoúri, A. 2012
1821 η αρχή που δεν ολοκληρώθικε: πότε και πως δημιουργηθήκε το κράτος οπου ζούμε σήμερα, Αθήνα.

Kastríti, K. 2006
Η Ελλάδα του '21 με τα μάτια των φιλελλήνων: Γαλλική φιλελληνική παραγωγή από τις συλλογές του Εθνικού Ιστορικού Μουσείο, Αθήνα.

Kennedy, J. 1830
Conversations on Religion, with Lord Byron and others, held in Cephalonia, a short time previous to his Lordship's Death, London.

Khatzilíras, A.-M. 2003
Η καθιέρωση της ελληνικής σημαίας. Hellenic Army General Staff, http://web.archive.org/web/20070402084632/http://www.army.gr/n/g/publications/articles/GreekFlag0/GreekFlag1/, accessed September 2018.

Kolokotronis, T. 1892
Kolokotrones the Klepht and the Warrior. Sixty Years of Peril and Daring. An Autobiography, London.

Koukíou-Mitropoúlou, D. 2007.
ADAM FRIEDEL Προσωπογραφίες Αγωνιστών της Ελληνικής Επανάστασης (Ιστορική και εθνολογική εταιρία της Ελλάδος) Αθήνα.

Koukíou-Mitropoúlou, D. 2014
Οι Έλληνες του Adam Friedel: προσωπογραφίες αγωνιστών της Ελληνικής Επανάστασης (Ιστορική και εθνολογική εταιρία της Ελλάδος) (Β' έκδοση επαυξημένη), Αθήνα.

Krarup, E. V. 1985
Dansk Filhellenisme. Dansk engagement i den græske frihedskamp 1821-1830, Thesis, University of Copenhagen.

Krøyer, H. 1870
Erindringer af Henrik Krøyers Liv 1821-1838, Kjøbenhavn.

Landfester, M. & R. Lessenich 2002
'Philhellenismus', *Der Neue Pauly Enzyklopädie der Antike* 15/2, Stuttgart & Weimar, 231-7.

Lausten, M. S. 2002
Oplysning i kirke og synagoge. Forholdet mellem kristne og jøder i den danske Oplysningstid (1760-1814) (Kirkehistoriske studier III Række nr. 8), København.

Lessen, A. F. 1823
Schilderung einer enthusiasmirten Reise nach Griechenland im Jahr 1822, Görlitz.

Macphail, J. St. M. 1928
'Baron Friedel, Artist', *Notes and Queries* 155, 27.

Mazarákis-Ainían, I.K. 1996
Σημαίες ελευθερίας. Συλλογή του Εθνικού Ιστορικού Μουσείου, Αθήνα.

Mandilará, A. B., G. V. Nikoláou, L. Phlioúris & N. Anastasópylos (eds) 2015
Φιλελληνισμός. Το ενδιαφέρον για την Ελλάδα και τους Έλληνές από το 1821 ως σήμερα, Αθήνα.

Marchand, L. A. (ed.) 1981
Byron's Letters and Journals Volume XI: 'For Freedom's Battle', 1823-1824, London.

Marchand, L. A. (ed.) 1994
Byron's Letters and Journals Supplementary Volume: 'What Comes Uppermost', London.

Michalídis, I. D. 2010
1821 Η γέννηση ενος εθνους-κράτος 3: Ο Αγώνας των ελλήνων. Πολιτικές επιλογές και στρτιωτικές επιχειρησείς, Νέο Φάληρο.

Nørgaard, L. 2000
'En græker i Bakkehuset – den unge Nikolaos Lunzi og Danmark', *Sfinx* 23, 114-8.

Papanikoláou-Krístensen, A. 2008
'Δανοί Φιλέλληνες στον αγώνα του 21', in *Das Bild Griechenlands Im Spiegel Der Voelker (17. Bis 18. Jahrhundert)*, E. Konstantinou (ed.), Frankfurt am Main, 287-96.

Papanikoláou-Krístensen, A. 2010
Το φιλελληνικό κίνημα στη Δανία, Αθήνα.

Parry, W. 1825
The Last Days of Lord Byron: with his Lordship's Opinions on Various Subjects, particularly on the Stage and Prospects of Greece, London.

Pelt, M. 2000
'Vi er alle sammen grækere: Den europæiske filhellenisme fra passion og politik til pædagogisk projekt', in *København-Athen tur/retur: Danmark og Grækenland i 1800tallet* (Meddelelser fra Ny Carlsberg Glyptotek Ny Serie 2), København, 30-42.

Pizánias, P. (ed.) 2009
Η ελληνική επανάσταση του 1821: ενα ευρωπαϊκο γεγονός, Αθήνα.

Quack-Eustathiades, R. 1984
Der deutsche Philhellenismus während des griechischen Freiheitskampfes 1821-1827, München.

Quack-Eustathiades, R. 2008
'Das Griechenbild der Deutschen zur Zeit der griechischen Revolution bis zur Mitte des 19. Jahrhunderts', in *Das Bild Griechenlands Im Spiegel Der Voelker (17. Bis 18. Jahrhundert)*, E. Konstantinou (ed.), Frankfurt am Main, 183-202.

Raybaud, L. M. 1824
Mémoires sur la Grèce pour servir a l'histoire de la guerre de l'Indépendance, accompagnes de plans topographiques (Vol. 2), Paris.

Richardson, E. 2013
Classical Victorians: Scholars, Scoundrels and Generals in Pursuit of Antiquity, Cambridge.

Romanoff, D. 1987
The Orders, Medals and History of Greece, Rungsted Kyst.

Ross, L. 1848
Reisen des Königs Otto und der Königinn Amalia in Griechenland (Vol. 1), Halle.

Schmidt Hansen, P. 2013
Kunsten & Litografien – udviklingen i Danmark gennem 200 år, Birkerød.

Senefelder, A. 1818
Vollstaendiges Lehrbuch der Steindruckerey, München.

St Clair, W. 2008
That Greece Might Still Be Free. The Philhellenes in the War of Independence (second edition), Cambridge.

Striebeck, K. T. 1834
Mittheilungen aus dem Tagebuche des Philhellenen. Nach dem Manuscript des Lieutenant Striebeck, Hannover.

Thackray, J. C. 1985
'Separately-published prints of fossils in nineteenth century Britain', *Archives of Natural History* 12, 175-99.

Tsigakou, F.-M. 1981
The Rediscovery of Greece: Travellers and Painters of the Romantic Era, New Rochelle & New York.

Twyman, M. 1967
'The lithographic hand press 1796-1850', *Journal of the Printing Historical Society* 3, 3-50.

Twyman, M. 1974/1975
'A Directory of London Lithographic Printers 1800-1850', *Journal of the Printing Historical Society* 10, 1-55.

Wade, R. J. 2012
Pedagogic Objects: The Formation, Circulation and Exhibition of Teaching Collections for Art and Design Education in Leeds, 1837-1857, PhD thesis, University of Leeds.

Woodhouse, C. M. 1973
Capodistria: The Founder of Greek Independence, London, New York & Toronto.

Zeuthen, H. G. 1893
'Hjelte, Jonas Christoffer Leonhard', in *Dansk Biografisk Leksikon* VII (second edition), C. F. Bricka (ed.), Kjøbenhavn, 467-8.

Images and Interactions:

Greece in Danish Public Life and Politics from the Revolution of 1821 to the Debt Crisis in the Second Decade of the 21st Century

MOGENS PELT

This article discuses three epochal episodes when Greece took a prominent position in public life in Denmark. The first is the period of the Greek national revolution and the first decade after the establishment of the Kingdom of Greece. The second episode is connected to King George I, the period around his accession to the throne and an evaluation by a prominent Danish reporter of his status during the 1897 Greek–Turkish war. The last episode concerns the reaction by the Danish public and politicians to the demise of Greek democracy in the crisis period of the early 1960s, culminating in the Colonels' coup on 21 April 1967. The article posits that the image of Greece in Denmark has been formed by a wide spectrum of representations, including those based on passions for the classical past, on compassion with fellow Christians and on solidarity with the ordinary Greeks based on universal values, as well as ones where curiosity about the exotic and otherness dominate.

Introduction

More than once, Greece has taken a prominent position in the public life in Denmark. Currents in international politics and public opinion constitute one important impetus that has brought Greece to the forefront of attention, in particular philhellenism. As for many other Europeans, philhellenism motivated many Danes to engage themselves in the Greek cause in the period around the Revolution of 1821, and it has never completely disappeared. Another crucial factor is the "special relationship" between the former Greek monarchy and the Danish one, as both institutions have been headed by kings and queens from the Glücksburg dynasty. Finally, the respective positions of the two countries on European issues and in international politics have also influenced the framing of Greece.

The aim of this article is to single out and define the watersheds that have determined the specific trends of images projected to the Danish public that have shaped the perception of Greece. A further aim is to investigate the interplay between the specific *Zeitgeist* in Denmark at the given time, the issues that made Greece topical and the role of cultural and political manifestations of Greek provenance that have found their way into the rather limited corpus of first-hand knowledge of Greece.

It should be mentioned that the public as a locus and sphere where opinions are formed in response to political or societal challenges or as demands for resistance, change or action is a phenomenon that underwent significant changes during the long period covered here. In the first place its locus moved from the coffee house, the club or the private circle of artists and intellectuals to the much broader sphere created by the emerging press and mass politics. This developmentwas also dependent, in turn, on the presence of censorship or its absence, i.e. on the degree of free expression that was allowed at any

141

given time. The Danish state and the nature of its regime underwent substantial changes during the period. At its outset the state was weak and the regime an absolute monarchy. Denmark did not get its first constitution until 1849, during an extremely turbulent period of internal upheaval that saw the Danish state confronting national movements in the duchies of Schleswig and Holstein in two wars that included Prussia. The regime issue continued to be a contentious one – reaching its most critical period between 1872 and 1901, when the king finally gave in to the principle that the leader who had the support of the majority of parliament should be called upon to form a government. It was in the same period that Denmark's modern mass politics and press was created.

The Revolution of 1821: A Threat to the European Order

The emergence of the modern Greek nation, not least the act of rising up against the Ottoman overlords and the prospects of a free Hellas, held a significant attraction for Danish intellectuals and artists. But it was also the first all-out Christian uprising aimed at complete independence from the Ottoman Empire. In this capacity it was a challenge to the Concert of Europe, the new conservative world order that was established after the defeat of Napoleon. The aim of this order was to roll back nationalism, liberalism and republicanism to prevent, in the words of Eric Hobsbawm, a second French Revolution, or even a European revolution on the French model.[1] The strongest proponent of this line was the Holy Alliance led by Russia, Austria and Prussia.[2]

In post-Napoleonic Europe Denmark was among the losers. The Treaty of Kiel 1814 had forced it to cede Norway to Sweden. This reduced the kingdom to a minor European power, as a result of which Copenhagen lost its role as an international mercantile and financial centre. There were also fears the country would not survive as an independent state. This was not least due to the fact that Holstein and Lauenburg were members of the German

Confederation, meaning that Prussia and Austria also had a say in what Copenhagen would consider local interests. It blurred the line between domestic and foreign affairs and in practical terms it made the Danish Monarchy a client of Austria in order to avoid possible constitutions in the duchies of Holstein and Lauenburg, in the northern part of what is now Germany.[3] In the domain of the normative aspirations for the new European order, Denmark would follow the Austrian statesman Prince Clemens von Metternich, the most powerful exponent of the reactionary intentions of the Holy Alliance.

Although the Ottoman Empire and its subject peoples, including the Greeks, were not a formal party of the Concert of Europe, in practical terms it was.[4] The Austrian stance on the Greek Revolution is perhaps best represented by a letter from Metternich to Prince Paul Esterhazy, the Austrian Ambassador in London, dated 21 September 1829. It was sent at a time when the great powers were discussing the future borders of Greece:[5]

What do we mean by the Greeks? Do we mean a people, a country, or a religion? […] If the third, then upwards of fifty million men are Greeks: the Austrian Empire alone embraces five million of them […] Long experience has taught us to realize that in racial denomination there may lie elements of trouble between empires and bones of contention between people and governments. And what a powerful and ever hostile weapon such denominations become in the hands of those who overthrow, or seek to overthrow, the existing order!

The official Danish stance towards the Greek Revolution was reflected in the press about a month after Alexandros Ypsilantis had crossed the Pruth River on 25 March, entering the Ottoman Empire. Presaging the words of Metternich and fully in line with his hostile stance on the Greek revolution, it read:

Recently a storm gathered over Italy that darkened its sky and spread its clouds to a wider area. And there were reasons to fear that the storm might have threatened the whole of Europe.

1   Hobsbawn 1962, 138.
2   Rodogno 2011, 20-2.
3   Bjørn & Due-Nielsen 2003 24-5; Schepelern 2008, 978.
4   Hanioglu 2008, 4.
5   MacFie 1989, 89.

But, then out of a sudden, it ceded and the sun of peace began to spread its beams.

The tenor of this metaphor is the 1820 revolutions in Naples and Sicily, as well as the actions of the Carbonari in the Kingdom of Sardinia – revolutions that were quelled by Austrian forces in February 1821 in the name of the Holy Alliance to restore the post-1815 European order. Such an end, the paper noticed, could only please the

just and neutral observer […] because the sort of freedom fanaticism which infected Italy and which a [small] clique wanted to instil in the masses of the people soon subdued. […] But now a new storm is gathering over Turkey […] that is of such a nature that it has the power to affect the course of political events in Europe.[6]

The storm over Turkey was the Greek revolution.
In the official Danish view, the Greek Revolution was dangerous. It had the potential to threaten the conservative European order and royal absolutism in Denmark. The immediate response was to restrict the circulation of news from Greece and prevent the spread of subversive appeals. Here Copenhagen followed Metternich, who pressed the German states to curb philhellenic activities.[7] From 1821 to the battle of Navarino in 1827, censorship banned any mention of the Greek Revolution that might contribute to the circulation of liberal and radical texts, and it was forbidden by law to take active part in the war.[8]

While Metternich was successful in closing down most organisational efforts to support the Greek revolution in Prussian and Austria and other German states – as well as preventing them from taking root in Denmark – the centres moved to London, Paris and Zürich.[9]

An End to Enslavement of Christians and a Return to Idealized Antiquity

Nevertheless, news from Greece did reach the Danish public. The notorious 1822 Ottoman massacre of the civilian Orthodox population on the island of Chios was mentioned a number of times in a broad array of papers, and, it would soon be clear, as Lord Palmerstone famously stated, that "Greece [was] an emotional word".[10] The state was unable to prevent intellectuals and artists responding. The most conspicuous exponent was Steen Steensen Blicher (1782-1848). He studied theology to become a priest and is considered among the major Danish authors of the early decades of the 19th century because of his status as the first realist in Danish literature, who gave a voice to those without a voice in his short stories, which narrated the lives of the ordinary people who lived on the great moor of Jutland.[11]

Blicher reacted immediately to the Greek Revolution. In 1821 he published a long poem *Til Det Gejnfødte Grækenland* [To the Reborn Greece] and in 1822 *Nygrækernes Sejreshymne* [Ode to the Victory of New Greeks], both celebrating the Greek uprising and its initial success. With no first-hand knowledge of Greece, Blicher depended on what news he could glean from the theatre of war. We do not know how he received his information, but one important source for news from abroad in Denmark was Hamburg. Another was private letters. Furthermore, it is obvious that Blicher's own imagination of Classical Hellas must also have had a strong influence on his perception of the emerging Greek nation, something betrayed by his representing the revolutionary Greeks of his age as the Ancients he knew so well from his schooling. In this way, Blicher's situation resembles that of most other Danes who became engaged in the Greek cause during the Revolution. They relied on information that in some way or another had passed through the censors, on news gathered by themselves or by their friends and in some cases, as we shall see, on private correspondence. As they had no first-hand knowledge, the images they created were

---

6   10 April 1821, *Den vestsjællandske Avis.*
7   Marchand 1996, 32-3.
8   Rostbøll 2015, 20-2.
9   Marchand 1996, 33.
10 Holland and Markides 2006, 1.
11 *Den store Danske Encyklopædi*, Steen Steensen Blicher.

dependent on this input and on what their education and upbringing had taught them about Greece, something which in practical terms meant Classical Hellas.

Blicher portrays the Greek struggle against the Turks as one in which the Olympic gods and the heroes of a resurrected Hellas fight the barbaric Turks. Blicher's Turk is the Persian at Thermopylae – but he is also the pirate of the Barbary Coast, and a trader of white slaves.[12] This was a character that would have been familiar to the Danish public from the Danish–Algerian War of 1769-72, also known as the Algerian Expedition. By combining his support of a free Greece with the fight against the white slave trade, Blicher followed the philhellenism of René Chateaubriand, a traveller and French minister of foreign affairs who famously framed the Greek struggle for freedom into the following more universal themes: "Christianity oppressed by Islam" and "the struggle of Christian civilization against Muslim obscurantism".[13]

Blicher responded to atrocities committed by the Ottomans and to pivotal events contributing to the achievement of Greek freedom. Indicative of this engagement are his poems *Ipsara*, published in 1824 and condemning the destruction of Psara by the Turks in the same year, and *Navarinoslaget* [the Battle of Navarino], celebrating the intervention by the Great Powers – Britain, France and Russia – at the Bay of Navarino, where their ships sank the Egyptian fleet and paved the way for Greek independence. It is indicative of the importance of the event for the Danish public that *Navarinoslaget* was first recited at the Royal Theatre in Copenhagen on 9 December 1827, before it was published in 1828.[14]

However, Blicher was no friend of revolution and social rebellion: he sided with the émigrés of the French Revolution and expressed his support of the nobility in the Saxon Peasants' Revolt in 1790.[15] For the same reasons, he never wavered in his support of the Danish absolute

monarchy.[16] While the latter qualifies him as a conservative, his support of the Greek cause dressed as if it were the Ancients who rose to reclaim themselves brings him close, if we follow Jonathan Israel's categories, to the so-called moderate enlightenment, which included figures like Voltaire who supported enlightened despotism.[17] Like the French *philosophe*, Blicher saw Ottoman rule in Greece as an expression of Oriental despotism and to him Greek freedom implied an end to the enslavement of Christians by Muslims and some kind of return to an idealised Antiquity. In this way Blicher's celebration of Free Greece seems to have belonged to what David Roessel has labelled "contemplative Hellenism", i.e. an approach that emphasises the exemplar value of Classical Greece as a source of moral introspection and self-improvement rather than demands for political change at home.[18]

This also indicates that Blicher's philhellenism did not expect, nor hope, that the revival of the Greeks would have the power to transform the lives and art of the world. His was not the kind of political and revolutionary philhellenism that was represented by the London Greek Committee, by Percy Bysshe Shelley or Lord Byron, whose list of demands, as Roessel reminds us, included Catholic emancipation, parliamentary reforms and abolition of slavery. In their wildest dreams they yearned for the revolution to spread from Greece to the rest of the world and undo the conservative world order embodied in the Holy Alliance.[19]

Revolutionary Philhellenism

Blicher was not alone among Danish intellectuals to react to the Greek cause. But because strict censorship prevented the exponents of political and revolutionary philhellenism publishing their thoughts, we have to look to private circles to find these trends. The most important circle was a salon, *Bakkehuset*, just outside of Copenha-

---

12   See his *A Voice on Ocean*, celebrating the Royal Navy's destruction of the port of Algiers in 1816 as an effort to end the white slave trade in the Mediterranean Sea.

13   Rodogno 2011, 39.

14   danskforfatterleksikon.dk/1850t/t1850dato1827.htm,6 January 2019.

15   On the political Blicher see Kjærgaard 2011, 49-65.

16   Kjærgaard 2011, 49-65.

17   Israel 2010, 1-36.

18   Roessel 2002, 28.

19   Roessel 2002, 28.

gen. *Bakkehuset* provided a forum for the discussion of liberal and radical ideas. Its friends were deeply engaged in contemporary European politics, as well as current social issues, not least the French Revolution and Napoleon's reforms. In 1814 Knud Lyhne Rahbæk introduced his friends at *Bakkehuset* to the works of Byron. In 1817 he would provide the Danish public with the first translation of the poet.[20] *Bakkehuset* was a venue for a vanguard of artists and intellectuals. The lady of the house, Kamma Rahbæk, received among many others her brother-in-law, the romantic poet par excellence in Denmark, Adam Oehlenschläger, as well as Christoffer Wilhelm Eckersberg, often referred to as the father of Danish painting or the founder of the Golden Age of Danish Painting, whose grand tour between 1813 and 1816 took him to Florence and Rome. The circle also counted the classical scholar P. O. Brøndsted and the young Hans Christian Andersen, who later became a famous writer of fairytales. They too saw Greek freedom as an end to the enslavement of Christians by Muslims and as some kind of return to an idealised Antiquity.[21]

But there was more to it, as the figure of Brøndsted shows. He made his grand tour of Greece between 1810 and 1812 where he met with Byron, held an interview with Ali Pasha, the de facto ruler of large tracts of today's Abania and Greece, and made the acquaintance of many Greeks who later took part in the Revolution.[22] In the following years, 18157, he would give public lectures about the political conditions in the Ottoman Empire and status of its Christian subjects.[23] He also brought Conrad Lunzi along with him, the son of count Anastacio Lunzi, the Danish consul on the isle of Zante.[24] Conrad Lunzi was his foster son and would become a close friend of Kamma Rahbæk. In 1818 Brøndsted went to Italy to serve as court

agent to the Papal State. However, his eager engagement in the revolutions in Naples and Sicily and his antipathy of the Austrian military suppression meant he fell into disgrace with the Danish king. In 1823 he left Rome.[25] He would not return to Denmark until after the establishment of the Kingdom of Greece in 1832. At that time Lunzi had returned to Zante, which, along with the other Ionian Islands, was under British rule, and functioned as a safe haven for Greek revolutionaries and a centre of intelligence regarding the development of their struggle against the Ottomans.

Brøndsted's deep engagement in the 1820 revolutions and his contacts with the friends of *Bakkehuset*, as well as Lunzi's correspondence with Kamma Rahbæk – his main source of information on the Greek War of Independence – kept the circle informed about the challenges to the conservative European order and about events in Greece. It also enabled them to place the Greek Revolution in its European context, and it is clear from the letters and artefacts at *Bakkehuset* that Kamma Rahbæk took a strong interest in the political aspects of the Greek cause.[26]

In spite of Metternich's pressure on the German states and Denmark to issue prohibitions on the mustering of volunteers, a few Danish philhellenes went to Greece to join the Revolution.[27] They were following a broader trend. Between November 1821 and August 1822, eight ships of German volunteers alone departed from Marseille – the main port of departure for volunteers going to Greece.[28] We know about ten Danes who went, and that most of them returned home disappointed by the "real" Greeks since they fitted so poorly with the idealised Ancients of their imagination, but their negative opinions did not seem to have influenced the image of the Greeks in any significant way.[29]

---

20 Rostbøll 2015, 16-22.
21 Ghazaleh 2005, 24. See also Krarup 1985, 24-36.
22 Isager 1999; Isager 2008, 115;127. See also Krarup 1985, 24-7.
23 Mejer 2008, 108-16.
24 Nørgaard, 2000; Rostbøll 2015, 18-22.
25 Schepelern 2008, 100-1.
26 Rostbøll 2015, 18-22.
27 Marchand 1996, 32-3.
28 St. Clair 2008, 69.
29 Ghazaleh 2005, 55.

The Battle of Navarino: an Intervention to Save Christians

The battle of Navarino in October 1827 buried any possibility of the Ottomans re-establishing sovereignty over the southern Greek lands; it tipped the balance of opinion among the European powers in favour of Greek independence and broke the solidarity between the five great powers. The decision by Britain, France and Russia to support the Greeks isolated Metternich, who was left alone with Prussia, which weakened his hand in European politics irreparably.[30]

This and the fact that the battle of Navarino was framed as an effort to save Christians, and retrospectively was portrayed as the first instance of modern humanitarian intervention, also made the Greek cause a much less contentious issue.[31] The official Danish response to these new realities was to lift censorship. In the wake of this decision various manifestations of support of the Greeks came out into the open. Among these we find Kamma Rabæk's close friend Frederikke Brun's humanitarian "Committee to support those who are suffering in Greece".[32] At about the same time Blicher announced a similar effort. While the result fell far short of his expectations, the text that accompanied one contribution saw the battle as one between Christians and Muslims almost in line with the iconic 1571 Battle of Lepanto: "Accept this humble contribution from a Christian to the Greek cause as an expression of a praise to the Lord for the holy victory by the Cross at Navarino October 20th."[33] There was even a publication that was solely dedicated to the Greek cause, *Grækervennen* [the friend of the Greek].[34]

Although philhellenism would continue to signal left liberalism well into the 1840s, it was becoming an increasingly inoffensive taste. When Brøndsted returned to Denmark, he was appointed director of the Royal Collections of Coins as well as professor in Philology and Archaeology. Here we should notice that his return in

May 1832 was synchronous with the decision of the great powers that independent Greece should be a Kingdom, meaning that Greece was beginning to lose its exemplar value for liberals: the new state soon developed into a de facto absolute monarchy.

Nevertheless, Greek affairs would continue to inspire Danes in the following decades. Some mainly focused on Greece as a battleground for a clash of civilisations, while others would take an interest in culture and fine arts rather than in politics.

Among the first group we find N. F. S. Grundtvig, a pastor, polymath and one of the most influential personalities in 19th-century Denmark. Among other things, he was the mastermind behind the Danish folk high schools, which were set up to give peasants and other underprivileged groups an education. In 1838 he held a series of public lectures on world history. On 2 and 5 November he spoke about the Greek war of independence, among other things. Here Grundtvig introduced his public to the names of its leading antagonists and the main events of the war. His approach is close to Chateaubriand's themes: "Christianity oppressed by Islam" and "the struggle of Christian civilization against Muslim obscurantism".[35] The clearest expression of this appears in the part concerning Ibrahim Pasha's 1825 campaign in Morea in the service of the Sultan. Ibrahim's intention, Grundtvig claimed, was to turn Morea into a "Colony of Negros".[36] The plan was to kill all the local Greeks or ship them off to sell them on the slave markets in Egypt, and settle "Negros" in Greece.[37]

Grundtvig must be referring to the scenario of the alleged plan – a non-existent so-called "barbarization project" – deliberately rumoured by the Russians by which Ibrahim was said to have intended to keep whatever part of Greece he could conquer, exterminate the whole Christian population or carry them off into slavery in Egypt and fill the country with Egyptians and Arabs – i.e. Grundt-

30   Tuncer 2014, 103-4.
31   Rodogno 2011, 69.
32   Rostbøll 2015, 22.
33   The Danish text reads: "Med tak til Gud for Korsets Hellige Seir ved Navarino den 20de Oktober oversendes vedlagte ringe Skjerv, som et Bidrag til Grækersagen, fra en Christen."
34   Published by Stockfleth 1828-9.
35   Rodognom 2011, 39.
36   The Danish text reads: "Negerkoloni".
37   Grundtvig 2016 http://www.grundtvigsværker.dk/tekstvisning/6450/43?keywords=kolokotronis#{"o":o,"k":43,"vo":o}, January 2019.

vig's "Negros". This rumour originated with the Russian Ambassador Christopher Lieven, who in October 1825 showed the British Ambassador to the Porte, Stratford Canning, a document that was supposed to prove the existence of such a plan. Even though the contemporary policy-makers knew that there was no policy of erecting a new "Barbary Power" in Europe, the "barbarization project" was among the important motivations for intervention at Navarino and it would survive in following decades in the public consciousness.[38]

Grundtvig also makes explicit that he was no friend of revolutionary philhellenism, or any of the other radical ideas that coalesced in a person like William Wilberforce – a member of the London Greek Society and a prime mover in the struggle that led to the Slave Trade Act of 1807, which abolished the slave trade in the British Empire.[39]

Philhellenism: An Inoffensive Taste

These developments made it possible to visit Greece to see the land first-hand – the architect Hans Christian Hansen and Hans Christian Andersen were among those who did.

Hansen set out for Italy and Sicily in 1831 and travelled to Athens in 1833, where he established himself on a more permanent basis. Here he won the favour of King Otto and was appointed court architect. A great part of his work in this capacity was to transform the new capital from an Ottoman village into a town on a par with its modern European counterparts. Together with his brother Theophilus, he had a lasting influence in Greece, giving the cityscape of Athens its distinct Classical touch.[40] The brothers' impact was not confined to Greece alone and their works contributed to an aesthetical interaction between Athens, Copenhagen, Trieste and Vienna, among other places.

Hans Christian Andersen, who as a young man had already made connections with the friends of *Bakkehuset*, would be the most influential Danish writer of the epoch

to visit Greece. He arrived in Athens in 1841. It was part of his grand tour of the Orient, when he visited Rome, Naples, Athens and Istanbul. In Athens he was received by King Otto and Queen Amalia, and Andersen wrote much about his experiences there. Its size reminded him of a medium Danish provincial town, while its sights still bore a clear testimony to its Ottoman past, such as in his encounter with a pair of black families who had been slaves when the Turks ruled the city. Andersen also wrote about touristic scenes and adventurous detours that would bring him in contact with locals. In this way, he introduced the Danish public to some aspects of the realities of modern Greece, first and foremost curiosities.[41] Like Hansen, Andersen primarily paid attention to forms and appearances and less to politics.

Considering the corpus of first-hand knowledge of Greece in Denmark around the mid-19th -century, only a very few translations of Greek texts existed. The first appeared in 1838 and was based on the German translation from 1837 of Alexandros Soutsos' novel *O exoristos tou 1831*, which was also the first translation into any foreign language of a Greek novel written and published in Greece after the foundation of the Greek state in 1830.[42] The scene is contemporary Greece in the very early period of independence, and it depicts the adventures of a young man who is unable to bear the tyranny of Capodistrias and is persecuted by those in power.

The image of Greece was informed mainly by non-Greek sources, mostly from Danish travellers, and by Danish literary and intellectual works. Many reflected a strong interest in the Classical past, and sometimes a longing for it to re-emerge with the Greek independence fighters battling the Turks as if they were King Xerxes' Persians. It was also common to represent the Greeks as fellow Christians enslaved by Muslims in shape of the well-known figure of the Pirate of the Barbary Coast. Others focused on the otherness of the new Greek world. It is worth noticing that this trend first appears among those who actually visited Greece, first of all in Andersen's work, where the Ottoman aspects of Athens caught his

---

38 Rodogno 2011, 78-80.
39 Grundtvig 2016 http://www.grundtvigsværker.dk/tekstvisning/6450/42?keywords=kolokotronis#{"o":o,"k":42,"vo":o}, 8 January 2019.
40 Papanicolaou-Christensen 1994; Haugsted 2009.
41 Andersen 2006, 161- 224.
42 Engberg 2000.

attention. The same aspects were also undoubtedly clear to the Hansen brothers, but their mission was different, namely to identify these aspects in order to remove them the cityscape and transform Athens into a European capital.

Revolutionary philhellenism never established itself in Denmark as an intellectual and political discourse in its own right, as in other places in Europe. But works by European philhellenes such as Byron and a genuine engagement by the friends of *Bakkehuset* in liberal and radical ideas in general and the Greek Revolution in particular meant revolutionary philhellenism became known among a small circle of artists and intellectuals. However, the dominant trend was contemplative Hellenism and humanitarian concern for fellow Christians in Greece. Overall, it was a development that was in harmony with the interest of the Danish absolute monarchy because it contributed to emasculating the utopian values of the Greek revolution and disconnecting it from its potential to challenge the illiberal regime in Copenhagen.

The trend was also in harmony with official Danish political interests in European affairs, seen through the prism of absolutism as they were. Although Greek independence dealt a blow to Metternich's standing and reduced Austria's role in the European balance of power, the Danish monarchy still needed its reactionary ally to stem a rising tide of demands for liberal constitutions and national independence. However, the 1830 July Revolution in France, Belgium's secession from the Netherlands and the Polish insurrection in the same year not only forced Metternich to accept Belgium's independence but also energised a number of political movements in Denmark demanding the abolition of absolute monarchy. During the 1830s and 1840s Danish kings strove to contain the most radical demands in a process of give-and-take that in 1834 would see the summoning of estates general with consultative powers and more room for public debate. The coup de grace for Danish absolutism came from the 1848 revolutions, from nationalism and from the imperative of the First Schleswig War (184851), where Denmark was fighting demands for self-determination in Schleswig and Holstein and the Prussian army. In 1849 the Danish king was forced to accept a constitution.[43]

The Greek Throne: An Exit from Denmark's International Impasse

The fact that the 1848 revolutions had driven Metternich into exile and turned Prussia against Denmark compelled Copenhagen to find new ways to balance its interests among the European great powers. This became all the more urgent in the following decade and a half, as tensions between German nationalism and the raison d'état of the Danish Kingdom in the duchies of Schleswig, Holstein and Lauenburg continued and caused increasing frictions between Denmark and an ever more powerful Prussia. While Austria was turning against Denmark and Russia was severely weakened as a result of its defeat in the Crimean War 1853-6, Denmark's nemesis from the Napoleonic Wars, Britain, was in the ascendant, which made an improvement of relations with London desirable.

Such an opportunity was offered by the internal situation in Greece. In 1862 King Otto was forced to leave Greece after he finally lost a protracted power-struggle with local magnates and politicians. In accordance with the principles of the Concert of Europe, Greece had to remain a kingdom. The challenge was to find a candidate who was acceptable to all the protective powers and would stand a chance of consolidating his position in Greece. To the British it was important to avoid a candidate who would serve French or Russian interests. After it became clear that the other powers would not accept Prince Albert, Queen Victoria's son, Prince Vilhelm of Denmark became their preferred candidate.[44] It was in this situation that King Christian IX agreed to send his son to Greece; in 1863 Vilhelm was enthroned as George I, King of the Hellenes. It was also part of larger political puzzle.

Orla Lehmann, one of the most important Danish politicians of the 19th century, offers a comprehensive analysis of the coronation's political implications for Denmark in a paper entitled *Den græske Thronfølgersag 1863* [the Question of the Succession to the Greek Throne in 1863]. As a member of the National Liberal Party, Lehmann had been a driving force in the fight against the absolute monarchy and one of the leading figures in the movement that resulted in the first Danish constitution in 1849. He was

43 Bjørn 7 Due-Nielsen 2003, 48-139.
44 Holland & Markides 2000, 63-7.

also the mastermind behind the fateful 1863 constitution that aimed to incorporate Schleswig, with its large German-speaking population, into the Danish nation state, a major trigger for the Second Schleswig War in 1864 between Denmark and Prussia, the first of three in the process that led to the unification of Germany in 1871.

In Prince Vilhelm's accession to the Greek throne Lehmann saw a great opportunity for Denmark to accommodate Britain, hoping that, in return, London would allow the union (enosis) of the Ionian Islands – a British protectorate since 1815 – in order to endear King George to the Greeks in a manner King Otto had never achieved. Lehmann's calculations were based on the observation that in the Eastern Question, Britain was less attentive to the interests of the Ottoman Empire than it had been prior to the Crimean War (18536), and London now seemed ready to support certain demands of the Greek Great Idea. It finally happened in March 1864, when the British ceded the Ionian Island to Greece.

Lehmann also regarded Prince Vilhelm's accession to the Greek throne as an opportunity for the Danish monarchy to increase its relative importance vis-à-vis the other royal families of Europe. This wish was fulfilled some years later, symbolically at least, when King George I's father, the Danish King Christian IX, became known as the father-in-law of Europe, as no fewer than four of his children were sitting on thrones – in Britain, Denmark, Russia and Greece – either as monarchs or as consorts, while his son Prince Valdemar was forced to decline the throne of Bulgaria.[45]

In all likelihood Lehmann wrote the paper around the time of Prince Vilhelm's accession to the Greek throne, but it was not published until 100 years later. It was too critical of the new king Christian IX, whom Lemann was said to have made look like a fool when Christian hesitated to agree to Vilhelm accepting the Greek throne out of fear of insulting the deposed King Otto's home country, Bavaria, and by proxy powerful German states like Austria and Prussia.[46]

Lehmann's analysis also demonstrates a good understanding of internal Greek affairs. His diagnosis of Otto's fall was that king had refused to listen to his people and local power-holders, and that he had been reluctant to rule on a constitutional basis. Lehmann was well versed in the history of the power game that had been going on since 1843, when the troops of the Athens garrison and a huge crowd forced King Otto to concede a constitution and the introduction of universal male suffrage.[47] For these reasons he believed George's survival as King of the Hellenes depended on his willingness to function as a constitutional monarch. This also made Lehmann one of the strongest opponents of Count W. Sponneck, the personal adviser to the young Prince Vilhelm. He believed Sponneck wanted to use his position in Greece as a platform to relaunch his career in Denmark and feared he was unable to grasp that his main task should be to advice the young king in accordance with the fact that Greece was a constitutional monarchy.[48] According to French historiography, when the new French minister to Greece, Arthur de Gobineau, arrived in Athens on 17 November 1864 Sponneck had taken over all the power from the young king, and by demonstrating his overt contempt for the Greek people he was putting the monarchy at risk. [49]In other words, this account substantiates Lehmann's fears that Sponneck's personal ambitions would jeopardise George's throne and thus the attempts to improve Danish–British relations, at a time when Denmark needed Britain as a counterweight to Prussia.

Later events seem to prove Lehmann's analysis right: although King George accepted a revised constitution in 1864 that was a more democratic document than its predecessor, his position was not secure until he gave in to Greek public opinion and dismissed Sponneck in November 1865. [50] In the process that followed George also demonstrated willingness – step by step – to accommodate the declaration of the constitution that all power derived from the people, until in August 1875 he finally accepted the principle that the leader who had the

---

45   Olden-Jørgensen 2003, 111-69.
46   Lehmann 1970, 10-1.
47   Lehmann 1970, 13-21.
48   Enemark 1988, 2-5.
49   Gobineau 1993, 20-1.
50   Enemark 1998, 2-5.

support of the majority of parliament should be called upon to form a government.[51] This concession is important because it was made in the same year a protracted constitutional crisis began in Denmark concerning the same principle, a crisis that would not end until 1901. It divided society and politics into two camps: the old order of landowners and the King, who were willing to overrule the majority of parliament in order to bar the agrarian party from forming a government, on the one hand, and the agrarian party and its intellectual supporters on the other.

The Greek King is a Danish Prince

The Greek monarchy would also become a focal point of broader Danish attention on Greece and somehow too in Danish diagnoses of the state of affairs in Greece. This is evident in the manner in which the Danish journalist Henrik Cavling covered the Greek–Turkish war of 1897. Cavling would become a towering figure in the Danish world of news because of his innovative style of journalism, and since 1945 one of the most prestigious journalism awards has carried his name: the Cavling Prize. Cavling was reporting from the Greek side, dispatching, as one would expect from a war correspondent, accounts from the front. But he also sent coverage of the daily life of Athens and interviews with various Greek political figures. Cavling's Athens was an emerging city and modern in a way that made it familiar to his Danish readers. The emphasis was on similarities between the Greek capital and other European cities, while his reports were devoid of any attempt of orientalising its otherness. In the cases where he brings up oddities in Athens he refers them to the Classical past, while he explicitly states that one would hardly find a single area of the city that could be labelled as 'oriental', bluntly stating that in the 34 years since King Otto was dethroned Athens has changed from an uncivilised city into the new Athens of King George's era.[52] It is difficult not to see his representation of Athens as a modern city as a simultaneous projection of his positive evaluation of King George: Cavling ded-

icated long articles to presenting him as a wise, stable and unifying force.

Here we should note that it was the newspaper *Politiken* that had sent Cavling to Greece. It happened in the midst of the worst political crisis in the modern history of Denmark, the so-called constitutional battle (1870-1901) that would decide the fate of the principles of parliamentary government. *Politiken* was established in 1884 as a result of this conflict. It originated among people close to the intelligentsia of the agrarian party in the peak years of the constitutional battle, which saw the government appointed by the King preparing for a violent confrontation with the oppositional forces.[53] Taking into consideration the fact that in Denmark *Politiken* and the monarchy constituted two opposed camps, it is worth pointing out that Cavling never questioned the legitimacy of the institution and the dynasty in Greece, whose Danish counterpart was undermining the principles Cavling's newspaper was fighting for. Quite the contrary: Cavling is pleased to inform his readers that King George was extraordinarily popular in spite of the fact that he acted as the sole authority and ruler of the country, a verity, Cavling is convinced, that would constitute a source of "the highest pleasure to any Dane". Cavling's attitude may well have been shaped by the fact that at the time King George had long since accepted what Cavling's newspaper demanded from the Danish king: that the leader who had the support of the majority of parliament should be called upon to form a government. Another reason may have been that Cavling was an early exponent of a modern style of reportage that was supposed to show the readers what the journalist came across in the field – in the case of George, a modern monarch at the helm of his country in time of war. It was a genre Cavling later would develop in cooperation with the palace in Copenhagen, when he covered the Danish prince Valdemar's voyage to the Far East.[54] Cavling concludes his article on the merits of King George in the following way:

It is strange that the oldest people of Europe in its fight for national resurrection has decided to entrust its fate to a Danish

---

51   Clogg 1979, 86.
52   *Politiken* 12 March 1897 cited in Kaarsted 1960, 44-7.
53   Hvidt, 1990, 293-8.
54   Schneider 2017, 240.

prince. In this moment of writing from my hotel room I can see the light in the King's studio, and I wish that this light will not be put out but that it will brighten the whole world.[55]

Although Cavling's piece clearly contains all the elements required by modern reportage, it is tempting also to see it as the expression of a pious wish that the light shining from King George's studio should reach the royal palace in Copenhagen to enlighten King Christian IX. While it must remain a moot point if Cavling was intending his King George to be a model for the king in Copenhagen, it is a fact that more than half a century later the Danish public would see the Danish monarchy as a model to be followed by the Greek one.

The Danish Constitutional Monarchy as Model for Greece

In Denmark the principle that the leader who had the support of the majority of parliament should be called upon to form a government was finally established 1901. But the new order was still so fragile that in the wake of Germany's defeat in the First World War conflicting visions between the King on the one hand and the elected government on the other as to what extent land which had belonged to the Danish Kingdom before the war of 1864 in the province of Schleswig should be claimed back unleashed a constitutional crisis in 1920. It called popular wrath upon the monarchy when King Christian X ousted the government – and at the end of the day, it forced him to undo his decision.[56] This also marked the last open confrontation between the monarchy and the elected institutions in Denmark.

Over the next almost three quarters of a century the Greek branch of the Glücksburg dynasty would face a number of crises similar to those the Danish monarchy experienced. In Greece the right of the king to appoint and dismiss ministers became a pivotal point in the confrontations between the elected politicians and the palace after King George was assassinated in 1913 in Thessaloniki by a Greek anarchist, Alexandros Schinas. As for the motive, apart from the fact that since the late 1880s regicide and the killing of members of royal families was not an

uncommon occurrence in Europe and that anarchists were often involved, we are at the mercy of speculations and conspiracy theories.

In contrast to the relative stability that characterised the 50-year reign of George I, instability would mark the course of his successors. In the following 61 years Greece would see five different kings, five plebiscites on the constitutional issue, the abolition of the monarchy, its restauration and its final abolition in 1974, as well as extreme polarisation of politics and society including a civil war in which the institution of the monarchy was a party.

In spite of this, neither the confrontations between King Constantine I and Prime Minister Eleftherios Venizelos in the period around the First World War, nor the controversies concerning George II's suspension of the parliament in 1936, and not even his controversial return to Greece in 1946 or the Greek Civil War made headlines in Denmark. Here we should recall that Denmark was neutral during the First World War and that the issue between Venizelos and Constantine was intimately connected to the issue of which side Greece should support. Support of Venizelos would indicate support of Britain, while support of Constantine would indicate support of Germany. George II's appointment in 1936 of the would-be dictator General Ioannis Metaxas was overshadowed by the Spanish Civil War, while the controversies regarding his return to Greece in 1946 took place in the shadow of the Cold War, where Denmark was on the side of the western great powers that supported George II.

In contrast, the clashes between the palace and the defenders of democratic principles in Greece that reached a new peak in the 1960s did arouse Danish public opinion. One important reason was undoubtedly that it was a well-known fact that the Danish princess Anne-Marie had fallen in love with Crown Prince Constantine of Greece, which a few years later would lead to their marriage. Another reason was probably that Danish public opinion had come to regard the monarchy as a non-political institution and expected a king to behave accordingly. Finally, the centre-left segment of Danish public opinion supported those Greeks who would no longer accept the political prerogatives of the kings, or any other unelected institu-

---

55 *Politiken* 12 March 1897, in Kaarsted 1960.
56 Olden-Jørgensen 2003, 182-7.

tion, and their meddling in political affairs. In doing so they followed a more global trend that found its expression in the so-called youth rebellion.

The opposition under the leadership of George Papandreou accused the unelected institutions of having tampered with the elections in 1961 and refused to accept the result.[57] The mood of this Greek opinion is the subject of a dispatch written by the West German Ambassador to Greece on the occasion of the 1963 official celebration of the centenary of the Glücksburg Dynasty in Greece.

The West German Ambassador seriously doubted the wisdom of the celebration, a sentiment he believed was shared by wide circles of the population and the diplomatic corps. After all, wrote the German Ambassador, fate had hardly smiled on a single Glücksburg King, and few had proved to have much dexterity in governing. The Glücksburg Centenary, the Ambassador went on, had been criticised in diplomatic circles and abroad as being well beyond the means of the state of Greece, a recipient country of foreign aid and one of the most exposed members of NATO.[58]

Faithful to its vow to avoid official dealings with the Royal Family and as a protest against the legitimacy of the government, the opposition had been absent from the Glücksburg Centenary. The Ambassador doubted that Prime Minister Constantine Karamanlis supported the idea of the Glücksburg Centenary wholeheartedly. After all, he would have been aware of the widespread criticism in Greece and abroad. Popular support for the royal family was not unlimited, and the sympathy with which the Greek population had met Anne-Marie was not necessarily directed at Constantine. Queen Frederica was criticised for meddling in politics. According to the German Ambassador, Frederika saw in the Karamanlis government a chance to have her own way. If she also in-

tended to realise her plans, the most severe consequences in terms of public opinion would ensue. One could only hope, however, as was widely desired in Athens, that the newly established close relationship with the Danish royal family would transmit some democratic thinking to the Greek court.[59]

As the German Ambassador warned relations between Karamanlis and the palace soon deteriorated, and dramatically so, as a consequence of an official visit by the royal couple to London planned for July 1963. On 11 June, after several abortive attempts to convince the King of the wisdom of staying at home as well as to avoid protest demonstrations, Karamanlis decided to resign while the King declared that he would not submit to the pressure of "a small minority".[60] As was widely expected, the royal couple was met with large demonstrations protesting against Greece's holding political prisoners and accusing the palace of having ordered the assassination of Grigoris Lambrakis, a deputy of the leftist party EDA who was murdered in Thessaloniki in May 1963 by thugs with links to the security forces.

The political role of the Greek monarchy also caused concern at the highest level in Danish politics. In his struggle with the palace, George Papandreou, who had become Prime Minister in 1963, attracted a certain sympathy from, among others, the Danish Minister of Foreign Affairs, Per Hækkerup. According the British Ambassador to Greece, Hækkerup should at the occasion of the royal wedding in Athens have personally lectured Queen Frederika on the virtues of constitutional monarchy. According to the British Ambassador in Copenhagen, there existed a "special relationship" between Denmark and Greece resulting from the marriage between Anne-Marie and Constantine and from Danish participation in the Cyprus UN force.

---

57 Pelt 2006, 257-9.

58 The wedding of Princess Sophia and Franco's heir, the Spanish Prince Juan Carlos in 1962, rendered the sources of royal income and state expenditures on behalf of the Royal Family subject to much public criticism. Sophia's dowry was established by a special law of an extra tax of 15 per cent. According to the German Embassy, it was seen as exorbitantly lavish and far in excess of the otherwise modest means at the disposal of the Greek state, not to mention those of an ordinary Greek person. In this way the Greek government also became entangled in the much-criticised financial conduct of the Royal Family, further contributing to the image of the prime minister as the 'King's puppet'.
Athens 28 March 1963, Jahrhundertfeier der Dynastie, Besuch des Dänischen Königspaares, Nationalfeiertag, Dynastische Prätensionen, Politisches Archiv des Auswärtigen Amtes, Abt. 2, Ref. 206, Bd. 153. Se also Kornetis, 2013, 16.

59 Athens 28 March 1963, Jahrhundertfeier der Dynastie, Besuch des Dänischen Königspaares, Nationalfeiertag, Dynastische Prätensionen, Politisches Archiv des Auswärtigen Amtes, Abt. 2, Ref. 206, Bd. 153.

60 Athens 15 January 1964, Greece: Annual Review for 1963, National Archives London, (hence NA, London) FO 371/174806. Regarding contemporary documents from Karamanlis' office and his own later account of his resignation, see *Konstantin Karamanli* 1994, 15-34.

On 16 September 1964, two days before the wedding, Hækkerup implied in an interview given to the Greek Press that Danish constitutional practice could also be followed "with advantage" by members of the Greek royal family, especially Queen Frederika. According to Hækkerup, it was possible in a modern democracy to combine the existence of a monarchy with the government of the people. "In Denmark", according to Hækkerup,

the King [has] no responsibility, direct or indirect, in the affairs of government […and] a Queen Mother [has] no status in the Danish constitution other than pertaining to a member of the Royal Family […] she [can] play no part at all in the political life of the country.

The British Ambassador regarded Haekkerup's statement as a token of solid support for Papandreou: "[a]lthough Haekkerup speaks very freely, he would not publicly have put his foot accidentally into a possible hornet's nest of this kind".[61]

Papandreou's forced resignation in July 1965 and the ensuing political crisis that was unleashed by Constantine's intervention and culminated in the coup d'état on 21 April 1967 only fuelled the protests in Denmark, not unlike reactions in Great Britain against the private visit by Queen Frederika to London in 1963 and the official one by the royal couple the same year. Seen in this context it is significant that the aversion to Constantine's role as a "political king" was so strong that it led to demonstrations at the royal palace in Copenhagen, reminiscent of those during 1920 crisis when the Danish king Christian X dismissed the elected government. [62]

Solidarity with the Greek Citizen

The Greek cause had mobilised a number of young people across a wide spectrum, from members of the so-called Appel Group on the extreme left to young Social Democrats. Among the latter, the most active was Mogens Camre, a young Social Democrat and three decades later a member of the European Parliament representing the National Conservative Dansk Folkeparti. He would soon become a celebrated source of contemporary Greek political realities. In Greece Camre was hosted by the Papandreou family when the Colonels took power on 21 April 1967, and it created headlines when the Danish press came to believe that he was being held prisoner by the Greek military, though these were false rumours.

Upon his return to Denmark he was called to brief the Prime Minister of the Social Democratic Government, Jens Otto Krag, and the leader of the German Social Democrats, Willy Brandt, who happened to be in Denmark at the same time. According to Camre's account Krag was very interested in the Greek cause. After all, it offered a most convenient opportunity to profile Denmark as a stiff opponent against tyranny and hypocrisy in the Western camp, at a time when America's war in Vietnam was increasingly becoming a rallying point for such attitudes in the public, not least among youth. And it is tempting to suggest that Krag took the Greek cause upon him as a substitute for the Vietnam cause, which divided the Social Democrat Party. Krag did take some quite unusual steps that would cement his public profile as a firm supporter of Greek democracy and political freedoms. In parliament he made it clear that the Danish government would not wish to see King Constantine present at the wedding of Crown Princess Margrethe on 10 June 1967.[63]

While successive Danish governments kept a relatively low profile in the case of Vietnam, the same governments would be very outspoken in their criticism of the Colonels' Greece, demanding its expulsion from the council of Europe and raising the question of the Greek problem in NATO in the name of universal human rights.[64] This made the major NATO powers nervous, in particular the United States and West Germany, fearing that in response Greece would leave the Western Alliance. In May 1970 the US Foreign Secretary William Rogers and his West German counterpart took up the matter and on 23 May Walther Scheel warned the Danish Minister of Foreign Affairs Poul Hartling of "the severe consequences that any discussion at the [NATO] meeting of the internal situation in Greece could have and I asked him [Hartling]

---

61   20 November 1964, British Embassy to Central Department, NA, London, PRO, FO 371/174837.

62   Olesen & Villaume 2005, 666-71.

63   Mogens Camre Papers; Camre 2007, 81-5; Olesen and Villaume 2005, 666-71.

64   Midtgaard 2010, 294-317.

to abstain from any criticism of the internal politics of the Greek regime". [65] Nevertheless Hartling did bring up the issue and voiced criticism against the Junta. He was supported by Norway and Holland. [66] This would be the policy line of Denmark until the collapse of the dictatorship in 1974.

The period of strong political engagement in the Greek cause and the struggle against royal intervention, dictatorship and abuse of human rights lasted from about 1963 well into the 1970s. It saw the translation of Greek poets and authors who often appeared or were cited in publications of a political nature to command attention to the situation in Greece. The tone was one of solidarity with the ordinary Greek citizen on the basis of universal political and human rights. The anthology *Med Solen i Ryggen*[67] [the Back against the Sun] from 1963 was the first published expression of this trend. It was edited by three prominent Danish writers from the Left, Halfdan Rasmussen, Ivan Malinovski and Erik Stinus, and presented to the sun-loving Danish public the unsavoury political realities of the popular holiday destinations of Greece, Spain and Portugal. In the approximately 100-page long section on Greece it brought fundamental aspects of post-war Greek history to the knowledge of the Danish reader for the first time, including the role of the strongest and Communist-led resistance movement, EAM/ELAS, during the Axis occupation of Greece and the ensuing Civil War. Its storyline follows the narrative of the Greek left and combines the events of the 1940s with the issues of political prisoners, the official silence on the role of EAM/ELAS in the resistance and the role of the shadow state and non-elected institutions like the palace and the army in the killing of Lambrakis. It also presented three poems translated into Danish. They are Yiannos Ritsos' *The Prison Tree and the Women*, Constantine Cavafy's *Waiting for the Barbarians* and George Seferis' *Edo telionoun*.

The Greek section was later published as a separate and extended edition in the wake of the Colonels' coup in 1967, entitled *Mørke over Akropolis*[68] [Darkness over Acropolis], and would interact with Costa-Gavras' 1968 French–Algerian film *Z* to expose the sinister aspects of Greek politics to a broader Danish public. The film was based on Vasilikos' work, which unravelled the involvement of the shadow state, from the level of street thugs to state officials at the highest level, in the assassination of Lambrakis. Featuring actors like Yves Montand and winning an Academy Award for the best foreign film, *Z* became an international common point of reference among young anti-establishment protesters.

While a single work of Kostis Palamas was translated in 1936 and the 1950s saw translations of some of Nikos Kazantzakis' works, it was not until the 1960s onwards that translations of modern Greek writers began to gain pace in earnest, giving the Danish public an opportunity to get acquainted with George Seferis, Antonis Samarakis, Constantine Cavafy, Yiannos Ritsos, Odysseas Elitis, Andreas Embirikos, Nikos Engonopoulos, Kostas Kariotakis, Vasilis Vassilikos and many others. In was in the same period that the Danish public became familiar with the music by Mikis Theodorakis and films by Theodor Angelopoulos.[69] It was these artists who first gave Greece its own voice in Denmark in any meaningful way. In addition, the decades of 1980s and 1990s would see a growing number of translations of modern Greek authors and poets.[70]

Otherness as a Source of (Mis)Understanding

In spite of this, when the issues of the Junta period began to fade from the headlines, so did the attitude of solidarity with the ordinary Greek. Instead images of the otherness of the Greeks began to appear. This can be explained among other factors by mass tourism, which would bring Danes to Greece in their hundreds of thousands. Some went to relax and enjoy the human qualities of the Greeks, others to explore the exotic. Indicative of this demand

65 Pelt 2006, 300-1.
66 Pelt 2006, 300-1.
67 Rasmussen, Malinovski & Stinus (eds) 1963.
68 Rasmussen, Malinovski & Stinus (eds) 1967.
69 Engberg 2000.
70 Engberg 2000.

is the reception of the 1981 book *Klokken i Makedonien* [The Bell in Macedonia] by the Danish author Knud H. Thomsen, which became a bestseller. The story takes place during the Axis occupation (1941-44) and the author portrays his fictive Greeks with Dionysian qualities, in the same cast as the popular *Zorba the Greek* or Henry's Miller's Katsimbalis, a main protagonist in *The Colossus of Maroussi*. His representation of the Greeks as unpredictable and driven by passion and zeal does not make them negative characters per se, but persons different from the Danes who according to similar stereotypes are cautious, inhibited and cold. And they apparently appealed to many of his readers who had gone to Greece to forget the routines of everyday life in Denmark or find their inner selves in the Aegean Shangri-La, in company with Miller's *The Colossus of Maroussi*.

On the political scene it was the period of the so-called Second Cold War. Once in a while Greece would find its way into the public debate as a troublesome ally, while Andreas Papandreou would be portrayed as an opportunistic populist. On the other hand, such representations were tempered by the fact that both countries were the main producers of the so-called footnotes in NATO, i.e. a pronounced critism on specific points in NATO's policy. Denmark left 23 footnotes, Greece 56, in the period 1982-6.[71] The important difference was that in the case of Greece, which was also by far the most vocal in its critism, the footnotes were the expression of government policy, while in Denmark they stemmed from the opposition, led by the Social Democracy, which was able to force its policy on a minority government.

In the same period Denmark and Greece had become partners in the EU and most business was routine. But the dissolution of the Soviet Union and the wars in Yugoslavia would bring Greek and Danish interests in conflict with each other. The attempts of the Baltic States to secede from the Soviet Union during 1991 were met with high-profile public support from the Danish government, which also saw it as a way of profiling it-self a pro-active government and distancing itself from the former foreign policy image of Denmark as a small state that would have to bow to great power interests.[72] In these attempts the same government also took the side of the Former Yugoslav Republic of Macedonia in its conflict with Greece regarding the name issue. The Danish Minister of Foreign Affairs Uffe Ellemann-Jensen made himself ignominiously famous in Greece when in a speech to the European parliament on 20 January 1993 he characterised the Greek position as "ridiculous" and expressed the hope that "the Security Council will very quickly recognize Macedonia". On television he asked the Greek government to decide whether Greece was a European country or a Balkan state.[73] This made headlines in the press, not unlike Jensen's one-liner just mentioned, expressing doubt about the sound judgment of the Greek government and ascribing its stance on the name issue more generally to the alleged otherness of the Greeks. In this context the otherness of the Greeks has a clear condescending meaning. Similar representations would reappear in the coverage of the protests against the austerity programme during the Greek debt crisis; a recent study of the coverage of the 2015 referendum by the right-of-centre Danish press labels this sort of representation as expressions of Orientalism and cultural racism.[74] There were also voices expressing solidarty with the ordinary Greek and expert criticism of the austerity progamme and its rationale.[75]

Conclusion

The image of Greece in Denmark appears in a wide spectrum of representations. The qualities ascribed to the modular value of Greece seem to a very large degree to have corresponded with the current trends in Danish domestic and foreign policy. Regarding the evaluation of the unfamiliar Greece, in times of harmonious Danish–Greek relations, its otherness has been associated with positive connotations and exotic attraction; in times of tension, the same features have been seen as less benign. Greek

71 Mariager 2015, 109-13.
72 *Den store Danske Encyklopædi*, Østblokkens opløsning og Danmark.
73 See *Berlingske Tidende* 1 July 2001.
74 Mylonas Noutsou, 2017.
75 E.g. Sørensen, 2015.

sources in the shape of translated literature, film and music only seem to have informed the dominating images of Greece, as if some kind of synergy existed between the Danish perceptions of Greece and the Greek sources.

During the Greek revolution the Danish absolute monarchy, as a client of one of the leading reactionary states in Europe, Austria, regarded the idea of "Greece" as outright dangerous, while liberals saw it as a source of inspiration. It was artists and intellectuals who took up the Greek cause.

The accession of George I to the Greek throne inspired Danes to take a political interest in Greece, which first of all concerned itself with the survival of the Greek monarchy during the first years after his coronation. Although the Greek–Turkish War in 1897 triggered some interest in internal Greek affairs, it was not until the 1960s that Greece would enter the public debate and political life as a major subject of concern and interest. While Greece of the 1820s was treated as model, in the 1960 and 1970s, it was the institutions and principles to which Denmark subscribed that were held up as models to be followed in Greece and as yardsticks to assess Greek affairs.

MOGENS PELT
Saxo Institute
University of Copenhagen
Karen Blixens Plads 8
DK-2300 Copenhagen
mpelt@hum.ku.dk

Bibliography

Unpublished Sources

Mogens Camre Papers
National Archives London, FO
371/174806, Athens 15 January 1964,
Greece: Annual Review for 1963
Politisches Archiv des Auswärtigen
Amtes, Abt. 2, Ref. 206, Bd. 153, Athens 28 March 1963, Jahrhundertfeier
der Dynastie, Besuch des Dänischen
Königspaares, Nationalfeiertag, Dynastische Prätensionen.

Published Sources

Isager, J. (ed.) 1999
Peter Oluf Brøndsted: Interviews with Ali Pasha of Joanina, Athens.

Kaarsted, T. (ed.) 1960
Henrik Cavling som Krigskorrespondent: Artikler og breve fra den græsk-tyrkiske krig 1897, Aarhus

Svolopoulos, Konstantinos (ed.) 1994
Konstantin Karamanlis: to archio: ghegonota ke kimena, stemma enandion kyvernisis (Vol. 6), Athens

Books and articles

Andersen, H. C. 2006
En Digters Bazar, Copenhagen.

Bjørn, C. & C. Due-Nielsen 2003
Fra Helstat til Nationalstat 1814-1914 (Bd. 3), Copenhagen.

Camre, M. 2011
Knus Tyrannerne: Erindinger, Copenhagen.

Clogg, R. 1979
A Short History of Modern Greece, Cambridge.

Enemark, I. B. 1988
W.Sponneck og den politiske udvikling i Grækenland 1863-1865, Copenhagen.

Engberg, S. 2000
Bibliography of Modern Greek literature, Simi.

Ghazaleh, M. Friis 2005
Danmark og den Græske Frihedskrig: Den danske philhellenske bevægelse i 1820'erne, Copenhagen.

De Gobineau, A. 1993
Au royaume des Hellènes, Paris.

Haugsted, I. 2009
Arkitekten Christian Hansen: "at vende tilbage til Fædrelandet med mange gode Erfaringer", Copenhagen.

Hanioğlu, M. S. year
A Brief History of the Late Ottoman Empire, Princeton.

Hobsbawn, E. J. 1962
The Age of Revolution: Europe 1789-1848, London.

Holland, R. & D. Markides 2006
The British and the Hellenes: Struggle for Mastery in the Eastern Mediterranean 1850-1960, Oxford.

Hvidt, K. 1990
Det folkelige gennembrud og dets mænd, 1850-1900 (Vol. 11), Copenhagen.

Isager, J. 2008
'P.O. Brøndsted, a Revolutionary?', in Rasmussen *et al.* (eds), page nos.

Israel, J. 2010
A Revolution of Mind: Radical Enlightenment and the Intellectual Origins of Modern Democracy, Princeton

Kjærgaard, K. 2011
'St.St. Blicher og Jøderne: Blichers politiske forfatterskab', *Kultur og Klasse* (Vol. 1), Copenhagen, 49-65.

Knudsen, P. Øvig 2007
Blekingegadebanden: Den danske celle, Copenhagen.

Kornetis, K. 2013
Children of the Dictatorship: Student Resistance, Cultural Politics and the "Long 1960s" in Greece, London and New York.

Krarup, E. V. 1985
Dansk filhellenisme: Dansk engagement i den græske frihedskrig 1821-1830, Copenhagen.

Lehmann, O. 1970
Den græske Thronfølgersag 1863, Kolding.

MacFie, A. L. 1989
The Eastern Quesion 1774-1923, London.

Marchand, S. L. 1996
Down from the Olympus: Archaeology and Philhellenism in Germany, 1750-1970, Princeton.

157

Mariager, R. 2015
'"Ostpolitikkens anden fase": Socialdemokratiet og sikkerhedspolitikken 1975-88', *Historisk Tidsskrift* 115, page nos.

Mejer, J. 2008
'The public lectures of P.O. Brøndsted', in Rasmussen *et al.* (eds), page nos.

Midtgaard, K. 2010
'En slags uafvendelig vanskæbne: Grækenlandssagen og dansk udenrigspolitik mellem politik og ret 1967-1970', *Nye Fronter i Den kolde Krig*, C. Due-Nielsen, R. Mariager & R. Schmidt (eds), Copenhagen, 294-317.

Mylonas, Y. & M. Noutsou 2017
'The Greek Referendum and Eurozone crisis in the Danish Press', *Class and Race* 59, 3.

Nørgaard, L. 2000
'En græker i Bakkehuset – den unge Nicolaos Lunzi og Danmark', *Tidsskriftet Sfinx* 3, page nos.

Olden-Jørgensen, S. 2003
Prinsessen og det hele kongerige: Christian IX og det glückborgske kongehus, Copenhagen.

Olesen, T. Borring & P. Villaume, 2005
I Blokopdelingens Tegn, 1945-1972 (Bd. 5), Copenhagen.

Papanicolaou-Christensen, A. 1994
Christian Hansen: Breve og tegninger fra Grækenland, Copenhagen.

Pelt, M. 2006
Tying Greece to the West: US–West German–Greek Relations 1949-74, Copenhagen.

Rasmussen, B. B., J. S. Jensen, J. Lund & M. Märcher (eds) 2008
Peter Oluf Brøndsted (1780-1842): A Danish Classicist in his European Context, Copenhagen.

Rasmussen, H., I. Malinovski & E. Stinus (eds) 1963
Med Solen i Ryggen, Copenhagen.

Rasmussen, H., I. Malinovski & E. Stinus (eds) 1967
Mørke over Akropolis, Copenhagen.

Rodogno, D. 2011
Massacre: Humanitarian Intervention in the Ottoman Empire 1815-1914, Princeton.

Roessel, D. 2002
In Bryon's Shadow: Modern Greece in the English and American Imagination, Oxford.

Rostbøll, G. 2015
Byron, Brøndsted og Bakkehuset, Frederiksberg.

Schepelern, O. C. 2008
'P.O. Brøndsted as Royal Danish court agent in Rome', in Rasmussen *et al.* (eds), page nos.

Schneider, M. M. 2017
The 'Sailor Prince' in the Age of Empire: Creating a Monarchial Brand in Nineteenth-Century Europe, London.

St. Clair, W. 2008
That Greece Might Still Be Free: The Philhellenes in the War of Independence, Cambridge.

Sørensen, C. 2015
Den græske Krise og Tysklands Korstfæstelse af Europa, Copenhagen.

Thomsen, K. H. 1981
Klokken i Makedonien, Copenhagen.

Tuncer, H. 2014
Das Osmannische Reich und Metternichs Politik, Berlin.

Reports on Danish Fieldwork in Greece

Topographical Work in Ancient Kalydon, Aitolia (2015-18)*

OLYMPIA VIKATOU, SØREN HANDBERG, NEOPTOLEMOS MICHAELIDES & SIGNE BARFOED

Abstract

This report presents the preliminary results of extensive topographical surveys of the entire archaeological area of the ancient city of Kalydon in Aitolia conducted in the years 2015-2018. The fieldwork has resulted in the creation of a new detailed topographical map of the city that includes all visible monuments within the archaeological area. One of the main aims of the survey project was to document the city's extensive necropoleis, and three distinct burial areas dating to the Hellenistic period surrounding the city were identified. Furthermore, the survey demonstrated the existence of graves situated on the slopes of the acropolis within the fortified area of the city, which may date to the Classical period. The report also includes a presentation of more detailed surveys of one of the city's gates and a stretch of the fortification wall where ancient repairs are visible. The first evidence ever found for olive oil production in the city and the discovery of Mycenaean pottery are also discussed in the report.

1. Introduction

In 2015, the Kalydon Archaeological Project initiated an extensive, diachronic, topographical survey of the ancient city of Kalydon in Aitolia.[1] The purpose of the survey was to produce a new and detailed topographical map of the ancient city that included all the known and visible archaeological monuments and other features within the archaeological area, as no such map had yet been made. This report presents the new map, produced by the Kaly-

don Archaeological Project after four consecutive field campaigns, which began in 2015, and highlights some of the results (Fig. 1).

The survey covered an area of 634,080 m², and included the entire area of the fortified city and the sanctuary plateau to the west of the city, as well as substantial areas outside the city walls that had not previously been surveyed in detail. Several different survey techniques, in-

---

* The Kalydon Archaeological Project is a collaboration between the Danish Institute at Athens and the Ephorate of Antiquities of Aitolia-Acarnania and Lefkada, under the direction of the Ephor Dr. Olympia Vikatou and associate professor at the University of Oslo Søren Handberg. The project is grateful to the Hellenic Ministry of Culture and Sports for granting the permission to carry out archaeological fieldwork in ancient Kalydon, and to the Carlsberg Foundation for generous financial support. Many thanks are also due to Giorgos Stamatis (archaeologist) and Giorgos Manthos (guardian of the archaeological site) from the Ephorate of Antiquities of Aitolia-Acarnania and Lefkada, who participated in the project. The project also wishes to express its gratitude to Giannis Dikaioulias and all the archaeology students from Denmark and Norway who participated in the fieldwork.

1 All the original data compiled during the survey is stored in the archives of the Danish Institute at Athens and the Ephorate of Antiquities of Aitolia-Acarnania and Lefkada.

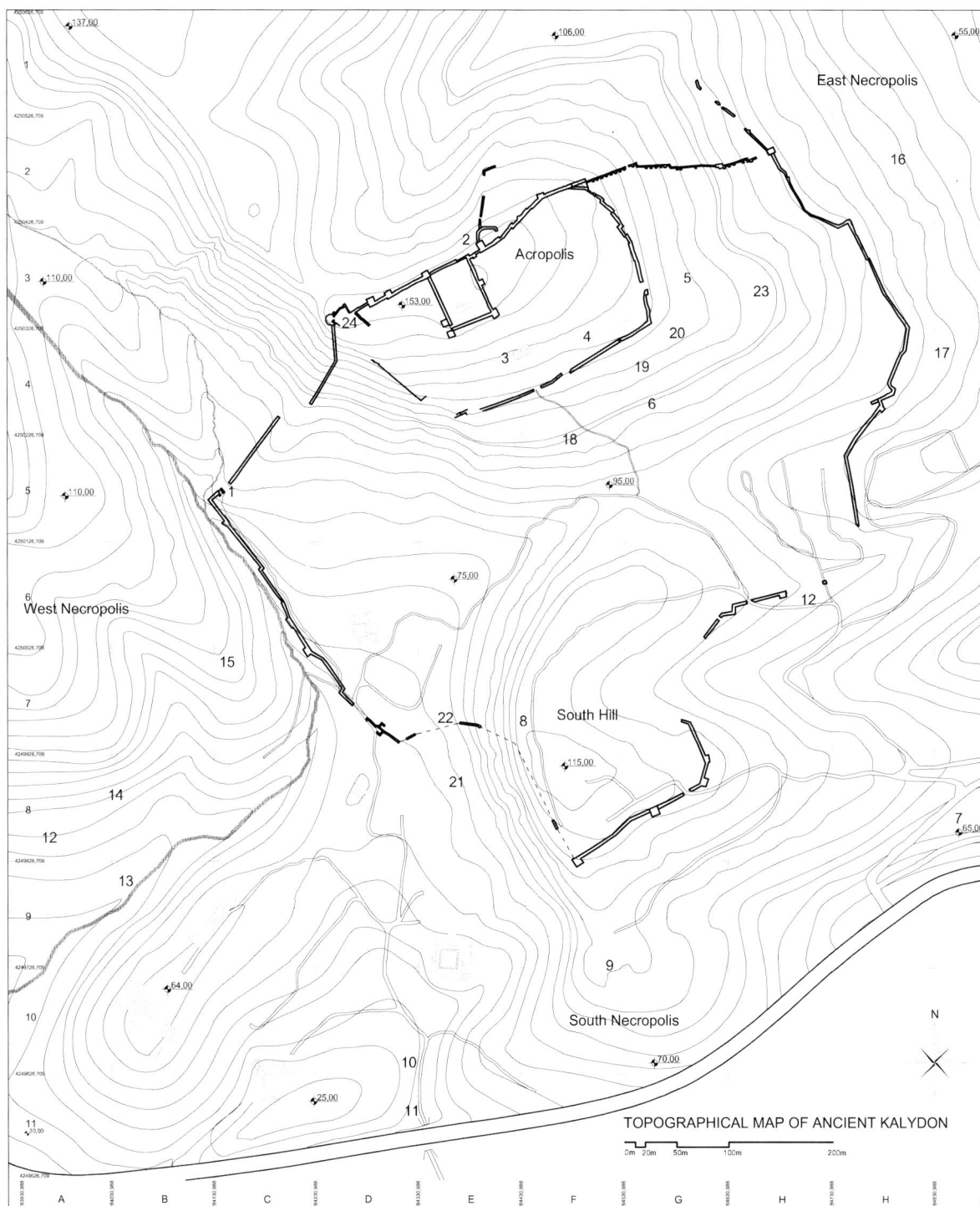

Fig. 1. *Topographical map of the archaeological area of ancient Kalydon. (N. Michaelides).*

cluding advanced digital surveying tools, were employed in the creation of the topographical map.

In total, 777 new features were identified and included on the map of the archaeological area, including buildings, wall sections, graves, quarries and individual finds. The new map adds significant information that allows for reinterpretations of many parts of the city's topography, urban structure and historical development.

2. Methodology

The archaeological site of Kalydon covers an area of more than 600,000 m², and the size of the area alone presented a challenge for the project. In addition, the terrain is hilly, and several areas are heavily overgrown with thick vegetation, such as *Calicotome villosa* L. and *Quercus coccifera* L., which makes terrestrial surveying difficult and time consuming. Furthermore, some areas were completely inaccessible to survey teams on the ground. To meet these challenges, the project employed a range of different terrestrial and aerial surveying methods, which are described below. Even so, it is important to state that despite the difficult terrain, pedestrian survey teams carefully explored almost the entire area. The survey teams, usually consisting of three persons, would traverse the landscape and record features such as modern terrace walls, ancient wall structures, roads, fences, tombs, outcropping bedrock, single finds such as pieces of architectural blocks, production debris, etc. The survey teams recorded all features encountered with a short description including basic measurements and photographs. In this way, a comprehensive catalogue of the visible features within the archaeological area was produced.

An important part of the survey was the creation of a completely new and detailed base-map of the area with height curvatures, since no detailed map existed beforehand. The first archaeological site plan of ancient Kalydon was made during the fieldwork carried out by Frederik Poulsen and Konstantinos A. Rhomaios in 1926, with help from the Greek military.[2] However, the height

curvatures on this old map are not detailed enough and a comparison between the map and the physical landscape reveals some discrepancies in the topographical layout of the area. During the archaeological fieldwork conducted in Kalydon in the years 2001-2005, a new survey of the main monuments of the city was undertaken and a new and valuable map was produced.[3] However, this map did not include detailed height curvatures and it showed almost exclusively excavated monuments.

2.1 UAV survey and the creation of a Digital Elevation Model of the archaeological site

Given the character of the pre-existing maps, the first step in producing a new topographical map of the archaeological area was therefore to create an entirely new base-map with detailed height curvatures. For this work, an Unmanned Aerial System (UAS) was used to produce a series of orthophotographs, which enabled the creation of a digital 3D point cloud of the site. From this cloud, a Digital Terrain-Terrestrial Model (DTM), a Digital Elevation Model (DEM) and a Digital Surface Model (DSM) covering c. 480,000 m² of the archaeological site were produced.[4]

Ground control points in the form of painted 20x20 cm aluminium targets were positioned in the surrounding landscape to mark significant alterations in altitude. In total, 70 control points were placed across the entire archaeological area during the 2017 summer campaign. The geographic positions of the control points' centres were recorded with the use of a Hi-Target V90Plus GPS (Fig. 2).[5] Subsequently, a series of aerial photographs were taken with a remote-controlled multi-copter/octa-copter following a preconfigured flight path at 186 m altitude.[6] The area was photographed with two different cameras, a Sony a7R II digital camera with 42.4 MP full-frame BSI CMOS sensor, which photographed the area vertically and laterally with 75% overlap of each photograph, and a Parrot Sequoia multispectral camera with 16 MP and 3 Bands (Blue 0.45-0.52, Green

---

2   Poulsen & Rhomaios 1927, 4-5 pl. 1, fig. 1.

3   See Dietz & Stavropoulou-Gatsi 2011a, 9-10, fig. 2.

4   For some examples of the use of UAV systems in monument surveys, see e.g. Achille *et al.* 2015; Colomina & Molina 2014; Nex & Remondino 2014.

5   The GPS receiver was adjusted to the EGSA-87 Greek reference system (EPSG:2100 GGRS87/Greek Grid).

6   The flight plan was created using the Ardupilot Mission Planner open source UAS Ground Station software, http://planner.ardupilot.com accessed 22 September 2018 (Avionics-Autopilot: Opensource Hardware Software PIXHAWK 2.1).

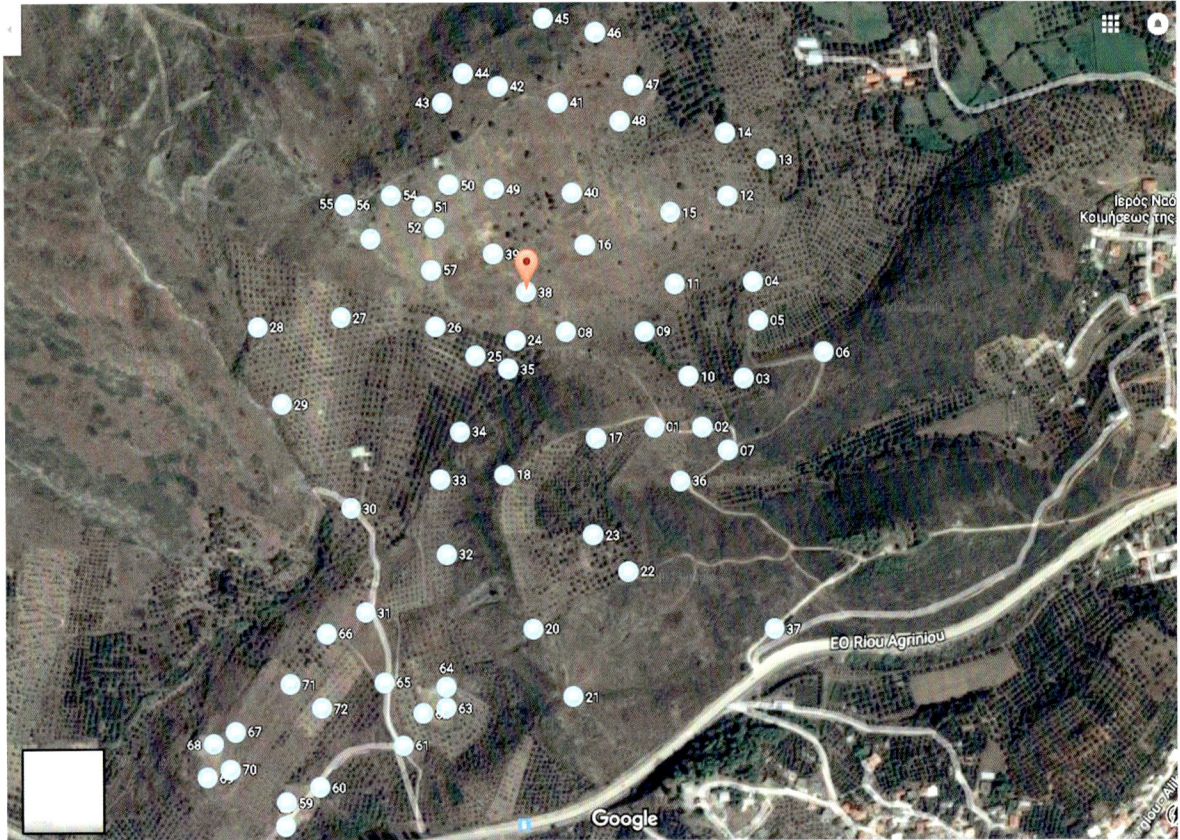

Fig. 2. *Geographic position of ground control points located within the archaeological area of Kalydon.*

0.52-0.60, Red 0.63-0.69).[7]

The digital 3D model of the site was created with Agisoft's Photoscan Professional photogrammetry software.[8] The photographs from the digital and multispectral cameras, as well as the GPS coordinates of all the ground control points, were uploaded to the program and the images carefully georeferenced and aligned with the exact coordinates of the ground control points. From these, a dense point cloud, a mesh and textures were generated. Using the information from the multi-spectral images,

dense point cloud manipulation and classification tools were used to isolate the level of the vegetation from the soil level, thereby producing a DEM of the ground surface (Fig. 3). This procedure was critical, since high vegetation distorts contour lines in DEMs.[9] A topographical basemap with detailed contour lines and an accuracy of 2.7 cm was finally extracted from the DEM.

---

7   280 photographs were taken with the Sony camera and 348 photographs with the multi-spectral camera. The following settings were used for the Sony Camera: image resolution (width/height): 7.952x5.304 pixels; shutter 1/2500; sensor (width/height) 35.814 x 23.876 mm; lens focal length: 22 mm.

8   Several other types of free and open source software, including freeware such as Regard3d, Meshlab, Autodesk ReMake, 3DF Zephyr Free and VisualSFM & OpenMVS, can be used in a similar way to produce photogrammetry models.

9   The final orthophotograph (3.75GB) consists of 40,448x44,836 pixels for a ground footprint of 1,426.88x1,581.71 m, so the ground resolution is 2.77 cm/pix. The DEM model resolution is 11.1 cm/pix with a point density of 81.4 points/m^2. The point cloud model of the archaeological site consists of 594,369 points and the 3D model of 5,812,493 faces.

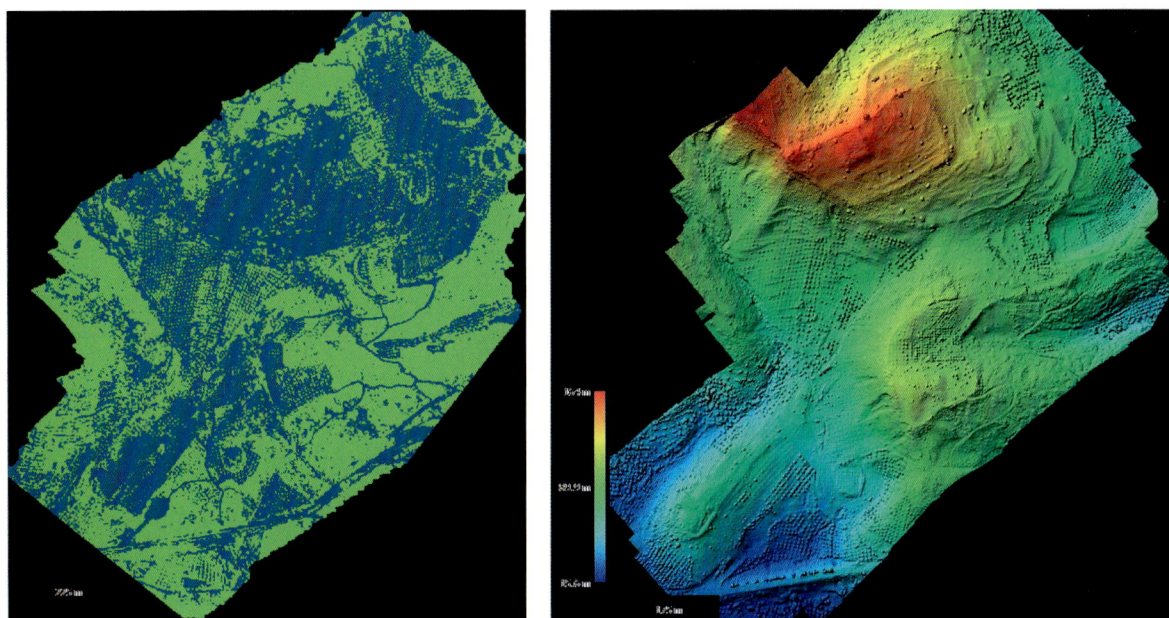

Fig. 3. A: *Infrared photomosaic of the archaeological area. B: Digital Elevation Model of the archaeological area.*

2.2 Mapping archaeological features within the archaeological site

The second step in the creation of the topographical plan involved the identification, recording and surveying of the visible archaeological features in the landscape. The whole archaeological area was divided into several smaller sections that were individually surveyed by survey teams, who traversed the area and recorded all visible features, both modern and ancient, in the landscape.

During the first two years of the survey (2015-2016), visible features in the landscape were recorded and surveyed with a Leica CS25 tablet with data corrections from Metrica's SmartNet through an installed SIM card, which allowed for an average accuracy between 1-3 cm. During those two years, mapping of the geographical position of visible archaeological remains on the entire acropolis hill was carried out using this system. However, the project experienced several operational difficulties with the system in the field, and the approach proved to be extremely time-consuming. Firstly, the tablet's battery quickly overheated in the warm Mediterranean conditions, demanding long breaks for the battery to cool down. Secondly, the satellite connection was unstable in the hilly area, which interrupted the work.

A different methodological approach was adopted for the surveys conducted in 2017 and 2018. During these two years, major features in the archaeological area were identified in the georeferenced orthophotographs and positioned on the topographical map. The features were then subsequently surveyed by teams on the ground, who also identified and mapped other features.

3. Preliminary Results of the Topographical Survey

The new topographical survey has considerably expanded our knowledge of the topographical layout and historical development of the ancient city of Kalydon. In this section, we will briefly highlight some of the preliminary results. One of the most noteworthy results is the identification and mapping of tombs and burial monuments. The mapping of the precise location of both known and previously unidentified graves shows that several distinct necropoleis, which include monumental chamber tombs, surrounded the ancient city. Many new monuments, especially wall sections of houses and other monuments, were also identified during the work. The survey also revealed the existence of several ancient sandstone quarries in the archaeological area. They were mostly identified by the traces of cut grooves in the bedrock, but in some quarries, ashlar blocks that were almost completely cut out from the bedrock can be observed. In addition, the city's

165

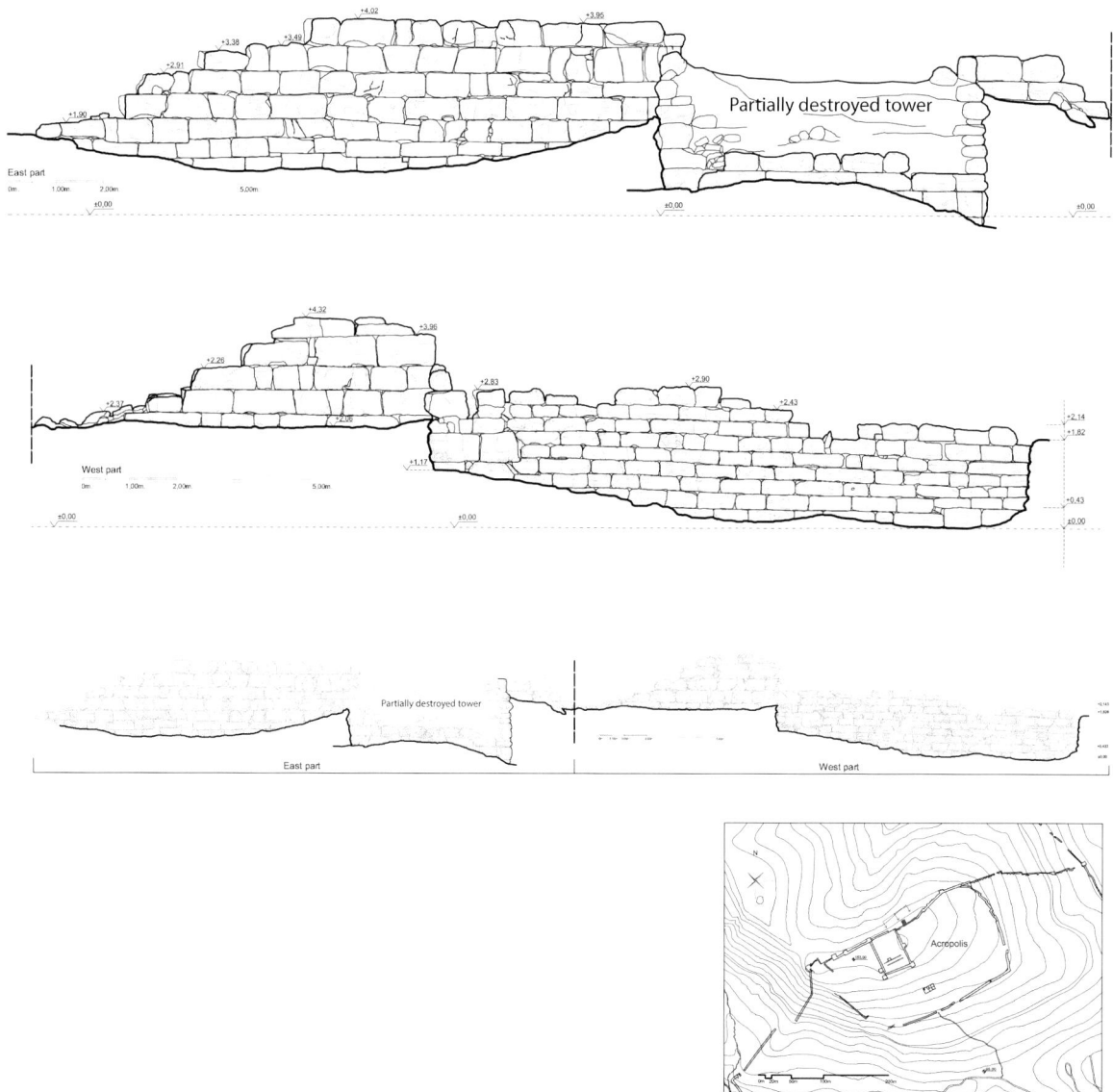

Fig. 4. *Section drawing of the exterior of part of the northern fortification wall west of the Central Acropolis. (Drawing: N. Michaelides).*

fortifications were also re-surveyed, and some areas and sections were investigated in greater detail. Finally, many important single finds were found scattered throughout the archaeological site. One of the most significant discoveries in terms of single finds was the Mycenaean pottery that was found at the highest point of the city in the northwestern corner of the acropolis. Another significant find is the first and, so far, only evidence for olive oil pro-

duction in the city in the form of a millstone from an olive crusher of the *trapetum* type.

3.1 The northern fortification wall and the Northwestern Gate

As part of the surveys of the fortification walls of the city, two separate parts of the fortifications were document-

Fig. 5. *The Northwestern Gate seen from the south. (Photograph: S. Handberg).*

ed in more detail: a stretch of the fortification wall on the northern side of the acropolis in 2017, and the so-called Northwestern Gate (or Gate A) near the northwestern corner of the fortifications in 2018 (Fig. 1, nos 1-2). These two areas were targeted for more detailed survey because they both provide new and important information about the construction and maintenance of the city's fortifications.

Repairs on the Northern Fortification

In 2017, a 50 m-long section of the exterior side of the fortification wall on the north side of the acropolis was surveyed in detail and a section plan was produced using photogrammetry and total station measurements (Fig. 4). This part of the fortification wall is particularly well-preserved with up to nine courses of sandstone ashlar blocks visible, and is particularly interesting because it provides

evidence for later repairs to the wall. Two different construction styles are clearly visible. In the western part, the wall is constructed with larger ashlar blocks; the blocks are smaller in the eastern part of the wall, where two courses of stones roughly correspond to one course in the western part. In one place, the smaller stones in the eastern part have been dressed to accommodate the larger blocks, and it is likely that the eastern part of the wall belongs to the Late Archaic–Early Classical fortifications of the acropolis, whereas the western part belongs to a later repair phase, which might be contemporary with the construction of the larger fortification enceinte of the city and the Northwestern Gate.[10] The survey of the wall section also clearly shows that the ground in the eastern part has sunk, causing the stone courses of the wall to slant slightly downwards towards the east.

---

10 The Early Classical construction date of the Acropolis fortification wall is based on the dating of the fill of part of the wall that was excavated in the summer of 2014; see Vikatou & Handberg 2017, 203-4, Vikatou & Handberg 2018, 309-10.

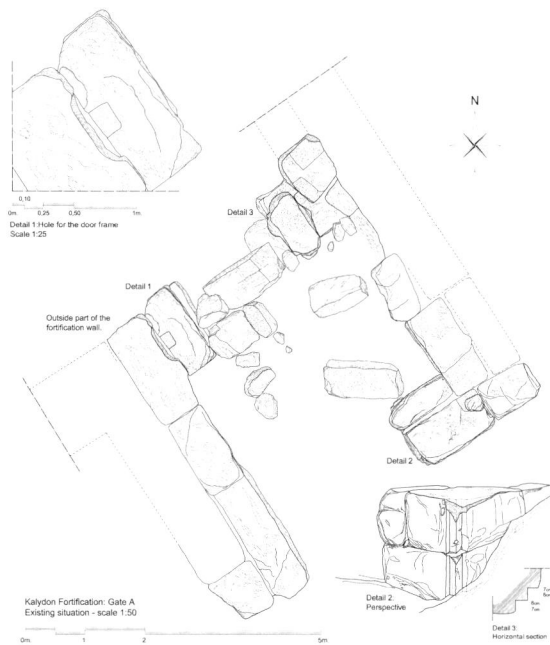

Fig. 6. *Plan of the Northwestern Gate with details of the threshold and the south-eastern ante. (Drawing: N. Michaelides).*

The Northwestern Gate

The Northwestern Gate is situated close to the northwestern corner of the city's fortification (Fig. 1, no. 1; Fig. 5). The main ancient road that ran along the interior of the western fortification wall led straight to the gate. The gate, which is not well-preserved, probably had a tower on its northeastern side (Fig. 6).[11] The course of the threshold, one course above and a foundation course below are preserved in the southwestern wall. The level of the threshold and two courses above are intermittently preserved in the northeastern wall.

The width of the gate's door opening is 2.57 m. A 47 cm-wide and 4 cm-deep recess has been cut into the stone block of the first course above and behind the threshold, and at the bottom of the recess there is a gap between the threshold block and the wall (Fig. 6 detail 1). The recess probably accommodated a wooden board that could be inserted into the cut at the bottom and thus fixed to the wall. The wooden post of the doorframe could

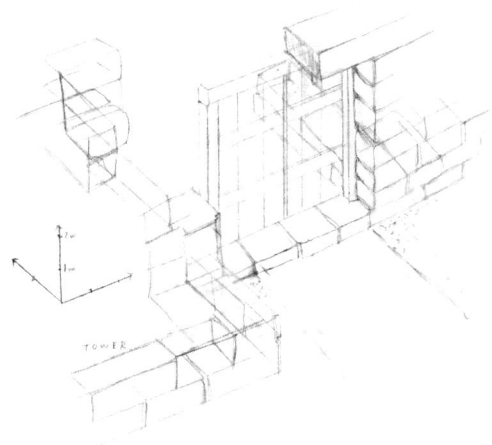

then have been fixed to the wooden board with nails, which would have secured the whole doorframe (Fig. 7). No similar cuttings for a doorframe on the other side of the gate opening were identified on any of the preserved stone blocks, and no holes for a locking mechanism could be identified.

There is some evidence to suggest that the gate was a later addition to the fortification wall. The practice of corner cuttings (or drafted margins) was used in the construction of the two antae in the northeastern side of the gate (Fig. 6, details 2-3). Furthermore, the ante at the second interior gate opening is not connected to the northeastern wall, but only built up against it.

The use of corner cutting in Greek fortifications is already attested from around the middle of the 5th century BC, but the practice becomes much more common in the Late Classical–Early Hellenistic period.[12] It is found in the fortifications of Messene, which probably date to around the second quarter of the 4th century BC, and at the fortifications at Pangali near Chalkis, which are most likely contemporary with the fortifications in Messene.[13] It has been suggested that the fortifications at Pangali could have been constructed during the Theban hegemony in

---

11   More extensive cleaning or even excavation is needed to understand how the gate is connected with the fortification wall.
12   Orlandos 1955-60, 258-9; Lawrence 1996, 168-9.
13   For Messene, see Müth 2014. For Pangali, see Mouritzen *et al.* 2016.

the Corinthian Gulf in the period 371-362/1 BC. The use of corner cuttings in Kalydon might therefore also suggest that the Northwestern Gate was installed after 367 BC, when Epaminondas "liberated" Kalydon from the Achaeans.[14] The use of corner cuttings is also found in the partially destroyed tower in the surveyed section of the northern fortification.

The gate conforms to Frederik Winter's Type I gate with a gate court, although at c. 9.5 m², it is small.[15] According to Winter, the gate court becomes more common during the 4th century BC.[16] The fact that the fortification of Kalydon did not take into consideration the higher ground on the hill to the west of the acropolis furthermore suggests that the fortifications were constructed before the development of catapults during the reign of Philip II (360/59-336 BC).[17] Considering the points raised above, a likely date for the construction of the outer fortifications enceinte in Kalydon would be in the 370-360s BC.

3.2. Houses on the Lower Acropolis

A *prostas* house, the first identified in Kalydon, was excavated on the Lower Acropolis plateau in the years 2013-2016 (Fig. 1, no. 3),[18] and during the survey, architectural remains that may belong to other houses of the same type were identified in several places on the acropolis hill. The remains of two such houses may be recognised in the southeastern area of the plateau (Fig. 1, no. 4). Traces of one or two other houses may perhaps be found immediately east of the Lower Acropolis fortification wall (Fig. 1, no. 5), and another house may be recognised on the south slope of the acropolis hill (Fig. 1, no. 6).

The reconstructed sizes of the two tentatively identified houses in the southeastern corner of the Lower Acropolis plateau correspond well with the size of the excavated *prostas* house (c. 160 m²). The dimensions of the other possible *prostas* houses are more difficult to estimate due to their poor state of preservation on the surface.

The results of both the excavation and the survey clearly show that the buildings on the acropolis and the slope closely followed the terrain, causing the buildings to have slightly different orientations. All around the acropolis, retaining terrace walls were constructed to create suitable spaces for the structures. This is especially clear in the area on the Lower Acropolis plateau directly below the Central Acropolis, where three terraced plateaus running in a southwestern/northeastern direction can be clearly observed. On the basis of geophysical surveys, a similar layout with houses located on terraced spaces around a hill has recently been proposed for ancient Chalkis, located c. 10 km east of Kalydon.[19]

3.3 *The necropoleis of Kalydon*

Few of Kalydon's known burials have ever been included in topographical maps of the ancient city. The absence of a detailed topographical map of the graves and tomb monuments has impeded a comprehensive understanding of the spatial setting, layout and development of the city's necropoleis. One of the priorities of the recent extensive survey was therefore to document and map both known and previously unidentified burials in the archaeological area. Now, for the first time, we have a complete topographical map with the location of almost all the known tombs in the city and the surrounding area. Since no coherent descriptions of the necropoleis of Kalydon exist, we will in this section give a brief diachronic summary of the available information.

The Bronze and Early Iron Age periods

The evidence for the earliest burial discovered near Kalydon comes in the form of a single vessel from a grave located close to the Evinos River, less than 1.5 km east of Kalydon's acropolis. Lazaros Kolonas and Gioulika Christakopoulou, who reported the discovery of the vessel, dated it to the Middle Helladic period.[20] The vessel

---

14   See Freitag 1999, 56; Mouritzen *et al.* 2016, 247-8. For the Achaians in Kalydon, see e.g. Bommeljé 1988.

15   See Winter 1971, 209-15 for this type. See also Dietz 2011a, 70-1, for a brief discussion of the gate.

16   Winter 1971, 215.

17   On this point see also Dietz 2011a, 66-7 with further references.

18   For preliminary reports on the excavation of the *prostas* house, see Vikatou & Handberg 2017; 2018.

19   Smekalova & Bevan 2016, 38-41, with fig. 16 (the buildings W2-W7) and the discussion in Dietz 2016.

20   Kolonas & Christakopoulou 2000, 240.

cannot be located today,[21] and no illustrations of the piece have ever been published, so its date cannot be confirmed, but since a couple of possible Middle Helladic pottery sherds have been found in Kalydon,[22] it would not be a great surprise to find contemporary graves, even if no other Bronze Age graves are attested in the area.

In 1965, Euthimios Mastrokostoas excavated 20 cist and pithos burials dating to the Protogeometric period in several discrete locations east and southeast of the city.[23] Unfortunately, the exact location of the burials seems not to have been recorded at the time of excavation, but most of them were located close to the modern water reservoir near the Antirrio-Ioannina road (Fig. 1, no. 7). A single grave was found near the old railway station in Evinochori around half a kilometre southeast of the reservoir grave plot, and another near the Evinos River. The existence of a grave in the modern village of Evinochori suggests that the necropolis area stretched around half a kilometre towards the southeast. During the recent rescue excavations in connection with the new Ionian Road, two Protogeometric–Early Geometric graves were found at the Chondreika plot and two at the Stoumpeika plot immediately northeast of Kalydon's acropolis.[24]

Combined, these finds reveal that in the Protogeometric–Early Geometric period, several burial clusters were located in an area stretching across a length of c. 1.5 km, from the centre of the modern village of Evinochori to the modern tunnel of the Ionian Road north of the city. No graves of the intervening period between the Protogeometric–Early Geometric and the Classical period have been identified with any certainty at Kalydon, except for one possible Archaic grave from the area of Evinochori (see the discussion below).

The Classical–Hellenistic necropoleis

Burials of the Late Classical–Hellenistic period are much better represented in Kalydon, and the recent survey has shown that three discrete necropoleis existed outside the area of the fortified city (Fig. 1). The South Necropolis covers the hill east of the so-called Heroon and the area towards the modern village of Evinochori. The West Necropolis is situated in the area north of the Laphrion Hill and on the southern spur of the Arakinthos mountain; this area has previously been described as the main necropolis of the ancient city, and might indeed continue much further beyond the city towards the west (see below).[25] The third and final burial ground that can be identified on the basis of the spatial distribution of the graves is the East Necropolis, located to the east and northeast of the Eastern Gate.

The South Necropolis

The most spectacular tomb known from the area of the South Necropolis is the underground chamber tomb of Macedonian type that was excavated underneath the northern exedra of the so-called Heroon by Poulsen and Rhomaios in 1926.[26] In the first publication from 1927, the excavators dated the Heroon complex to the second century AD based on the letterforms on inscriptions found in the building.[27] However, in the final publication from 1934, they revised the date based on the architectural elements, especially preserved column fragments, the floral decoration on a footstool in the burial chamber, and pottery from the foundation fill of the building, where, among other things, fragments of a mould-made bowl was found.[28] Considering these arguments, the excavators dated the construction of the complex, and hence the tomb, to somewhere between the late 2nd century BC and the foundation of Nikopolis in 27 BC, when according to

21   Stavropoulou-Gatsi 2011, 279 n. 17.
22   Stavropoulou-Gatsi & Dietz 2011, cat. no. 229, 275, 460, pl. 44. Another possible Middle Helladic sherd was found among the pottery assemblage from the Artemis Laphria sanctuary. Publication of this sherd is forthcoming by S. Barfoed.
23   Mastrokostas 1967, 320; Stavropoulou-Gatsi 2011.
24   Vikatou 2017, 33-8; forthcoming; Gatsi 2010a.
25   See Dietz 2011a, 66, where the hypothesis that the West Necropolis was the main necropolis of Kalydon is presented.
26   Poulsen & Rhomaios 1927, 51-84; Dyggve, Poulsen & Rhomaios 1934.
27   Poulsen & Rhomaios 1927, 53-5, fig. 84.
28   Dyggve, Poulsen & Rhomaios 1934, 397-414, 425. For details of the pottery found in the Heroon excavations see Dyggve, Poulsen & Rhomaios 1934, 415-27.

Fig. 8. *A: Ceramic cremation urn from the burial chamber below the Heroon (after Poulsen et al. 1934, 127). B: Fragmented vessel found in Room 1 in the prostas house on the Lower Acropolis. (Photograph: S. Handberg).*

ancient written sources Augustus moved the population of Aitolian towns to that city.[29]

The tomb had unfortunately been robbed prior to the excavations, but a ceramic cremation urn was found inside the tomb chamber; the excavators did not propose a date for this particular urn (Fig. 8a).[30] During the excavations of a *prostas* house on the Lower Acropolis in the years 2013-16, a somewhat similar vessel was found in Room 1 of the house in a context that predominantly dated to the period from c. 250-125 BC (Fig. 8b).[31]

The best argument for the later date has been the tendril-scroll decoration on a footstool in the burial chamber, but later research has clearly shown that this specific type of floral decoration is also found earlier in the Hellenistic period.[32] A chamber tomb of Macedonian type from New Pleuron, which was cleaned by E. Mastrokostas in 1967, included a stone *kline* with legs and pillows very similar to the decoration of the *kline* in the chamber tomb in Kalydon. The tomb yielded a single find, a silver Silenus with a comic face.[33] New Pleuron was founded after the destruction of Old Pleuron in 235/4 BC by Demetrios II, so it is very likely that the tomb dates to after this period. The comic masks appear to be most common in the 3rd-century BC Athenian black-glossed pottery,[34] adding further evidence that might support a somewhat earlier date for the tomb in Kalydon.

The *terminus post quem* for the construction of the Heroon finally depends on the fragments of the mould-made bowl found in the fill layer underneath the southern part of the Heroon complex.[35] However, the original publication did not include any detailed information about the exact find context or the stratigraphy of the area, so the question of the date of the Heroon cannot be considered completely resolved.

---

29   For a discussion of the date of the Heroon building, see Charatzopoulou 2006, 76-85. For a discussion of the foundation of Nikopolis and the translocation of populations of the Aitolian cities to Nikopolis, see Isager 2009.

30   Dyggve, Poulsen & Rhomaios 1934, 425-7, cat. no. 36, fig. 147. The whereabouts of the urn is currently unknown.

31   For preliminary reports of the excavation of the *prostas* house, see Vikatou & Handberg 2017; 2018. Work on the finds from the *prostas* house is still ongoing, and the chronological limits of the context in Room 1 should be understood as preliminary at this stage.

32   See, for instance, Nalimova 2017; Kullberg 2014. Similar floral designs can also be observed on the Tertia Horaria from Rheneia, dated to the 2nd century BC; see Palagia 2016, 379-80, fig. 26.4.

33   Mastrokostas 1960, 195; Mastrokostas 1967, 321 pl. 228b; Zapheiropoulou 1976, 169 pl. 119a. See also Stamatis 2018, 129-30 for the find of a grave stele with the name "Drakon" and further discussions of the grave.

34   See *Agora* 29, 92 and e.g. cat. nos 119-20, 126, 147, 172-3, 235, 255.

35   Dyggve *et al.* 1934, 419-27, cat. no. 40, figs 148-9.

Distinct but sporadic clusters of tombs have been recorded in the areas to the east and south of the Heroon. Some of these tombs were already identified and included on a map published in 1934.[36] One tomb complex, consisting of a larger burial chamber with two sarcophagi and two accompanying cist tombs located outside the chamber, is situated on the low hill northeast of the Heroon (Fig. 1, no. 8). These tombs were published by Ejnar Dyggve in 1951.[37]

The location of another two tombs on a small spur at the western edge of the hill east of the Heroon is also marked on the 1934 topographical plan of the area, but not discussed in any detail in the publication (Fig. 1, no. 9). In 2018 when these tombs were photographed, and their exact location mapped, it became clear that one of the marked graves was in fact a larger tomb with two chambers connected by an anteroom (Fig. 9). The existence of another group of three graves on the 1934 map (Fig. 1, no. 10) could not be verified during the recent survey, but another cist tomb (Fig. 1, no. 11) was identified further south near the tunnel of the modern Antirrio-Ioannina road. In 2018, two additional tombs were also located in a very overgrown area between the fortification wall and the modern dirt road that cuts through the ancient fortifications (Fig. 1, no. 12).

The low hill east of the Heroon and the surrounding area is today mostly covered by thick vegetation, which is often impenetrable, but scattered groups of burials across the area suggest that it was covered with burial monuments and cist tombs in Antiquity. The larger and more prominent tombs probably had grave markers, such as columns, stelai or even sculptural groups to be visible from afar, even if no tangible evidence for this practice has so far been found in the area.

Today private properties of the residents in the village of Evinochori cover the area opposite the road from the archaeological site and the Antirrio-Ioannina road cuts through the southern spur of the hill, separating the village from the archaeological site. However, in 1972 a cluster of seven Early Hellenistic cist tombs were found on the opposite (southern) side of the road,[38] which shows

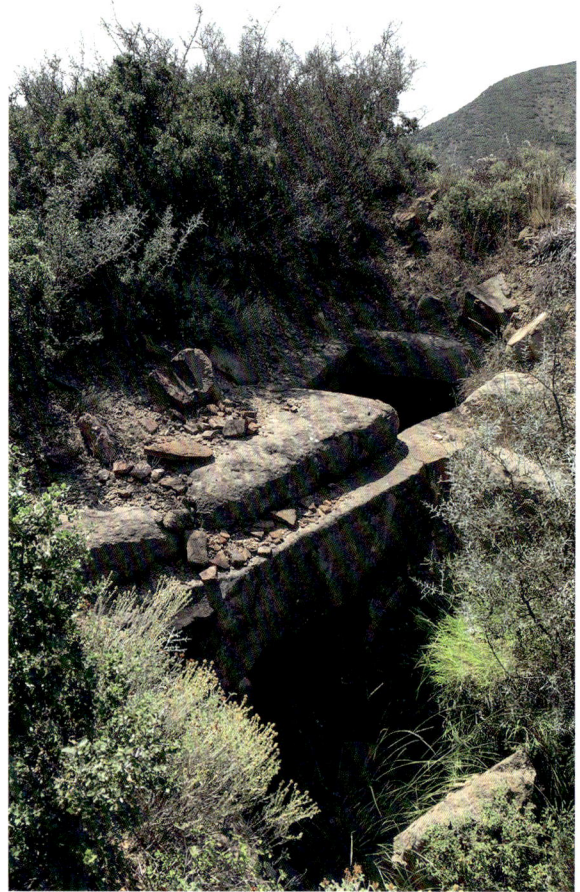

Fig. 9. *Monumental chamber tomb on the hill east of the Heroon. (Photograph: S. Handberg).*

that the necropolis originally stretched further towards the southeast. Four vessels (an Archaic Corinthian kotyle, two Classical lekythoi and a Hellenistic unguentarium) published by Jonas Eiring in 2004 are reported to have come from the garden of a private property in Evinochori, somewhere in the general vicinity of the seven excavated tombs c. 400 m southeast of the Heroon.[39] Eiring was convinced, mainly due to the vessels' good state of preservation, that they originated from graves. If that is indeed the case, the grave that contained the Corinthian kotyle must be considered unique, since it would be the only known grave dating to the Archaic period so far identi-

---

36   Dyggve *et al.* 1934. 12, fig. 6.

37   Dyggve 1951, 361-2, fig. 2.

38   Papapostolou 1972. The exact geographic location of the seven graves remains unknown.

39   Eiring 2004. The exact find spot of these four vessels is not reported by Eiring.

Fig. 10. *Entrance to the so-called Heroon II burial chamber in the Western Necropolis. (Photograph: G. Stamatis. @ Ephorate of Antiquities of Aitolia-Acarnania and Lefkada).*

fied in Kalydon.[40] Furthermore, graves of the Hellenistic period and two inscribed grave stelai have been reported from Kryoneri on the coast at the foot of the Varasova mountain, c. 5.5 km further southeast of Kalydon.[41]

The West Necropolis

In 1935, Dyggve found a monumental chamber tomb north of the Laphrion Hill across the so-called Kallirrhoë stream, which he named the "Heroon II" (Fig. 1, no. 13.[42] The tomb is covered by an earth tumulus mound with a diameter of c. 25 m and consists of a single chamber with three sarcophagi (Fig. 10). When the project re-visited

the grave in 2018, cuttings for a cist tomb were found at the southern border of the tumulus. Additionally, a fragment of a fluted Doric column was found on top of the large stone slabs that constitute the roof of the chamber (Fig. 11). It is possible that the tomb had a grave marker in the form of a column similar to the column that marked the large memorial monument (*sema*) at Rigaiika c. 2.5 km west of Kalydon discovered in 2015.[43] Another single cist grave was found close to "Heroon II" near the Kallirrhoë stream (Fig. 1, no. 14).

Approximately 120 m northeast of the "Heroon II", a peribolos grave was found in 2018 (Fig. 1, no. 15). Only one course of the ashlar blocks of the peribolos wall is exposed

---

40 It is possible that the four vessels actually come from the Laphria sanctuary; both Archaic Corinthian pottery and several lekythoi were found during excavation in the sanctuary area. It is well known, however, that there are ancient graves in the area of the private houses in Evinochori, and an Archaic site is known at Kryoneri on the coast at the foot of the Varasova mountain. The Kryoneri site remains unpublished, but Stavropoulou-Gatsi (2013) provides a preliminary report.

41 Mastrokostas 1967, 320 (Kryonerion).

42 Dygve 1951.

43 Vikatou 2017, 44-5; forthcoming; Vikatou & Michaelides, forthcoming.

Fig. 11. *Fragment of a fluted column found at the Heroon II during survey in 2018. (S. Handberg).*

Fig. 12. *Stele bases from the West Necropolis most likely stemming from peribolos tombs. (Photographs: A: S. Handberg; B: N. Michaelides).*

on the surface and part of the monument remains buried at the foot of the hill. In front of the peribolos wall, half of a foundation stone for a grave stele, which was probably set up on top of the peribolos wall, was found (Fig. 12a). Such peribolos tombs with retaining walls enclosing cist tombs are well known from, for instance, nearby New Pleuron[44] and Rigaiika.[45] Further up the hill of the West Necropolis, another stele foundation base was found (Fig. 12b; Fig. 1, no. 16), and it is likely that the whole hill was covered in peribolos tombs in Antiquity.[46]

Another well-preserved peribolos tomb was excavated in 2011 by the Ephorate of Antiquities of Aitolia-Acarnania and Lefkada at the Fraxos plot, around half a kilometre west of Kalydon.[47] The encircling peribolos measures 12.75x2.70 m and is preserved to a height of 1.35 m. The peribolos contained six cist graves and a Macedonian-type tomb with a small antechamber as well as a grave stele. All the graves were found in undisturbed condition and contained a variety of objects dating to the Late Classical–Hellenistic period, among which were a gold earring, a silver disc and a bronze mirror and bucket.

The East Necropolis

During survey work in 2018, the project identified at least 17 cist tombs to the east of the city, immediately outside the fortification wall (Fig. 1, nos 17-18; Fig. 13). Spatially the graves are situated in two discrete clusters; the southern one, consisting of 13 graves, is located close to the East Gate, whereas the northern and smaller cluster of four graves is close to the northeastern corner of the fortification wall. The layout of the tombs suggest that they lined an ancient road leading out of the East Gate and branching off towards the north. Other graves were

---

44 For a well-preserved periobolos tomb outside Gate A in New Pleuron, see Stamatis 2018, 127-9, 137-8, figs 2-3. For peribolos tombs in general, see e.g. Palagia 2016; Closterman 2007; Garland 1982.

45 Gatsi 2010b, 1057-8, figs 15, 18-9.

46 Frederik Poulsen and Konstantinos A. Rhomaios published the inscriptions of three grave stelai found in the fields of the wine orchards around Kalydon and from the Artemis Laphria sanctuary, see Dyggve & Poulsen 1948, 296 with further references. Leake also reported a grave stele from Kalydon, see Leake 1935, 112. Several grave stelai are also known from New Pleuron, see Stamatis 2018, 130 n. 21-22; Zapheiropoulou 1976, 169 fig. 119b; Moschos 1999, 272.

47 Vikatou 2011; 2012; 2017, 46-47; forthcoming.

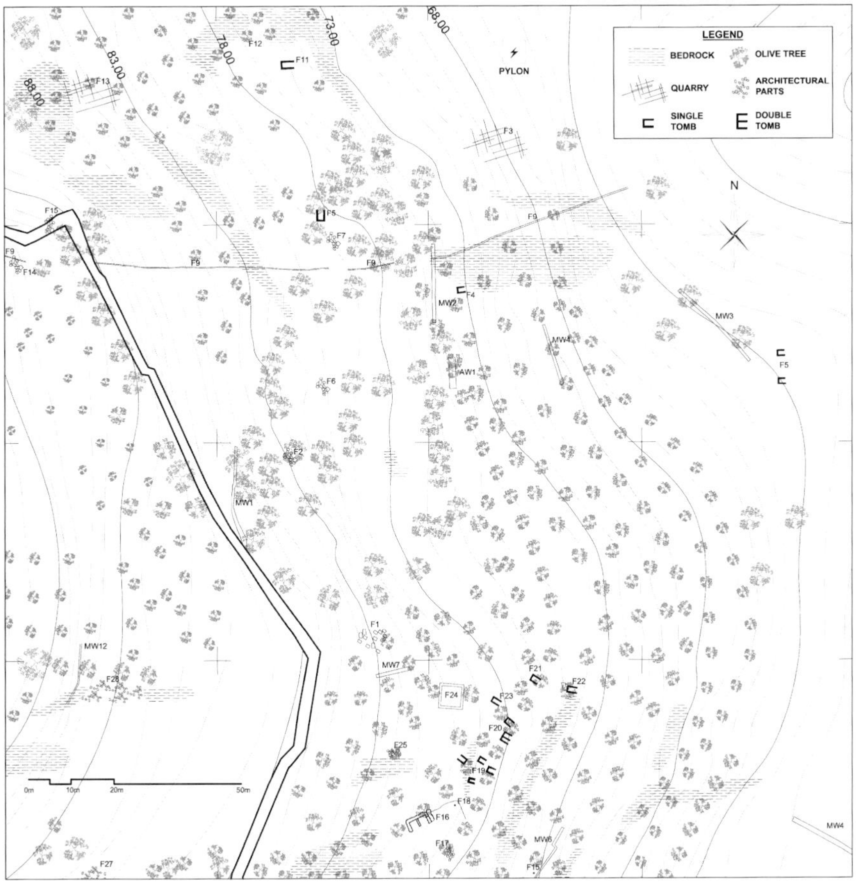

Fig. 13. *Map of a part of the East Necropolis. (N. Michaelides).*

presumably located between the two clusters, but no clear evidence for tombs was found in this area.

Unfortunately, all the tombs had been disturbed and only the foundation cuttings in the bedrock, and in some cases the lower stone courses, are preserved (Fig. 14). The tomb walls would originally have been built up of larger dressed sandstone blocks, like the smaller tomb found behind the large burial memorial monument at Rigaiika and other tombs known from Macedonia.[48] Fragments of limestone stelai and porolithos stones, the stone normally used for columns and other architectural elements in Kalydon, were found scattered among the tombs of both the northern and southern clusters of graves.

During rescue excavations for the new Ionian Road, archaeologists from the Ephorate of Antiquities of Aitolia-Acarnania and Lefkada found eight cist graves dating to the Hellenistic period at the Chondreika site c. 400 m

north-northeast of the northern cluster of tombs.[49] One of the graves is a 3x4 m-large cist tomb of Macedonian type with a *thalamos*. The tomb had been disturbed, but not robbed, and the grave goods included, among other objects, a golden *danake* and three bronze coins. Another grave contained five black-glossed vessels dating to the Early Hellenistic period. The existence of these graves shows that the East Necropolis covered an area of at least half a kilometre along the eastern border of the outer fortification wall.

The lower courses of several ancient walls belonging to smaller buildings or enclosures were found near the tombs. It is possible that these structures are family grave periboloi, or they could stem from smaller buildings or enclosures for burial associations. A terracotta antefix was found in one of the tombs in the southern cluster (Fig. 15). The provenience of this piece is very problem-

---

48 For Rigaiika, see Vikatou 2017, 45 fig. 7. For Macedonia, see e.g. Themelis & Touratsoglou 1997.
49 Vikatou 2017, 33-8; forthcoming.

Fig. 14. *Monumental cist tomb in the East Necropolis. (Photograph: S.T. Tomter).*

atic, but its presence in the tomb should probably be understood as a result of post-depositional processes. Even so, the existence of an antefix in the area is significant, since it signals the existence of a larger building in the area. A similar antefix, which was almost certainly produced from the same mould, has been found in upper stratigraphical layers in the excavation of the Peristyle House in the Lower Town.[50] In style it is close to the antefixes from the South Stoa in Corinth and should therefore most likely be dated to the Early Hellenistic period.[51]

A necropolis on the slope of the Acropolis in the Classical period

One of the most surprising results of the recent survey was the discovery of burials on the south slope of the acropolis hill inside the fortified area of the city. In 2018, two cist tombs were found on the south slope of the

acropolis (Fig. 1, nos 19-20). The two graves are constructed in the same fashion with larger stone slabs set vertically in the ground to form the cist (Fig. 16a-b).

In front of the western tomb, remains of an ancient wall can be traced for a length of 7.25 m. The wall might have served as a peribolos wall for one or more tombs, but the visible remains are too sparse to verify this. A stele fragment was found further down the slope, however, which might support the existence of a peribolos tomb on the acropolis slope.[52]

No finds that could directly indicate the date of the two graves were found. However, in terms of construction, they are similar to the 5th-century BC graves at the Rigaiika necropolis, located c. 2.5 km west of Kalydon, that were recently excavated during salvage excavations in connection with the construction of the new Ionian Road.[53] The generic similarity might suggest a similar date for the two graves in Kalydon. Even though this idea must remain tentative, two circumstances support

---

50   Dietz 2011c, 378, cat. no. 8.
51   Broneer 1954, pl. 21.1a.
52   For Classical period peribolos tombs in Pharsalos, see Stamatopoulou & Katakouta 2013.
53   Vikatou 2017, 39-44; Stauropoulou-Gatsi 2010.

Fig. 15. *Terracotta antefix from the East Necropolis. Find no. 18-1010. (Photograph: S. Handberg).*

a date in the Classical period. First, since the graves are found inside the fortified area of the city, it is reasonable to suppose that they belong to the period before the construction of the outer fortification enceinte, which, as discussed above, was probably constructed in the Late Classical period. Secondly, during the excavations on the Central Acropolis in 2001-05, a pit burial probably dating to the Classical period was found. The pit, which was underneath the walls of the Hellenistic "palace", is reported to have contained a human skeleton placed on the bedrock. The pottery from the pit is described as dating to the Classical period, and a gold finger ring found nearby might originally have belonged to the grave assemblage.[54] Unfortunately, none of the finds from this pit have been published, so its date must remain an open question.

In 2016, a stone urn was found directly southeast of the southeastern corner of the fortification wall (Fig. 1, no. 21, Fig. 17). Typologically the urn belongs to a series of cremation urns referred to as *osteotheken*, which are well known from the Kerameikos necropolis in Athens, where 50 examples have been documented.[55] A few examples of the type are known from Leukas, but it is rare outside Athens.[56] The stone used for the urn does not appear to be

Fig. 16. *Cist graves on the south slope of the acropolis hill. (Photographs: A: S. Handberg; B: N. Michaelides).*

local, and it is possible that it was imported to Kalydon, possibly even from Athens. Morphologically the urn from Kalydon is closest to urns that can be dated around the middle of the 4th century BC, as well as one example

---

54 Dietz 2011, 229 (Pit HS43). For mention of the finds from the pit, see Bollen 2011a, 465 (H8).

55 Torben Kessler has recently compiled a convenient typology of the osteotheken from Kerameikos, see Kessler 2014/2015.

56 Kessler 2014/2015, 190. For Leukas, see Andreou 1980, 75 fig. 2.

Fig. 17. *Stone cremation urn (osteothek) found in the slope of the acropolis hill. (Photograph: A.D.K. Høj).*

Fig. 18. *Plan and section drawing of rotary crusher stone. (Drawing: N. Michaelides).*

found in a Roman context.[57] However, the urn found in a Roman context in Athens might have been an earlier mortar that was re-used as a funerary urn, and another urn that is almost identical to the one from Kalydon has been found in a Hellenistic context in Kallipoli.[58] Since such *osteotheken* were often re-used mortars, it remains an open question whether the Kalydonian urn is in fact a mortar originating in a Hellenistic house on the acropolis slope or a funerary urn, and, if so, what period it should be ascribed to.[59] However, the surface treatment of the Kalydonian vessel conforms to a treatment that is often found in the Late Classical and Hellenistic examples in Athens.[60]

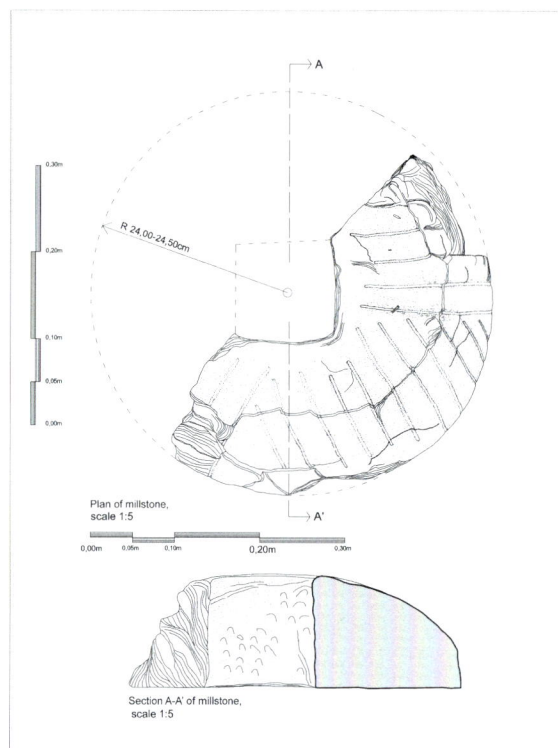

Concluding remarks

It is clear that at least 90 individual burials can be identified in Kalydon, most of which had not previously been included on a topographical map of the ancient city. The detailed recording of the spatial distribution of the tombs now allows us to identify three distinct necropoleis outside the fortification walls, and to presume the existence of earlier tombs on the acropolis hill within the fortified area. Comparatively few tombs are yet known from ancient Kalydon, and it remains difficult to say more about the spatial development of the necropoleis. However, two points can tentatively be made. First, it appears that the more elaborately constructed cist and chamber tombs are located closer to the city walls and along prominent roads, whereas simpler cist graves, such as those found in the modern village of Evinochori, are located further away

---

57 Compare the urn from Kalydon with Kessler, cat. no. 8 (mid-4th century BC) and cat. no. 11 (Roman period).

58 Themelis 1980, 274 pl. 42.

59 For the re-use of mortars such as *osteotheken*, see Kessler 2016, 188-9.

60 Kessler 2014/2015, 190.

from city. Secondly, the most elaborate tombs appear to be placed in topographically very conspicuous places, such as the "Heroon II" in line of sight from the main sanctuary, the two-chamber tomb on the hill above the Heroon, and the chamber tomb excavated by the Ephorate in 2011, which lined the ancient road towards New Pleuron.

The tombs found on the slope of the acropolis are particularly interesting since they suggest that in an earlier period the city was confined to the acropolis. The recent excavations of a small section of the acropolis wall provided evidence for a *terminus post quem* of 500-480 BC, and it is likely that it was constructed in the Early Classical period.[61] The new evidence from the excavations and survey provides significant information about the character and urban development of Kalydon in the pre-Hellenistic period, contributing to the scholarly debate about urban development in Aitolia in general, and specifically the question of the so-called refuge fortifications mentioned by ancient sources.[62]

In Giorgos Sotiriades' report on his archaeological work in Kalydon, published in 1908, he mentions that he found fragments of gold leaf foil in a grave north of the Laphrion hill, and when Dyggve investigated the "Heroon II", he considered that this might have been the tomb where Sotiriades found the gold fragments.[63] Fragments of gold leaves, presumably from a gold wreath, were also reported to have been found on the floor of the burial chamber underneath the Heroon.[64] The gold earring found in the undisturbed chamber tomb in 2011, the gold ring from the pit/grave on the Central Acropolis and the gold and silver objects found in the graves at the Chrondreika site are further testimonies of the wealth found in the Kalydonian tombs. Even though almost all the graves from Kalydon were found in a robbed condition at the time of excavation, we can begin to form a picture of the

elaborate and rich chamber and cist burials, which offer us a glimpse of the riches of Aitolia in the Hellenistic period as described in written sources.[65]

3.4. Evidence for the production of olive oil in Kalydon in the Hellenistic or Roman period

During the survey in 2018, evidence for oil production was identified for the first time in Kalydon. A large fragment of a rotary olive crusher millstone made of the local sandstone (*psamitis*) of the *trapetum* type was found north of the Heroon and just outside the fortified area of the South Hill (Fig. 1, no. 22).

Only about half of the round millstone is preserved (Fig. 18). It has a hemispherical shape with a maximum height of 13 cm near the centre, which tapers towards the edge. The centre of the stone has a square hole to accommodate a wooden beam. There are clear traces of use-wear on the edges, but its reconstructed diameter is 48-9 cm. A series of shallow grooves are cut into the surface of the spherical side. The *trapetum* type of olive mill worked with two such hemispherical crushers that squeezed the olives into a pulp in a large stone mortar with a concave bottom. The grooved surface of the millstones and the mortar facilitated the crushing when the millstones were rotated around the mortar (Fig. 19).[66]

The millstone from Kalydon was not found in its original context, but on the ground surface at the foot of the South Hill, where it seemed to have been moved. No obvious traces of buildings or a corresponding mortar were identified in the vicinity of the find spot, and it cannot be excluded that it eroded down from the South Hill, although the hill would not seem to be an ideal location for the processing of olives.[67] An area with many roof tiles and pottery dating to the 2nd century BC was found c. 50 m northwest of the crusher (Fig. 1, no. 23).

---

61   For the excavations at the acropolis fortifications, see Vikatou & Handberg 2017a, 203-5; 2018, 309-10.

62   For the question of fortified hills in Aitolia, see e.g. Funke 1987.

63   Sotiriades 1908, 100; Dyggve 1951, 361. For the mention of gold in graves at Kalydon, see also Dawkins 1909, 355.

64   Dyggve, Poulsen & Rhomaios 1934, 347.

65   For the riches of the Aitolian tombs, see also Grainger 1999, 188 n. 2.

66   For this type of crusher, see e.g. Foxhall 2007, 165-77.

67   During the recent survey, evidence for the existence of public buildings on the top of the South Hill was found. During an earlier intensive survey a few pottery sherds were found on the hill, and the area was especially void of finds dating to the Late Hellenistic and Roman periods. This has led the former director of the archaeological fieldwork in Kalydon, Søren Dietz, to propose that the South Hill was used as a grazing area inside the fortified area of the city in this period. See Dietz 2011b, 79.

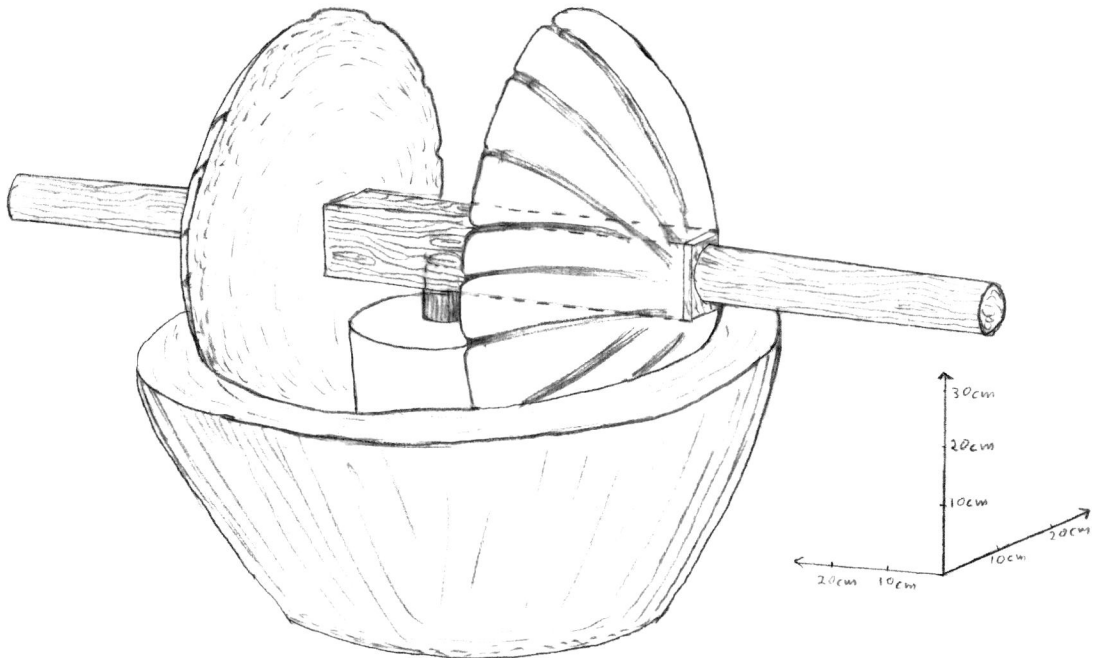

Fig. 19. *Reconstruction drawing of an olive crusher of the* trapetum *type. (Drawing: N. Michaelides).*

The millstone cannot be directly associated with this assemblage of pottery and roof tiles, but at least we can say that it was found in an area with Middle Hellenistic material.

Few rotary crushers have so far been reported from western Greece, but one has been found in a house in Arta in Epirus.[68] The context of this millstone can only be dated between the 2nd century BC and the 1st century AD. Another example has recently been reported from a farmhouse in Sitaralona in Aetolia.[69]

The chronology and morphological development of rotary crushers is not well documented. The type was most common in Roman times, but several examples dating to the Late Classical and Hellenistic periods are known from Greece.[70] The crushers of the Classical and Hellenistic periods seem generally to have been twice the size of the crusher from Kalydon.[71] The well-preserved crusher stones found in a Hellenistic house on the acropolis of Argilos in Macedonia appear to be slightly smaller than the ones from Olynthos.[72] A millstone crusher very similar to the one from Kalydon but with a diameter of 60 cm has been found in a Roman villa dated between the 1st century BC and the 1st century AD at Akraphia in Boeotia, and the crushers generally appear to be smaller in the Roman period compared to the earlier Greek examples.[73]

The only other indication we have of olive cultivation in Kalydon is the few charred olive stones that were found in a predominantly 2nd-century BC context in Room 1 in the *prostas* house on the Lower Acropolis.[74] That olive

---

68 Morgan 20092010, 113 (Arta, Garouphilia Street); Aggeli 1999, 4602; 2000, 546-7.

69 Gatsi 2010c; Gerolumou 2013.

70 E.g. from Chios, see Boardman 1958-9, 304; from Olynthos, see e.g. Isager & Skydsgaard 1995, 63 pl. 3.10-11; from Delos, see Bruneau & Fraisse 1981.

71 Foxhall 2007, 168-9.

72 Bonias & Perreault 1997, 544-8.

73 For the millstone crusher from Akraiphia, see Vlachoyanni 2013, 494 fig. 9b. For the decrease in size in the Roman period, see Foxhall 2007, 168-70; Mattingly 1990, 85. See also White 1975, 229.

74 Vikatou & Handberg 2017, 194 fig. 5.

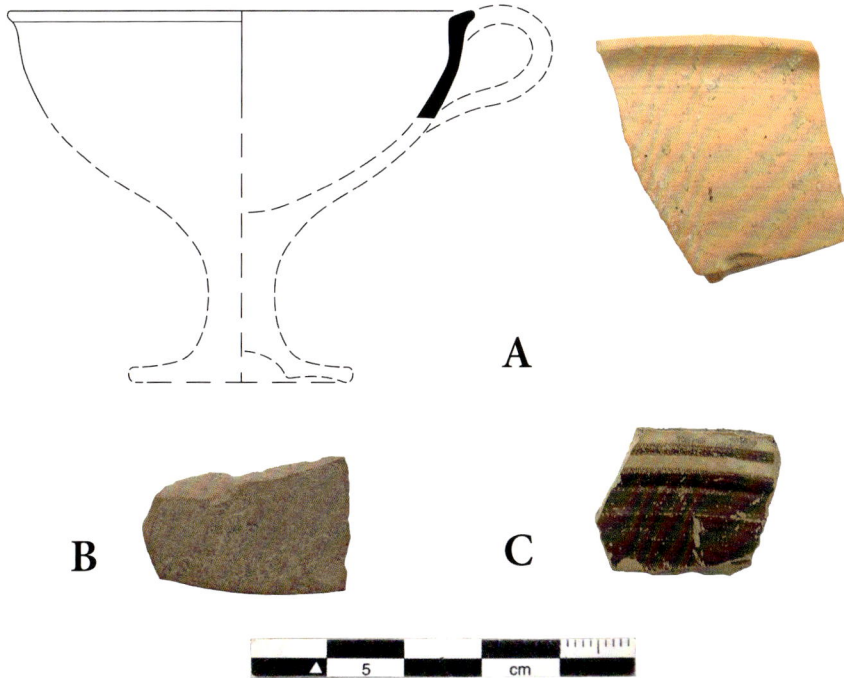

Fig. 20. A: Rim sherd of a Late-Helladic IIIA1 kylix and reconstruction drawing (drawing not to scale). (Drawing: J. Melander). B: Body sherd possibly from a Middle-Helladic vessel. C: Body sherd of a Geometric? Vessel. (Photographs: K.E. Vinther).

oil was produced in the Late Hellenistic or Early Roman period in Kalydon can perhaps be supported by the find of three pieces of an *opus spicatum* floor that might originally have been part of a pressing floor. The pieces were found in the eastern part of the city (Fig. 1. no. 24). During the period from the 2nd century BC to the 1st century AD, this type of floor was widely used as the surface of pressing floors in the central Adriatic region in Italy.[75] The piece of *opus spicatum* floor was not found in any obvious connection with architectural remains, and no base blocks for the pressing lever, decantation tanks, or larger storage vessels were found in the surrounding area, which would have strengthened the idea that these floor pieces were indeed from a pressing floor.

If the millstone originally belonged to a processing facility north of the Heroon, which seems likely, it provides valuable information about the organisation of land use in ancient Kalydon, since no farmhouses have so far been identified in the *chora*. Surely, it would have been more efficient to process the olives closer to the olive groves, rather than transporting them back to the city.[76] In Halieis, for instance, many presses have been found inside the town, but no rotary crushers, which could suggest that the crushing of the olives into pulp took place in the countryside.[77] The existence of a millstone in Kalydon might therefore reinforce our current picture of a countryside devoid of farmhouses, which is indeed noteworthy in comparison to the many Late Hellenistic and Roman farmhouses that are known from the countryside of Patras.[78]

3.5. A Mycenaean "platform"

In 1908, the archaeologist Giorgos Sotiriades explored Kalydon and made a small excavation in the northwestern corner of Kalydon's acropolis.[79] There he discovered walls that he interpreted as belonging to a Mycenaean defensive tower. He supported the date with reference

---

75   Van Limbergen 2011, 75-80.

76   Foxhall 2007, 198-9.

77   Ault 1994, 200; 1999, 652-4; Jameson 1969, 324; 2001, 283-4. For a discussion, see also Foxhall 2007, 143-8.

78   See most recently Stavropoulou-Gatsi & Alexopoulou 2013.

79   Sotiriades 1908, 99-100.

to the presence of Mycenaean and Geometric pottery sherds.[80] However, in his brief report he did not include any illustrations of the walls or the pottery. In 2018, Sotiriades' excavation trenches and "tower" in the northwestern corner of the acropolis were re-surveyed and a small rectangular "platform" was identified (Fig. 1, no. 25). Like Sotiriades, the survey team found Mycenaean pottery on the surface near this "platform", which included a handful of plain-ware body sherds and a rim fragment of a Late Helladic IIIA1 kylix (Fig. 20a). Additionally, a body sherd possibly dating to the Middle Helladic period was found (Fig. 20b), as well as a fragment of an open vessel that could date to the Geometric period (Fig. 20c). In the years 2001-2004, a few Mycenaean sherds were found in the same area during an intensive survey in the city.[81] A few additional sherds were also found in the excavations on the Central Acropolis,[82] and one sherd comes from the excavations of a kiln in the Lower Town.[83] It remains uncertain whether Sotiriades' walls are indeed of Mycenaean date, but any clarification of this question would require extensive cleaning of the area and perhaps excavations.

An ongoing research project that aims at a full publication of the pottery from F. Poulsen, K. A. Rhomaios and E. Dyggve's excavation in the Artemis Laphria sanctuary in the 1920s and 30s has shown that a substantial amount of Mycenaean pottery was found in the sanctuary area.[84] The number of Mycenaean finds known from Kalydon has thus been steadily growing ever since exploration of the site began, and we are now able to suggest that occupation at the site in this period was more than just intermittent.

4. Conclusion

Through the extensive surveys conducted in the archaeological area of Kalydon over four summer campaigns, the project produced a new and more detailed topographical map, which will be an invaluable tool for future exploration of the city and research into its development.

The important work of mapping Kalydon's necropoleis likewise adds new essential evidence for the character of burial customs, not just in Kalydon but also across the region of Aitolia.

The new survey of the city's monuments has allowed for some corrections of the topographical plan of the sanctuary on the Laphrion hill, which was surveyed during the excavations conducted there in the 1920s and 30s. A comparison between the old plan and the results of the new survey shows that the location of some of the monuments in the old plan was offset by up to two metres.

The discovery of a few Mycenaean ceramic sherds in the northwestern part of the Acropolis, and the few additional sherds found at various locations on the site, combined with the larger group of Mycenaean pottery excavated in the sanctuary in the 1920s and 30s, are clearly powerful indications of the Mycenaean habitation of Kalydon, and future excavations may confirm the strong Mycenaean mythological background of the ancient city.

OLYMPIA VIKATOU
Ephorate of Antiquities of Aetolia-Acarnania and Lekada
Ag. Athanasiou 4
GR-302 00 Mesolonghi
ovikatou@culture.gr

SØREN HANDBERG
Department of Archaeology, Conservation and History
University of Oslo, P.O. Box 1019, Blindern
N-0315 Oslo
soren.handberg@iakh.uio.no / shhandberg@hotmail.com

NEOPTOLEMOS MICHAELIDES
5 Mavromixali, P. Peteli
P.O. Box GR-15236 Athens
nemosmich@yahoo.com

80   Sotiriades 1908, 100.
81   For the survey, see Methenithis 2011. The Mycenaean sherds found in the northwestern corner of the Acropolis are discussed in Stavropoulou-Gatsi & Dietz 2011, 275.
82   In the trenches H1 and H6, Stavropoulou-Gatsi & Dietz 2011, 275.
83   Bollen 2011 (the kiln pottery), cat. no. 2, 201, fig. 140.
84   Barfoed 2019.

SIGNE BARFOED
University of Kent
School of European Culture and Languages, Department
of Classical & Archaeological Studies Canterbury,
UK-CT2 7NF Kent
sb711@kentforlife.net / barfoed.signe@gmail.com

183

Bibliography

Abbreviations

Agora 29 = S. I. Rotroff, *Hellenistic Pottery, Athenian and Imported Wheelmade Table Ware and Related Material* (The Athenian Agora 29), Princeton NJ, 1997.

Achille, C., A. Adami, S. Chiarini, S. Cremonesi, F. Fassi, L. Fregonese & L. Taffurelli 2015
'UAV-based Photogrammetry and Integrated Technologies for Architectural Applications-Methodological Strategies for the After-Quake Survey of Vertical Structures in Mantua (Italy)', *Sensors (Switzerland)* 15.7, 15520-39.

Aggeli, A. 2000
'Οδός Γαρουφαλιά (οικόπεδο Χ. Θεοδώρου)', *AD* 55, Chronika Β΄, 1β, 546-7.

Aggeli, A. 1999
'Οδός Γαρουφαλιά (οικόπεδο Χρ. Θεοδώρου)', *AD* 54, Chronika Β΄, 1β, 460-2.

Andreou, H. 1980
'Αρχαιολογική Συλλογή Λευκάδας', *AAA* 13, 74-84.

Ault, B. A. 1994
'Koprones and Oil Presses: domestic installations related to agricultural productivity and processing at classical Halieis', in *Structures Rurales et Société Antiques*, P.N. Doukellis & L.G. Mendoni (eds), Paris, 197-206.

Ault, B. A. 1999
'Koprones and Oil Presses at Halieis: interactions of town and country and the integration of domestic and regional economies', *Hesperia* 68, 549-73.

Barfoed, S. 2019
'Rediscovering Artemis Laphria at Kalydon. Preliminary results', *Proceedings of the Danish Institute at Athens* 9, page nos.

Boardman, J. 1958-9i
'Excavations at Pindakas in Chios', *BSA* 53-4, 295-309.

Bollen, E. 2011a
'Pottery, Lamps and Miniatures from the Central Acropolis', in *Kalydon in Aitolia I. Reports and Studies: Danish/Greek fieldwork 2001-2005,* (Monographs of the Danish Institute at Athens 12.2), S. Dietz & M. Stavropoulou-Gatsi (eds), Aarhus, 455-518.

Bollen, E. 2011b
'The Kiln Pottery', *Kalydon in Aitolia I. Reports and Studies: Danish/Greek fieldwork 2001-2005,* (Monographs of the Danish Institute at Athens 12.2), S. Dietz & M. Stavropoulou-Gatsi (eds), Aarhus, 199-200.

Bommeljé, S. 1988
'Aeolis in Aetolia: Thuc. 3.102.5 and the Origins of the Aetolian "ethnos"', *Historia: Zeitschrift für Alte Geschichte* 37, 297-316.

Bonias, Z. & J. Perreault 1997
'Άργιλος, ανασκαφή 1997', *Το Αρχαιολογικό Έργο στη Μακεδονία και στη Θράκη* 11, Α.-Β. Polyxeni (ed.), Thessaloniki, 539-47.

Broneer, O. 1954
The South Stoa and its Roman Successors (Corinth 1.4), Athens.

Bruneau, Ph. & Ph. Fraisse 1981
'Un pressoire à vin à Délos', *BCH* 105, 128-69.

Charatzopoulou, C. 2006
'L'héroon de Kalydon revisité', in *Rois, cites, necropolis. Institutions, rites et monuments en Macédoine. Actes des colloquies de Nanterre (Décembre 2002) et d'Athens (Janvier 2004).* (Meletimata 45), A.-M. Guimier-Sorbets, M. B. Hatzopoulos & Y. Morizot (eds), Athens, 63-87.

Closterman, W.E. 2007
'Family Ideology and Family History: the function of funerary markers in Classical Attic peribolos tombs', *AJA* 111.4, 633-52.

Colomina, I. & P. Molina 2014
'Unmanned Aerial Systems for Photogrammetry and Remote Sensing: a review', *ISPRS Journal of Photogrammetry and Remote Sensing* 92, 79-97.

Dawkins, R.M. 1909
'Archaeology in Greece (1908-1909)', *The Journal of Hellenic Studies* 29, 354-65.

Dietz, S. 2011a
'The Fortification Walls, Towers and Gates', in *Kalydon in Aitolia I. Reports and Studies: Danish/Greek fieldwork 2001-2005*, (Monographs of the Danish Institute at Athens 12.2), S. Dietz & M. Stavropoulou-Gatsi (eds), Aarhus, 65-76.

Dietz, S. 2011b
'The City – inside and outside the walls', in *Kalydon in Aitolia I. Reports and Studies: Danish/Greek fieldwork 2001-2005*, (Monographs of the Danish Institute at Athens 12.2), S. Dietz & M. Stavropoulou-Gatsi (eds), Aarhus, 77-81.

Dietz, S. 2011c
'Architectural Terracottas', in *Kalydon in Aitolia I–II. Reports and Studies: Danish/Greek fieldwork 20012005*, (Monographs of the Danish Institute at Athens 12.1-2), Aarhus, 375-97.

Dietz, S. 2011d
'General Stratigraphy', in *Aitolia I–II. Reports and Studies: Danish/Greek fieldwork 2001-2005*, (Monographs of the Danish Institute at Athens 12.1-2), Aarhus, 213-36.

Dietz, S. 2016
'Changing Space and Habitation Pattern', in *Chalkis Aitolias III. The Emporion. Fortification systems at Aghia Triada and the Late Classical and Hellenistic habitation in Area III. The Fortifications at Pangali,* (Monographs of the Danish Institute at Athens 7.3), S. Dietz & L. Kolonas (eds), Aarhus, 45-52.

Dietz, S. & M. Stavropoulou-Gatsi 2011a
'General Introduction', in *Kalydon in Aitolia I–II. Reports and Studies: Danish/Greek fieldwork 2001-2005,* (Monographs of the Danish Institute at Athens 12.1-2), Aarhus, 9-12.

Dietz, S. & M. Stavropoulou-Gatsi 2011
Kalydon in Aitolia I–II. Reports and Studies: Danish/Greek fieldwork 2001-2005 (Monographs of the Danish Institute at Athens 12.1-2), Aarhus.

Dyggve, E. 1951
'A Second Heroon at Calydon', *Studies Presented to David Morre Robinson on His Seventieth Birthday*, G. E. Mylonas (ed.), St. Louis, 360-3.

Dyggve, E. & F. Poulsen 1948
Das Laphrion, der Tempelbezirk von Kalydon, (Arkæologisk-kunsthistoriske Skrifter 1.2), Copenhagen.

Eiring, J. 2004
'Calydonian Strays: Four Vases and a Cemetery', *Mediterranean Archaeology* 17, (Festschrift in Honour of J. Richard Green), 35-42.

Foxhall, L. 2007
Olive Cultivation in Ancient Greece. Seeking the ancient economy, Oxford.

Freitag, K. 1999
Der Golf von Korinth. Historisch-topographische Untersuchungen von der Archaik bis in das 1. Jh.v.Chr., Munich.

Funke, P. 1987
'Zur Datierung befestigen Stadtanlangen in Aitolien Historisch-philologische Anmerkungen zu einem Wechselverhältnis zwischen Siedlungsstruktur und politischer Organisation', *Boreas* 10, 87-96.

Garland, R.S.J. 1982
'A First Catalogue of Attic Peribolos Tombs', *BSA* 77, 125-76.

Gatsi, M. 2010a
'Έργο: "Αυτοκινητόδρομος Δυτικής Ελλάδας – Ιόνια Οδός". Θέση Στουμπέικα, βόρεια της αρχαίας Καλυδώνας, Χ.Θ. 25+960, *AD* 65, Chronika Β´, 1β, 1058-9.

Gatsi, M. 2010b
'Έργο: "Αυτοκινητόδρομος Δυτικής Ελλάδας – Ιόνια Οδός". Ρηγαίικα Μεσολογγίου, Χ.Θ 27+200Χ.Θ. 27+530-550', *AD* 65, Chronika Β´, 1β, 1057-8.

Gatsi, M. 2010c
'Έργο: "Αναμόρφωση Αρδευτικού Δικτύου ΤΟ.Ε.Β. Παμφίας Τριχωνίδας". Τομέας Κ17, Σιταράλωνα', *AD* 65, Chronika Β´, 1β, 1052.

Gerolumou, V. 2013
'Αγροικία στα Σιταράλωνα Αιτωλοακαρνανίας: Αγροτική και Εργαστηριακή Παραγωγή', *Villae Rusticae. Family and Market-Oriented Farms in Greece under Roman Rule, Proceedings of an international congress held at Patrai, 23-24 April 2010, MELETHMATA 68A*, D. Rizakis & I. P. Touratsoglou (eds), Athens, 682-703.

Grainger, J. D. 1999
The League of the Aitolians, Leiden.

Isager, J. 2009
'Destruction or Depopulation of the Cities in Pausanias. Nikopolis, Aetolia, and Epirus', *Proceedings of the Danish Institute at Athens 6*, 201-15.

Isager, S. & J. E. Skydsgaard 1995
Ancient Greek Agriculture: an introduction, London.

Jameson, M. H. 1969
'Excavations at Porto Cheli and Vicinity, preliminary report I: Halieis 1962-8', *Hesperia* 37, 311-42.

Jameson, M. H. 2001
'Oil Presses of the Late Classical/Hellenistic period', in *Technai, Techniques et sociétés méditerranéennes. Hommage a' Marie-Claire Amouretti*, J.-P. Brun & P. Jockey (eds), Paris, 281-99.

Kessler, T. 2014/2015
'Die Osteotheken im Kerameikos', *AM* 129/130, 163-96.

Kolonas L. & G. Christakopoulou 2000
'Οδός Ευηνοχωρίου – Αγίου Γεωργίου (οικόπεδο Τριώτη)', *AD* 50 (1995), Chronika Β΄, 1β, 240.

Kullberg, J. B. 2014
'Flowers and Garlands of the Alsos. Verdant themes in the architectural sculpture of Labraunda', in *ΛΑΒΡΥΣ. Studies Presented to Pontus Hellstöm*, L. Karlsson, S. Carlsson & J. B. Kullberg (eds), Uppsala, 19-41.

Lawrence, A. W. 1996
Greek Architecture, New Haven.

Leake, W. M. 1835
Travels in Northern Greece (Vol. 1), London.

Mastrokostas, E. I. 1960
'Αιτωλία', *AD* 16, 195.

Mastrokostas, E. I. 1967
'Ἀρχαιότητες καὶ Μνημεῖα

Αἰτωλοακαρνανίας', *AD* 22, Chronika Β΄, 2β, 318-22.

Mattingly, D. J. 1990
'Paintings, Presses and Perfume Production at Pompeii', *Oxford Journal of Archaeology* 9, 71-90.

Methenithis, K. 2011
'1.3. The Field Survey – a preliminary report', in *Kalydon in Aitolia I. Reports and Studies: Danish/Greek fieldwork 2001-2005*, S. Dietz & M. Stavropoulou-Gatsi (eds), Aarhus, 59-64.

Morgan, C. 20092010
'Archaeology in Greece 2009-2010', *AR* 56, 1-201.

Moschos, I. 1999
'Πλευρώνα', *AD* 54, Chronika Β΄, 1β, 272.

Mouritzen, M., L. Kolonas & S. Dietz 2016
'The Late Classical Fortifications at Pangali', in *Chalkis Aitolias III. The Emporion. Fortification systems at Aghia Triada and the Late Classical and Hellenistic habitation in Area III. The Fortifications at Pangali*, (Monographs of the Danish Institute at Athens 7.3), S. Dietz & L. Kolonas (eds), Aarhus, 237-48.

Müth, S. 2014
'The Historical Context of the City Wall of Messene: preconditions, written sources, success balance, and social impacts', *Proceedings of the Danish Institute at Athens* 7, 105-22.

Nalimova, N. A. 2017
'The Origin and Meaning of Floral imagery in the Monumental Art of Macedonia (4th–3rd centuries BC)', in *Македония – Рим – Византия:

искусство Северной Греции от античности до средних веков, материалы научной конференции: научное издание, электронное издание сетевого распространения*, N. A. Nalimovoj, T. P. Kižbali & A.V. Zacharovoj (eds), Moscow, 13-35.

Nex, F. & F. Remondino 2014
'UAV: platforms, regulations, data acquisition and processing', in *3D Recording and Modelling in Archaeology and Cultural Heritage: Theory and Best Practices*, F. Remondino & S. Campana (eds), Oxford, 73-86.

Orlandos, A. K. 1955-60
Τα υλικά δομής των αρχαίων Ελλήνων και οι τρόποι εφαρμογής αυτών κατά τους συγγραφείς, τας επιγραφάς και τα μνημεία, Αθήναι, 258-9.

Papapostolou, I. A. 1972
'Ἀρχαιότητες καὶ Μνημεῖα Αἰτωλίας-Ἀκαρνανίας. Καλυδών', *AD* 27, Chronika Β΄, 2β, 434-6.

Poulsen, F. & K. A. Rhomaios 1927
Erster vorläufiger Bericht über die dänisch-griechischen Ausgrabungen von Kalydon, Copenhagen.

Poulsen, F., E. Dyggve & K. A. Rhomaios 1934
Das Heroon von Kalydon, Copenhagen.

Smekalova, T. & B. Bevan 2016
'A Magnetic Exploration of Chalkis Aitolias', in *Chalkis Aitolias III. The Emporion. Fortification systems at Aghia Triada and the Late Classical and Hellenistic habitation in Area III. The Fortifications at Pangali*, (Monographs of the Danish Institute at Athens 7.3), S. Dietz & L. Kolonas (eds), Aarhus, 33-44.

Sotiriades. G. 1908
'Anaskafi en Aitolia kai Akarnania', *PAE* 1908, 95-100.

Stamatis, G. 2018
'Τα νεκροταφεία της αρχαίας Πλευρώνας. Πρώτη παρουσίαση', *Το Αρχαιολογικό Έργο στην Αιτωλοακαρνανία και τη Λευκάδα, Πρακτικά 2ου Αρχαιολογικού και Ιστορικού Συνεδρίου, Μεσολόγγι 6-8 Δεκεμβρίου 2013*, O. Vikatou (ed.), Mesolonghi, 127-40.

Stamatopoulou, M. & S. Katakouta 2013
'Ταφικοί περίβολοι κλασικής περιόδου στα Φάρσαλα', in *Griechische Grabbezirke klassischer Zeit. Normen und Regionalismen. Akten des Internationalen Kolloquiums am Deutschen Archäologischen Institut, Abteilung Athen*, K. Sporn (ed.), Munich, 83-94.

Stavropoulou-Gatsi, M. 2013
'Κρυονέρι, θέση Σπηλιές', *AD 60* (2005), Chronika Β΄, 1β, 473-4.

Stavropoulou-Gatsi, M. 2010
'Από την Καλυδώνα στην Αλίκυρνα: Η πορεία του αρχαίου δρόμου και άγνωστο νεκροταφείο κάτω από τη σημερινή Ιόνια Οδό', *Τα Αιτωλικά 15*, 79-88.

Stavropoulou-Gatsi, M. 2011
'Thirty Protogeometric Vases from Kalydon in Aitolia', in *Kalydon in Aitolia I. Reports and Studies: Danish/Greek fieldwork 2001-2005*, (Monographs of the Danish Institute at Athens 12.2), S. Dietz & M. Stavropoulou-Gatsi (eds), Aarhus, 279-99.

Stavropoulou-Gatsi, M. & G. Alexopoulou 2013
'Αγροικίες της Πάτρας και της χώρας της', *Villa Rusticae. Family and Market-Oriented Farms in Greece under Roman Rule. Proceedings of an International Congress held at Patrai, 23-24 April 2010* (Meletimata 68), 88-153.

Stavropoulou-Gatsi, M. & S. Dietz 2011
'Pre-Archaic Finds from Inside and Outside the City Wall', in *Kalydon in Aitolia I. Reports and Studies: Danish/Greek fieldwork 2001-2005*, (Monographs of the Danish Institute at Athens 12.2), S. Dietz & M. Stavropoulou-Gatsi (eds), Aarhus, 275-7.

Themelis, P. 1980
'Ausgrabungen in Kallipolis (Ost-Aitolien) 1977-1978', *AAA 13*, 245-79.

Themelis, P. G. & I. P. Touratsoglou 1997
Οι τάφοι του Δερβενίου, Athens.

Van Limbergen, D. 2011
'Vinum picenum and oliva picena. Wine and oil presses in Central Adriatic Italy between the Late Republic and the Early Empire. Evidence and Problems', *BABesch 86*, 71-94.

Vikatou, O. 2011
'Το Έργο της ΛΣΤ' Εφορείας Προϊστορικών και Κλασικών Αρχαιοτήτων κατά το έτος 2011', *Τα Αιτωλικά 17*, 50-2.

Vikatou, O. 2012
'Το Έργο της ΛΣΤ' Εφορείας Προϊστορικών και Κλασικών Αρχαιοτήτων κατά το έτος 2012', *Τα Αιτωλικά 20*, 157-8.

Vikatou, O. 2017
'Νεκροταφείο στη θέση "Ρηγαίικα" Μεσολογγίου', in *Διαχρονικό ταξίδι στην Ιόνια Οδό. Ο θησαυρός των ευρημάτων της*, εκδ. Κέντρο Λόγου & Τέχνης "Διέξοδος" – Ιστορικό Μουσείο, O. Vikatou, F. Saranti & G. Stamatis (eds), Mesolonghi, 39-47.

Vikatou, O. forthcoming
'Από τη ζωή στον θάνατο. Ανιχνεύοντας έθιμα ταφής και πρακτικές στην Αιτωλοακαρνανία με αφορμή την εκτέλεση των μεγάλων δημοσίων έργων οδοποίίας', in *Τα αποτελέσματα των σωστικών αρχαιολογικών ερευνών της Αρχαιολογικής Υπηρεσίας (Προϊστορικές και Κλασικές Αρχαιότητες). Τόμ. I. Τα νεκροταφεία: Χωροταξική οργάνωση – Ταφικά έθιμα – Τελετουργίες*, Ταμείο Αρχαιολογικών Πόρων και Απαλλοτριώσεων, El. Kountouri & A. Gadolou (eds). City of publication and page nos.

Vikatou, O. & S. Handberg 2017
'The Lower Acropolis of Kalydon in Aitolia. Preliminary report on the excavations carried out in 2013-15', *Proceedings of the Danish Institute at Athens 7*, 191-206.

Vikatou, O. & S. Handberg 2018
'Excavations on the Lower Acropolis Plateau in Kalydon', in *Το Αρχαιολογικό Έργο στην Αιτωλοακαρνανία και τη Λευκάδα, Πρακτικά 2ου Αρχαιολογικού και Ιστορικού Συνεδρίου, Μεσολόγγι 6-8 Δεκεμβρίου 2013*, O. Vikatou (ed.), Mesolonghi, 309-23.

Vikatou, O. & N. Michaelides forthcoming
'Αποτύπωση, Τεκμηρίωση και Αναπαράσταση Μνημείων κατά μήκος του άξονα της Ιόνιας Οδού, με χρήση σύγχρονων τεχνολογιών (3d laser scanner, animation, κα.) και δημιουργία ψηφιακού αρχείου Μνημείων',

187

Πρακτικά επιστημονικού συνεδρίου: "Ἀρχαιολογικές Ἔρευνες και Μεγάλα Δημόσια Ἔργα", Athens.

Vlachoyanni, E. 2013
Ἀγροικία ρωμαϊκών χρόνων στην αρχαία Ακραιφία (Ακραίφνιο Βοιωτίας),' *Villa Rusticae. Family and Market-Oriented Farms in Greece under Roman Rule. Proceedings of an International Congress held at Patrai, 23-24 April 2010* (Meletimata 68), 486-509.

White, K. D. 1975
Farm Equipment of the Roman World, Cambridge.

Winter, F. E. 1971
Greek Fortifications, Toronto & Buffalo.

Zapheiropoulou, F. 1976
'Πλευρώνα', *AD* 31, Chronika B´, 1β, 169.

188

Rediscovering Artemis Laphria at Kalydon:

*Preliminary Results**

SIGNE BARFOED

Abstract

This report presents the preliminary results of the research project "Rediscovering Artemis. A comprehensive re-examination of the Artemis Laphria Sanctuary in Kalydon, Aitolia". The project concerns the study and publication of the finds, such as pottery and votives, from the Artemis Laphria sanctuary excavations, which were carried out in the 1920s and 30s. "Rediscovering Artemis" is hosted by the Danish Institute at Athens; its principal support comes from the Carlsberg Foundation, and it has also been awarded a number of Danish and Norwegian grants. The project is a collaboration with the National Archaeological Museum at Athens (NAM).

Research History

In 1926 a Danish–Greek collaboration began exploring the Artemis Laphria sanctuary in Kalydon, the extra-mural sanctuary of the city, as well as a Hellenistic palaestra, the so-called "Heroon".[1] The team consisted of the then director of the Ny Carlsberg Glyptotek in Copenhagen, Frederik Poulsen, the renowned Greek archaeologist Konstantinos Rhomaios and the famous Danish architect Ejnar Dyggve. Explorations in Kalydon have continued intermittently up to the present day. Søren Dietz excavated at the central acropolis, a Hellenistic peristyle house in the Lower Town, and the Hellenistic theatre from 2001-06;[2] Rune Frederiksen completed the excavation of the Hellenistic theatre from 2011-14;[3] and in 2013 Søren Handberg initiated excavations at the Lower Acropolis of Kalydon and found a Hellenistic house,[4] carried out new excavations at the fortification wall in order to estab-

*   I am very grateful to the Hellenic Ministry of Culture and Sports for the permit to study and publish the Artemis Laphria assemblage, and the National Archaeological Museum, especially Dr Giorgos Kavvadias, who has made all my campaigns enjoyable and smoothly running. A warm thank you also goes to the Friends of the National Archaeological Museum, the many guards who accompanied me in the apothiki, and to the conservators in the NAM conservation laboratory for their extraordinary work on cleaning and restoring a selection of the pottery assemblage. A heartfelt thank you also goes out to the Danish Institute at Athens and their help with acquiring the permit, Søren Dietz and Popi Sarri, and to Katja E. Vinther, Joos Melander, Trine B. Pedersen and Søren Handberg for their company and help in the storerooms where they created technical drawings of some of the pottery. Last but not least, I am extremely grateful to the Carlsberg Foundation, the Elisabeth Munksgaard Foundation, the Svend G. Fiedler and Wife Foundation, and the Travel Stipend of the Norwegian Institute at Athens for their generous financial support.

1   Poulsen, Dyggve & Rhomaios 1934. Excavations were carried out in the years 1926, 1928, 1932 and 1935.

2   Dietz & Stavropoulou-Gatsi 2011.

3   Vikatou, Frederiksen & Handberg 2014.

4   http://www.carlsbergfondet.dk/da/Forskningsaktiviteter/Forskningsprojekter/Andre%20forskningsprojekter/Soeren%20Hanberg_THE%20
KALYDON%20ARCHAEOLOGICAL%20PROJECT

lish its date and, additionally, instigated the demanding undertaking of creating a precise topographical plan of Ancient Kalydon.[5]

The excavations of the 1920s and 30s were later published by Poulsen, Rhomaios and Dyggve.[6] The topography and architectural elements of the Artemis Laphria sanctuary were extensively treated in this 1948 publication, but it did not include the studies of the small finds such as pottery, protomes, figurines and coins.[7] Poulsen intended to publish this material later, but his work was interrupted by WWII and he died in 1950 before he could finish the task; the present author is working on completing it.

Evidence of a Mycenaean Settlement?

The unpublished assemblage from the excavations of the Artemis Laphria sanctuary consists of more than 30 large wooden trays containing pottery and terracotta figurines of humans, fruit and animals, as well as terracotta protomes. After five study seasons at the National Archaeological Museum in Athens spread out over more than a year, it seemed that the assemblage spanned from the Geometric to the Roman period, with most datable objects between the Archaic and Classical periods. However, one box of finds led to a revision of this impression. This specific box contained about 108 individual vessels dating to the Bronze Age period.

As shown in Table 1, most shapes are different cup types, for instance, kylikes (Fig. 1). The second most prominent shape group comprises different types of jugs, such as stirrup jars, and other jug types (Fig. 2) as well as different types of bowls where some are preserved in full profile (Fig. 3). Kraters of different sizes are also found (Fig. 4). The pottery is currently under close study for publication, but it seems that the assemblage consists of shapes belonging to a settlement, or perhaps related to feasting activities. Most of the vessels can be dated to the LH III period (c. 1400-1050 BCE), and further studies will reveal additional details of the shapes as well as a more

Kylix	35
Other cup type	14
Jug/Jar	21
Bowl	21
Krater	5
Dipper	4
Lamp	2
Basin	1
Alabastron	1
Unknown	4
Total	**108**

Table 1. *Distribution of Mycenaean pottery shapes.*

precise chronology of the Mycenaean pottery from the Artemis Laphria assemblage.

There is no explicit mention of Mycenaean pottery in the publications or the unpublished excavation diaries, but Poulsen refers to finds of "greyish pottery", which he compared to Prehistoric finds from the Apollo sanctuary at Thermon, further north – it is plausible that he is talking about the pottery in this box. A meticulous reading of the excavation diaries makes it clear that the Mycenaean pottery was only found in the area of the Structures G and H in the southeastern part of the Artemis Laphria sanctuary, which according to the published architectural studies are the earliest structures in the sanctuary (Fig. 5).[8] It is possible that these structures are of Mycenaean date, and are perhaps the remains of a so-called Megaron structure. These remains could be the only Bronze Age structures so far identified in Kalydon. The complete lack of prehistoric figurines and other cult equipment on the entire sanctuary plateau could suggest that it was not a cultic

---

5   Vikatou & Handberg forthcoming; Vikatou & Handberg 2017. In 2017 the Lower Acropolis project moved into study season and publication is planned for the near future. See also Vikatou, Handberg, Michaelides & Barfoed, this volume.

6   Poulsen & Rhomaios 1927; Dyggve & Rhomaios 1934; Dyggve & Poulsen 1948; Rhomaios 1951.

7   Dyggve & Poulsen 1948.

8   Dyggve & Poulsen 1948, 26-81.

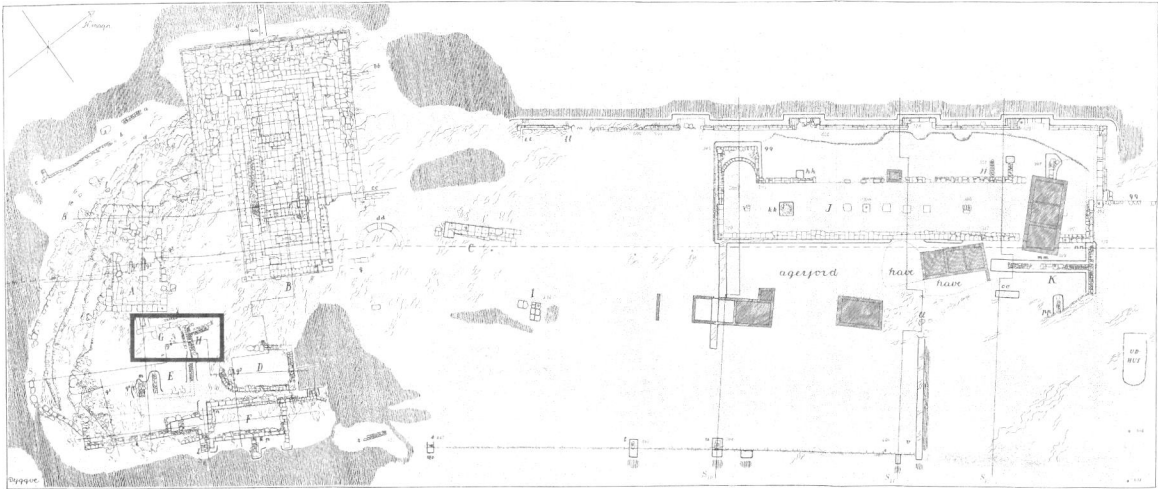

Fig. 5. *Plan of the Artemis Laphria sanctuary drawn by E. Dyggve. Structures G, g4 and H are inside the box (after Dyggve & Poulsen 1948, pl. 1; reproduced courtesy of the Royal Danish Academy of Sciences and Letters).*

area in this period, but instead the location of a Bronze Age settlement.

The Extramural Sanctuary of Artemis Laphria (Geometric–Hellenistic period)

The sanctuary of Artemis Laphria is believed to have existed since the Geometric period, which is also confirmed by the descriptions of the excavation finds in Poulsen's notebooks. He mentions that they found Geometric pottery near the apsidal building, Building D, on the east side of the plateau (in front of the later Artemis temple), and the structure named g4 south of structure H (Fig. 5).

The date of the apsidal building has been debated, but based on the pottery now discovered, it seems clear that it belongs to the Late Geometric period. The Late Geometric pottery is very important for our understanding of the development of the sanctuary, because it clearly suggests that the apsidal building predates the earliest phase of temple construction in the sanctuary.

Late Geometric pieces have been identified among the pottery in the assemblage stored in the National Archaeological Museum at Athens. They are a small group of sherds of so-called Thapsos Ware dating to the second half of the 8th century BCE, believed to have been produced in the Ancient region of Achaea, across the Corinthian gulf from Kalydon (Fig. 6).[9] Thus, in this early period pottery was already being imported to Kalydon. Metal figurines from the Artemis Laphria sanctuary are on display in the Bronze Collection of the National Archaeological Museum in Athens and also attest to activity in the Geometric period,[10] when Laphria plateau may have been used as a meeting place for chieftains from Aitolia and the region Achaea across the gulf, and other neighbouring regions.

Evidence from both the Artemis Laphria assemblage and the recent excavations at the Lower Acropolis proves that this significant import pattern continued throughout the 7th, 6th and 5th centuries BCE. In the Artemis Laphria assemblage the period is represented by, for example, conical oinochoai and figure-decorated aryballoi from Corinth (Fig. 7). Corinthian pottery was imitated in Kalydon, both Corinthian terracotta figurines of the well-known "standing kore" type and miniature pottery in various shapes (Fig. 8).[11] Preliminary studies of the different clay types represented in the Artemis Laphria assemblage suggest that the moulds of some terracottas may have come from Corinth, perhaps via Aitolian Chalkis

---

9   Gadolou 2011.

10   In the Bronze Collection of the National Archaeological Museum, the display called "Aitolian Sanctuaries".

11   For more on the miniatures and cult in Kalydon, see Barfoed 2017.

191

approximately 15 km from Kalydon, which according to Thucydides was a Corinthian town.[12]

Most of the Attic pottery from the Artemis Laphria assemblage can be dated to the Classical period. Oil vessels such as lekythoi are especially popular – black-figure (Fig. 9), red-figure, white ground and black-glazed lekythoi are all found. There were also fragments of fine pieces of an Attic red-figure column krater with an inscription to Artemis, [ΑΡΤΕ]ΜΙΔΟΣΗΙΑΡΟΣ (Fig. 10), one of the few pieces of pottery mentioned in the first publication by Poulsen and Rhomaios.[13] Was this specific krater an exclusive piece used for ritual activities, perhaps ritual dining, in the sanctuary during the early Classical period?

The relatively large amount of Attic pottery found in the assemblage is perhaps not surprising, considering the city of Naupaktos' close relations with Athens in the 5th century BCE.[14] Naupaktos is located only 35 km from Kalydon; it would take about a day to walk between them. As Søren Dietz also suggested, it is possible that the sanctuary of Artemis Laphria was an important regional sanctuary,[15] and therefore fine Attic pottery was used and dedicated there. Despite the uncertainties concerning the sampling and the lack of stratified contexts in the sanctuary, it is interesting to note that the assemblage contains a large amount of Attic figure-decorated pottery. This suggests a conspicuous consumption of Attic pottery, especially since contemporary figure-decorated pottery is sparse elsewhere in the city.[16]

Concluding Remarks

In this report some preliminary results and tentative interpretations of the unpublished Artemis Laphria assemblage from the 1920s and 30s excavations in Kalydon in Aitolia were presented. Working with excavation material from a time when excavations were not carried out stratigraphically has proved to be problematic for determining both the precise location and the dating of the finds. Furthermore, in the processed boxes containing pottery, there are few body sherds. One may assume that the majority of pottery body sherds were sorted from the diagnostic sherds during the excavations and left behind in piles on or near the site.

The discovery of Mycenaean pottery in the Artemis Laphria assemblage means that Kalydon now can be counted among the few Mycenaean settlement sites in the region of Aitolia.[17] From as early as the 8th century BCE Kalydon had established networks in the region of Achaea, and slightly later in the city of Corinth. This "new" material establishes that the Artemis Laphria sanctuary in Kalydon was of great importance, possibly in the entire region, from an early period onwards, throughout the Archaic to the Hellenistic period and eventually declining in the Roman period.

SIGNE BARFOED
Honorary Research Fellow
University of Kent
School of European Culture and Languages, Department of Classical & Archaeological Studies Canterbury,
UK-CT2 7NF Kent
sb711@kentforlife.net / barfoed.signe@gmail.com

12 This is a pattern also seen in the terracotta figurines from Dietz' excavations; Barfoed 2017, 140; Mayerhofer Hemmi & Dietz 2011, 531; Thuc. 1.108; Mackil 2016, 52.

13 The krater rim with the graffito was mentioned by Poulsen & Rhomaios 1927, 9 fig. 3.

14 Badian 1990; Merker 1989.

15 Dietz 2011, 133.

16 Just seven Attic fragments are mentioned in the publications of Dietz' work in Kalydon; see nos. 10, 137, 191, 226, 255, 329, 351 in Bollen 2011, 313-48.

17 Nine possible Mycenaean sites in Aitolia (including Kalydon) were documented by a Dutch survey carried out in the 1980s (the sites are Thermon, Agios Ilias (south of Stamna), Kryonerion (Kryoneri), Pleuron, Lithovounion (Ano Votinou), Kato Vasiliki, Marathias, Tolofon; see Bommeljé & Doorn 1987.

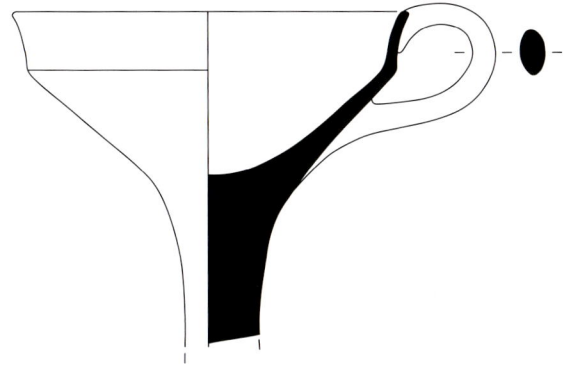

Fig. 1. *Kylix, Mycenaean (Temp. inv. no. 1928/7.1, drawing and inking: K. E. Vinther; photo: I. Dalla).*

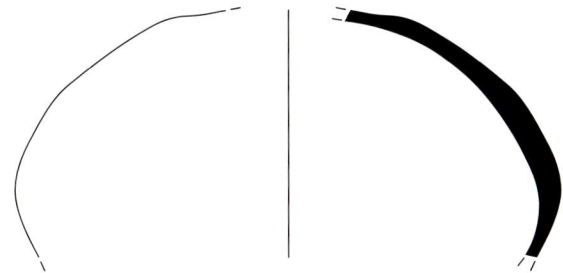

Fig. 2. *Stirrup jar, Mycenaean (Temp. inv. no. 1928/7.107, inking: K. E. Vinther; drawing and photo: S. Barfoed).*

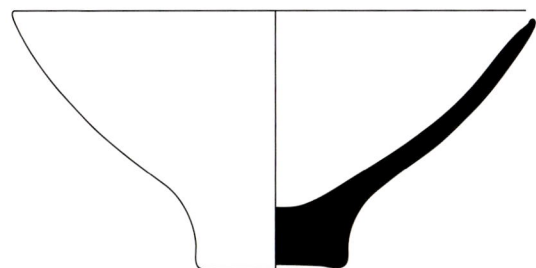

Fig. 3. *Bowl, Mycenaean (Temp. inv. no. 1928/7.39, drawing: J. Melander; inking: K. E. Vinther; photo: I. Dalla).*

193

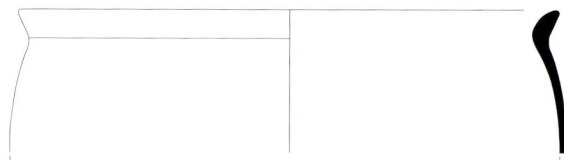

Fig. 4. *Krater, Mycenaean (Temp. inv. no. 1928/7.2, drawing: S. Handberg; inking: K. E. Vinther; photo: S. Barfoed).*

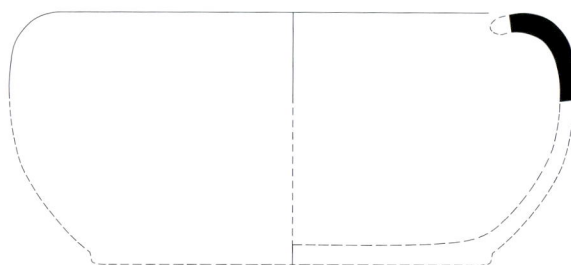

Fig. 6. *Pyxis, Thapsos ware (temp. inv. no. 1928/2.92, drawing: S. Handberg; photo: S. Barfoed; inking: K. E. Vinther).*

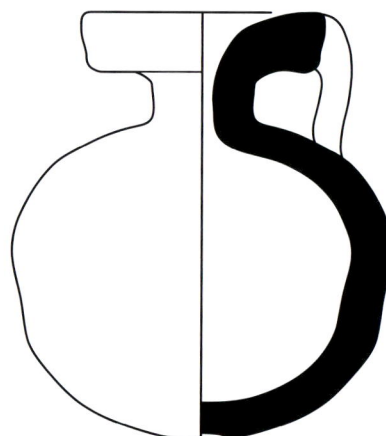

Fig. 7. *Corinthian aryballos (Temp. inv. no. 1928/8.6, drawing: S. Barfoed; inking: K. E. Vinther; photo: I. Dalla).*

Fig. 8. *Local miniature kotyle (Temp. inv. no. 1928/4.43, drawing and photo: S. Barfoed; inking: K. E. Vinther).*

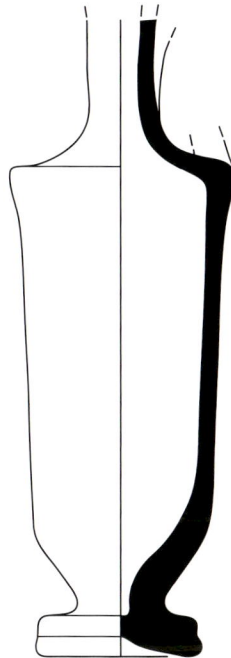

Fig. 9. *Attic black-figure lekythos (Temp. inv. no. 1928/4.150, drawing: T. B. Pedersen; inking: K. E. Vinther; photo: S. Barfoed).*

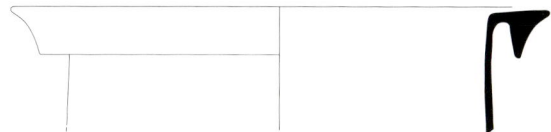

Fig. 10. *Attic column-krater rim (Temp. inv. no. 1928/8.3, drawing and photo: S. Barfoed; inking: K. E. Vinther).*

195

Bibliography

Badian, E. 1990
'Athens, the Locrians and Naupactus', *The Classical Quarterly* 40, 364-69.

Barfoed, S. 2017
'The Cults of Kalydon. Reassessing the Miniaturised Votive Objects', *Proceedings of the Danish Institute at Athens* 7, 131-48.

Bollen, E. 2011
'The Pottery of Kalydon', in S. Dietz & M. Stavropoulou-Gatsi (eds), Aarhus, 313-48.

Bommeljé, S. & P. K. Doorn 1987
Aetolia and the Aetolians: Towards the Interdisciplinary Study of a Greek Region, Utrecht.

Dietz, S. 2011
'The Cult-Room in its Context', in S. Dietz & M. Stavropoulou-Gatsi (eds), Aarhus, 133-6.

Dietz, S. & M. Stavropoulou-Gatsi (eds) 2011
Kalydon in Aitolia I–II. Reports and Studies: Danish/Greek fieldwork 2001-2005, (Monographs of the Danish Institute at Athens 12), Aarhus.

Dyggve, E. & F. Poulsen 1948
Das Laphrion, der Tempelbezirk von Kalydon, Copenhagen.

Gadolou, A. 2011
Thapsos-Class Ware Reconsidered: The case of Achaea in the Northern Peloponnese. Pottery workshop or pottery style?, Oxford.

Mackil, E. M. 2016
Creating a Common Polity: Religion, Economy, and Politics in the Making of the Greek Koinon, Berkeley.

Mayerhofer Hemmi, S. & S. Dietz 2011
'Terracotta Figurines,' in S. Dietz & M. Stavropoulou-Gatsi (eds), Aarhus, 519-48.

Merker, I. 1989
'The Achaians in Naupaktos and Kalydon in the Fourth Century', *Hesperia. The Journal of the American School of Classical Studies at Athens* 58, 303-11.

Poulsen, F. & K. A. Rhomaios 1927.
Erster vorläufiger Bericht über die dänisch-griechischen Ausgrabungen von Kalydon, Copenhagen.

Poulsen, F., E. Dyggve & K. A. Rhomaios 1934
Das Heroon von Kalydon, Copenhagen.

Rhomaios, K. A. 1951
Keramoi tes Kalydonos. Symbole eis akribesteran theoresun tes hellenikes technes, Athens.

Vikatou, O. & S. Handberg forthcoming
'Excavations on the Lower Acropolis Plateau in Kalydon', *20 Διεθνές Αρχαιολογικό και Ιστορικό Συνέδριο Αιτωλοακαρνανίας*, Mesolongi.

Vikatou, O. & S. Handberg 2017
'The Lower Acropolis of Kalydon in Aitolia. Preliminary report on the excavations carried out in 201315', *Proceedings of the Danish Institute at Athens* 8, 191-208.

Vikatou, O., R. Frederiksen & S. Handberg 2014
'The Danish–Greek Excavations at Kalydon, Aitolia. The Theatre: preliminary report from the 2011 and 2012 campaigns', *Proceedings of the Danish Institute at Athens* 7, 221-34.

Preliminary Report on the Excavation at the Papachristodoulou-Karika Plot in Rhodes

ANASTASIA DRELIOSSI-HERAKLEIDOU
& LISA BETINA

Abstract

This report gives a first overview of the different building phases recorded at the Papachristodoulou-Karika plot in the central necropolis of Rhodes Town. Between the 4th century BC and the 1st century AD, the function and use of the site changed considerably: initially serving as a burial ground, later on it became a building complex, with a courtyard and triclinia; after the building was abandoned, refuse was dumped on its ruins. We will present preliminary results of the study of the architectural remains and finds, as well as discussing the scientific objectives of the ongoing interdisciplinary research programme.

The excavation

Important remains of various chronological phases, as well as uses, spanning the 4th century BC to the 1st century AD[1] were revealed in the rescue excavation conducted by the 22nd Ephorate of Prehistoric and Classical Antiquities in two adjacent plots, properties of Evangelos Papachristodoulou and Christos Karikas (at the corner of K. Tsaldari and Ithakis streets), in the central sector of the Hellenistic necropolis of Rhodes (Fig. 1), between 1977 and 1981.[2]

The initial use of the space was as a burial ground; burials of the late 4th/early 3rd century BC were uncovered. These constitute the eastward continuation of the extensive cemetery of rectangular pit and cist graves, densely arranged in clusters, that has been brought to light over many years of investigation by the Ephorate. Towards the end of the Hellenistic period, the use of space changed

radically when a large building complex was erected at this site (Fig. 2, left). Organised around an oblong peristyle court are rooms, some of which are interpreted as assembly and symposium halls, that is, *andrones*. This is indicated by the built Π-shaped couches (triclinia), coated on the outside with fine stucco. The particular architectural form of the building, unique to date within the large Rhodian necropolis, is appropriate to funerary triclinia or *andrones* mainly of the Roman period, known from other places such as Alexandria and Anemurium in Tracheia Cilicia.[3]

There is mention of a funerary *andron* in the Rhodian decree of the association (*koinon*) of Sabaziastai, one of the numerous associations active in cosmopolitan Rhodes, particularly during the 2nd/1st century BC, which played

---

1   It is interesting to note the occasional presence of ceramics dating to the 2nd–3rd centuries AD, as well as post-antique vessels.
2   Δρελιώση-Ηρακλείδου 2018; Παπαχριστοδούλου 1979.
3   Adriani 1966, 174-5, pl. 97, fig. 328-9 and pl. 98, fig. 330-1 (Alexandria); Rosenbaum 1971, 93, 103 (Anemurium); Πατσιαδά 2013, 170-1, 177, 210.

Fig. 1. *Location of the excavations studied in the course of* The Rhodes Centennial Project; *(1) indicating the Papachristodoulou-Karika plot (map adapted from StepMap by L. Betina).*

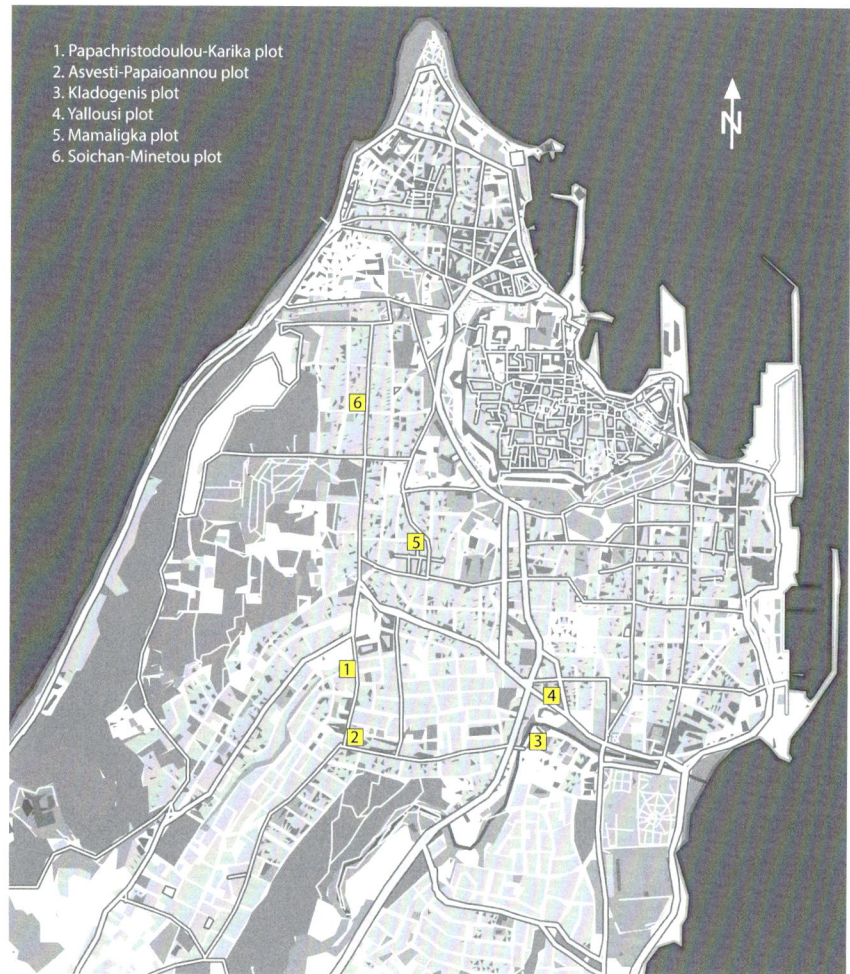

an important role in the economic and social life of the city.[4] According to the inscription, in the *andron* of the Sabaziastai the members of the association would gather to celebrate the *nekysia* (festival for the dead), where, after the symposium, they would honour a certain Ariston from Syracuse for the virtue and the solicitude he showed regarding the graves of the *koinon*. These references led various researchers to the hypothesis of a possible association of the inscription with the building on the Papachristodoulou-Karika plot.[5] This hypothesis was based on the fact that the decree of the Sabaziastai was found not far away, in the excavation of another tomb complex, which, however, according to epigraphic testimonies found in its investigation, belonged to families of Rhodian citizens.

In a later phase, when the building had ceased to be used, perhaps because of some natural disaster, huge infills of greyish-black earth (*mavra chomata*) with traces of burning and copious mortuary and domestic refuse were thrown into the area of the court and the south part of the complex. Excavation of these spaces showed that the deposits, which at some points were as deep as 3.65 metres, covered fissures in the friable rocky subsoil, a rock-cut descent into an underground space and possibly remnants of a cavernous construction. The debris fill (Fig. 2, right) included finds from emptying and arranging earlier graves and tomb complexes (abundant potsherds from grave goods and intact urns, cinerary vases, bones and minor objects), as well as finds originating from the city

---

4   Kontorini 1983, 71-9 no. 8, pl. X.

5   Different interpretations: Kontorini 1983, 73; Gabrielsen 1997, 123-4, footnote 52; Πατσιαδά 2013, 211 n. 587 and 240 n. 715.

Fig. 2. *Left: View of the excavation at the Papachristodoulou-Karika plot from the east . Right: Cinerary urn, lamp and unguentaria in the course of excavating the* mavra chomata *(photo credit: A. Dreliossi-Herakleidou, Ephorate of Antiquities of the Dodecanese).*

(a large quantity of sherds from cooking vessels, braziers, fragments of amphorae with a large number of stamped handles, imported and local pottery [see further below], roof-tiles, clay loom-weights, figurines, pigments, fragments of architectural members, plaster, minor objects of glass, metal and bone, coins, stone vessels, workshop wasters and so on).

Outstanding among the host of finds retrieved from the *mavra chomata*, and dating mainly from the 4th century BC to the 1st century AD, is a significant number of inscribed ostraca (potsherds mainly from amphorae) of the Late Hellenistic period. These are precious specimens of written communication between estate owners and their authorised employees, probably including slaves. These inscribed ostraca are part of one or more archives whose content attests lively commercial activity in connection with the circulation of agricultural produce (figs, cucumbers, gourds and so on), while at the same time pointing to an organised rural economy.

An unexpected find among the refuse of the *mavra chomata* was a lovely erotic epigram of the late 3rd to early 2nd century BC. Written in black ink on the surface of a potsherd, it lyrically recounts the bittersweet cares of love, which Glykere from Samos desired to cast off, by making a wish and dedicating to the deity – whose identity eludes us – a painting that depicted night-long revels.[6]

Study of the excavation and the finds

In April 2016 the systematic conservation and study of the finds from the Papachristodoulou-Karika plot commenced, in the framework of *The Rhodes Centennial Project*, a joint programme of the Ephorate of Antiquities of the Dodecanese and the University of Copenhagen.[7] An interdisciplinary team of scientists (archaeologists, historians, philologists, architects, conservators) is studying the early cemetery, the building complex and the funerary triclinia, the refuse deposit, the pottery, the stone

---

6   Δρελιώση-Ηρακλείδου – Λίτινας 2009-11.
7   Project director: V. Gabrielsen. Funding: Carlsberg Foundation.

inscriptions, the series of inscribed ostraca and the rest of the finds.

In 2017, in the course of conserving finds yielded by the *mavra chomata* fill, a rare case of textual testimony was observed on the surface of a small unguentarium (E 7769). The inscription, written in black ink, begins from the lower part of the neck and is developed in at least 10 lines down to the base of the vase. Preliminary study of the text shows that the content of the vase, an unguent/ medicinal mixture, was intended for a woman.[8]

Arrangements have been made for an analogous photographing, in the Centro di Papirologia Achille Vogliano, of the series of inscribed ostraca, which are not well preserved; the ink has faded away in places, meaning the reading and study of the inscriptions is difficult.

Interpretative approaches – aims of the study

Apart from the morphological and typological study of the architectural remains and finds, study of the excavation in the Papachristodoulou-Karika plot will concentrate on investigating the following issues:

- The duration of use of the cemetery that pre-existed the building complex, involving study of the grave goods and the rest of the excavation data. The chronological and typological affinity of the graves with those found in neighbouring excavations will also be examined.
- The exact dating of the change of function of the space and the way in which this was affected by the construction of the building complex. Also the circumstances of the disturbance, ascertained in the excavation, of the preceding cemetery.
- The architectural form and function of the building and of its individual spaces.
- The significance of the two small inscribed altars of Lartian stone, which appear to have been found *in situ* between two rectangular couches in a room of the building complex.

- The possible correlation of the building with the *koinon* of Sabaziastai, including the probable use of the building by the said association and the possibility of its availability for use by other associations for celebrating postmortem rituals.
- The importance of the building complex's function for the social life of the city of Rhodes.
- The duration of operation of the building complex, when it ceased to be used and the causes of this.
- The provenance of the archive (or archives) of inscribed ostraca.
- Interpreting the *mavra chomata* fill in its entirety: examining the provenance of the refuse as well as its collection and transportation to the site; determining when the refuse was deposited, after the assemblage of finds from it has been studied.

Analysis of the pottery finds from the *mavra chomata* accumulation

As already mentioned, the *mavra chomata* accumulation is a mixed, non-stratified deposit of refuse, which is also reflected in the character of the ceramics discovered in the layer. Due to the formation process of the deposit, certain limitations in the interpretation of the ceramic material do apply.

Firstly, the establishment of a typo-chronology of Rhodian ceramics is restricted, as vessels dating from the 4th century BC to the early 1st century AD are randomly combined. When middens or waste deposits are built up gradually over longer periods of time, one might expect to encounter older artefacts in the lower levels and more recent finds in the upper layers. However, at the Papachristodoulou-Karika plot no chronological order in the arrangement of the pottery finds has been observed and, therefore, the various types of Rhodian pottery cannot even be set in a relative chronological order. A comparison with ceramics from other plots investigated with a clear archaeological stratigraphy might help to confine the span of use of certain vessel types; similarly, published ceramics of Hellenistic tomb contexts

---

8   The full reading and study of the inscription, which is effaced at several points, will be completed with the scheduled special photographing of the object in the studio, specially equipped for this purpose, of the Dipartimento di Studi letterari, filologici e linguistici (Papirologia) at the Centro di Papirologia Achille Vogliano in Milan.

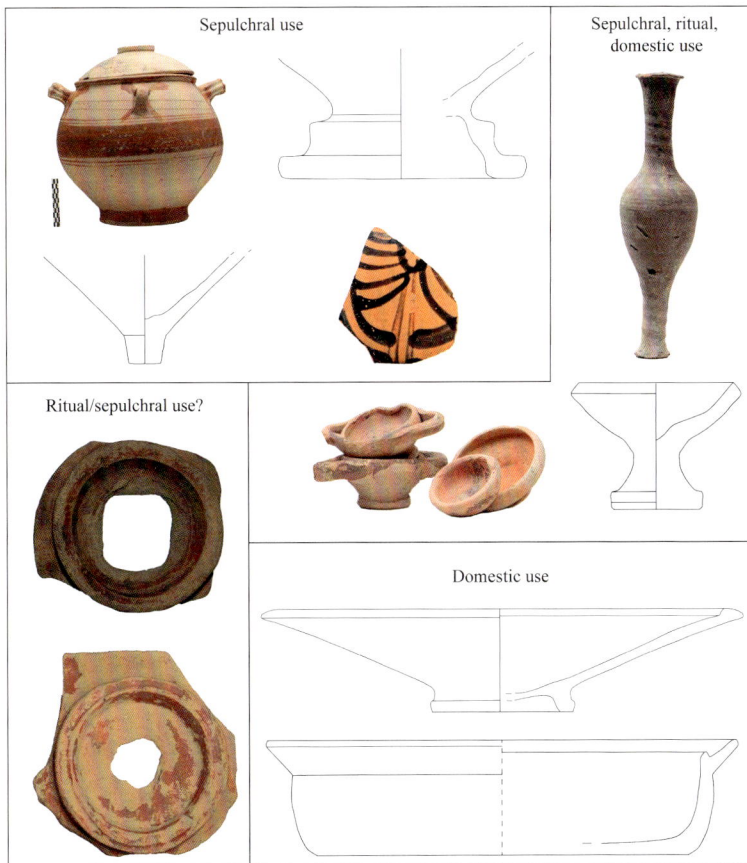

Fig. 3. *Reconstructing the original context of use of the ceramics from the* mavra chomata *accumulation. Vessels connected to sepulchral use (cinerary urn, base of a Hadra hydria, base of an amphoriskos, body sherd of an aryballos/lekythos); sepulchral, ritual or domestic use (unguentarium, thymiaterion, miniature vessels); ritual/ sepulchral use (bases of table ware); domestic use (profile drawing of a plate and a lopas). Illustrations not to scale (photo credit: G. Kasiotis; drawings: L. Betina,* © The Rhodes Centennial Project*).*

excavated in Rhodes can be consulted as references for dating purposes. However, imported ceramics are the most reliable indicator for dating the assemblage.[9]

Secondly, the original context of use and consumption of the ceramics can only be hypothesised based on the character and function of the vessels. In other words, the ceramics cannot be linked to specific building structures or locations in the city of Rhodes.

Besides determining the overall character of the assemblage and establishing a chronological framework for the deposit, the scientific analysis of the ceramics focuses on the reconstruction of local, regional and foreign trade relations, cultural exchange and transfers, and the comprehensive evaluation of Rhodian pottery traditions. These research objectives require an interdisciplinary approach, combining archaeological, archaeometric and ethnoarchaeological methods. A classification of the ceramics by ware, function

and fabric forms the basis for differentiating local/regional and imported vessels. Rhodian pottery production will be investigated systematically by applying petrographic and geochemical scientific techniques, aiming to create references and solid criteria for identifying Rhodian ceramics with certainty outside of the island. While the distribution of Rhodian amphorae in the Mediterranean is relatively well studied, table wares originating from Rhodian workshops have only been recognised sporadically in the archaeological record e.g. in Delos and Alexandria – probably also due to the absence of appropriate comparative data. Besides allowing an attribution of ceramics to the island of Rhodes in general, it is hoped that the establishment of archaeometric reference data will enable ceramics to be assigned to individual landscapes or workshops. Natural-scientific analyses have the potential to reveal the degree of compositional homogeneity or heterogeneity of clay pastes native to the island, crucial for such an endeavour.

---

9   Betina (forthcoming).

During the 2017 and 2018 study seasons, the major share of the ceramics constituting the *mavra chomata* assemblage has been processed through statistical analysis, photographic documentation, technical drawings and descriptive database entries. Selected ceramic wares or groups have already been studied in more detail. Preliminary results and ideas on the four main topics of the research programme are presented briefly below.

a) Consistency of the ceramic assemblage

The character of the ceramics constituting the deposit is diverse (Fig. 3). A few vessel shapes can be associated with a sepulchral context, namely cinerary urns, Hadra hydriae, amphoriskoi and the fragment of a lekythos or aryballos. Some vessels, such as the unguentaria and lagynoi, cannot be categorised with certainty as they might have served multiple functions and therefore could perhaps be related to both sepulchral and domestic use. The same applies to miniature vessels (skyphoi, bowls) and thymiateria, which can appear in burial, ritual or domestic spaces. A peculiarity of the assemblage is the consistent presence of holes or perforations in the central portion of several ceramics (e.g. cups, bowls, plates). In a few cases, the holes have been drilled or cut out carefully, testifying to this phenomenon being an intentional practice, while on other ceramics the edges of the holes can have an irregular shape. It is likely this practice relates to a secondary use of the vessels, e.g. in the context of funerary rituals, as libations for the deceased. Table ware such as bowls, plates and jugs, common and cooking wares, lamps and storage vessels might be associated with dining and daily activities – and probably belonged in a domestic sphere. Lastly, several elongated rods (kiln furniture) and a tool (possibly a scraper) might originate from a ceramic workshop. The ceramics deposited in the *mavra chomata* can be associated with different spheres of consumption, with pottery attributed to domestic contexts clearly dominant.

b) Rhodian and imported pottery

Until now, focus had been placed on the imported wares in the archaeological analysis of ceramics from the Papachristodoulou-Karika plot. This is due to the fact that imported pottery is straightforward to identify and date, based on the state of publications on Mediterranean ceramics,

while for Rhodian pottery this framework still needs to be established in the course of the ongoing project. Classifying the local and regional ceramics reliably requires an initial assessment of the entire ceramic assemblage, which, due to the vast amount of pottery fragments in the *mavra chomata* (c. 90,000 sherds), has not been accomplished yet. Rhodian pottery represents around 85 % of the total ceramic assemblage, attesting to autonomous and self-sustainable ceramic production on the island.

The bulk of the imports can be assigned to production centres in central Western Asia Minor (Knidos, Ephesos, Pergamon). Moreover, a considerable quantity of Eastern Sigillata A or sporadic Italian imports (thin-walled ware) has been noted. The evaluation of several hitherto non-classified fine ware objects (e.g. sigillata) is currently underway.

One group of ceramics already analysed in more detail is the unguentaria. Another vessel category that would be worth analysing comprehensively is the cinerary urns that occur at the Papachristodoulou-Karika plot in three variants. It remains to be seen whether the three variants represent different chronological phases, as their shape, adornments and even ceramic fabrics can differ.

c) Raw materials and vessel functionality

Ceramics from Rhodes or of Rhodian provenance have rarely been analysed with natural-scientific methods in the past, and on those occasions the studies hardly ever comprise, apart from amphorae, examples of the Hellenistic and Roman periods. A key component of *The Rhodes Centennial Project* is the compositional characterisation of Rhodian ceramics with petrographic and geochemical methods.

Macroscopic observations on the ceramic fabrics indicate specific choices in clay pastes for particular vessel shapes and functions. For instance, cooking pots are exclusively manufactured from a red clay, while white clays were exploited for various functional groups (table ware, common ware, miniature vessels, etc). Coarse light reddish clays enriched with large dark reddish clasts were used in the production of large storage containers. The performance properties of the individual clays might have influenced this deliberate selection.

Ethnoarchaeological research has been initiated on the central Eastern shoreline of Rhodes in the area of

Fig. 4. *State of preservation of the ceramic artefacts. Collection of (almost) fully-preserved ceramics versus decorated pottery in poor condition, only attested in individual sherds (photo credit: G. Kasiotis and L. Betina, © The Rhodes Centennial Project).*

Archangelos in order better to understand the selection criteria of certain clays. The village of Archangelos and the adjacent coastal settlement of Stegna were in operation as a large potting centre in the late 19th and 20th centuries. By interviewing contemporary potters in June 2017, information on the clay extraction sites appropriate for pottery production and on the clay mixtures utilised in the manufacture of different functional ceramics has been gained. A geological field survey conducted in March 2018 targeted the sampling of clay, sand and rock samples around Arch-

angelos and the city of Rhodes, forming the starting point for a detailed characterisation and the establishment of differentiation criteria for Rhodian clays.

d) Chronological frame and deposition process

Our preliminary results indicate that the main share of the ceramics of the *mavra chomata* accumulation dates to the late 2nd and particularly the 1st century BC. Amongst the

203

earliest finds, going back to the late 4th or 3rd century BC, is (Attic) black gloss pottery, though there is very little of it. Eastern Sigillata A might give an indication of the lower chronological boundary of the assemblage in the late 1st century BC or early 1st century AD, with a few more recent finds. Surprisingly, the latter cannot be rated as residual finds scattered on the surface of the *mavra chomata* accumulation, but have been found embedded in the ceramic assemblage. The ongoing studies will help to explain this pattern and contribute to the understanding of the formation process of the assemblage.

The state of preservation of the ceramic artefacts (Fig. 4) also needs to be explained. Several ceramics are either fully preserved – for example, most of the cinerary urns and their lids and some table ware – or at least can be assembled to relatively complete vessels when broken. Other vessels, however, are represented by single fragments measuring a few centimetres only; this is most recognisable with painted and decorated ceramics,

e.g. lagynoi with vegetal decoration or West Slope Ware, where matching pieces would be easily identifiable. The co-existence of well- and poorly-preserved artefacts needs to be further investigated and specific patterns screened, since it might be related to the chronology or the original context of use of the individual items.

ANASTASIA DRELIOSSI-HERAKLEIDOU
Ephorate of Antiquities of the Dodecanese
Odos Hippoton
GR-85100 Rhodes
anastasia.drel@yahoo.gr

LISA BETINA
Saxo Institute
University of Copenhagen
Karen Blixens Plads 8
DK-2300 Copenhagen
peloschek@hum.ku.dk

Bibliography

Adriani, A. 1966
Repertorio d'arte dell' Egitto Greco-Romano (Serie C, volume I-II), Palermo.

Betina, L. forthcoming
'Rhodes and the Eastern Mediterranean in the Late Hellenistic-Early Imperial Periods: The Ceramic Evidence', *Proceedings of the 19th International Congress of Classical Archaeology 22-26 May 2018*, Cologne/Bonn.

Δρελιώση-Ηρακλείδου, Α. & Ν. Λίτινας 2009-2011
'Ροδιακό όστρακο με ερωτικό επίγραμμα', *ΕΥΛΙΜΕΝΗ* 10-12, 135-54.

Δρελιώση-Ηρακλείδου, Α. 2018
'Από τη ροδιακή νεκρόπολη: τόποι ταφής, χώροι συγκεντρώσεων και τελετών, αποθέσεις απορριμμάτων', *Πρακτικά of the ΚΗ΄ Congress of Στέγη Γραμμάτων και Τεχνών Δωδεκανήσου* June–July 2017, Rhodes 208-24.

Gabrielsen, V. 1997
The Naval Aristocracy of Hellenistic Rhodes (Studies in Hellenistic Civilization 6), Aarhus.

Kontorini, V. 1983
Inscriptions inédites relatives à l'histoire et aux cultes de Rhodes au IIe et au Ier s. av. J. C. (Rhodiaka I), Louvain-La-Neuve.

Παπαχριστοδούλου, Ι. Χ. 1979
'Οικόπεδα Ευανγ. Παπαχριστοδούλου και Χρ. Καρίκα', *ΑΔ* 34, Β2- Χρονικά, 43538, σχ. 6, πίν. 232 β–δ, 233 α–β.

Πατσιαδά, Β. 2013
Ρόδος III. Μνημειώδες ταφικό συγκρότημα στη νεκρόπολη της Ρόδου. Συμβολή στη μελέτη της ελληνιστικής ταφικής αρχιτεκτονικής, Ρόδος-Αθήνα.

Rosenbaum, E. A. 1971
The necropolis of Anemurium, Ankara.